Greek Writing from Knossos to Homer

Greek Writing from Knossos to Homer

A Linguistic Interpretation of the
Origin of the Greek Alphabet
and the Continuity of
Ancient Greek Literacy

ROGER D. WOODARD

New York   Oxford
Oxford University Press
1997

Oxford University Press

Oxford   New York
Athens   Auckland   Bangkok   Bogota   Bombay   Buenos Aires
Calcutta   Cape Town   Dar es Salaam   Delhi   Florence   Hong Kong
Istanbul   Karachi   Kuala Lumpur   Madras   Madrid   Melbourne
Mexico City   Nairobi   Paris   Singapore   Taipei   Tokyo   Toronto

and associated companies in
Berlin   Ibadan

Copyright © 1997 by Roger D. Woodard

Published by Oxford University Press, Inc.
198 Madison Avenue, New York, New York 10016

Oxford is a registered trademark of Oxford University Press

Library of Congress Cataloging-in-Publication Data
Woodard, Roger D.
Greek writing from Knossos to Homer : a linguistic interpretation of the origin of the
Greek alphabet and the continuity of ancient Greek literacy / by Roger D. Woodard.
p. cm.
Includes bibliographical references and index.
ISBN 0-19-510520-6
1. Greek language—Alphabet.   2. Written communication—Greece—History.   3. Language
and culture—Greece—History.   4. Greek language—Written Greek.   5. Literacy—Greece—
History.   6. Greek language—Writing.   I. Title.
PA273.W66   1997
481'.1—dc20   96-7447

9 8 7 6 5 4 3 2 1
Printed in the United States of America
on acid-free paper

For Paul

בן חכם ישמח אב

υἱὸς σοφὸς εὐφραίνει πατέρα

Preface

Of the many splendid achievements of the ancient Greeks, the alphabet was perhaps the most marvelous and certainly the most influential. Like practically all great intellectual and technological achievements, this one was no creation *ex nihilo*. The alphabet stands on the shoulders of the consonantal script of the Phoenicians, as is well known. However, in the following pages I argue that one alphabetic foot also rests on a shoulder of the syllabic script of the Cypriot Greeks. That this is so only comes to light when the question of the origin of the alphabet is examined in a manner which cuts across individual disciplinary boundaries. Because of the cross-disciplinary nature of this investigation, some of the territory traversed will be unfamiliar to one or another group of readers. The phonetic and phonological discussions and the careful examinations of earlier attempts to elucidate certain spelling strategies of the Greek syllabaries will, for example, be new ground for some. These matters are, however, crucial in discovering that there is indeed a continuum of Greek literacy from Mycenaean Knossos to Homer. Perhaps those readers less familiar with linguistics may even wish to begin reading the book with chapter 6 and, after completing chapter 8, go back and read the book from the beginning. Readers may also wish to consult the phonetic glossary and charts which appear following chapter 8.

This is a work which has taken shape over some time. While I would hesitate to provide an exhaustive list of everyone who has offered constructive comments along the way, lest some individuals be unintentionally omitted, there are particular persons and organizations to whom I must express heartfelt appreciation. I am yet again deeply grateful to the Andrew W. Mellon Foundation, which provided partial support for the research underlying this book. I would like to express my appreciation to Marshall Cohen, former dean of the Humanities Division of the College of Letters, Arts and Sciences at the University of Southern California, for granting to me a semester's leave during a critical stage in the writing of this book. For reading the manuscript and offering guidance and encouragement, I particularly thank Professors Thomas Palaima, Laurence Stephens, and William Thalmann. For his assistance with Russian language and many kind suggestions, I am most grateful to my former Johns Hopkins colleague and friend, the late Professor James W. Poultney. I am deeply indebted to Oxford University Press and to Elizabeth Maguire, Elda Rotor, Susan Chang, Rahul Mehta, and Robert Dilworth for the wonderful editorial assistance which they have provided. Last and most importantly of all, I thank my wife and son for their unfailing support, without which this undertaking could not have come to fruition. Whatever errors and oversights remain herein are solely my own.

Contents

Abbreviations

NK   *The Nymphaeum of Kafizin* (= Mitford 1980)
RP   *Revue de philologie*
SMEA   *Studi micenei ed egeo-anatolici*
SPA   "Handbook of Phonological Data from a Sample of the World's Languages: A Report of the Stanford Phonology Archive" (= Crothers et al. 1979)
TAPA   *Transactions of the American Philological Association*
TPS   *Transactions of the Philological Society*

Greek Writing from Knossos to Homer

Introduction

1.0 Overview

This is a book about the origin of the Greek alphabet (at least that is my perception). But I cannot begin this book with the alphabet, for it was not with the advent of that script that the Greeks first began to write. Hundreds of years before the conception of α, β, γ, and so on, Greek scribes had already taken stylus in hand and were engaged in giving orthographic expression to their language. In the following pages I argue that it is only within the broader context of Greek literacy that the origin of the Greek alphabet can be rightly perceived. The Linear B syllabic script, the syllabary of the Cypriot Greeks and the alphabet each stand as points along an unbroken continuum of Greek literacy which stretches from the Mycenaean era to the present.

The continuity of Greek literacy only comes to light upon examining certain aspects of prealphabetic Greek orthography in exacting detail, and I undertake such an examination in the ensuing four chapters. In chapter 2 an overview is presented of the two ancient Greek syllabaries (i.e., scripts in which each character has a value equivalent to a syllable rather than a single consonant or vowel sound).[1] These two scripts are Linear B, the second millennium B.C. writing system of the Mycenaean Greeks, and the slightly later Cypriot Syllabary. Chapters 3 and 4 are devoted to an analysis of the various modern interpretations of the Linear B and syllabic Cypriot spelling strategies which were used for writing sequences of consonants. As each character in the syllabic scripts has a built-in vowel component (since every syllable contains a vowel), special mechanisms had to be devised for spelling phonetic strings of consonants. Though we would most certainly not have anticipated it, we will first encounter here, in these syllabic strategies for spelling consonant clusters, telling evidence that the Greek alphabet was developed by individuals who were already literate—literate in the tradition of a syllabic writing system. This initial discovery of a bridge between the Greek syllabic and alphabetic traditions is the object of a detailed investigation in chapter 5.

We at last turn our attention fully on the alphabet in chapter 6. Here I explore the Greek adaptation of the characters of the Phoenician consonantal writing system (which is, of course, the source of the Greek alphabetic script), focusing on the Phoenician sibilant letters (*zayin, samek, ṣade,* and *shin*) and their Greek counterparts (*zeta, xi, san,* and *sigma*). Recent investigators have characterized the devolutionary relationship between these particular Semitic and Greek characters as confused and problematic. Closely examining phonetic, typological, and historical-phonological evidence, I argue that the presence of *zeta, xi,* and *san* (alongside *sigma*) in the Greek alphabet is reasonably and convincingly motivated only within the framework of a Greek adaptation of the Phoenician script in which the adapters were persons already literate in the syllabic Cypriot orthographic tradition. Moreover, within such a framework the relationship between the Phoenician sibilant characters and their Greek analogues is not confused but straightforward.

Chapter 7 is concerned with Cyprus as the place of origin of the alphabet. Here I identify additional evidence supporting the thesis that the alphabet was the product of Cypriot scribes and explore a scenario of early developments of the alphabet on Cyprus which would account for variations in the local alphabets of Greece. Within recent years the date assigned to the origin of the Greek alphabet has ranged from the eighth to the fifteenth centuries B.C. I argue that the model of a Cypriot origin of the alphabet establishes for this process a *terminus post quem* of the early to mid-ninth century B.C. and that the development of the alphabet at the hands of scribes trained in the syllabic writing system of Cyprus is responsible for the occurrence in the alphabet of certain features which some investigators have interpreted to be evidence for a second-millennium date of origin. Chapter 7 concludes with a survey of the findings of those investigators who have proposed Cyprus as the place at which the Greek alphabet was devised, followed by an examination of other proposed sites for this process.

In chapter 8, I will summarize my findings which point to the Greek adaptation of the Phoenician script at the hands of scribes accustomed to spelling the Greek language with the syllabic script of Cyprus. Recent work on the origin of the Greek alphabet has invoked a causative relationship between the advent of the alphabet and the recording of Homeric verse, an issue I also address in chapter 8. My study concludes with an examination of the nature of the exportation of the alphabet out of Cyprus to points west.

1.1 The Greek Syllabaries

Before proceeding to chapter 2 and its survey of the orthographic principles of the Mycenaean and Cypriot syllabic scripts, I offer a few remarks toward placing those scripts within the context of their historical development. Linear B, the name that the British archaeologist Sir Arthur Evans coined at the turn of the century for the syllabic Mycenaean script, survives primarily on clay tablets recovered from the ruins of the Mycenaean palace at Knossos and at Khania[2] on the island of Crete, as well as from various Mycenaean sites on the Greek mainland, chiefly Pylos, Mycenae, Tiryns, and Thebes (see figure 1.1). The materials from Knossos are most often dated to about 1400 B.C. and those from the mainland sites to about 1200 B.C. The Linear B script almost certainly developed from the as yet undeciphered Minoan script which Evans called Linear A; the advent of the Linear B script is probably to be placed in the fifteenth century B.C.[3] Linear A, in turn, had likely evolved out of the also undeciphered script known as Cretan Hieroglyphic. The former is attested from about 1750 to 1450 B.C., and the latter appears to have spanned the Middle Minoan period (ca. 2000–1600).[4]

The Greek syllabic writing system of Cyprus, the Cypriot Syllabary, first attested in the middle of the eleventh century B.C., appears to be a Greek adaptation of one of the Cypro-Minoan scripts, so called because they are believed to be descended from a Cretan writing system, quite probably Linear A.[5] The Cypro-Minoan scripts have been traditionally identified as Cypro-Minoan 1, 2, and 3; a fourth script, sometimes called Archaic Cypro-Minoan, is attested on

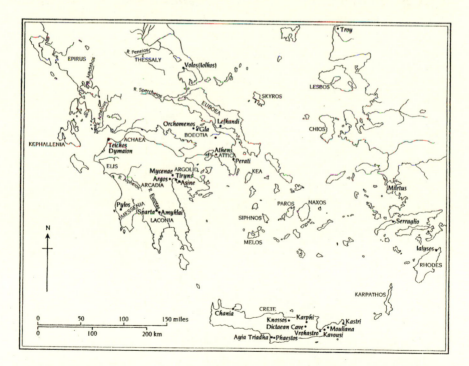

FIGURE 1.1 Map of the Bronze Age Aegean. From Barry Cunliffe, *The Oxford Illustrated Prehistory of Europe* (Oxford University Press, 1994). Reprinted by permission of Oxford University Press.

a single document of ca. 1500 B.C. and is perhaps the immediate predecessor of Cypro-Minoan 1, the probable source of the Greek Cypriot Syllabary. Cypro-Minoan 1 inscriptions are attested approximately from the late sixteenth to the twelfth centuries B.C. Cypro-Minoan 2 and 3 are known from thirteenth-century documents, the latter having been recovered thus far only at the site of the Syrian coastal trading center of Ugarit.[6]

1.2 Miscellanea

I have anticipated that this book's audience will include classicists, linguists, and specialists in Near Eastern studies and have undertaken to write in such a way that the work will be accessible to the full array of its readers. The result of so doing may be that at points in the study, one subset or another of the readership may encounter exhaustive discussion of matters which, for that subset, seem patently obvious. I would implore each group of specialists to exercise tolerance and long-suffering in the midst of such trials, so that perhaps in the end some common benefit will be realized.

All Greek and Semitic words cited in the text are phonetically transcribed and glossed. The mode of transcribing Greek vowels which I have adopted is that of W. S. Allen 1974 (see figure 1.2):[7]

(1) ι = high front unrounded /i/ and /i:/
    υ = high front rounded /ü/ and /ü:/
    $o\upsilon$ = high back rounded /u:/
    $\varepsilon, \eta, \varepsilon\iota$ = mid front unrounded /e/, /ẹ:/, and /ẹ:/, respectively
    o, ω = mid back rounded /o/ and /ọ:/, respectively
    α = low central unrounded /a/ and /a:/

The decision was made to transcribe, by convention, all Greek vowels as they would have been pronounced in fifth-century Attic (a procedure which admit-

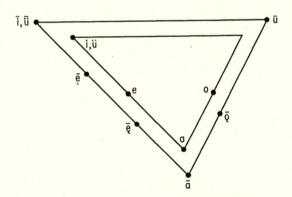

FIGURE 1.2 The vowels of Classical Attic Greek. From W. S. Allen, *Vox Graeca: A Guide to the Pronunciation of Classical Greek,* 2nd ed. (Cambridge University Press, 1974). Reprinted by permission of Cambridge University Press.

tedly has often resulted in anachronistic transcription), except where it was necessary to make dialectal vowel values explicit for the sake of the discussion or argument at hand.

Notes

1. Of course, there are characters in the Greek syllabaries which represent single vowels, as a vowel alone can constitute a syllable. It is at this one point that the values of characters of syllabic scripts and alphabetic scripts overlap.

2. On the tablets from Khania, see E. Hallager, M. Vlasakis, and B. Hallager, 1990, "The First Linear B Tablet(s) from Khania," *Kadmos* 29:24–34; 1992, "New Linear B Tablets from Khania," *Kadmos* 31:61–87; J.-P. Olivier, 1993, "KN 115 = KH 115. Un même scribe à Knossos et à La Canée au MR IIIB: Du soupçon à la certitude," *BCH* 117:19–33.

3. On the development of the Linear B script from Linear A, see T. Palaima, 1988, "The Development of the Mycenaean Writing System," in *Texts, Tablets and Scribes: Studies in Mycenaean Epigraphy and Economy Offered to Emmett L. Bennett, Jr.,* ed. J.-P. Olivier and T. Palaima (supplement to *Minos,* no. 10), pp. 269–342.

4. For an overview of the Cretan and Cypriot scripts, see R. Woodard, forthcoming, "Linguistic Connections Between Greeks and Non-Greeks," in *Greeks and Barbarians,* ed. J. Coleman and C. Walz. On Linear A see Y. Duhoux, 1989, "Le linéaire A: Problèmes de déchiffrement," in *Problems in Decipherment,* ed. Y. Duhoux, T. Palaima, and J. Bennet (Louvain-La-Neuve: Peeters), pp. 59–120; Y. Duhoux, ed., 1978, *Études minoennes I: Le linéaire A* (Louvain: Éditions Peeters); L. Godart, 1976, "La scrittura lineare A," *La parola del passato* 31:31–47. On Cretan Hieroglyphic see J.-P. Olivier, 1989, "The Possible Methods in Deciphering the Pictographic Cretan Script," in Duhoux et al. 1989:39–58; 1976, "La scrittura geroglifica cretese," *La parola del passato* 31:17–23.

5. See T. Palaima, 1989a, "Ideograms and Supplementals and Regional Interaction among Aegean and Cypriote Scripts," *Minos* 24:29–54; J. Chadwick, 1979, "The Minoan Origin of the Classical Cypriot Script," in *Acts of the International Archaeological Symposium "The Relations Between Cyprus and Crete, ca. 2000–500 B.C."* (Nicosia: Nicolaou and Sons), pp. 139–143.

6. On the Cypro-Minoan scripts, see especially T. Palaima, 1989b, "Cypro-Minoan Scripts: Problems of Historical Context," in Duhoux et al. 1989:121–187 (with extensive bibliography of earlier work); E. Masson, 1974, *Cyprominoica* (Göteborg: Paul Åströms Forlag). Palaima disputes the traditional four-way classification of the Cypro-Minoan scripts.

7. However, I utilize the *colon* to mark long vowels in phonetic transcription, while Allen uses the *macron.*

The Syllabaries

2.0 Structure of the Syllabaries

2.0.1 Symbol Types

The two syllabaries in which ancient Greek was written share the trait of consisting almost entirely of two types of symbols: (1) symbols representing simply *vowels*[1] (i.e., V characters); and (2) symbols representing sequences of *consonant + vowel* (i.e., CV characters). In figure 2.1 the symbols of Linear B are presented; as indicated, the only characters having a value other than V or CV are the *dental + glide* characters *twe, two, dwe, dwo, nwa* (and perhaps *swa* and *swi*), *tya, rya, ryo,* and the double stop character *pte.* It is true that the consonantal component of the characters transcribed as *za, ze,* and *zo* does correspond etymologically to the alphabetic Greek character *zeta* (ζ) and that *zeta* represents the sound sequence [zd] (i.e., *zeta* is a CC *alphabetic* character); however, the phonetic value of *zV* in the second-millennium script of Mycenaean Greek was almost certainly not the same as that of first-millennium *zeta.* This problem is addressed in chapter 6.

Figure 2.2 illustrates the characters of the Cypriot Syllabary. In addition to V and CV characters, the Cypriot system possesses the CCV symbols *kse* and *ksa.*[2] Unlike the CCV characters of Linear B, these symbols have a *phonetic analogue* in the Greek alphabet: namely, the letter *xi* (ξ), also having the value [ks]. This "coincidence" will prove to be of considerable significance and is discussed at length in chapter 6. Of course, the Greek alphabetic symbol *zeta* (ζ) which was mentioned above could be said to be an *analogue* of the Linear B *zV* symbols, but only to the extent that the consonantal sound spelled with *zV* in the second-millennium script of Linear B evolved into the sound spelled with ζ in the alphabetic script of the first millennium; as indicated above, they

BASIC VALUES

A	E	I	O	U
DA	DE	DI	DO	DU
JA	JE		JO	
KA	KE	KI	KO	KU
MA	ME	MI	MO	MU
NA	NE	NI	NO	NU
PA	PE	PI	PO	PU
QA	QE	QI	QO	
RA	RE	RI	RO	RU
SA	SE	SI	SO	SU
TA	TE	TI	TO	TU
WA	WE	WI	WO	
ZA	ZE		ZO	

SPECIAL VALUES

HA	AI	AU	DWE	DWO
NWA	PTE	PHU	RYA	RAI
RYO	TYA	TWE	TWO	

FIGURE 2.1 The symbols of the Linear B syllabic script. From Oliver Dickenson, *The Aegean Bronze Age* (Cambridge University Press, 1994). Reprinted by permission of John Chadwick.

are almost certainly not phonetically identical. On this point, note that figure 2.2 includes syllabic Cypriot symbols transcribed as *zo* and *za*. These also correspond etymologically to alphabetic *zeta* and are considered in chapter 6, along with the Mycenaean *zV* symbols.

2.0.2 Ill-Suited Systems

A syllabic writing system consisting almost entirely of V and CV symbols would be quite well suited for representing languages such as Japanese and those of the Polynesian branch of the Austronesian linguistic family, that is, languages in which closed syllables and consonant clusters occur infrequently or are absent altogether. Japanese is, in fact, written syllabically (at least in part[3]), and the Kana syllabaries used for this purpose consist almost solely of V and CV characters. The Greek language is quite a different matter, however; the phonotactics of Greek are such that closed syllables and consonant clusters abound. Greek is not a language for which one would expect a syllabary consisting of only V and CV characters to be most naturally devised. It would clearly seem to be the case that the Greeks adopted syllabic scripts which had been originally designed for writing a language, or languages, phonotactically quite unlike Greek.

FIGURE 2.2 The symbols of the Cypriot syllabic script.

2.0.3 Linear B

As a consequence of the significant disparity between the syllable structure of Greek and the sign structure of its syllabic scripts, special strategies had to be devised by the scribes for graphically treating sequences of consonants and word-final consonants. In the case of Linear B, these scribal strategies are of two basic types (though there is a third type, discussed later, which is quite restricted in application). On the one hand, a consonant may simply not be written, as, for example, in the following forms:

(1) A. *pe-mo* for σπερμο ([spermo], 'seed')
     B. *pa-i-to* for Φαιστος ([pʰaistos], a place name)

In (1A) there are two consonant clusters, a word-initial [sp-] and a word-internal [-rm-], and in neither case is the first member of the cluster spelled. The same treatment is exhibited in the case of the [-st-] cluster in (1B); that is, only the second member of the cluster is actually written. I refer to this strategy of underrepresentation of clusters as *partial spelling*. Notice that the word-final fricative of (1B) is also not represented orthographically. This is the regular treatment of word-final consonants in Linear B.

On the other hand, in some cases a consonant which precedes another consonant is in fact written, and to do this a CV symbol is used whose vowel component must be understood to have *no phonetic reality*. This spelling strategy is exemplified by forms such as the following:

(2) A. *te-ko-to-ne* for τεκτονες ([tektones], 'carpenters')
     B. *de-so-mo-i* for δεσμοις ([desmois], 'with bindings')

In (2A) the word-internal sequence [-kto-] is spelled -*ko-to*-. In other words, the first consonant is represented by using a CV symbol, and, as there is no vowel pronounced after the stop [k], the vowel component of the symbol -*ko*- must be understood as a merely orthographic, nonphonetic "empty" vowel. Notice that the particular vowel chosen for this purpose is the one which is identical to the vowel that phonetically follows the [-kt-] cluster. The strategy for representing the [-sm-] cluster of (2B) is the same; the first consonant is written -*so*-, using an empty vowel identical to the vowel that is pronounced after the [-sm-] cluster. I refer to this type of spelling as *plenary spelling*. [4]

2.0.4 The Cypriot Syllabary

Both of these Mycenaean strategies for representing consonant clusters were also employed by the scribes of the syllabic Cypriot script. The use of partial spelling, however, is limited to clusters whose first member is a nasal, as seen in the following examples:

(3) A. *pa-ta* for παντα ([panta], 'all')
     B. *a-to-ro-po* for ανθρωπω ([antʰrɔːpɔː], 'of man')

In these and many other forms, a preconsonantal nasal is simply omitted from the spelling. It was pointed out above that an omission strategy is also used for word-final consonants in Linear B. Greek is phonotactically constrained in such a way that a word[5] is only permitted to have as a final consonant either [-r], [-n], or [-s]. A word-final [-r] is regularly spelled in the Cypriot Syllabary. In some instances word-final [-n] and [-s] are spelled as well; in other instances the latter two are omitted.[6] In the event that a word-final consonant is written, it is conventionally represented by using a CV character whose vowel component is *e*, as in the forms presented in (4):

(4)   A. *ka-re* for γαρ ([gar], 'for')
      B. *-pa-i-to-ne* for παιδων ([paidǫ:n], 'of (the) children')
      C. *ka-si-ke-ne-to-se* for κασιγνητος ([kasignę:tos], 'brothers,' accusative
         plural)

I term this type of spelling *arbitrary vowel spelling*.

Examples (3B), *a-to-ro-po* for ανθρωπω ([antʰrǫ:pǫ:]), and (4C), *ka-si-ke-ne-to-se* for κασιγνητος ([kasignę:tos]), also illustrate the use of the *progressive spelling* strategy in the Cypriot Syllabary: the first member of each of the clusters [-tʰr-] and [-gn-] is spelled with a symbol whose vocalic component is identical to the vowel which follows the cluster. This procedure is identical to Linear B *plenary spelling*.

In addition to partial spelling, arbitrary vowel spelling and progressive spelling, a fourth strategy is widely used for representing consonant clusters in the Cypriot Syllabary, as is illustrated by the following examples:

(5)   A. *mi-si-to-ne* for μισθων ([mistʰǫ:n], 'of a fee')
      B. *a-ra-ku-ro* for αργυρω ([argürǫ:], 'of silver')

In example (5A), the first member of the word-internal cluster [-stʰ-] is written by utilizing a CV character (*-si-*) whose vocalic component must be read as an empty vowel, just as we have seen in the case of progressive spelling. In this instance, however, the empty vowel is not identical to the vowel which phonetically follows the cluster ([-ǫ:-]), as in progressive spelling; instead, its identity is with the vowel which phonetically precedes the cluster ([-i-]). In the same way, the first member of the [-rg-] cluster of (5B) is spelled *-ra-*, that is, with the symbol whose vowel component matches the vowel occurring before the cluster. I term this spelling strategy *regressive spelling*.

2.0.5 Final Clusters in Linear B

Regressive spelling also occurs in Linear B orthographic practice, but in this script, unlike the syllabic Cypriot system, it has a quite limited application. As indicated above, word-final consonants are not written in Linear B. If a word ends in a consonant cluster, however, the consonant preceding the final one may be written, and if it is, this writing is effected by employing the regressive spelling strategy. Specifically, the clusters involved in this kind of representation are those of the type *stop + fricative:*

(6)   A. *wa-na-ka*, ϝαναξ ([wanaks], 'king')
      B. *a₃-ti-jo-qo*, Αιθιοqʷς ([aitʰiokʷs], a man's name)[7]

As (6A) and (6B) illustrate, a word-final [-s] is simply deleted from the orthography (which as we have seen is the regular Linear B treatment of word-final consonants), and a preceding stop is represented using the CV character whose vocalic component is identical to the vowel which phonetically precedes the word-final cluster.

2.0.6 Geminate Clusters

An idiosyncrasy of consonant cluster spelling which is shared by Linear B and the Cypriot Syllabary is found in the spelling of geminate clusters:

(7) *Linear B*
  A. *e-ne-wo* for ϵννϵϝο ([ennewo], 'nine')
  B. *mi-to-we-sa* for μιλτοϝϵσσα ([miltowessa], 'painted red')

  Cypriot Syllabary
  C. *wa-na-sa-se* for ϝανασσας ([wanassas], 'of the lady')
  D. *a-po-lo-ni* for Απολλωνι ([apollǫ:ni], 'for Apollo')

As these examples reveal, only one member of such clusters is actually written; that is, a type of partial spelling is employed.

2.0.7 Word-Initial Clusters

My remarks up to this point have addressed only word-internal and word-final clusters and single word-final consonants; some attention must now be given to word-initial clusters. In the case of Linear B, word-initial clusters are treated just as word-internal clusters; that is, whatever strategy is used to represent a cluster occurring word-internally is also used to spell that cluster when it occurs at the beginning of a word. This equal treatment of clusters word-internally and word-initially in Linear B marks a fundamental difference between this script and its Cypriot counterpart. In the case of the latter, word-initial clusters are written using progressive spelling, *regardless* of the type of strategy employed in representing the same cluster when it occurs word-internally. Consider the Cypriot treatment of the cluster *[s] + stop* when it occurs word-internally (8A) and word-initially (8B):

(8) A. *ka-te-se-ta-se* for κατεστασε ([katestase], '(s)he placed')
  B. *sa-ta-sa-to-ro* for Στασανδρω ([stasandrǫ:], a man's name, genitive)

As example (8A) illustrates, and as we have seen already (note example (5A)), regressive spelling is used to represent a word-internal cluster of *[s] + stop*; however, when this cluster occurs word-initially, as in (8B), it is written with progressive spelling.

2.0.8 Summary of Spelling Strategies

Perhaps it would be helpful at this point to summarize the types of strategies utilized by the Mycenaean and Cypriot scribes for spelling consonant clusters and word-final consonants:

(9) A. Partial Spelling
      Linear B: (i)   certain word-internal and word-initial clusters
                (ii) word-final consonants
                (iii) geminate clusters

Cypriot Syllabary:	(i)	certain clusters beginning with a nasal
	(ii)	some occurrences of word-final [-n] and [-s]
	(iii)	geminate clusters

B. Plenary / Progressive Spelling

Linear B:	(i)	certain word-internal and word-initial clusters
Cypriot Syllabary:	(i)	certain word-internal clusters
	(ii)	word-initial clusters

C. Regressive Spelling

Linear B:	(i)	stops before word-final [-s]
Cypriot Syllabary:	(i)	certain word-internal clusters

D. Arbitrary Vowel Spelling

Cypriot Syllabary:	(i)	word-final [-r]
	(ii)	some occurrences of word-final [-n] and [-s]

For the sake of summation, I include geminate clusters under the heading *partial spelling,* since in the case of geminates, as in other instances of this type of spelling, only one member of a biconsonantal cluster is actually written. However, I do not necessarily claim that it is the *second* member of the geminate cluster which is being written, as is indeed the practice with nongeminate clusters; for at least Linear B geminates such a claim would be moot. Also included beneath this heading are word-final consonants, which, as we have seen, are simply not written in Linear B and, in some instances, in the Cypriot system as well. Perhaps these clusters seem out of place here, but, as I argue later, the nonspelling of word-final consonants actually conforms to partial spelling practice.

2.0.9 Other Orthographic Practices

As the preceding discussion and summary are admittedly rather imprecise at points, let us next turn our attention to a more detailed consideration of which strategies are used for which clusters. We will do this by initially examining the treatments of Mycenaean and syllabic Cypriot spelling of consonant clusters which have been offered in the Greek handbooks. Before so doing, however, there are a few other general principles of Linear B and Cypriot orthography which should be mentioned. First of all, as the reader is perhaps already aware from considering the examples above, no orthographic distinction is made in the Cypriot Syllabary between plain voiceless stops, voiceless aspirated stops, and voiced stops. In other words, each of the sounds [p, p^h, b] is represented by CV symbols conventionally transcribed as *pV*; [t, t^h, d] by *tV*; and [k, k^h, g] by *kV*. The same principle is utilized in Linear B spelling, except that the voiced dental stop [d] is distinguished (transcribed *dV*) from the voiceless stops [t, t^h] (transcribed *tV*). Linear B preserves an additional set of stops, the labiovelars [k^w, k^{wh}, g^w], and these are each spelled with the symbols transcribed *qV*. The Mycenaean script, though not the Cypriot, also fails to distinguish the two liquids [l] and [r], both of these sounds being represented in the former system by symbols arbitrarily transcribed as *rV*.[8]

2.1 Previous Accounts

2.1.1 Linear B

The specific applications of the above discussed Linear B strategies for representing consonant clusters are conventionally presented in the various handbooks of Mycenaean Greek[9] as sets of "spelling rules." For example, in the second edition of Ventris and Chadwick's *Documents,* Chadwick offers the following consonant spelling rules:

(10)   A. *Final -L, -M, -N, -R, -S*
      At the end of a syllable these sounds are omitted from the spelling.
      . . . In *-sm-*, however, the *s* is regularly noted.

    B. *Initial S . . .*
      Before a consonant initial *s-* is generally omitted . . . but *sm-* is treated
      as in medial syllables. . . .

    C. *Consonant clusters*
      Doubled consonants are not distinguished. Where a plosive consonant
      [i.e., a stop] precedes another consonant, it is written with the vowel of
      the succeeding syllable. . . . A few irregularities are found with *-kt-*
      . . .
      x (ξ) *ps* (ψ) and *qᵘs* [i.e., *kʷs*] are treated as *k-s-, p-s-, q-s-.* . . . *When*
      final, they shed the -s and take the vowel of the preceding syllable . . .
      m is preserved in *mn-* . . . *r* in *-rw-* is usually omitted. . . .
      The group *-nw-* may be written either *-nu-w-* or with the vowel of the
      following syllable supplied with *n.* . . . In the group *-sw-,*
      s is normally written . . .[10]

2.1.2 The Cypriot Syllabary

The principal work treating the syllabic Cypriot materials is Olivier Masson's *Les inscriptions chypriotes syllabiques.*[11] Masson's interpretation of the application of the various basic strategies for the spelling of consonant clusters in this script is thoroughly syllable-based. According to Masson:

(11)   Les groupes consonantiques initiaux sont *tautosyllabiques.*[12]

In the case of word-internal clusters, he states:

(12)   A. Quand les deux consonnes forment un groupe *tautosyllabique,* le traitement est le même qu'à l'initiale. . . . [L]a première consonne est rendue par le signe comportant la voyelle qui accompagne la seconde.
    B. Quand les deux consonnes sont *hétérosyllabique,* la première consonne est rendue par le signe comportant la voyelle qui figure dans la syllabe précédente.[13]

Somewhat more summarily, in his *CAH* article on the Cypriot Syllabary (coauthored with T. B. Mitford), Masson writes:

(13)   In the case of consonantal clusters, several rules are in use, based on the principle that the first consonant is rendered by the sign containing the vowel of the syllable to which this consonant belongs.[14]

This syllable-dependent analysis of consonant cluster spelling in the Cypriot Syllabary, first offered by Richard Meister (1894),[15] is commonly reported. For example, Buck states:

(14)   For groups of consonants, the first is indicated by the sign containing the vowel of the syllable to which this consonant belongs.[16]

But not all investigators have explicitly linked Cypriot spelling of word-internal clusters with tautosyllabicity and heterosyllabicity. Consider Friedrich's treatment:

(15)   Auch anlautende und inlautende Konsonantengruppen werden durch nur graphische Hilfsvokale beseitigt, und zwar erhält beim Anlaut das erste Silbenzeichen den Vokal des zweiten . . . , bei inlautender Gruppe ebenfalls den Vokal des zweiten Konsonanten, falls die Gruppe auch anlautend vorkommen kann . . . , andernfalls den vor der Gruppe stehenden Vokal.[17]

We could rephrase the second half of Friedrich's formulation using the terminology introduced above in this way:

(16)   A word-internal cluster will be represented with progressive spelling if the cluster is also capable of occurring word-initially; otherwise regressive spelling will be used word-internally.

Rather than tying the choice of symbols used to represent the first consonant of a cluster to syllable membership, Friedrich interprets Cypriot spelling of consonant clusters essentially as a matter of analogy, with the mode of cluster representation in word-initial position serving as the analogical model. Friedrich does not indicate his reasons for adopting this analysis, but it is an attractive analysis to the extent that it avoids positing the problematic premise, which is required by a syllable-based analysis such as Masson's, that certain word-internal biconsonantal clusters are tautosyllabic (see (12A); why this premise is problematic is discussed below). Friedrich's analysis is mistaken, however. According to (15/16), word-internal clusters of the type *[s]* + *stop* should be written with progressive spelling since such clusters are capable of occurring at the beginning of a word, as is illustrated within the examples of (8), repeated here as (17):

(17)   A.   *ka-te-se-ta-se* for κατεστασε ([katestase], '(s)he placed')
       B.   *sa-ta-sa-to-ro* for Στασανδρω ([stasandrọ:], a man's name, genitive)

Contrary to (15/16), when the *[s]* + *stop* cluster-type occurs within a word, as in (17A), it is represented by utilizing *regressive* spelling.[18]

Returning to Masson's presentation of the consonant spelling rules of the Cypriot Syllabary, we see that in addition to (11) and (12), he states:

(18)   A. Les consonnes géminées sont écrites sans exception comme des simples.

      B. Les consonnes finales sont rendues régulièrement à l'aide des signes syllabiques de la série en -*e*.[19]

Some attention has already been given to both of these rules in the foregoing discussion. Masson continues:

(19)   A. Les nasales placées devant consonne (occlusive ou sifflante) ne sont jamais notées à l'intérieur d'un mot ou d'un groupe nominal.[20]

      B. Un cas particulier est posé par les groupes $\chi\sigma$ [k^{h}s] (ξ) et $\pi\sigma$ [ps] (ψ). On exprime ces groupes de deux manières différentes: à l'intérieur, par la décomposition en deux syllabes, comme dans les autres cas; mais en finale, et à notre connaissance seulement pour -$\xi\varepsilon$ [-kse], -$\xi\alpha$ [-ksa], par les signes spéciaux *xe, xa*.[21]

Each of these rules, particularly (19B), is considered in detail in chapter 5.

The conventional treatments of the spelling of consonant clusters and word-final consonants in the syllabic scripts of ancient Greek, such as those of Ventris and Chadwick and of Masson, are reasonably adequate for the mere description of the spelling used to represent any particular consonantal configuration, given the assumptions about Greek syllable structure which each makes.[22] It would be highly desirable, however, to discover some general principle, or at least a very minimal set of such principles, which underlies the spelling rules of each script and which is perhaps even common to both the Mycenaean and Cypriot systems. There have been a number of attempts to do so, and a consideration of these efforts is the subject of the next two chapters.

Notes

1. Including in some instances diphthongs.

2. One might expect that CCV characters with the consonantal value [ps] would have likewise occurred; however, such are not as yet attested among the syllabic Cypriot documents. We will return to this matter below.

3. Logographic symbols (i.e., characters representing words rather than single syllables) also occur as a component of Japanese orthography; see I. Gelb, 1963, *A Study of Writing*, 2nd ed. (Chicago: University of Chicago Press), pp. 159–165, for discussion.

4. This spelling practice is identical to the syllabic Cypriot strategy which I call *progressive* spelling. It seems preferable to use the term *plenary* for the Linear B treatment, however, since the Mycenaean strategy is one of *absence versus presence* of graphemes; in the Cypriot system, as we shall see, the corresponding strategies oppose *directionality* of spelling.

5. With the exception of the proclitics; we will return to the matter of proclitics in chapter 5.

6. O. Masson, 1983, *Les inscriptions chypriotes syllabiques* (Paris: Édition E. de Boccard), pp. 73–74.

7. With the latter example compare classical Greek Αἰθίοψ ([ait^{h}íops], 'Ethio-

pian'). Mycenaean preserves the labiovelar stop, which has become a bilabial by the time of the earliest alphabetic materials.

8. See also the remarks below on the representation of diphthongs in Linear B and the Cypriot Syllabary.

9. For example, L. Palmer, 1963, *The Interpretation of Mycenaean Greek Texts* (Oxford: Oxford University Press), pp. 24, 26; A. Thumb, 1959, *Handbuch der griechischen Dialekte,* part 2, 2nd ed., ed. A. Scherer (Heidelberg: Carl Winter), pp. 318–319; M. Ventris and J. Chadwick, 1973, *Documents in Mycenaean Greek,* 2nd ed. (Cambridge: Cambridge University Press), pp. 45–46, 390; E. Vilborg, 1960, *A Tentative Grammar of Mycenaean Greek* (Göteborg: Almqvist and Wiksell), pp. 36–38.

10. *Docs.*:45–46, 390. The empty vowel ⟨-u⟩ may be used before [w] and ⟨-i⟩ before [y].

11. See n. 6 above.

12. Ibid., p. 74.

13. Ibid., pp. 75–76.

14. T. Mitford and O. Masson, 1982, "The Cypriot Syllabary," in *CAH,* 2nd ed., ed. J. Boardman and N. Hammond (Cambridge: Cambridge University Press), vol. 3, part 3, p. 78.

15. R. Meister, 1894, "Zu den Regeln der kyprischen Silbenschrift," *IF* 4:175–186.

16. C. Buck, 1955, *The Greek Dialects* (Chicago: University of Chicago Press), p. 210. See also M. Lejeune, 1982, *Phonétique historique du mycénien et du grec ancien* (Paris: Klincksieck), p. 285; Thumb-Scherer, pp. 153–155.

17. J. Friedrich, 1954, *Entzifferung Japanese orthography; see I. Gelb, 1963, A Study of Writing,* 2nd ed. (Chicago: University of Chicago Press), pp. 159–165, for discussion.

4. This spelling practice is identical to the syllabic Cypriot strategy which I call *progressive* spelling. It seems preferable to use the term *plenary* for the Linear B treatment, however, since the Mycenaean strategy is one of decipherment; the inadequacy of his analysis at this point may well be more a matter of brevity than oversight.

19. O. Masson, 1983:73.

20. Ibid., p. 74.

21. Ibid., p. 76.

22. Though, as we shall see, these assumptions are problematic.

3

Syllable-Dependent Approaches

The various attempts to uncover a minimal principle (or set of principles) for the representation of consonant clusters and word-final consonants in the Mycenaean and Cypriot syllabic scripts are essentially of two basic types: (A) analyses constructed on the premise that such representation is dependent upon syllable structure; and (B) analyses which hold that such representation is not dependent upon syllable structure but is instead sensitive to a set of hierarchical relations. In this chapter we will consider approaches of the *syllable-dependent* type and turn our attention to the *hierarchical* approaches in chapter 4.

3.0 Householder

An early attempt to formulate a more general expression of the Mycenaean scribes' strategy for spelling consonant clusters was presented by F. W. Householder[1] at the 1963 "Wingspread" Mycenaean Colloquium (the Third International Colloquium for Mycenaean Studies).[2] After summarizing the Mycenaean spelling rules as presented in the first edition of Ventris and Chadwick's *Documents,* Householder suggests what he calls an "alternative formulation":[3]

(1) All syllable codas are omitted except *w* (written -*u*-), and *n* (rarely *r-l*) before *w*. A "coda" . . . is a phoneme which closes a syllable[4] (and does not open a new syllable).[5]

In his remarks concerning syllable-final *w* in the first portion of this statement, Householder is referring to the second element of the Greek diphthongs which we may broadly transcribe as [eu], [ou],[6] and [au]. These diphthongs are normally spelled in full in Linear B, as opposed to the diphthongs [ei], [oi], [ai]. In the case of the latter three, the second vocalic element is occasionally represented in spelling but is normally omitted.[7] I consider the second component of the diphthongs [eu], [ou], and [au] to be fundamentally vocalic rather than consonantal—as is indicated by the regular use of the V symbol *u* for its representation—and, consequently, its representation is a phenomenon distinct from consonant cluster spelling.

By this analysis all consonant clusters which are completely spelled, other than [-nw-] (and occasionally [-rw-] and [-lw-]), should be tautosyllabic, while all other clusters should be heterosyllabic. For example, both consonants of the sequence [-sm-] in (2A) would fall within the final syllable; but in (2B), [-r-] would belong to the initial syllable and [-m-] to the final:

> (2)   A. *de-so-mo* for δεσμοις ([de$smois], 'with bindings')
>   B. *pe-mo* for σπερμο ([sper$mo], 'seed')

At least this would be the regular case; Householder indicates that there are a few exceptions in which "a fuller writing" is employed for heterosyllabic clusters.[8]

One problem with this interpretation of the consonant cluster spelling rule, which Householder acknowledges, arises in the instance of a word-final cluster of the type *stop* + *[s]*.[9] By rule (1) neither consonant of the cluster should be written, since both belong to the coda of the final syllable. The word-final [-s] of this cluster, just as predicted by rule (1), is not represented; we saw in chapter 2 that this is the regular treatment of word-final consonants in Linear B. However, contrary to Householder's formulation, a stop preceding the final [-s] can be written. Thus, we find Mycenaean spellings such as the following (already encountered in chapter 2):

> (3)   *wa-na-ka*, ϝαναξ ([wanaks], 'king')
>   *a₃-ti-jo-qo*, Αιθιοqʷς ([aitʰiokʷs], a man's name)[10]

The means by which Householder extracts himself from this difficulty is rather ad hoc and strikes one as suspicious—and it seems clear that Householder is aware that this is so. He suggests that by convention a word-final sequence [-ks] is spelled *-ka* and that a word-final sequence [-kʷs] is spelled *-qo* "no matter what vowel preceded."[11] It would presumably be coincidental that in the attested forms [-ks] is preceded by [-a-] and [-kʷs] by [-o-]. There is more to be said about this matter, and we shall return to it in chapters 4 and 5.

There is, however, a far more serious problem with Householder's interpretation. By his analysis the Linear B spelling of consonant clusters is dependent upon syllable structure. The syllable structure which is required by this analysis, however, is contradicted by what we otherwise know about the construction of the Greek syllable. That is to say, Householder must posit that in the case of some word-internal clusters of two consonants, both consonants have membership in the same syllable (as in (2A)). Yet, as is well known, the evidence afforded by Greek meter indicates that it is generally the case that the members of any given word-internal cluster of two consonants will each belong to a *different* syllable—regardless of what those consonants are. This is of course revealed by the metrical weight of syllables.

The meter of Greek is quantitative; that is, metrical patterns are created by arranging *heavy* and *light* syllables in particular sequences. In the metrical structure of Greek, a syllable is heavy (A) if it contains a long vowel or a diphthong[12] or (B) if it is a closed syllable (i.e., a syllable which ends in a consonant).[13] *When a vowel is followed by two consonants,*[14] the syllable to which that vowel belongs counts as a heavy syllable regardless of whether its vowel is long or short.[15] This is because a vowel preceding a biconsonantal cluster occurs in a closed syllable, with the syllable being closed by, and having as its final member, the first consonant of the cluster. Thus, a syllable-boundary separates the two members of a word-internal cluster.[16] A syllable is light if it contains a short vowel and is open.

In addition to the testimony of meter, phonological evidence also exists which reveals that the members of a word-internal cluster belong to two different syllables. An often cited set of examples evidencing this syllabification pattern is provided by comparative and superlative formation of *o*-stem adjectives.[17] If the syllable preceding the stem vowel is light (i.e., an open syllable containing a short vowel), the addition of the comparative suffix -τερος and the superlative suffix -τατος is accompanied by lengthening of the stem vowel, as in the following examples:

(4)   νέ-ο-ς ([né-o-s], 'new')
      νε-ώ-τερος ([ne-ǫ́:-teros], 'newer')
      νε-ώ-τατος ([ne-ǫ́:-tatos], 'newest')

If, however, the syllable preceding the stem vowel -*o*- contains a long vowel or a diphthong, and thus is heavy, there is no lengthening of the stem vowel:[18]

(5)   ὠμ-ό-ς ([ǫ:m-ó-s], 'raw')
      ὠμ-ό-τερος ([ǫ:m-ó-teros], 'rawer')
      ὠμ-ό-τατος ([ǫ:m-ó-tatos], 'rawest')

In the same way, if the stem vowel is preceded by a consonant cluster, then the vowel again is not lengthened, regardless of whether the vowel preceding the cluster is long or, as in the following examples, is short:

(6)   A. λεπτ-ό-ς ([lept-ó-s], 'thin')
         λεπτ-ό-τερος ([lept-ó-teros], 'thinner')
         λεπτ-ό-τατος ([lept-ó-tatos], 'thinnest')

      B. μακρ-ό-ς ([makr-ó-s], 'long')
         μακρ-ό-τερος ([makr-ó-teros], 'longer')
         μακρ-ό-τατος ([makr-ó-tatos], 'longest')

Such examples reveal of course that the syllable preceding the stem vowel is heavy, just as in (5). Since in each case the vowel of the heavy syllable is short, the syllable must be heavy by position; in other words, the initial consonant of the cluster [-pt] in (6A) and [-kr-] in (6B) closes, and thus belongs to, the syllable preceding the stem vowel [-o-] (i.e., λεπ$τός etc., μακ$ρός etc.).[19]

Further evidence for the heterosyllabicity of word-internal clusters is provided by the accentuation pattern of trisyllabic neuter nominals ending in -ιον

([-ion]).[20] When the syllable preceding the -ιον formant is light, the accent generally falls on this syllable, as in the following examples:

(7)   κόρ-ιον ([kóp-ion], 'little girl')
      λίθ-ιον ([líthᵸ-ion], 'little stone')
      πτύχ-ιον ([ptükᵸ-ion], 'folding tablet')

However, when the preceding suffix is heavy as a consequence of containing a long vowel or a diphthong, the accent occurs on the first vowel of the formant:[21]

(8)   κλειδ-ίον ([klẹ:d-íon], 'little key')
      ψωμ-ίον ([psọ:m-íon], 'little morsel')
      παιδ-ίον ([paid-íon], 'little child')

As would be expected, the same pattern of accentuation is found when the syllable preceding -ιον is heavy as a consequence of being closed:

(9)   καρφ-ίον ([karpʰ-íon], 'little twig')
      λυχν-ίον ([lükʰn-íon], 'lamp(stand)')
      τεκν-ίον ([tekn-íon], 'little child')

These examples again evidence, contra Householder, that a syllable-boundary separates, and does not precede, a word-internal consonant cluster (i.e., λυχ-$-víov[22] etc.).[23]

These two changes (*o*-stem vowel lengthening and the accent shift which accompanies -ιον suffixation), and hence the syllable structure which they require, belong to an ancient period of Greek. This syllable structure is, in fact, identical to that of Vedic Sanskrit, as revealed by Vedic meter, concerning which Antoine Meillet states:

(10)   La prosodie, c'est-à-dire l'ensemble des règles suivant lesquelles se définissent les syllabes longues et les syllabes brèves, est la même en grec et en védique. Est longue toute syllabe dont l'élément vocalique est long, ce qui arrive quand cet élément est soit une voyelle longue soit une diphtongue; est longue également toute syllabe où une voyelle brève est suivie de deux consonnes. Chez Homère comme dans les védas, tout groupe de consonnes détermine ainsi une syllabe longue.[24]

This agreement in prosodic structure between two of the most ancient Indo-European dialects suggests that the heterosyllabicity of a word-internal consonant cluster was a syllable trait inherited from their common parent Proto-Indo-European.[25] Since this syllable structure characterizes both pre-Greek and the first-millennium literary language, we would certainly expect it to be a characteristic of the intervening second-millennium Greek dialects for which the syllabic scripts were adapted.

In summary, Householder's rule (1) requires that when both members of a word-internal cluster are written, as in (2A), both members of the cluster lie within a single syllable. This analysis is undermined by extensive metrical and phonological evidence which reveals just the opposite, that is, that members of word-internal clusters belong to different syllables.

3.1 Beekes

A somewhat more broad-based attempt to discover the underlying systematic principle of consonant cluster representation in Linear B was offered by R. S. P. Beekes in 1971. Beekes rightly saw that the strategy utilized by the Mycenaean scribes for this purpose was fundamentally parallel to that used by their Cypriot counterparts. In beginning his discussion, he presents a list of the various types of consonant clusters which he has identified as occurring in the Linear B and syllabic Cypriot materials (though he indicates that fewer cluster-types are found in the latter materials; thus, these clusters constitute only a subset of those occurring in the former). In the scheme he offers, which follows, T stands for "stop" and R for "resonant"; he identifies the latter as consisting of the liquids *l* and *r*, the nasals *m* and *n*, and the glides, which he writes as *i* and *u*:

(11) I geminates
      II A I T + T
           2 T + R
         B I R + T
           2 R + R
              a_1 liqu. + liqu.
              a_2 liqu. + nas.
              a_3 liqu. + *i, u*
              b_1 nas. + liqu.
              b_2 nas. + nas.
              b_3 nas. + *i, u*
              c *i, u* + R
              d_1 *r + l*
              d_2 *l + r*
              e_1 *m + n*
              e_2 *n + m*
              f_1 *i + u*
              f_2 *u + i*
      III A I *s* + T
            2 *s* + R
          B I T + *s*
            2 R + *s*[26]

Beekes first considers syllabic Cypriot spelling practice, setting out two rules:[27]

(12) Geminates are written singly.

(13) A consonant before another is written with the vowel of the syllable to which the consonant belongs.

Rule (13) is, of course, the interpretation encountered in the handbooks (summarized in chapter 2), which holds that the syllabic Cypriot spelling of consonant clusters is dependent upon syllable structure.

In his discussion at this point (pp. 339–340), Beekes only explicitly associates rule (13) with the clusters of his group II (see (11)), even though he refers to (13) as "the general rule for Cyprian." His silence here on the applicability of rule (13) to group III appears to be the consequence of several factors. First of all, he states that there are no instances in the syllabic Cypriot materials of two of the four clusters in group III: the missing clusters are *s* + R (III A 2) and R + *s* (III B 2); however, on both counts Beekes has committed an oversight. An instance of the former type of cluster occurs, for example, in the participle *i-na-la-li-si-me-na, ιναλαλισμεναν* ([inalalismenan], 'engraved'), and an occurrence of the latter is found, for example, in the verb *e-ke-re-se, εκερσε* ([ekerse], '(s)he carved'). Concerning a third cluster-type in his category III, the cluster T + *s* (III B I), Beekes remarks that "the treatment is not clear."[28] While there is some variation in the strategy used for representing clusters of this type in the Cypriot Syllabary, we will see in chapter 4 that a general treatment can be reasonably identified.[29] The remaining cluster in Beekes' group III is *s* + T. As I show later, this cluster-type proves to be quite problematic for Beekes' analysis of Linear B and syllabic Cypriot spelling.

Beekes next proceeds to consider Linear B spelling of consonant clusters and, like Householder, contends that "the general principle is that writing of consonant groups in Mycenaean was determined by the syllabic structure of the word."[30] The spelling rule which Beekes offers for Linear B representation of consonant clusters is the following:

(14)   Consonants at the beginning of a syllable are written, those at the end are not.[31]

He then correctly observes that in those instances in which the Cypriot Syllabary uses regressive spelling, Linear B employs partial spelling (utilizing the terminology which I introduced in chapter 2), and that in those instances in which the former uses progressive spelling, the latter does likewise (i.e., it uses plenary spelling). We will further consider these correspondences in chapter 4, but for the present I simply offer two of Beekes' examples as illustrations:

(15)   A. R + T (resonant + stop)
        Cypriot *a-ra-te-mi-ti, Αρτεμιτι* (artemiti), 'to Artemis': regressive spelling
        Mycenaean *a-te-mi-to, Αρτεμιτος* (artemitos), 'of Artemis': partial spelling

       B. T + R (stop + resonant)
        Cypriot *pa-ti-ri, πατρι* (patri), 'to father': progressive spelling
        Mycenaean *e-ru-ta-ra, ερυθρα* (erüt[h]ra), 'red': plenary spelling

A qualification which must be attached to the preceding generalization (14) is that it holds only for word-internal clusters. As I indicated above in my introductory discussion of Linear B and syllabic Cypriot spelling practices, special strategies exist for word-initial and *nasal* + *consonant* clusters in the Cypriot Syllabary and for word-final clusters in both Linear B and the syllabic Cypriot script.

Thus, Beekes advocates that consonant cluster spelling in both Linear B and the Cypriot Syllabary is sensitive to syllable structure: the type of strategy used to represent the first member of a word-internal cluster is determined by whether that consonant belongs to the same syllable as the second member of the cluster ([-V\$C$_1$C$_2$V-], plenary/progressive spelling used in both scripts) or whether it belongs to the preceding syllable ([-VC$_1$\$C$_2$V-], partial spelling used in Linear B and regressive spelling in the Cypriot Syllabary). Beekes' analysis is precisely that one which we have immediately above seen advocated by Householder—Beekes has just extended its application to the Cypriot Syllabary, and in fact this is the very interpretation which we have seen to be offered by the handbooks on the syllabic Cypriot materials. We found, however, that this interpretation comes up short when viewed in the light of what we otherwise know about Greek syllable structure, as revealed by metrical and phonological phenomena.

Beekes is aware of the contradiction between his interpretation of Greek syllable structure and the evidence, and he is aware of the seriousness of this discrepancy.[32] He enumerates the cluster sets affected as follows:[33]

(16) II A 1   T + T
             2   T + R
      II B 2 b$_3$ n + w
             e$_1$ m + n
      III A 2 s + R
          B 1   T + s[34]

Toward rectifying this discrepancy, Beekes proposes that in the case of the clusters of (16) the syllable-boundary falls *within* the first consonant rather than simply before or after it. In other words, he contends that an intervocalic cluster[-C$_1$C$_2$-] is syllabified [-C$_1$/C$_1$C$_2$-]. For support of this analysis, he adduces evidence from alphabetic Greek inscriptions. It is not uncommon that inscriptional forms containing a word-internal consonant cluster are spelled with a doubling of the first member of the cluster, as in the following examples:

(17)   Ἔκκτωρ for Ἔκτωρ ([hékto̧:r], proper name)
       τέθαππται for τέθαπται ([tétʰaptai], '(s)he is honored with funeral rites')[35]

Concerning this spelling practice, Beekes states, "This is generally assumed to indicate that the syllabic trench lay within the first consonant."[36] Beyond that he contends, "It is remarkable that these cases [of double spelling] occur exactly where we would expect them."[37] That is to say, they coincide with those clusters which, according to his analysis, are revealed to be tautosyllabic by the spelling practices of the syllabaries (i.e., the clusters of (16)); though, as he points out, the cluster n + w is an exception to this coincidence: "There are no parallels in alphabetic inscriptions, probably because the groups had disappeared."[38]

Beekes' account of the alleged, unexpected tautosyllabic structure of the clusters of (16) is a quite interesting one. Certain theoretical phonologists have claimed in a somewhat similar fashion that some word-internal consonants—not only consonants found in clusters but also consonants occurring singly—"overlap" syllable-boundaries.[39] Moreover, as Beekes suggests, classical philologists and linguists other than himself have previously conjectured that the double spelling of consonants in Greek alphabetic inscriptions is a consequence of dual syllabic membership, though in instances with some qualification. For example, Buck states:

> (18)   A single consonant is often written double, this indicating a syllable division by which it was heard at the end of one syllable and the beginning of the next. But not all the examples . . . can be understood in this way.[40]

(Buck does not indicate which forms he would interpret otherwise, however.) In his influential work on Greek syllable structure, Eduard Hermann writes:[41]

> (19)   Die Schreibung zeigt somit auf zwei Silben verteilt die Gruppen 7 [*s + stop*], 8 [*s + nasal*], zum Teil auch 1 [*stop + stop*], 3 [*stop + nasal*], 12 [*nasal + nasal*], vielleicht auch 4, 5 [both groups *stop + liquid*]. Unter allen Gruppen, die nicht durch Assimilation usw. beseitigt waren, ist also nur allenfalls Verschußlaut + σ ausgenommen.[42]

There are, however, other scholars who have proposed a different interpretation for this graphic doubling of initial consonants in clusters. For example, Michel Lejuene remarks:[43]

> (20)   [L]es géminées étant toujours hétérosyllabiques, il arrive dans les inscriptions que soit redoublée la consonne initiale d'un groupe, pour mieux marquer ainsi le caractère hétérosyllabique du groupe.[44]

Given this interpretation of dual syllabic alignment for the first member of certain biconsonantal clusters, Beekes' proposed rule (14) for the Linear B spelling of consonant clusters, repeated here as (21), still appears adequate:

> (21)   Consonants at the beginning of a syllable are written, those at the end are not.

For example, a form such as *τεκτονες*, which would now have the syllabic structure [tekktones], should be and is spelled *te-ko-to-ne* (i.e., only the syllable-initial consonants are written as prescribed by (21)). However, by introducing this interpretation of Greek syllable structure, a complication is created for his rule (13) of consonant cluster spelling in the Cypriot Syllabary, repeated here as (22):

> (22)   A consonant before another is written with the vowel of the syllable to which the consonant belongs.

Consider, for example, that the name *Τιμοϝανακτος* would have the syllabic structure [timowanakktos] and by rule (22) should be spelled **Ti-mo-wa-na-ka-ko-to-se* rather than *Ti-mo-wa-na-ko-to-se,* as it actually is spelled. Presumably, Beekes would link this nonrepresentation of the first occurrence of the consonant having dual affiliation (here the initial [k] of [k$kt]) with rule

(12), which prohibits the spelling of both members of a geminate cluster. While not addressing this matter directly, Beekes does speculate as to why in clusters of the proposed type $C_1\$C_1C_2$ it is the second occurrence of C_1 which is spelled rather than the first: "That the part of the consonant which belonged to the next syllable was chosen is probably caused by the fact that the explosion was 'stronger' than the implosion."[45] By "implosion" he is apparently referring to the production of the articulatory closure (as opposed to the release of the closure).[46]

We have already seen that the idea of a syllable-boundary falling within the first consonant of a cluster has hardly been embraced by all previous commentators on the double representation of consonants in inscriptions. Beyond this fact, however, there are two specific objections which must be raised. The first is directed both toward this interpretation of the inscriptional spellings and, following from that, toward Beekes' analysis of the "tautosyllabic" clusters of Mycenaean and Cypriot Greek (i.e., the clusters of (16)). The second, more serious objection, is directed only toward Beekes' analysis.

The first objection concerns clusters of three consonants. In the Linear B materials, we find occurrences, for example, of clusters of the type *stop + stop + liquid,* as in the following:

(23) *ra-pi-ti-ra₂*, ῥάπτριαι ([hraptriai], 'seamstresses')
re-u-ko-to-ro, Λευκτρον ([leuktron], place-name)

As these examples indicate, in the case of this type of cluster, all three members of the cluster are written. This means, of course, that by Beekes' analysis these forms would be syllabified as follows:

(24) hrap$ptri$ai
leuk$ktron

Here, as before, the inscriptions could be appealed to for support, for such spellings occur as

(25) ἐκκπρᾶξαι ([ekkpraksai], 'to levy')[47]

The syllabic analysis of (24) seems quite improbable, however. The prosodics of Greek are such that only a single type of word-initial triconsonantal cluster is allowed, that cluster being *[s] + stop + liquid or nasal.*[48] As the cluster-type *stop + stop + liquid* cannot occur word-initially,[49] it is highly improbable that such a cluster could occur at the beginning of a word-internal syllable. The same point holds true in the case of the cluster-type *stop + fricative + nasal,* as in the Mycenaean form

(26) *a₃-ka-sa-ma*, αιξμανς ([aiksmans], 'points')[50]

in which the use of progressive spelling to represent the sequence [ksm] would again, by Beekes' analysis, indicate a tautosyllabic cluster. Compare the inscriptional spelling

(27) εξσμνεαι for εξμνεαι ([heksmneai], 'six minas')[51]

which would suggest a syllable-initial cluster of the type *[s]* + *nasal* + *nasal,* another impossible word-initial cluster. The examples of (23) through (27) and others of the same type pose a significant problem for those investigators who would interpret these syllabic and alphabetic orthographic practices as evidence for Greek syllable structure.

A second problem concerns the cluster-type *[s]* + *stop.* By far, most of the examples of double spelling of the initial consonant of a word-internal cluster in inscriptional materials involve this type of cluster. Thus, Hermann writes:

> (28) Gegenüber allen andern Verdoppelungen ragen an Zahl weit heraus die Ver-
> bindungen von σσ vor Verschlußlaut. . . . Die Fälle sind so außerorden-
> tlich zahlreich (390 Belege), daß an Versehen ganz und garnicht zu denken
> ist.[52]

Similarly, Threatte states:

> (29) Consonants forming the first element of a cluster are not infrequently dou-
> bled out of a confusion as to whether they go with the following syllable
> or the preceding. Such geminations are well attested in the case of the
> sibilant. . . . The gemination of [s] is very frequent, especially before τ, κ
> and θ.[53]

He then goes on to offer eighty-nine examples of *[s]* + *stop* clusters occurring in Attic inscriptions in which the *s* is doubled.[54] This same cluster-type *[s]* + *stop* is the most frequently occurring consonant cluster in the Linear B materials (451 occurrences) and the second most frequently occurring word-internal cluster among the syllabic Cypriot materials (sixty-three occurrences).[55] Given the alleged correspondence between the inscriptional practice of consonant doubling and the progressive spelling of consonants in the syllabic scripts, we should find that in both Linear B and the Cypriot Syllabary the [-s-] of word-internal *[s]* + *stop* clusters is represented using progressive spelling. This is not the case. In every instance of this cluster in Mycenaean, the [-s-] is omitted; that is, partial spelling is used. Similarly, in all but one occurrence of the cluster in Cypriot, the [-s-] is written using regressive spelling and not the predicted progressive type. This is a critical distinction and can reasonably be interpreted to show that whatever the phonetic significance of the inscriptional practice of consonant doubling may be, this practice is fundamentally different from the use of the progressive spelling strategy in the syllabic scripts.

This conflicting treatment of *[s]* + *stop* clusters which is exhibited by the syllabic scripts vis-à-vis the alphabetic inscriptions has not escaped Beekes' attention, though he has perhaps deemphasized its significance. For him the conflict is all the more problematic because the quite similar cluster-type *s* + R shows the orthographic treatment which he would expect; he writes:

> (30) Here we have a problem. In *s* + R we find that the *s* is written in Myce-
> naean [and in syllabic Cypriot as well; see above]. . . . As this group
> makes position, it seems probable that the syllabic trench fell within the *s,*
> and this is confirmed by inscriptional forms. . . . The problem, however,
> is that both Cyprian and Mycenaean treat *s* before a stop (A I) as not
> belonging to the second syllable.[56]

Beekes proposes to account for the troublesome word-internal treatment of *[s]* + *stop* clusters by appealing to their treatment in word-initial position, stating, "I think that it must be connected with the fact that *s* before a stop was also not written at the beginning of the word."[57] While this is certainly the case in Linear B, it is not the case in the Cypriot Syllabary. In fact, in the latter script, word-initial *[s]* + *stop* is written using progressive spelling, the very spelling which Beekes' analysis would predict for word-internal occurrences of this cluster, but the spelling which is *not* used there. It is clearly the case that word-initial treatment cannot be responsible for word-internal treatment in the Cypriot Syllabary.

We will find again and again that the cluster *[s]* + *stop* is problematic for any attempt to account for the representation of consonant clusters in Linear B and the Cypriot Syllabary on the basis of syllable structure. Beekes takes a step toward what I believe to be the proper solution when, speculating on the nonrepresentation of [s-] in word-initial *[s]* + *stop* clusters (which occurs only in Linear B, as pointed out above), he suggests that "it is more probable that the reason must be found in the nature of the group *s* + stop: the aperture of *s* is greater than that of the stop, so that a syllabification *s|per-* could be expected."[58] As we will discover, the notion of aperture is critical not only for the representation of word-initial *[s]* + *stop* clusters but for the spelling of all clusters in both Linear B and the Cypriot Syllabary.

3.2 Sampson

In a book which appeared in 1985, Geoffrey Sampson presents a general treatment of writing systems. For his chapter on syllabic writing, he chooses to investigate Linear B, identifying it as "a relatively pure example of syllabic writing." Among the issues to which Sampson pays particular attention is the spelling of consonant clusters. He first offers a general rule of consonant cluster spelling which he identifies as being essentially a close approximation:

> (31)   Consonants are written (if necessary, with borrowed vowels) whenever they precede the vowel of their syllable, and are omitted whenever they follow the vowel of their syllable.[59]

By the phrase *borrowed vowel* he is denoting what we have called an empty vowel, and he is referring here to that type of spelling which we have identified as plenary. Sampson's rule looks quite familiar to us because it is essentially the same as the general rules for spelling consonant clusters in Linear B which Beekes and Householder offered; Beekes' rule (14) and Householder's rule (1) are repeated here as (32A) and (32B) respectively:

> (32)   A. Consonants at the beginning of a syllable are written, those at the end are not.
>   B. All syllable codas are omitted except *w* (written *-u-*), and *n* (rarely *r-l*) before *w*. A "coda" . . . is a phoneme which closes a syllable (and does not open a new syllable).

Sampson is accordingly faced with the very same set of problems with which his predecessors had to deal, and he immediately addresses two of these: (A) the matter of word-final *stop* + *[s]* clusters; and (B) that of *[s]* + *stop* clusters.

3.2.1 The *Stop* + *[S]* Problem

As we have already seen, if a word ends in the consonantal sequence *stop* + *[s]*, the final fricative [-s] is not written and the preceding stop is spelled by utilizing the symbol whose vocalic component is identical to the vowel which precedes the cluster. The examples considered earlier are repeated here as (33):

(33)   A. *wa-na-ka*, ϝαναξ ([wanaks], 'king')
       B. *a₃-ti-jo-qo*, Αιθιοqʷς ([aitʰiokʷs], a man's name)

In the case of these clusters a stop is written which *does* follow the vowel of its syllable, contrary to Sampson's rule (31) (and contrary to Beekes' and Householder's rules, of course). Sampson suggests that the stops are "exceptionally" noted in this context because, given his formulation, this would be the *only position* in a word in which stops would not be spelled: "[S]ince the general rule led to the overwhelming majority of stops being written, the rule was expanded so as to require all stops to be written."[60] Sampson thus opts for a kind of analogical solution to this problem.

3.2.2 The *[S]* + *Stop* Problem

Clusters of the type *[s]* + *stop* are equally problematic (as we have already seen quite clearly), because the fricative is not written, even though, in Sampson's terms and given his assumptions concerning Greek syllable structure, the fricative does "precede the vowel of its syllable." Sampson illustrates this difficulty with the following examples:

(34)   A. /sperma/ 'seed' = <pe-ma>
       B. /statʰmos/ 'farmstead' = <ta-to-mo>
       C. /ksunstrokʷʰaː/ 'aggregate' = <ku-su-to-ro-qa>

With respect to (34C) he states, "the syllabification must surely be /ksun\$s-tro\$kʷʰaː/."[61]

3.2.3 A Reformulation

Due to these problematic exceptions to rule (31), Sampson reformulates his rule as follows:

(35)   A consonant which is not a stop is omitted if it occurs after the vowel of its syllable, and (in the case of /s/)[62] if it immediately precedes a stop; otherwise all consonants are written, with borrowed vowels where necessary.[63]

In addition to the examples of (34), Sampson offers a number of other Linear B spellings in the course of his discussion, among which are the following:

(36) A. /kʰalkos/ 'bronze' = <ka-ko>
      B. /korwos/ 'boy' = <ko-wo>
      C. /amni:sos/ (a place name) = <a-mi-ni-so>
      D. /aksones/ 'axles' = <a-ko-so-ne>
      E. /alektruo:n/ 'cock' = <a-re-ku-tu-ru-wo>

His revised formulation (35) is supposed to predict correctly the spelling of the forms of (34) and (36). However, as we have seen already, this is only the case if a syllable-boundary should precede those clusters which are fully spelled (i.e., represented with plenary spelling) and should fall within those clusters which are partially spelled. In other words, the examples of (34) and (36) must be syllabified as follows:

(37) A. /sper$ma/
      B. /sta$tʰmos/
      C. /ksun$strokʷʰa:/
      D. /kʰal$kos/
      E. /kor$wos/
      F. /a$mni:sos/
      G. /a$ksones/
      H. /ale$ktruo:n/[64]

To justify his analysis of the fully spelled clusters (i.e., those of (37B, C, F, G, and H)) as tautosyllabic, Sampson claims that *clusters which are capable of occurring word-initially are preceded by a syllable boundary when they occur word-internally.*[65] Yet, as he himself points out,[66] the cluster [-ktr-] of (37H), which he claims to be tautosyllabic, is *not permitted* word-initially; for that matter, neither is the cluster [-tʰm-] of (37B).[67] In contrast, [-tr-] is a frequently occurring initial cluster, so by Sampson's own analysis a syllabification [-k$tr-] (and a spelling other than *a-re-**ku**-tu-ru-wo?*) would be expected.[68]

3.2.4 A Further Problem

There is, however, a far more serious and pervasive problem with Sampson's analysis, and that is, of course, the very one which I have identified in my arguments against Householder's and Beekes' analyses: namely, there exists a great body of metrical and phonological evidence which shows that a syllable-boundary occurs *within* a word-internal cluster and *not before* it, even if such a cluster is capable of occurring at the beginning of a word. Sampson does not ignore this problem completely; but neither does he give it the serious attention which it requires (as Beekes does to some degree). After pointing out that the problem exists, he states, in referring to his principle of syllable-division which locates a boundary before an internal cluster that is capable of occurring initially, "If [this] traditional principle of syllable-division must be rejected, then it seems that the relatively simple spelling-rule I have given [i.e., (35)] could be defended only if there were evidence in Greek for differences between shallow and deep syllabification."[69] In the following section we will more closely examine this recurring problem for those various attempts to systematize consonant cluster spelling in the syllabic scripts.

3.3 Ancient Tradition

3.3.1 Inscriptional Word-Division

As I noted in the preceding paragraph, Sampson refers to the idea that a syllable-boundary precedes any word-internal cluster which is capable of occurring
word-initially as the *"traditional principle* of syllable division" (emphasis is
mine). This theory can be rightly identified as "traditional" in that it has its
roots in antiquity. We find, for example, that it is essentially this principle
which was utilized for dividing words at the end of lines in Greek inscriptions.[70] According to Threatte,[71] Attic inscriptions are found as early as the
sixth century B.C.[72] which attempt to divide words at "syllable" boundaries;[73]
some of these divisions involve consonant clusters. For the sixth and fifth centuries the evidence is not abundant as compared to later periods, but on the
basis of what evidence there is, Threatte reports that internal word-division
usually does not conform closely to what will emerge as canonical practice in
the third century B.C. The inscriptional evidence from the fourth century, which
is somewhat more plentiful, also shows an absence of the later regular treatment until the last quarter of the century: two Athenian naval catalogues dated
ca. 326–324 B.C. contain divided words which are "syllabified" according to
practices observed with regularity beginning in the third century (the period
during which a large body of evidence first becomes available).[74]

The third-century (and later)[75] practices of internal word-division which
involve segmentation at or within a consonant cluster are formalized by
Threatte[76] as the following rules:[77]

(38)   A. Division normally takes place before a single consonant (also ξ [ks],
        ψ [ps]).
        B. Geminated consonants are normally divided (including γγ [ŋg], κχ
        [ŋkʰ]).
        C. A combination of a stop and a liquid or a nasal [i.e.,]
            [pl], [pr],
            [pʰl], [pʰr]
            [bl], [br]
            [tr]
            [tʰl], [tʰm], [tʰn], [tʰr]
            [dn], [dr]
            [kl], [km], [kn], [kr]
            [kʰl], [kʰm], [kʰn], [kʰr]
            [gm], [gn], [gl], [gr][78]
        is almost never divided; normally both consonants go on to the second
        line.
        D. The cluster [mn] is not divided and division precedes it.
        E. . . . combinations of liquid or nasal plus stop are normally divided.
        F. The clusters [bd], [gd], [kʰtʰ], [pt], [pʰtʰ], [kt] are not divided.
        G. The final [-k] of the preposition ἐκ is more often carried to the next
        line than not. . . .

H. Clusters of *[s]* + *stop* are sometimes divided and sometimes have division before them.

I. The cluster [sm] is generally divided, but examples of division before it and even after it are attested.

J. The prepositions εἰς [ẹ:s] and πρός [prós] and the definite article ending in [-s] do not permit division before the final *sigma.*

K. Clusters of three or more consonants divide after the first consonant. . . . When the first of the three consonants is *sigma,* failure to divide the cluster is more frequent.

From these rules of Athenian inscriptional orthography, it is possible to abstract a general (though not exceptionless) principle of word-division:

(39)   A word-internal sequence of consonants will not be divided at the end of a line if, and only if, that sequence is an instance of a cluster-type which is capable of occurring in word-initial position; in such instances word-division precedes the consonant sequence.

The cluster-types of (38) which are capable of occurring word-initially and which are not divided at the end of a line are, of course, *stop* + *[s]* (38A); *stop* + *sonorant* (38C); *stop* + *stop* (38F); and the cluster [mn] (38D). It is necessary to use the term *cluster-type* in (39) because not all of the *specific clusters* which are preserved intact in the process of word-division actually occur at the beginning of a word. For example, while clusters of the general type *stop* + *stop* and *stop* + *nasal* are capable of occurring in word-initial position, the specific clusters [gd], [km], [kʰm], and [gm], among others, are not found word-initially in Greek. As indicated in (38), however, each of these occurs word-medially and when it does so is treated like other clusters of the same *type* which do in fact occur word-initially.[79]

There is one quite obvious exception to the generalization (39): namely, particular clusters of the type *[s]* + *consonant.* The sequence [sm] is capable of occurring word-initially in Greek, hence by (39) we would expect that word-division would precede the cluster. However, according to Threatte (38I), word-division at the end of a line most often separates the two members of the cluster, though there is some degree of variation in the treatment. Threatte's observations are supported by findings offered previously by Hermann:[80] in an investigation of inscriptions written in a variety of dialects, Hermann identified 130 instances in which the cluster [sm] is divided at the end of a line, as opposed to only twenty-nine in which word-division precedes the cluster. The cluster *[s]* + *stop,* which occurs frequently in Greek in word-initial position, is reported by Threatte as showing a variable treatment, being preserved without division at times (as we would expect on the basis of (39)) but divided at others.[81] Hermann's data again corroborate Threatte's observations, though they indicate a preference for separation of the two members of the cluster, contrary to (39). Hermann found 850 instances of word-division involving the word-internal cluster *[s]* + *stop.* In 547 cases the division occurs after the [s]; in the remaining 303 instances, division precedes the cluster.

We saw immediately above that the cluster-type *[s]* + *stop* was also problematic in the case of Sampson's analysis of Linear B spelling. The nature of the problem is a bit different in the two instances, however. In the alphabetic inscriptions, sequences of word-internal *[s]* + *stop* (as well as [sm] clusters) *are not* treated in a parallel fashion to word-initial clusters of the same type, to the extent that word-division more often than not *divides* the [s] from the following consonant. In Linear B, on the other hand, word-internal *[s]* + *stop* clusters *are* treated in the same fashion as identical clusters which occur at word-beginning: in both positions the cluster is written using partial spelling; that is, the [s] does not appear in the spelling (see examples (1A) and (1B) in chapter 2). The Linear B cluster is exceptional for Sampson in that it does not conform to his principle that clusters which are capable of occurring word-initially, and so by his analysis are preceded by a syllable-boundary, are represented with plenary spelling (see (34)), and thus he is compelled by this cluster (along with word-final sequences of the type *stop* + *[s]*) to formulate the less general strategy (35). The syllabic Cypriot treatment presents an analogue to the alphabetic inscriptional practice: word-internally and word-initially *[s]* + *stop* clusters are treated differently (with progressive spelling initially, regressive spelling internally), as we have seen.

Following from (39), it is the case that consonant clusters which *cannot* occur word-initially should normally be divided at the end of a line in Attic inscriptions.[82] This is thus the treatment utilized for geminate clusters (38B) and for clusters of the type *sonorant* + *stop* (38E).

Threatte's observation that clusters of three or more consonants are usually divided between the first and second consonants (38K) also follows from the generalization (39). Each of the examples of a three- or three-plus-member cluster which Threatte cites from the Attic inscriptions, with the exception of clusters of one particular type, is a cluster which cannot occur word-initially. Instead, these clusters are composed of some initial consonant followed by a sequence of consonants which *can* occur word-initially, as, for example, in the following:

(40)   A. ἀνέγ|κλητος ([anéŋklẹ̄tos], 'blameless')
       B. συν|πρόεδροι ([sün|próedroi], 'joint-presidents')[83]

Word-division occurring after the initial consonant of the cluster is then in keeping with (39). The particular three-member cluster-type alluded to above which is a common exception to division after the initial consonant is the sequence *[s]* + *stop* + *sonorant*. There is in Greek only one type of three-member cluster which is capable of occurring at the beginning of a word: namely, this very sequence *[s]* + *stop* + *sonorant*. Given the general principle (39), it would only be expected that words containing an internal cluster of, for example, [-str-] would show division before the cluster. However, just as there is variation in the manner of dividing *[s]* + *consonant* clusters (sometimes divided before the [s], sometimes after), so there is variation in the division of these *[s]* + *consonant* + *consonant* clusters.

The two remaining rules offered by Threatte ((38G) and (38J)) deal with morphologically conditioned exceptions to the regular treatment of [kC] and [sC] clusters. I will return to this matter later.

3.3.2 Greek Grammarian Syllable-Division

Explicit principles of a process that is identified as *syllable-division* and which are almost identical to these inscriptional strategies for dividing words at the end of lines are found in the writings of the Greek grammarians. The most extensive surviving treatment of this subject is that of the second-century A.D. grammarian Herodian, who writes of clusters as being either ἐν συλλήψει ([en süllḗ:psẹ:], 'in conjunction') or ἐν διαστάσει ([en diastásẹ:], 'in separation'). Among the "syllable-division" rules which he proposes, utilizing these two notions, are the following general principles for grouping consonants according to syllable membership:

(41) The consonants which are found at the beginning of a word are found *in conjunction* [i.e. are not divided] when they occur word-medially. For example, in [ktệ:ma] the [kt] is at the beginning of the word, and in [étikton], where they occur in the middle of the word, the consonants stand together.[84]

(42) Such consonants as are unable to be pronounced at the beginning of a word are to be separated from one another when they occur word-medially: for example, [ánthos], [érgon].[85]

(41) and (42) define the very principle of syllable-division which we have seen Sampson utilizing in his analysis of Linear B spelling (see chapter 3, n. 65): a syllable-boundary stands before a word-internal cluster-type which is capable of occurring word-initially.

According to Herodian, however, certain clusters constitute "exceptions" to the patterns of (41) and (42); these he specifies as the following:

(43) [thm], [phn], [gd], [khm], [km], [sg], [sd]: for these, though they are nowhere found in combination at the beginning [of a word], are not separated from one another medially, for example, [íthma], [aphnẹ:ós], [ógdoos], [aikh-mé:], [akhmé:], [phásganon], [theósdotos]. For if a word is not found beginning with [sd] in everyday Greek, it is in fact [found] in Aeolic,[86] for example, <sdügós> instead of <zügós>.[87]

Whatever the reason that Herodian chose to make specific reference to these particular clusters, it is clear that what he is doing is generalizing the treatment of *cluster-types* capable of occurring word-initially (*stop + nasal, stop + stop, fricative + stop*) to specific permutations of those types which are not found at the beginning of words.[88] Recall that we have already seen the exact same generalizing of cluster-types at work in the dividing of words at line-end in inscriptions; in fact, five of the seven clusters which Herodian specifies are also explicitly identified by Threatte as clusters which are preserved by word-division occurring before the cluster (see (38C) and (38F)).[89] Here we see a Greek grammarian making specific use of the notion of "manner of articulation."

Beyond (43), Herodian addresses the treatment of other specific cluster-types and individual clusters which either can or cannot occur word-initially. We are told, for example:

(44)   Stops before liquids are *in conjunction*; that is to say the two are together, neither the stop nor the liquid is separate: for example, [akmę́:], [atmós], . . . [agrós], [óklaion], [étʰnę:skon], [épleon], [habrós].[90]

Notice that the term ἀμετάβολον ([ametábolon], 'liquid') designates not only those sounds which in contemporary phonetic terminology are referred to as liquids (i.e., [l] and [r] (for Greek)) but also nasals (i.e., [m], [n], and [ŋ] (for Greek)). The Latin grammarians translated ἀμετάβολον as *liquidus* and limited its application to [l] and [r].[91]

(45)   Liquids [occurring] before stops are *in separation* [i.e., are divided]: for example, [hérpǫ:] (the [one meaning] 'to walk'), [hélkǫ:], [ántʰos], [ártos], [érgon], [émbolos], [súmpʰǫ:non], [súmponos].[92]

(46)   A liquid does not precede a liquid according to *conjunction* but according to *separation:* for example, [arnós], [hermȇ:s], [hálmę:], [érnos], [hólmos]. Note that in the case of these, one liquid is the terminal [sound] of the syllable coming first and the other is the initial [sound] of the ensuing [syllable], and [the two liquids] are not together.[93]

Herodian's rule (46) provides us with our first insight into the relationship between his notions *in conjunction* and *in separation* and his interpretation of syllable membership: consonants which are *in separation* are members of different syllables; and, we can infer, consonants which are *in conjunction* are members of the same syllable (this is explicitly stated in (49)). The latter has, of course, already been implied by Herodian's identification of ability to occur in word-initial position, and hence in syllable-initial position, with occurrence *in conjunction*. The grammarian goes on to tell us that there is, however, an exception to (46):

(47)   It is necessary to except [m] and [n], for these are found according to *conjunction* as in [mnâ], [mnę:mȇ:on]; here the [m] and the [n] are together.[94]

Herodian's remarks concerning *liquid + liquid* clusters are subsumed beneath a more general statement:

(48)   A continuant[95] does not precede a continuant according to *conjunction* but according to *separation.*[96]

The cluster [-mn-] is of course also an exception to this rule, as well as the cluster [-sm-] and word-final clusters:

(49)   It is necessary to except [m] and [n], [s] and [m], and syllables occurring at the end of a word; for in the case of these, continuants are found preceding continuants according to *conjunction:* in the case of [m] and [n] as in [mnâ], [mnę:mȇ:on]; in the case of [s] and [m] as in [smǫ̂:], [smilíon], and

[kósmos]; and in the case of syllables occurring at the end of a word, for example, [háls], [mákars], [tîrüns], and [hélmins]. Note that in the case of these, continuants are found preceding continuants according to *conjunction,* since they do not have an ensuing vowel, which is requisite to effect the combination of one consonant [i.e., to separate it from the other consonant].[97]

Rules (44), (45), (46), and (48) (as well as rule (50) below), when considered together with their respective "exceptional case" rules, are in compliance with the general principle that a syllable-boundary precedes a word-internal cluster if, and only if, it is capable of occurring word-initially. Word-final (*continuant + continuant*) clusters are a different matter for the reason pointed out by Herodian. Notice that in stating that sequences of continuants which are located within word-final *syllables* occur according to *conjunction* (49), Herodian now makes an explicit connection between tautosyllabicity and being *in conjunction.*

3.3.2.1 [s] + Stop *Clusters Yet Again*

We saw in the preceding section that the *[s] + stop* clusters, as well as sequences of *[s] + [m],* depart from the regular inscriptional treatment of clusters which are capable of occurring word-initially, in that in the majority of instances word-division separates the two members of these clusters rather than occurring before the clusters as would be expected. Herodian's analysis of [-sm-] clusters, presented in rule (49), thus contradicts the inscriptional practice to the extent that Herodian assigns to [-sm-] clusters the same treatment that he assigns to other clusters which are permitted at the beginning of a word (see (41)); that is, a syllable-boundary is said to precede the clusters when they occur word-internally. According to Herodian, the same is the case with clusters of the type *[s] + stop:*

(50) An [s] before all of the stops is *in conjunction,* that is to say the two are together—the [s] and the following stop—for example, [ésbese], [pʰásganon], [tʰeósdotos], [askós], [asté:r], [aspís], [astʰené:s], [askʰe:mosûne:], [heǫ:spʰóros]. Note that in the case of these, the [s] is together with the following stop.[98]

Although Herodian interprets word-internal *[s] + stop* and [-sm-] clusters as tautosyllabic, this was certainly not an interpretation which was shared by all grammarians. For example, in elaborating upon the area of grammatical study identified as σύνταξις ([súntaksis]), one grammarian writes:

(51) And σύνταξις is when we seek in which syllable we should construe sounds,[99] for example, in [astʰené:s], whether the [s] is the terminal [sound] of the first syllable or the initial [sound] of the second.[100]

That disagreement in this matter existed among the grammarians is made unmistakably plain by the skeptic Sextus Empiricus (ca. second-century A.D.). In *Against the Professors,* the philosopher-physician chides the grammarians:

(52)　For they say orthography occurs in three methods: quantity, quality and division. . . . On division: whenever we should query concerning the word [óbrimos], whether at times the [b] is at the beginning of the second syllable or the end of the preceding [syllable], and concerning the name [aristíǫ:n], where the [s] is to be assigned. But again, systematic treatment such as this (not considering even thornier issues which we could dredge up) appears to be worthless, first because of disagreement and then because of the results themselves. Because of disagreement, since the grammarians battle one another and will battle [one another] to eternity; concerning the very same thing, some insist on writing this way and others that way. . . . Therefore, guidance in orthography from the grammarians is not needed.

　　Refutation such as this then is based on disagreement; that [refutation] which is based on results is self-evident. Indeed we are not harmed . . . in the case of the name [aristíǫ:n] if we should place the [s] in the preceding syllable or if we should arrange it in the following [syllable]. For if, . . . because the [s] . . . is arranged this way and not that way, [aristíǫ:n] became [dẹ:pníǫ:n] (just as some witty person says), it would be appropriate not to be indifferent. But if . . . [aristíǫ:n] is always [aristíǫ:n], whether we should place the [s] with the [i] or with the [t], then what is the need of the lengthy and empty moronic discourse of the grammarians concerning these things?[101]

These remarks leave little room for doubt that the significant variation in the treatment of *[s] + stop* clusters which we observed in the inscriptional practices of word-division was paralleled by a disagreement among the grammarians as to the proper placement of "syllable"-boundaries with respect to such clusters. Herodian simply chose to present his own particular (and certainly not unbiased) view.

That Sextus Empiricus should indicate that there was also debate among the grammarians over syllable-division involving [-br-] clusters is most interesting, though not surprising. The classical Attic dialect (about which the grammarians were principally concerned) was characterized by a prosodic peculiarity traditionally termed *correptio Attica,* or Attic shortening. Metrical evidence reveals that in this dialect certain, though not all, word-internal clusters of the type *stop + liquid* and *stop + nasal* have become tautosyllabic; clusters of the type *[voiced stop] + nasal* and *[voiced stop] + [l]* usually remain heterosyllabic. The cluster [-br-] thus belongs to the subset which is prone to tautosyllabicity.[102] Several clusters having [w] as their second member also tend to be tautosyllabic in Attic (prior to the disappearance of the glide [w] from the dialect): namely, *liquid + [w], [-nw-], [-sw-]* and perhaps *[-dw-].*[103]

3.3.3 Morphologically Conditioned Variation

Before leaving Herodian's discussion of syllable-division, some attention should be given to his formulations which treat morphologically conditioned exceptions to his general principles of syllabic membership. Following his remarks on the tautosyllabicity of *stop + liquid* clusters (see (44)), Herodian adds:

(53) It is necessary to except [clusters] which come about from the prefixing of [ek(s)].[104] For these hold a stop with a following liquid *in separation*; that is to say, [they have] the stop in one syllable and the liquid in the other, for example, [eklúsai], [ekneurísai], [ekreûsai], [ekmáksai].[105]

Similarly, he appends to his discussion of *[s]* + *stop* clusters (see (50)) the following qualification concerning the prefixes εἰς, πρός, and δυς:

(54) It is necessary to except [clusters] which come about from the prefixing of the adverbs [ẹ:s], [prós], and [düs]; for these hold [s] with a following stop *in separation*; that is to say, they have the [s] in one syllable and the following stop in the other, for example, [ẹ:spʰérọ:], [prospʰorá], [düstükʰẹ́:s].[106]

The morphologically induced exceptions of (54) are of the same sort as those identified by Threatte for the process of word-division in Athenian inscriptions (see (38J), repeated here as (55)):[107]

(55) The prepositions εἰς [ẹ:s] and πρός [prós] and the definite article ending in [-s] do not permit division before the final *sigma*.

3.3.4 An Impasse?

On one hand, the inscriptional practices of word-division suggest and, much more explicitly, the teachings of the grammarians reveal an ancient theory of syllable membership which held that a syllable-boundary precedes a word-internal cluster which is of a type that is capable of occurring word-initially (though there is disagreement concerning the position of the syllable-boundary when the cluster involved is *[s]* + *stop* or *[s]* + *[m]*). On the other hand, metrical evidence no less clearly reveals that it is generally the case that a syllable-boundary divides any given word-internal cluster, regardless of whether the cluster is capable of occurring word-initially. How are these conflicting accounts to be reconciled?

Whatever phenomenon it was that the grammarians were treating when they discussed the division of words into "syllables," it almost certainly was some phenomenon *other than* syllable structure. That this is so is revealed by a set of quite remarkable statements made by the Alexandrian grammarian Hephaestion (second century A.D.) in his treatise on meter. The opening portion of the *Handbook of Meters* is devoted to a discussion of what Hephaestion refers to as "syllable length"; here the grammarian states that a syllable may be either long by nature (i.e., it may contain a long vowel or a diphthong)[108] or long by position.[109] With regard to the latter type of syllable, he writes:

(56) They are long by position when more than one simple consonant falls between a short or shortened[110] vowel and the vowel of the next syllable. This occurs in five ways.
A. Either [the syllable] ends in two consonants, for example, . . . [mákars]. . . .
B. Or these [two consonants] are in the next syllable, for example, [hékto̜:r]. . . . It is to be noted that here the first [consonant] should not

be a stop and the second a liquid: such [syllables] are *common,*[111] as
will be mentioned further along.

C. Or [the syllable] ends in one [consonant] and the next [syllable] begins
with another, for example, [ál-los],

D. or it ends in a double consonant,[112] for example, [héks],

E. or the next [syllable] begins with a double consonant, for example,
[é-ksǫ:].[113]

When Hephaestion writes of "long syllables" he is referring to what we have
called heavy syllables; the ancient grammarians unfortunately used the terms
μακρός ([makrós], 'long') and βραχύς ([brakʰűs], 'short') to designate both
vowel duration and syllable weight.[114] Hephaestion's claim (56B) could thus
be restated as follows:

(57)   A syllable containing a short vowel is heavy if the next syllable begins
with two consonants, for example, [hé-ktǫ:r].

Hephaestion is of course correct in identifying this type of syllable as metrically heavy. However, the very reason that such a syllable is heavy is that the
first of the two consonants which "follow" is—contrary to Hephaestion's
claim—*not* in the succeeding syllable: to take his example, the initial syllable
of [hék-tǫ:r] is heavy only because [k] falls within it, thus closing the syllable
and rendering this initial short-voweled syllable quantitatively equivalent to one
which contains a long vowel.[115] Notice, in fact, that Hephaestion must qualify
his statement (57) by excepting *stop + liquid* clusters (see (56B)),[116] because
it is in this case that both consonants following the short vowel actually can
occur in the succeeding syllable, (e.g., as in ἄ-κρον ([á-kron])), at least in the
Attic dialect; thus, the syllable containing the short vowel may be light.[117]

Hephaestion's analysis of syllable quantity ("length" in his terms) and his
interpretation of the positioning of word-internal syllable-boundaries are *mutually exclusive notions*. It is his analysis of syllable quantity which is accurate;
consequently, his interpretation of the positioning of word-internal syllable-
boundaries, which, as we have already seen, is the conventional account offered
by the grammarians, must be ill-conceived.

As W. S. Allen has argued, the grammarians' rules for the division of words
into syllables, and so the parallel rules of word-division evidenced in inscriptional materials, must be formulations which are principally orthographic in
origin and not devised for the phonetic description of syllable structure.[118] This
interpretation is supported, Allen points out, by morphologically motivated exceptional divisions. We have encountered such exceptions both in the Athenian
inscriptions (see (38J)) and in Herodian's grammatical treatise (see (53) and
(54)); for example, Herodian instructs his readers that εἰσφέρω ([ę:spʰérǫ:], 'I
carry into'), where [ę:s] is the preposition meaning 'into') is to be divided [ę:s
$ pʰérǫ:], rather than [ę: $ spʰérǫ:] as his treatment would otherwise have it. If
the grammarians' practice of syllable-division were phonetically based, exceptions such as these would not be expected.

That the spelling of consonant clusters in the syllabic scripts, word-division
in alphabetic inscriptions and the "syllable-division" doctrine of the grammari-

ans should show general agreement and should each depart from actual Greek syllable structure is quite remarkable and is most unlikely to be simply a matter of coincidence. In all probability a historical link exists between these orthographic phenomena, and this linkage has not gone unnoticed by other investigators.[119]

3.4 Ruijgh

The idea that the type of "syllable-division" found in alphabetic inscriptions and advocated by the grammarians is orthographic in nature, rather than phonological or phonetic, has been utilized by C. J. Ruijgh in his interpretation of the Linear B spelling of consonant clusters.[120] Ruijgh takes the phonological/orthographic disparity inherent in this system of word-division to its systematic end, proposing that in the case of the alphabetic spellings of the first millennium, a distinction is to be made between "phonological (or phonetic) syllabification," on the one hand, and "orthographic syllabification," on the other. Phonological syllables are the prosodic units evidenced by Greek meter and the various types of phonological changes discussed above, while orthographic syllables are spelling units which are defined on the basis of possible word-initial and word-final sounds and sound sequences. Thus, to use Ruijgh's example, $\lambda\varepsilon\pi\tau\acute{o}\varsigma$ ([leptós], 'fine, thin') has the phonological syllabification $\lambda\varepsilon\pi$-$\tau\acute{o}\varsigma$ ([lep-tós]) but the orthographic syllabification $\lambda\varepsilon$-$\pi\tau\acute{o}\varsigma$ ([le-ptós]); the latter is determined by the occurrence in Greek of the word-initial sequence [#pt-] and is reinforced by the nonoccurrence of word-final [-p#] (and hence by the absence of a word-final sequence such as [-lep#]).

Ruijgh proposes that a notion of orthographic syllabification analogous to that which existed in the first millennium was utilized for spelling with the second-millennium syllabic script of the Mycenaeans. The spelling of Linear B proceeds according to orthographic, not phonological, syllables:

> (58) En principe, le premier segment d'un groupe de consonnes constituant le début d'une syllabe orth. s'exprime de la même façon qu'au début du mot, tandis qu'une consonne constituant le segment final d'une syllabe orth. n'est pas exprimée.[121]

To this formulation, Ruijgh appends:

> (59) Les occlusives sont toujours exprimées, même après la voyelle d'une syllabe final.[122]

Thus, for example, corresponding to the first-millennium word-division $\lambda\varepsilon$-$\pi\tau\acute{o}\varsigma$ ([le-ptós]), we find the equivalent Linear B spelling *re-po-to*, where the medial cluster [-pt-] is spelled in full (just as it is when it occurs word-initially), since it stands at the beginning of an "orthographic syllable"; word-final [-s] is not written, since it occurs at the end of such a syllable unit. Contrast with this the spelling *ka-ko* for $\chi\alpha\lambda$-$\kappa o\varsigma$ ([kʰal-kos], 'bronze'). The medial cluster [-lk-] is not a possible word-initial sequence of Greek, hence [-l-] occurs at the end of one orthographic syllable and [-k-] at the beginning of the next (i.e., the orthographic syllabification is here identical to the phonological syllabification). Since [-l-] occurs at the end of an orthographic syllable, it is not written, in accordance with (58).

Ruijgh's analysis of the Linear B representation of consonant clusters is in spirit essentially identical to the analyses of Householder, Sampson, et al. Ruijgh circumvents the problematic impermissible syllable structure required by these latter analyses by making the critical structures upon which spelling is based orthographic units which differ from actual syllable structure; in other words, Ruijgh's orthographic syllabification is equivalent to Householder's and Sampson's phonological syllabification. Ruijgh is also able to avoid the difficulties of *[s] + stop* clusters with which Sampson labors (see (34) and the accompanying discussion). He does so by simply stating (see (58)) that clusters which occur at the beginning of a word-internal orthographic syllable, among which are clusters of the type *[s] + stop,* are normally spelled just as they are when they occur in word-initial position; since such clusters are represented with partial spelling word-initially, they are so represented word-internally. However, his formulation (58) provides no insight into why in word-initial position, unlike other clusters, *[s] + stop* sequences are represented with partial—and not plenary—spelling.

On the other hand, Ruijgh's and Sampson's analyses are alike in that Ruijgh also must make explicit reference to the behavior of stops; in other words, his formulation (59) does not follow from (58), but is required because of word-final *stop + [s]* clusters of the type presented in (3), repeated here as (60):

(60)   *wa-na-ka,* ϝαναξ ([wanaks], 'king')
       a₃-ti-jo-qo, Αιθιοqʷς ([aitʰiokʷs], a man's name)

With respect to word-final clusters, it should also be pointed out that strictly interpreted, (58) is not sufficient in that it predicts that the nasal in the word-final sequence [-ns#] would be written, when in fact it is not, as is illustrated by the following examples:

(61)   *si-a₂-ro,* σιhαλονς ([sihalons], 'fat hogs,' accusative plural)
       -pa, πανς ([pans], 'all,' nominative singular)[123]

Ruijgh's analysis is again like the other syllabic interpretations of Linear B spelling which we have considered above in that, as he points out, it is able to account automatically for the partial representation of geminate clusters. For any particular word-internal geminate cluster, given Ruijgh's notion of orthographic syllabification, one member of the cluster would occur at the beginning of one orthographic syllable and the other at the end of the preceding orthographic syllable (since word-initial geminate clusters are generally not permitted in Greek[124]). Consequently, by (58), the first member of a geminate cluster would not be expressed. For example, in the case of the Mycenaean forms

(62)   *i-to-we-sa,* ἱστοϝεσσα ([histowessa], 'having a beam/mast')
       e-ne-wo-, εννεϝο- ([ennewo-], 'nine')

Ruijgh's orthographic syllabification would be

(63) [hi-sto-wes-sa]
      [en-ne-wo-]

and, therefore, only the second member of the cluster is actually noted. In the case of the analyses of Householder, Sampson, et al., the syllable structure of these forms would be the same as Ruijgh's orthographic syllabification (recall that their phonetic syllables are equivalent in structure to Ruijgh's orthographic syllables); consequently, only one member of the geminate clusters would be written (for the reason that only one member precedes the vowel of its syllable[125]). However, if Ruijgh's analysis were extended to the Cypriot Syllabary, as he suggests it should be,

(64) Dans l'écriture chypriote, une telle consonne finale de syllabe orth. est exprimée au moyen d'une voyelle 'morte', à savoir la voyelle précédente dans le cas d'une consonne non finale de mot, la voyelle e dans le cas d'une consonne finale de mot.[126]

it would not account for the nonrepresentation of geminates here, since in this script, unlike Linear B, consonants appearing at the end (except nasals), as well as those at the beginning, of "orthographic syllables" are spelled; the same observations can be made of course for the treatments of Householder, Sampson, et al.

3.5 Morpurgo Davies

Beneath the rubric of "syllable-dependent analyses" can also be placed the work of A. Morpurgo Davies,[127] whose ideas are in spirit quite similar to those of Ruijgh which we have just examined. Like Ruijgh, Morpurgo Davies is well aware of the massive difficulties faced by an interpretation of Greek syllable structure which holds that a syllable-boundary precedes any word-internal cluster-type which is capable of occurring word-initially; yet the strategies of consonant cluster spelling in the syllabic scripts which she appears to embrace are essentially those which we have identified with Householder, Sampson, Buck, et al.: in the case of Linear B, the first member of a cluster is spelled if it is preceded by a "syllable-boundary" (with the noted exceptions of *s* + *stop* and word-final *stop* + *s* clusters); in the Cypriot system the initial member of a cluster is written with the CV symbol whose vocalic component is identical to the vowel of the "syllable" to which that consonant belongs. Morpurgo Davies suggests, much like Ruijgh, that the determination of syllable-boundaries which is requisite for the application of these strategies was not one which was based purely on " 'phonetic' reality";[128] instead, perception of syllable structure was colored (or, perhaps more accurately, skewed) by analogy with possible word-initial and word-final consonant arrangements. In other words, since a syllable-boundary is clearly perceived as preceding a word-initial cluster and following a word-final cluster (or simply a word-final consonant), the various

possible configurations of consonants occurring at word-extremities were utilized as coordinates for mapping the location of word-internal syllable-boundaries: [pn-] occurs word-initially, and [-p] does not occur word-finally, so a
word-internal sequence [-Vpn-] is "syllabified" [-V$pn-], not [-Vp$n-]. Thus,
the scribes of the syllabic scripts and, in turn, the grammarians and other practitioners of alphabetic spelling possessed something of a linguistically naive
notion (or a folk-linguistic notion) of "syllable" which was utilized in designing
strategies for syllabic spelling and word-division. Unlike Ruijgh, Morpurgo Davies stops short of explicitly identifying a discrete orthographic entity—the orthographic syllable—which is distinct from the phonological or phonetic syllable, though this would be a small step for her to take.[129]

The phonotactic restrictions of Greek permit only three consonants to occur
at the end of a word, namely, [-s, -r, -n].[130] Morpurgo Davies points out that
[s] is fundamentally different from [r] and [n] in that, in addition to occurring
word-finally, it can appear as the first member of a word-initial consonant cluster. As a consequence, given her proposal that "syllable-division" is based upon
analogy to possible word-initial clusters *and* to possible word-final consonants,
the proper division of word-internal [-sC-] clusters would be ambiguous:
[-V$sC-] is supported by analogy to word-initial position but [-Vs$C-] by analogy to word-final position (as well as to word-initial position, since the consonant following [s] could occur initially). With regard to the latter and the former
division respectively, she surmises: "Here it is conceivable that those who opted
for a division of the type ἄρισ/τος were swayed by 'phonetic' factors, though
for Herodian's view at least the model provided by the word initial clusters was
more important."[131] In other words, it is perhaps a competition between phonetic and analogical factors which underlies both the varying treatment of
word-internal [-sC-] clusters exhibited within the alphabetic inscriptions[132] and
the conflicting analyses of the grammarians concerning the division of such
clusters.

3.5.1 Scribal Continuity

In her analysis of syllabic spelling, Morpurgo Davies stresses the continuity
which she perceives to exist between the second-millennium syllabic scripts
and the first-millennium alphabetic tradition; this continuity, as I have already
suggested, is revealed by the idiosyncratic nature of "syllable-division" in these
traditions—that is, by a common departure from phonetic reality.[133] She suggests that the aforementioned variation in the division of word-internal [-sC-]
clusters which is manifest within the alphabetic inscriptions and the grammatical treatises is likely to be tied to the varying orthographic treatments accorded
these clusters by the two syllabic scripts: "[T]he *s*-clusters provide us with the
best evidence we have that we are on the right track in linking the writing
practice of Linear B, Cyprian and alphabetic Greek."[134] She proposes that the
treatment of *[s]* + *stop* clusters in Linear B is like that advocated by Herodian
to the extent that such clusters receive the same treatment word-initially and
word-internally. In both contexts, *[s]* + *stop* clusters are represented with par-

tial spelling by the Linear B scribes; in a parallel fashion, for Herodian a syllable-division precedes *[s]* + *stop* clusters word-internally just as it does word-
initially. In contrast, while *[s]* + *stop* clusters are represented with progressive
spelling word-initially by the scribes of the Cypriot Syllabary, within the word
the [-s-] of such clusters is written using the regressive spelling strategy. This
disparate treatment within the Cypriot tradition is to be likened, says Morpurgo
Davies, to that exhibited by those grammarians (about whom Sextus Empiricus
tells us) who disagree with Herodian and by the scribes of the alphabetic tradition who divide *[s]* + *stop* clusters word-internally while, of course, treating
them as tautosyllabic at word-beginning.[135]

While I believe that Morpurgo Davies is correct in linking syllabic script
representation of *[s]* + *stop* clusters with the later variable alphabetic treatment
of these sequences, her formulation of this equation is not altogether accurate.
Though there is disagreement among the grammarians and within alphabetic
inscriptions as to the proper "division" of word-internal *[s]* + *stop* clusters,
such *word-internal* clusters receive comparable treatment in the two syllabic
scripts. In the Mycenaean system they are represented by partial spelling and
in the Cypriot system by regressive spelling (recall that partial spelling is the
Linear B equivalent to Cypriot regressive spelling). The variation in the representation of *[s]* + *stop* clusters in the syllabic scripts occurs not internally but
in *word-initial* position: Linear B shows partial spelling again, while the Cypriot Syllabary utilizes progressive spelling. As I have pointed out, this variation
arises as a consequence of the Cypriot orthographic practice of more fully representing consonants—of spelling all initial clusters progressively regardless of
the type of representation they receive word-internally. Notice that this progressive spelling is not a necessary strategy given the Cypriot script's propensity
for fuller consonantal representation; an arbitrary empty vowel like that one
used for spelling word-final consonants could have been utilized for writing the
initial consonant.

Morpurgo Davies argues that continuity between the syllabic and alphabetic
traditions is further revealed by a common notion of "word." In so doing she
is responding in part to the long-offered claim that the Greeks had no concept
"word" prior to the fourth century B.C., as their language appears to have had
no term which conveys that meaning unambiguously.[136] That the Greeks indeed
possessed such a notion, she contends, is clearly indicated by the regular Mycenaean scribal practice of separating individual words with a word-divider.[137]
Moreover, she notes that clitics—both proclitics and enclitics—are not graphically separated from the orthotonic forms with which they form an accent unit,
as in the following examples:[138]

(65)   *da-mo-de-mi,* δαμος δε μιν ([da:mos de min], 'but [the] community')
       o-u-pa-ro-ke-ne-[to], ου παρογενετο ([u: parogeneto], 'he was not on
       hand')

Thus, she concludes, the Mycenaean notion of "word" was one which was
accentually based: "[T]he word-divider is used to separate accentual groups,
i.e. speech sequences characterized by one main accent."[139] A word-divider is

likewise found in the syllabic Cypriot system though its use is infrequent;[140] however, the end of a word which terminates in a consonant is regularly marked graphically, as we have seen, by the use of the empty vowel -*e*. Though the interpretation of the total evidence is somewhat less straightforward than in the case of Linear B, syllabic Cypriot spelling also indicates an accentually based notion of "word": "[A] 'word' was either an orthotonic word or a sequence of orthotonic and unaccented elements."[141] Based on a preliminary examination of the materials, Morpurgo Davies notes that the use of punctuation for regular word-division in alphabetic inscriptions is uncommon but not unknown. Punctuation so used occurs in several archaic inscriptions of the sixth and fifth centuries B.C., in which case, just as in the syllabic traditions, "the general pattern of 'word-division' is relatively consistent; . . . a 'word' is either an orthotonic word or a sequence of proclitics—orthotonic word—enclitics."[142] She here contends that such an accentual unit of clitic plus orthotonic form was also recognized by Greek scribes, grammarians and other authors of the first-millennium alphabetic tradition.

Morpurgo Davies thus identifies a continuity of tradition stretching from Linear B to the Greek alphabet, and she is surely correct in doing so. Beyond that, she makes what I believe to be a crucially important point in identifying the Cypriot Syllabary as the intermediary agent in the chain of continuity which connects these systems: "Cyprian is important in that it may provide us with the link we need between the Linear B and the alphabetic texts."[143] Exactly what she perceives the nature of this continuity to be is not altogether clear, however. After mentioning the idiosyncratic "syllable-division" of the grammarians which we have discussed at length (i.e., the type of [hé$kto:r] rather than [hék$to:r]), she states:

(66)   The last facts I have mentioned reveal a continuity of linguistic, or perhaps folk-linguistic, reactions, which lasted in Greece for more than one millennium and survived through a violent disruption such as that which signed the end of the Mycenaean civilization and a cultural renewal such as that marked by the introduction of the alphabet and the new literacy.[144]

And on the accentually based notion of the word, she writes:

(67)   Continuity of school between Mycenaean and alphabetic writing is probably to be excluded; if so, we ought to reach the conclusion that the Mycenaean, Cyprian and alphabetic writers based their principles of word-division on a common response to speech which consciously or more probably unconsciously, analysed it on the basis of accentual criteria.[145]

Such an unlearned continuity of "reactions" or "responses" would in effect be no continuity at all. Instead, it would merely be a sequence of orthographic coincidences sprung generation after generation from intuitive language knowledge. On the other hand, however, in a slightly more recent work Morpurgo Davies observes:

(68)   From the point of view of Greek culture another interesting point emerges. If the syllabification adopted by the Mycenaean and Cyprian scribes and

by the later Greek grammarians had been based on purely phonetic facts, it would have been easy to suppose that independent processes of analysis had reached the same results. We now assume that this is not the case and that other factors were relevant. If so, it was not only the main features of the Greek language that survived the collapse of Mycenaean civilization; some fundamental linguistic or folk-linguistic notions survived too—the recognition of basic units such as the word and the "syllable" and the criteria used in identifying those units.[146]

Here it seems that the connections which she envisions are of a much more continuous, historical nature.[147]

The continuity of scribal tradition proceeding from the second millennium to the first, I will argue, is indeed historical. It arises as a consequence of the incorporation of certain Mycenaean orthographic features into the Cypriot Syllabary at the time this script was devised for spelling Greek. In turn, various features of the syllabic Cypriot writing system were introduced into the Greek alphabetic tradition.

3.5.2 *[S]* + *Stop* Again and Other Problems

As we have seen again and again, the representation of *[s]* + *stop* clusters is a problem that plagues those analyses of consonant cluster spelling which assume that such spelling is sensitive to syllable structure (whether the structure is claimed to be actual or perceived). Morpurgo Davies's analysis is no different, and she herself indicates that these clusters are problematic for her interpretation: "We still do not understand why in an initial or internal cluster of *s* + *stop* s is not written; we must simply make do with the observation that, whatever the reason, it is interesting that the same rule applies in Linear B to the initial and the internal cluster."[148]

A second recurring difficulty for syllable-based interpretations of Linear B spelling—one which has required proposing additional, ad hoc spelling conventions—is that of the representation of word-final *stop* + *[s]* clusters (the mirror image of word-initial *[s]* + *stop* clusters). Again, Morpurgo Davies points out that the spelling of these sequences is likewise problematic for her interpretation: "Why does Linear B write some word-final stops when followed by (unwritten) *-s* (*wa-na-ka* etc.)? . . . [W]hy *wa-na-ka* etc. and not *wa-na* . . . ?"[149]

There is yet another problem with syllable-based analyses, one which I have not thus far broached but to which Morpurgo Davies briefly refers.[150] As we have seen, Herodian contends that a syllable boundary precedes certain word-internal clusters even though they do not actually occur word-initially (see (43)). In each case, however, the cluster is of a *type* which does occur word-initially (*stop* + *nasal, fricative* + *stop* etc.). Are there *types of clusters* which are not found at the beginning of a word yet are treated as if a syllable-boundary preceded them when they occur word-internally?

Such clusters are attested in Linear B. For example, the Mycenaean scribes use progressive spelling to represent the word-internal sequence [-nw-]:

(69)   *ke-se-ni-wi-jo[*, ξενϝιον ([ksenwion], 'for guests')
       pe-ru-si-nu-wo, περυσινϝον ([perüsinwon], 'last year's')

According to syllable-based interpretations, a syllable-boundary should precede [-nw-] since the initial member of the cluster is written; however, by these same interpretations, syllable-boundaries should only precede word-internal clusters which can occur word-initially, yet neither the sequence [nw-] nor the cluster-type *nasal + glide*[151] is found in word-initial position.[152]

3.6 Concluding Remarks

Syllable-based interpretations of consonant cluster spelling in the Mycenaean and Cypriot syllabic scripts falter beneath the weight of a completely untenable assumed syllable structure. Certain investigators who have adopted syllable-based approaches have recognized the enormity of this problem and have attempted to circumvent it in various ways: by proposing syllable-boundaries which fall within (not before) the first member of the cluster; by postulating either orthographic units distinct from actual syllable structure or analogical processes which make reference to word-initial and word-final consonantal arrangements. In some cases there are glaring problems even with these adjustments; but *in every case* the analysis is incapable of dealing effectively with *[s] + stop* clusters and word-final *stop + [s]* clusters. If, however, we reject the syllable-based approach, we find a credible solution, to which I attend in chapter 4.

Notes

1. F. Householder, 1964, "A Morphophonemic Question and a Spelling Rule," in *Mycenaean Studies*, ed. E. Bennett, Jr. (Madison: University of Wisconsin Press), pp. 71–76.

2. Other early interpretations of this aspect of Linear B spelling which are essentially identical to that one offered by Householder are to be found in the following: C. Gallavotti, 1956, *Documenti e struttura del greco nell'età micenea* (Rome: Edizioni dell' Ateneo), p. 16; M. Doria, 1965, *Avviamento allo studio del miceneo* (Rome: Edizioni dell' Ateneo), pp. 43–47; A. Heubeck, 1966, *Aus der Welt der frühgriechischen Lineartafeln* (Göttingen: Vandenhoeck und Ruprecht), pp. 15–16. See also M. Lejeune, 1958, *Mémoires de philologie mycénienne*, vol. 1. (Paris: Centre National de la Recherche Scientifique), pp. 258–259. For a brief summary of each of these, see R. Viredaz, 1983, "La graphie des groupes de consonnes en mycénien et cypriote," *Minos* 18:127–128.

3. Householder 1964:73.

4. By this definition of *coda*, the vowel (syllabic nucleus) of an open syllable would also be a syllable coda; the definition should of course be emended to specify that only consonants in the coda are omitted.

5. It should be noted that Chadwick had already offered essentially the same rule. In the first edition (as in the second) of *The Decipherment of Linear B* (1958 (Cambridge: Cambridge University Press), pp. 74–75), Chadwick writes: "The basic principle

is that the language has to be represented in the form of open syllables; when two or more consonants begin a syllable they have to be shown by doubling the vowel; but when a consonant stands at the end of a syllable before a consonant at the beginning of the next, it is omitted altogether."

6. Though still a diphthong during the Mycenaean era, [ou] had been monophthongized and raised to [u:] in Attic by perhaps the fifth century B.C. See W. S. Allen, 1974, *Vox Graeca,* 2nd ed. (Cambridge: Cambridge University Press), pp. 73–75, 156.

7. In contrast, both [Vu] and [Vi] diphthongs are regularly spelled in full in the Cypriot Syllabary.

8. Householder 1964:75. As an example of this fuller spelling of a heterosyllabic cluster, he offers *po-ni-ki-pi,* [pʰoinikʰpʰi], 'with palm trees'. He appears to analyze the cluster [-kʰpʰ-] as heterosyllabic because this cluster does not occur in word-initial position in Greek. It is generally held that in the Mycenaean dialect a dental stop occurring before [pʰ] was assimilated to this bilabial; Ventris and Chadwick interpret *po-ni-ki-pi* as a possible etymological spelling of a foreign word which is designed to eliminate confusion (see *Docs.:*82–83, 400). In this paper Householder is questioning the idea that stops are assimilated before [pʰ]. His spelling rule, as he points out, leaves open the possibility that assimilation did not occur in such clusters; this is because by his analysis any *stop* + *[pʰ]* cluster would be heterosyllabic (as such clusters are not found word-initially), and, consequently, the first member of the cluster would not be represented. By the analysis of Ventris and Chadwick, both members of a *stop* + *stop* cluster should be spelled (see (10) in chapter 2); the spelling of a *stop* + *[pʰ]* cluster with only a single -*p*- thus suggests a geminate cluster and, hence, an assimilated cluster.

9. Householder 1964:74.

10. Householder also mentions as examples the names *po-ki-ro-qo* and *wo-no-qo* (p. 74); Ventris and Chadwick, however, question the interpretation of these forms.

11. Ibid., p. 75.

12. Such syllables are traditionally called "heavy by nature." For matters of Greek prosody in general, see the excellent treatment in A. Devine and L. Stephens, 1994, *The Prosody of Greek Speech* (Oxford: Oxford University Press).

13. Such syllables are traditionally called "heavy by position."

14. Word-internal sequences of more than two consonants are also heterosyllabic. Such clusters will be discussed below in chapter 5.

15. In other words, a cluster of consonants "makes position."

16. An exception to this generalization occurs in the instance of *correptio Attica* or Attic shortening. As will be further considered in the discussion below, the consonantal sequences traditionally referred to as *muta cum liquida,* that is, *stop* + *liquid* and *stop* + *nasal,* do not make position in certain poetic works written in the classical Attic dialect.

17. On which, see, among other works, Allen 1974:98; P. Chantraine, 1984, *Morphologie historique du grec,* 2nd ed. (Paris: Klincksieck), pp. 113–114; E. Hermann, 1923, *Silbenbildung im Griechischen* (Göttingen: Vandenhoeck und Ruprecht), pp. 8–12.

18. This is usually analyzed as a kind of rhythmic lengthening. See, for example, Lejeune 1982:221, 291.

19. Notice that example (6B) indicates the heterosyllabicity of word-internal clusters of the form *stop* + *liquid;* see above, n. 16.

20. See J. Vendryes, 1904, *Traité d'accentuation grecque* (Paris: Klincksieck), pp. 165–166; C. J. Ruijgh, 1985, "Problèmes de philologie mycénienne," *Minos* 19:120. For a morphological interpretation, see J. Kurylowicz, 1968, *Indogermanische Grammatik,*

vol. 2 (Heidelberg: Carl Winter), p. 102, and 1958, *L'accentuation des langues indo-européennes* (Kraków: Wroclaw), pp. 139–140.

21. The second-century A.D. Greek grammarian Herodian writes of this accent placement. He states concerning the three syllables in such ὑποκοριστικά ('diminutives'), εἰ μέντοι ἡ πρώτη τούτων μακρὰ ὑπάρχοι . . . παροξύνεται; "if the first of these should be long . . . the acute accent falls on the penult" (A. Lentz, ed., 1867, *Grammatici Graeci,* part 3, vol. 1 (Leipzig: Teubner), p. 356, 10–11.

22. Notice that the example λυχν-ίον ([lük^{h}n-íon]) again shows the heterosyllabicity of a *muta cum liquida* cluster—in this case *stop + nasal.*

23. Among additional phonological evidence for the heterosyllabicity of word-internal clusters which could be offered are the formulations known as Wheeler's Law and Vendryes' Law. Wheeler's Law states that *if a word originally had an acute accent on its final syllable and if it ends in the syllabic sequence heavy-light-light, i.e., ends in a dactyl, then the accent was retracted to the penultimate syllable,* as in ἀγκύλος ([aŋkúlos]), 'crooked,' compare Sanskrit *ankurás,* 'a young sprout' (B. Wheeler, 1885, "Der griechische Nominalakzent" (Strassburg: Ph.D. diss.), pp. 60ff). According to Vendryes' Law, *in the Attic dialect, if a word originally had a circumflex accent on the penultimate syllable, the accent was retracted to the preceding syllable (in which case the accent automatically becomes acute) if that syllable was light,* as may be seen by comparing Attic ὅμοιος ([hómoios]), 'like' (Ionic and Old Attic ὁμοῖος) and ἀστεῖος ([asteîos]), 'polite' (Vendryes 1904:263). The legitimacy of both of these formulations has been questioned by some scholars. For a recent discussion and bibliography, see N. Collinge, 1985, *The Laws of Indo-European* (Philadelphia: John Benjamins), pp. 199–202, 221–223.

24. A. Meillet, 1965, *Aperçu d'une histoire de la langue grecque,* 7th ed. (Paris: Klincksieck), p. 145.

25. On Proto-Indo-European meter, see, among other works, A. Meillet, 1923, *Les origines indo-européennes des mètres grecs* (Paris: Les Presses Universitaires de France); G. Nagy, 1974, *Comparative Studies in Greek and Indic Meter* (Cambridge: Harvard University Press); C. Watkins, 1963, "Indo-European Metrics and Archaic Irish Verse," *Celtica* 6:194–249; M. L. West, 1973, "Indo-European Meter," *Glotta* 51:161–181.

26. R. Beekes, 1971, "The Writing of Consonant Groups in Mycenaean," *Mnemosyne* 24: 338–339.

27. Ibid., p. 339.

28. Ibid., p. 340.

29. In fact, Beekes seems to suggest this himself, but his position is unclear. On p. 345 he states that the spelling of T + *s* clusters is "irregular" and at the same time that "both Cyprian and Mycenaean write the consonant with the following vowel."

30. Ibid., p. 342.

31. Ibid., p. 344.

32. Ibid., pp. 343, 346.

33. Ibid., p. 345.

34. Beekes states (p. 345), "As to the metrical evidence, in Homer each syllable followed by a consonant group is long, whatever the structure of the group. It is evident that this asks for comment in cases II A and II B 2 b_3 and e_1. In *all other cases* [emphasis is mine] the metrical evidence is in agreement with the Cyprian and Mycenaean evidence, but in the cases mentioned it seems contradictory." Beekes curiously excludes the clusters of III A 2 and III B I from this statement of discrepant clusters, even though he has included them in his list of tautosyllabic clusters (16). However, in

his discussion of III A 2 (pp. 348–349) and III B I (p. 347) he includes these clusters among those which syllabify by his analysis in a way other than that expected given the metrical and phonological evidence.

35. Ibid., p. 346. Less commonly, it is the second member of the cluster which is doubled. For a discussion and presentation of extensive data, see Hermann 1923:110–123. See also L. Threatte, 1980, *The Grammar of Attic Inscriptions,* vol. 1 (Berlin: De Gruyter), pp. 527–535.

36. Beekes 1971:346.

37. Ibid.

38. Ibid., p. 347.

39. See, for example, two works by J. Anderson and C. Jones: 1974, "Three Theses Concerning Phonological Representations," *JL* 10:1–26; 1977, *Phonological Structure and the History of English* (Amsterdam: North-Holland).

40. Buck 1955:75.

41. Hermann 1923:123.

42. It is far from obvious why these double spellings would be used as an indicator of syllable structure in some cases but not in others.

43. Lejeune 1982:286.

44. See also R. Viredaz 1983:134–135. Viredaz criticizes Beekes' interpretation of the spelling of the clusters of (6) and suggests that the doubled consonants in the inscriptional forms are an indication of the greater length of the first consonant of the cluster.

45. Beekes 1971:346.

46. None of the consonants involved are likely to be implosive in the sense in which the term is currently used by phoneticians. Linking the nonrepresentation of initial C_1 in clusters of the form $C_1\$C_1C_2$ to the rule prohibiting complete representation of geminate clusters would offer the advantage of automatically accounting for the particular choice of consonant to be represented: just as it appears to be the second geminate only which is spelled in the syllabic Cypriot script, so it is the second occurrence of C_1 only which is spelled.

47. Hermann 1923:111.

48. See W. S. Allen, 1973, *Accent and Rhythm* (Cambridge: Cambridge University Press), p. 208.

49. Beyond that, Greek does not show a word-initial sequence [kp-].

50. That the form is accusative plural, as here indicated, is uncertain, however.

51. Hermann 1923:113. With this compare the curious spelling Σέξκτον ([séksk-ton], with two occurrences cited by Hermann) for Σέξτον ([sékston]).

52. Ibid., p. 119.

53. Threatte 1980:527.

54. Ibid., pp. 527–530. In a few instances the [-s] occurs at the end of a word and the stop at the beginning of the following word.

55. Only word-internal clusters are included for Cypriot because, as mentioned above and as will be discussed below, word-initial clusters are subject to a different spelling strategy (and *[s]* + *stop* clusters do not occur word-finally in Greek). There are fifty-six occurrences of this cluster word-initially in the Cypriot materials. These totals are drawn from my extensive database which is described in the ensuing chapter.

56. Beekes 1971:348.

57. Ibid., p. 349.

58. Ibid.

59. G. Sampson, 1985, *Writing Systems* (Stanford: Stanford University Press), p. 69.

60. Ibid.

61. Ibid.

62. It is unclear why Sampson places this restriction within parentheses, as this clause is added to the rule for the purpose of excepting *[s]* + *stop* clusters from the more general statement (31).

63. Ibid.

64. Ibid., pp. 67–68.

65. Sampson states: "/aksones/ 'axles' is syllabified /a\$kso\$nes/ because in Greek / ks-/ is a permitted, indeed common initial cluster" (p. 69); and "a syllable-boundary is placed as far to the left as is compatible with the limitations on permissible initial clusters" (p. 70).

66. Ibid., p. 69.

67. Though [tm-] and [dm-] occur word-initially.

68. Sampson does not mention that [tr-] is a commonly occurring word-initial cluster; he attempts to justify his syllabic analysis /ale\$ktruo:n/ by making recourse to the possible configurations of word-final consonants He states that "/-k, -kt, -ktr/ are all quite impossible in word-*final* position" (p. 69). This is of course absolutely correct; but then his analysis of Greek syllabification also produces syllable-final consonants which are not permitted in word-final position, such as the syllable-final [-l] of his example (37D) /kʰal\$kos/.

69. Ibid., p. 70.

70. For recent works which take note of the similarities between alphabetic word-division and consonant cluster spelling in the syllabic scripts, see Ruijgh 1985:121–126 and especially A. Morpurgo Davies, 1987, "Mycenaean and Greek Syllabification," in *Tractata Mycenaea,* ed. P. Ilievski and L. Crepajac (Skopje: Macedonian Academy of Sciences and Arts), pp. 91–103; 1986a, "Folk-Linguistics and the Greek Word," in *Festschrift for Henry Hoenigswald,* ed. G. Cardona and N. Zide (Tübingen: Gunter Narr Verlag), pp. 266–271; 1986b, "Forms of Writing in the Ancient Mediterranean World," in *The Written Word,* ed. G. Baumann (Oxford: Oxford University Press), pp. 67–68. For earlier works which discuss the relationship between word-division practices in alphabetic inscriptions and syllabic Cypriot spelling, see Hermann 1923:181–185 and R. Meister 1894:178–186. We will return to this matter.

71. Threatte 1980:64–73.

72. The earliest Attic inscription, that of the Dipylon Oinochoe, dates to perhaps 740 B.C. See B. Powell, 1988, "The Dipylon Oinochoe and the Spread of Literacy in Eighth-Century Athens," *Kadmos* 27:65–86.

73. The use of quotation marks around *syllable* is mine, not Threatte's. As will be argued below, it is quite likely that in most cases the division is not actually made at a syllable break. It is clearly the case, however, that a principled means for dividing words is being utilized which has some phonetic/phonological basis.

74. However, two lengthy Athenian naval catalogues from the same period show no indication of the use of any sort of rule-governed word-division: "a glance at either shows so many wrong divisions that it is clear that no effort is being made to end the lines with syllables." Moreover, Threatte goes on to say, "These texts fall into a group of large late fourth-century inventories, which, although they are non-stoichedon, are nevertheless non-syllabified" (p. 72). Among the Athenian naval catalogues which exhibit some attempt at "syllabification," according to Threatte, "there seems to be a clear chronological development" toward regular use of third-century strategies (p. 73).

75. Threatte states that his observations are based upon an examination of "texts dating ca. 300 B.C.–ca. 300 A.D. in which the laws of syllabification are generally ob-

served. During this period there are also texts which avoid the rules altogether, or contain numerous infractions of them" (p. 69).

76. Ibid., pp. 66–69. In citing Threatte's rules, I have in some instances replaced his use of Greek script with phonetic transcription.

77. Similar, if less explicitly enumerated, rules have been offered by other investigators on the basis of examination of inscriptions written in a variety of dialects; see, for example, H. Stuart-Jones, 1901, "The Division of Syllables in Greek," *CR* 15:396–401.

78. I have changed the order in which these various clusters are presented from an alphabetic order (Threatte) to a phonetic one.

79. The matter of the recognition of segment types by the Greek scribes is an extremely interesting one which will be further considered below.

80. Hermann 1923:132–176; see especially pp. 174–175.

81. Threatte reports that both treatments are even attested within a single document.

82. And this practice is general for inscriptions in all dialects; see, *inter alios*, Stuart-Jones 1901:397.

83. Threatte 1980:68. In the case of Λαμ|πτρέα ([lam|ptréa]) it is not the entire sequence [-ptr-] which can occur word-initially but only [-pt-], the first pair of consonants which follows the division, though the sequence [-tr-] is also permissible at the beginning of a word.

84. A. Lentz, 1867–1868, *Grammatici Graeci*, part 3, vol. 2 (Leipzig: Teubner), p. 393, 33–36: Τὰ σύμφωνα τὰ ἐν ἀρχῇ λέξεως εὑρισκόμενα, καὶ ἐν τῷ μέσῳ ἐὰν εὑρεθῶσιν, ἐν συλλήψει εὑρίσκονται, οἷον ἐν τῷ κτῆμα τὸ κτ ἐν ἀρχῇ λέξεως ἐστίν, ἀλλὰ καὶ ἐν τῷ ἔτικτον εὑρεθέντα ἐν τῷ μέσῳ τὸ κ καὶ τὸ τ ὁμοῦ ἐστιν·

85. Ibid., p. 396, 1–2: ὅσα σύμφωνα μὴ δύναται ἐν ἀρχῇ λέξεων ἐκφωνεῖσθαι, ταῦτα καὶ ἐν μέσῃ λέξει εὑρεθέντα χωρισθήσεται ἀλλήλων· οἷον ἄνθος, ἔργον.

86. A transcription of the *spelling* of the Aeolic and Attic forms is offered rather than a phonetic transcription since the initial portion of the two words is almost certainly phonetically identical ([zd-]); that is, the use of σδ– as opposed to ζ– is an orthographic, not phonetic, difference, and hence a phonetic transcription would obscure the claim which Herodian is offering.

87. Ibid., p. 396, 5–10: θμ, φν, γδ, χμ, κμ, σγ, σδ· ταῦτα γὰρ οὐδέποτε ἐν συμπλοκῇ ἐν ἀρχῇ εὑρισκόμενα, ἐν μέσῳ ἀλλήλων οὐ χωρίζονται οἷον ἴθμα, ἀφνειός, ὄγδοος, αἰχμή, ἀκμή, φάσγανον, θεόσδοτος· εἰ γὰρ παρὰ τοῖς κοινοῖς οὐχ εὕρηται λέξις ἀπὸ τοῦ σδ ἀρχομένη, ἀλλὰ παρὰ τοῖς Αἰολεῦσίν ἐστιν οἷον σδυγός ἀντὶ τοῦ ζυγός.

88. Moreover, as just pointed out, the phonetic value of σδ, <sd>, is identical to that of the character *zeta* (ζ).

89. The remaining two clusters are -sg- and -sd-; while Threatte finds *[s] + stop* clusters to have a variable treatment in the inscriptions, Herodian prescribes a consistent treatment, as will be seen below.

90. Ibid., p. 393, 4–6: τὰ ἄφωνα πρὸ τῶν ἀμεταβόλων ἐν συλλήψει εἰσὶν ἤγουν ὁμοῦ εἰσιν, καὶ οὐκ ἔστι χωρὶς τὸ ἄφωνον καὶ χωρὶς τὸ ἀμετάβολον οἷον ἀκμή, ἀτμός, . . . ἀγρός, ἔκλαιον, ἔθνησκον, ἔπλεον, ἁβρός·

91. For discussion, see Allen 1974:38.

92. Ibid., p. 394, 33–34: τὰ ἀμετάβολα πρὸ τῶν ἀφώνων ἐν διαστάσει εἰσὶν οἷον ἕρπω τὸ βαδίζω, ἕλκω, ἄνθος, ἄρτος, ἔργον, ἔμβολος, σύμφωνον, σύμπονος.

93. Ibid., p. 395, 10–13: ἀμετάβολον ἀμεταβόλου οὐ προηγεῖται κατὰ σύλ–

ληψιν, ἀλλὰ κατὰ διάστασιν οἷον ἀρνός, Ἑρμῆς, ἅλμη, ἔρνος, ὅλμος. ἰδοὺ ἐπὶ
τούτων τὸ ἓν ἀμετάβολον ληκτικόν ἐστι τῆς προηγουμένης συλλαβῆς καὶ τὸ
ἕτερον ἀρκτικὸν τῆς ἐπιφερομένης καὶ οὐκ εἰσὶν ὁμοῦ.

94. Ibid., p. 395, 13–15: δεῖ προσθεῖναι χωρὶς τοῦ μ̄ καὶ ν̄, ταῦτα γὰρ εὑρίσκονται κατὰ σύλληψιν ὡς ἐν τῷ μνᾶ, μνημεῖον· ἐνταῦθα γὰρ τὸ μ̄ καὶ τὸ ν̄
ὁμοῦ εἰσιν.

95. The term here translated as 'continuant' is ἡμίφωνον ([hε:míphǫ:non]); however, strictly speaking, not all ἡμίφωνα are continuants. In addition to the liquids, nasals, and [s], the grammarians included in this group the sounds represented by the so-
called double letters of the Greek alphabet: namely, ζ ([zd]), ξ ([ks]), and ψ ([ps]).

96. Ibid., p. 395, 16–17: ἡμίφωνον ἡμιφώνου οὐ προηγεῖται κατὰ σύλληψιν,
ἀλλὰ κατὰ διάστασιν.

97. Ibid., p. 395, 20–28: δεῖ προσθεῖναι χωρὶς τοῦ μ̄ καὶ τοῦ ν̄ καὶ τοῦ σ̄ καὶ
τοῦ μ̄ καὶ τῶν συλλαβῶν τῶν οὐσῶν ἐν τέλει λέξεως· ἐπὶ τούτων γὰρ εὑρίσκονται ἡμίφωνα ἡμιφώνων προηγούμενα κατὰ σύλληψιν, καὶ ἐπὶ μὲν τοῦ μ̄ καὶ ν̄
ὡς ἐπὶ τοῦ μνᾶ καὶ μνημεῖον, ἐπὶ δὲ τοῦ σ̄ καὶ μ̄ ὡς ἐπὶ τοῦ σμῶ καὶ σμιλίον
καὶ κόσμος· ἐπὶ δὲ συλλαβῶν τῶν οὐσῶν ἐν τέλει λέξεως οἷον ἅλς, μάκαρς,
Τῖρυνς, ἕλμινς. ἰδοὺ ἐπὶ τούτων εὑρέθησαν ἡμίφωνα ἡμιγώνων προηγούμενα
κατὰ σύλληψιν, ἐπειδὴ οὐκ ἔχουσι φωνῆεν ἐπιφερόμενον τὸ ὀφεῖλον τοῦ ἑνὸς
συμφώνου τὴν σύνταξιν ἀναδέξασθαι.

98. Ibid., p. 393, 16–19: τὸ σ̄ πρὸ πάντων τῶν ἀφώνων ἐν συλλήψει ἐστίν,
ἤγουν ὁμοῦ εἰσι τὰ δύο, τὸ σ̄ καὶ τὸ ἐπιφερόμενον ἄφωνον, οἷον ἔσβεσε, φάσγανον, θεόσδοτος, ἀσκός, ἀστήρ, ἀσπίς, ἀσθενής, ἀσχημοσύνη, ἑωσφόρος· ἰδοὺ ἐπὶ
τούτων τὸ σ̄ μετὰ τῶν ἐπιφερομένων ἀφώνων ὁμοῦ ἐστι.

99. Or perhaps "letters."

100. Bekker, ed., 1814–1821, *Anecdota Graeca,* 3 vols. (Berlin: Reimer), 3:1127:
καὶ σύνταξις μέν ἐστιν ὅταν ζητῶμεν ποίᾳ συλλαβῇ συντάξωμεν τὰ στοιχεῖα,
οἷον ἐν τῷ ἀσθενής τὸ σ̄ πότερον ληκτικόν ἐστι τῆς προτέρας συλλαβῆς ἢ ἀρκτικὸν τῆς δευτέρας·

101. M:1.169–174: τὴν γὰρ ὀρθογραφίαν φασὶν ἐν τρισὶ κεῖσθαι τρόποις,
ποσότητι, ποιότητι, μερισμῷ. . . . μερισμῷ δέ, ἐπειδὰν διαπορῶμεν περὶ τῆς
ὄβριμος λέξεως, πότερόν ποτε τὸ β τῆς δευτέρας ἐστὶ συλλαβῆς ἀρχὴ ἢ τῆς
προηγουμένης πέρας, καὶ ἐπὶ τοῦ Ἀριστίων ὀνόματος ποῦ τακτέον τὸ σ.
πάλιδ ὐ᾽ ἡ τοιαύτη τεχνολογία, ἵνα μηδὲν τῶν ἀπορωτέρων κινῶμεν, μάταιος
εἶναι φαίνεται, πρῶτον μὲν ἐκ τῆς διαφωνίας, ἔπειτα δὲ καὶ ἐξ αὐτῶν τῶν ἀπο-
τελεσμάτων. καὶ ἐκ μὲν τῆς διαφωνίας, ἐπείπερ οἱ τεχνικοὶ μάχονταί τε καὶ εἰς
αἰῶνα μαχήσονται πρὸς ἀλλήλους, τῶν μὲν οὕτως τῶν δὲ ἐκείνως τὸ αὐτὸ γράφ-
ειν ἀξιούντων. . . . οὐκ ἄρα χρειώδης ἐστὶν ἡ περὶ ὀρθογραφίας παρὰ τοῖς
γραμματικοῖς ὑφήγησις.

ἀλλ᾽ ὁ μὲν ἀπὸ τῆς διαφωνίας ἔλεγχος τοιοῦτος, ὁ δὲ ἀπὸ τῶν ἀποτελεσ-
μάτων ἐμφανής. οὐδὲν γὰρ βλαπτόμεθα . . . ἐπὶ τοῦ Ἀριστίων ὀνόματος ἐὰν
τε τῇ προηγουμένῃ συλλαβῇ τὸ σ προσμερίζωμεν ἐάν τε τῇ ἐπιφερομένῃ τοῦτο
συντάττωμεν. εἰ μὲν γὰρ . . . παρὰ τὸ τοῦ Ἀριστίων ὀνόματος οὕτως ἀλλὰ μὴ
ἐκείνως συντάσσεσθαι τὸ σ ὁ Ἀριστίων, καθώς φησί τις τῶν χαριεντιζομένων,
Δειπνίων γίνεται, ἥρμοζε μὴ ἀδιαφορεῖν. εἰ δ᾽ . . . ὅ τε Ἀριστίων ἀεί ποτέ
ἐστιν δ᾽ Ἀριστίων, ἐάν τε τῷ ι ἐάν τε τῷ τ τὸ σ προσμερίζωμεν, τίς χρεία τῆς
πολλῆς καὶ ματαίας παρὰ τοῖς γραμματικοῖς περὶ τούτων μωρολογίας;

102. Contrast the remarks of Hermann (1923:131) concerning the reference to
[óbrimos] in Sextus Empiricus's work.

103. See the discussion of *correptio Attica* in Allen 1973:210–216. Allen notes that

the phenomenon occurs more frequently in Attic comedy than in tragedy and states that it "may be presumed to reflect the spoken colloquial of the time; the alternatve treatment might be seen as due to the influence of epic tradition, which would appropriately be stronger in tragedy" (p. 211).

104. In Attic Greek this preposition occurs as the allomorphic variants [eks] and [ek]. The former appears before an ensuing vowel and the latter before a consonant. There is also indication of a variant [ekʰ] occurring before aspirated consonants and [eg] before voiced consonants. See Buck 1955:83.

105. Lentz, 393, 8–11: δεῖ προσθεῖναι χωρὶς τῶν ὄντων ἀπὸ τῆς ἐξ προ–
θέσεως. ταῦτα γὰρ ἐν διαστάσει ἔχουσι τὸ ἄφωνον μετὰ τῶν ἐπιφερομένων
ἀμεταβόλων, ἤγουν ἐν ἄλλῃ συλλαβῇ τὸ ἄφωνον καὶ ἐν ἄλλῃ τὸ ἀμετάβολον
οἷον ἐκλῦσαι, ἐκνευρίσαι, ἐκρεῦσαι, ἐκμάξαι.

106. Ibid., p. 393, 20–24: δεῖ προσθεῖναι χωρὶς τῶν ὄντων ἀπὸ τῆς εἰς προ–
θέσεως καὶ ἀπὸ τῆς πρός καὶ ἀπὸ τοῦ δυς ἐπιρρήματος· ταῦτα γὰρ ἐν διαστάσει
ἔχουσι τὸ σ μετὰ τῶν ἐπιφερομένων ἀφώνων, ἤγουν ἐν ἄλλῃ συλλαβῇ ἔχουσι
τὸ σ καὶ ἐν ἄλλῃ τὸ ἐπιφερόμενον ἄφωνον οἷον εἰσφέρω, προσφορά, δυστυχής.

107. However, contrast with (54) Threatte's comment in (38G): "The final [-k] of the preposition ἐκ is more often carried to the next line than not."

108. Though it need not concern us here, if this long vowel or diphthong is not followed by a consonant, Hephaestion classifies the syllable as "common" rather than long (see n. 111).

109. Or "by convention" (θέσει, [tʰésẹ:]); on the meaning of θέσει in this use, see Allen 1973:54.

110. By the term "shortened (βραχυνόμενον, [brakʰünómenon]) vowel," the grammarians designated long vowels which are not orthographically distinct from their short counterparts (i.e., long α, ι, and υ).

111. On the notion of common (κοινή) syllables, see Allen 1974:101.

112. The so-called double consonants being, of course, ζ ([zd]), ξ ([ks]), and ψ ([ps]), as I indicated earlier.

113. *Ench.*, pp. 2–3: θέσει μακραὶ γίνονται, ὅταν βραχέος ὄντος ἢ βραχυνο–
μένου φωνήεντος σύμφωνα πίπτῃ μεταξὺ αὐτοῦ καὶ τοῦ τῆς ἑξῆς συλλαβῆς
φωνήεντος πλείονα ἑνὸς ἁπλοῦ. γίνεται δὲ τοῦτο κατὰ πέντε τρόπους. ἤτοι γὰρ
λήξει εἰς δύο σύμφωνα οἷον . . . μάκαρς. . . .

ἢ ἐν τῇ ἑξῆς ἐστι ταῦτα συλλαβῇ οἷον Ἕ–κτωρ. . . . ἔνθα καὶ δεῖ παρ–
ατηρεῖν, μὴ τὸ μὲν πρότερον ἄφωνον ᾖ, τὸ δὲ δεύτερον ὑγρόν· αἱ γὰρ τοιαῦται
κοιναί, ὡς ἑξῆς εἰρήσεται.

ἢ λήγει μὲν εἰς ἕν, ἔχει δὲ καὶ τὴν ἑξῆς ἀρχομένην ἀπὸ ἑτέρου οἷον ἄλ–
λος,

ἢ εἰς διπλοῦν λήγει οἷον ἔξ,

ἢ τὴν ἑξῆς ἔχει ἀπὸ διπλοῦ ἀρχομένην οἷον ἔξω.

114. See Allen 1973:53–55; 1974:97–99.

115. The same argument can of course be made in the case of (56E).

116. That is, *muta cum liquida,* and hence *stop + liquid or nasal*; see above for the sense of Greek *liquid.*

117. Hephaestion's description of syllables which are long by position is almost identical to that offered by the grammarian Dionysius Thrax (second century B.C.) in his *Techne Grammatike.* However, with regard to the syllable-type treated by Hephaestion in (56B)/(57) (i.e., the type of the initial syllable of [héktọ:r]), Dionysius Thrax's treatment differs in that he does not explicitly state that the two consonants following the short vowel occur in the next syllable: "a syllable is long . . . by position . . . when

two consonants follow a short or shortened vowel, for example [agrós]." (μακρὰ συλ–λαβὴ γίνεται . . . θέσει . . . ὅταν βραχεῖ ἢ βραχυνομένῳ φωνήεντι ἐπιφέρηται δύο σύμφωνα, οἷον ἀγρός·) (DT 633.9). Note, in addition, that the example given by Dionysius Thrax, [agrós], is actually of the type excluded by Hephaestion (see (56B)) (the vowel is followed by a *stop* + *liquid* cluster), thus underlining the variableness of the position of the syllable-boundary in *muta cum liquida* clusters of Attic.

118. Allen 1973:29–30; 1974:98–99.

119. See the references in n. 70 above.

120. Ruijgh 1985:105–126.

121. Ibid., p. 124. As can be seen, identity with possible word-initial clusters is used *both* to divide words into orthographic syllables *and,* that division having been made, to determine the type of spelling to be used for representing a word-internal cluster.

122. Ibid.

123. In all probability, the word-final sequence [-Vns#] had not already been reduced to [-V:s#] in Mycenaean. Notice that in Attic this change was relatively late, not occurring until after the raising of $\bar{a}$ to η ([a:] → [æ:] → [ẹ:] (*νικανς (*[nikans]) → νίκᾱς ([níka:s], 'victories')) and not *νίκης (*[níkẹ:s])); on this change, see, *inter alios,* O. Szemerényi, 1968, "The Attic 'Rückverwandlung' or Atomism and Structuralism in Action," in *Studien zur Sprachwissenschaft und Kulturkunde,* ed. M. Mayrhofer (Innsbruck: Leopold-Franzens-Universität), pp. 139–157; W. S. Allen, 1987, "The Development of the Attic Vowel System: Conspiracy or Catastrophe?," *Minos* 20–22:21–32. The ambiguity inherent in the Linear B writing system, which nowhere fully spells nasals occurring before [s], makes it impossible to verify that word final [-Vns#] remained intact; see Lejeune 1982:11, 131–132.

124. I say "generally" since, in synchronic terms, it is the case that an underlying word-initial geminate cluster can surface when the preceding word ends in a vowel. Such clusters are historically the result of some type of assimilation. See Ruijgh 1985:122, 124–125; for a general discussion see Lejeune 1982:119–120, 274–275, 303–305.

125. The same can be said of Beekes' analysis, though for him the syllabification of the first form in (63) would presumably be [his-sto-wes-sa].

126. Ruijgh 1985:124, n. 62.

127. Morpurgo Davies 1987:91–104.

128. Ibid.

129. Note, however, her comment of p. 104, n. 1: "It may be argued that there is no reason why we should use the word 'syllable' for anything but a phonetic concept. . . . If so, we shall speak of something different for the syllable of the grammarians. Yet the real problem in my view is whether we can attribute to Mycenaean, Cyprian, and later Greek writers the awareness of some linguistic unit smaller than the word but larger than the phoneme and definable according to some rules. If this is so, then we can dispute whether these units did overlap, in part at least, with the real syllables—as I think they did."

130. Though a final stop may occur on a proclitic; see Buck 1933:156.

131. Morpurgo Davies 1987:102.

132. Aside from the fully expected spelling variation occurring in inscriptions, as Thomas Palaima has reminded me.

133. Ibid., pp. 102, 104; 1986b:67.

134. Ibid., p. 101.

135. Morpurgo Davies also indicates that there is significant irregularity in the orthographic treatment of *[s]* + *stop* clusters within the two syllabic scripts, especially

within the Cypriot Syllabary. For example, she states concerning the spelling practices of the latter: "Word-internal *s* + *stop* is normally (but as we have seen, there are numerous exceptions) written in the 'disyllabic' way" (p. 99). As we will see below, there is actually very little variation in the representation of such clusters in the syllabic scripts.

136. On this matter, see the comments of W. S. Allen (1973:23; 1974:113, n. 1).

137. Morpurgo Davies 1986a:266–269.

138. Morpurgo Davies 1987:96; 1986a:267.

139. Ibid.

140. See O. Masson 1983:68–69.

141. Morpurgo Davies 1986a:270; she appends, "[I]t may be safer to retain from this discussion one conclusion only: accentual factors played a considerable part in determining the notion of word which was influential in Cyprian spelling."

142. Ibid., p. 271. Morpurgo Davies goes on to argue for the occurrence of an accentually based notion of the word in the work of classical authors and grammarians; see pp. 271–275.

143. Ibid., p. 270.

144. Morpurgo Davies 1986b:68. Elsewhere on the same page she speaks of a "continuity, as revealed by writing, in what I should like to call metalinguistic reactions, from the period of the syllabic scripts down to the period of full alphabetic literacy."

145. Morpurgo Davies 1986a:271.

146. Morpurgo Davies 1987:104.

147. This does not appear to be the result of a progression in theory, as, in this same work (1987), she remarks, "[I]t is just this accentually based notion of word which gives us the evidence we need to establish a form of continuity in the Greek *reactions* to language from the Mycenaean to the late Hellenistic period" (p. 103; emphasis is mine).

148. Ibid., p. 103.

149. Ibid.

150. Ibid.

151. The same may hold true for at least one additional cluster-type—*nasal* + *liquid*—though there is uncertainty regarding the Mycenaean form in which it has been identified; moreover, this cluster-type did occur at word-beginning in *Proto-Greek*. The cluster [-mr-] is represented with progressive spelling, as shown in *o-mi-ri-jo-i,* 'Ομρι–οιhι ([omrioihi], 'for the Rain Spirits'), if this form has been properly etymologized. The Proto-Greek sequence *nasal* + *liquid* is eventually disrupted by the intrusion of an excrescent consonant (which is homorganic with the nasal), for example,*γαμρος* ([*gamros]) → γαμβρός ([gambrós], 'son-in-law etc.'), *άνρος* ([anros]) → ἀνδρός ([andrós], 'of man'). In the case of the cluster beginning with a dental nasal, *[-nr-], (there are no instances of Proto-Greek *[nl]), the change appears to be pre-Mycenaean, as indicated by *a-di-ri-ja-te,* ανδριαντει ([andriantẹ:], 'with the figure of a man'). There is some indication, however, that the sequence [mr] is in certain dialects preserved into the early alphabetic period (see Viredaz 1983:143, 205; R. Arena, 1972, "Greco ὄμ–βρικος : βάκχος e miceneo *o-mi-ri-jo-i,*" *Minos* 13:182–191; A. Heubeck, 1970, "Nochmal zu griech. –μρ–/–μβρ–," *Glotta* 48:67–71). Word-initially, the nasal in clusters of the type *nasal* + *liquid* was lost after the introduction of the excrescent consonant, as in *μροτος (*[mrotos]) → *μβροτος (*[mbrotos]) → βροτός ([brotós], 'mortal'). On these changes generally see, *inter alios,* Lejeune 1982:154.

152. See now the syllable-dependent approach of G. Miller, 1994, *Ancient Scripts and Phonological Knowledge* (Amsterdam: John Benjamins), pp. 13–37.

Non-Syllable-Dependent Approaches

In contrast to the interpretations of Linear B and syllabic Cypriot spelling discussed in chapter 3, there are other analyses of these phenomena which are either not dependent upon syllable structure or, in one instance, only partially dependent upon such structure. It is this latter, "mixed system" of analysis which we shall consider first.

4.0 Tronsky

It appears that the earliest example of a non-syllable-based approach to interpreting the Mycenaean and Cypriot strategies for representing consonant sequences is found in a work by the Russian philologist and linguist I. M. Tronsky. In a 1962 article entitled "The Syllable Structure of the Ancient Greek Language and Greek Syllabic Writing" (a work apparently not widely known among Western scholars, owing to its publication only in Russian)[1] Tronsky briefly considers Linear B and syllabic Cypriot spelling practices and treats them as, at least in part, a function of the phonological property of *sonority*.

4.0.1 Sonority and the Sonority Hierarchy

Sonority is a quite basic and noncontroversial (if not altogether explicitly defined) notion utilized by phoneticians and phonologists in describing sounds and their arrangement within syllables. Perhaps most fundamentally, the term *sonority* refers to the acoustic energy, or loudness, with which a sound is produced: Ladefoged, for example, defines the sonority of a sound as "its loudness relative to that of other sounds with the same length, stress, and pitch."[2] It is generally held that the sounds which have the greatest sonority are low vowels while those which have the least sonority are voiceless stops. Other sounds range in between these two end-points. On the basis of sonority, sounds can then be arranged in a scalar fashion, the resulting scale usually being dubbed the *sonority hierarchy*. Most typically, the hierarchy which is encountered is of the following form, where sonority increases progressively from top to bottom:

(1)   stop
       fricative
       nasal
       liquid
       glide
       high vowels
       mid vowels
       low vowels

   It is generally the case that within a syllable, the sound or sounds with high sonority occur at the very core of the syllable; any sounds which may precede this syllabic nucleus are arranged according to progressively increasing (or at least not decreasing) sonority, and any sounds which may follow the nucleus are arranged according to progressively decreasing (or at least not increasing) sonority. Thus, for any given syllable there is a peak of sonority at the heart of the syllable, with an optionally occurring preceding crescendo and/or ensuing decrescendo. Consider, for example, the following forms from Greek, Latin, and English, respectively:

(2)   δρῦς ([drûs], 'tree, oak')
       grus ('crane')
       brass (phonetically [bræs])

Each of these monosyllabic words has the same phonetic structure: in terms of major sound classes, the *onset* (that portion of the syllable which precedes the vowel) consists of the sequence *stop + liquid,* while the *coda* (that portion which follows the vowel) contains a fricative. In passing from the beginning of the syllable to its vowel there is a progressive increase in sonority; that is, a stop is less sonorous than a liquid, which is in turn less sonorous than a vowel. Conversely, between the vowel and the final segment of the syllable, the fricative [-s], there is a net decrease in sonority.

   There is, however, a widespread violation of the generalization presented in the preceding paragraph. In many of the world's languages, syllables may begin with the sequence *[s] + stop* and end with the sequence *stop + [s],* as in the following monosyllabic words from Greek, Latin, and English respectively:

(3)   Στύξ ([stúks], the river Styx)
       stips ('offering')
       spots

At the beginning of each of these words, a segment with higher sonority, [s], precedes one with lower sonority, [t] or [p]; that is, there is a fall in sonority in an environment in which sonority is expected to be progressively increasing.

At the end of each form the violation is simply the reverse: [k], [p], or [t] is followed by [s]; that is, an increase in sonority is found where a progressive decrease in sonority is expected.

We saw in chapter 3 that sequences of *[s]* + *stop* and word-final *stop* + *[s]* are problematic for those interpretations of the Linear B and syllabic Cypriot spelling of consonant clusters which hold that such spelling is based upon syllable structure. *That these clusters are the very ones which also violate that arrangement of consonants within a syllable which is expected on the basis of the sonority hierarchy can hardly be an accident.* We shall return to this matter later.

4.0.2 Tronsky's Analysis

Utilizing the notion of sonority, Tronsky proposes that Linear B spelling of consonants is guided by the following strategy set:

(4)   A single consonant preceding a vowel is written.

(5)   The consonants of the syllable coda are not written.

(6)   In the syllable onset, consonants in a sequence which are arranged in order of progressively increasing sonority, and only these, are written (using the appropriate CV symbols).[3]

The appropriate CV symbols would be those which have a vocalic component that is identical to the vowel of the syllable. Given this strategy, the only consonants occurring in word-initial position which are not actually written are instances of [s-] which precede a stop, as in the following (Tronsky's) example:

(7)   *pe-ma,* σπερμα ([sperma], 'seed')[4]

In this example the fricative [s-] is not written because it is not arranged in an order of progressively increasing sonority with respect to the ensuing consonant, the stop [-p-]; that is, the sonority of a stop is *less* than that of a fricative. Sonority does increase between the stop and the following vowel.

The spelling of word-initial clusters is straightforward. For word-internal clusters, however, Tronsky indicates two possible interpretations of the attested Mycenaean spelling practice. He appears to favor the interpretation that the mode of spelling word-initial clusters was simply applied to medial clusters. In other words, the spelling of a word-initial onset serves as a template which is replicated whenever a matching sequence of consonants occurs elsewhere in the word. Tronsky does not, however, develop this proposal systematically. The evoking of analogy to word-initial position is a process we encountered in the analyses offered by Ruijgh and Morpurgo Davies, discussed in chapter 3.

The second possible interpretation is—in contrast to the first and to other interpretations discussed subsequently in this chapter—one which is dependent upon syllable structure, like those considered in chapter 3. Earlier in his article, prior to discussing the spelling of consonant clusters,[5] Tronsky had mentioned

Kuryłowicz's proposition that in forms such as ὀκτώ ([oktǫ́:], 'eight') the initial stop of the medial cluster is bisyllabic; in other words, the syllable structure is as follows:

(8) [ok-$-ktǫ́:][6]

This is of course the very same proposal developed by Beekes and discussed at length in chapter 3. Tronsky seems to discount Kuryłowicz's idea but indicates that if it were to turn out to be the proper interpretation of syllable structure, then it would obviously be the case that clusters occurring in word-internal syllable onsets (such as [-$kt-] in (8)) are spelled in the way that clusters occurring word-initially are spelled, that is, by exercising strategy (6). In accordance with (5), the consonant of the coda of the preceding syllable (such as [-k$-] in (8)) is not written. Note that this interpretation of the Linear B spelling of word-internal clusters is in effect identical to that of Householder, Sampson, et al., except that Tronsky utilizes the sonority hierarchy to account for the omission of [s] when it precedes a stop in syllable-initial position.

Proposal (5), which states that the consonants of the syllable coda are not written, is introduced by Tronsky apart from any consideration of Kuryłowicz's interpretation of Greek syllable structure. He extends this principle to account for the nonrepresentation of the second element of diphthongs. As I pointed out in chapter 2, however, it is only those diphthongs which end in [-i] that are regularly spelled by omitting the second element of the diphthong. Appealing to the nonrepresentation of syllable codas will not, then, in itself account for the omission of the second element in the orthographic expression of certain diphthongs. Furthermore, Tronsky does not consider that stops occurring before word-final [-s] (and hence in the coda of the final syllable) are represented with plenary spelling. As we shall see below, an orthographic principle explicitly stating that those consonants which follow the vowel of their syllable are omitted is neither necessary nor desirable if Linear B spelling is interpreted solely as a function of sonority.

Tronsky gives only brief attention to syllabic Cypriot spelling. He states that the Cypriot script preserves "the principles of syllabic division inherited from the Mycenaean period,"[7] by which he means that those members of a word-internal consonant cluster which are represented by plenary spelling in Linear B are represented by progressive spelling in the syllabic Cypriot system (with the exception of preconsonantal nasals, of course). We have already seen that this is so.

In contrast to the interpretation offered by Tronsky, the next three systems of analysis to be discussed in this chapter are more purely nonsyllabic. Each of these analyses was conceived independently of the other two and, it would appear on all counts, without knowledge of the earlier work of Tronsky.

4.1 Woodard

In Woodard 1994 I presented for the first time in print,[8] and more summarily than here, a non-syllable-dependent interpretation of the spelling of consonant clusters in Linear B and the syllabic Cypriot script which is dependent upon a scaler notion that I dubbed the *hierarchy of orthographic strength*. This interpretation has been constructed upon the basis of a careful quantitative investigation of the Mycenaean and syllabic Cypriot materials.

4.1.1 Data Collection

Before presenting the results of my investigation, a word should be said regarding the collection of the data. Linear B forms were collected from the glossary of Ventris and Chadwick 1973. The actual number of occurrences of each form collected was determined by an examination of the appropriate entry in Olivier et al. 1973.[9] As a precaution a form was not utilized if Ventris and Chadwick indicate that its identification is uncertain; furthermore, no form was counted which Ventris and Chadwick indicate to be only partially legible or partially preserved. The Cypriot data were collected by examination of the inscriptions which appear in Masson 1983; Mitford 1980 and 1971; and Traunecker, Le Saout, and Masson 1981.[10] Again, forms were systematically excluded on the basis of uncertain interpretation and incomplete representation.[11] This principled screening of the Mycenaean and Cypriot data has led to the exclusion of forms which almost certainly exhibit recognizable sequences of consonants and which would generally have provided additional support for my arguments; however, erring on the side of conservatism in such an endeavor is preferable to constructing a hypothesis upon questionable data.

4.1.2 Consonant Clusters in Linear B

The statistical results of my investigation of the occurrence of consonant clusters in the vocabulary of the Linear B materials appear in table 4.1. In the leftmost column is listed in terms of manners of articulation each type of two-member consonant cluster which could occur in the Mycenaean Greek dialect given its consonantal inventory. The number of consonant clusters of each type which are represented using plenary spelling (<CC>; that type of spelling in which both members of the cluster are actually written) is indicated in the middle column. The column on the right contains the number of occurrences of consonant clusters which are written using partial spelling (<ØC>; that type of spelling in which only the second member of a phonetic cluster actually appears in the orthography). Word-final clusters and geminate clusters are not included in table 4.1 since their representation is governed by the above discussed special constraints. The number of occurrences of word-final and geminate clusters is given in the notes to the table.

The data reported in table 4.1 reveal that with few exceptions it is the case that for any particular type of consonant cluster, that cluster is *either* written with plenary spelling *or* it is written with partial spelling; that is, there is little variation in the particular strategy used for representing any given cluster-type.

Upon the basis of the data reported in table 4.1, the diagram of figure 4.1 can be offered. The consonants listed in the left margin of the diagram specify the initial member of a cluster-type, while those which appear across the top of the diagram specify the second member. The diagonally lined boxes represent cluster-types for which plenary spelling predominates; the horizontally lined boxes represent cluster-types for which partial spelling predominates (I use the term *predominates,* though as indicated immediately above the distribution of plenary and partial spelling is almost completely *complementary*). Those cluster-types which are *only* evidenced by geminate clusters (i.e., *fricative + fricative* and *liquid + liquid*) are so marked; those cluster-types for which no examples are found are marked with the null set symbol (∅).

As proposed in Woodard 1994, the distribution of the spelling strategies utilized for the various types of clusters is such that a spelling-boundary is suggested; this boundary is indicated by the bold line in figure 4.1. It is the general case that

(9)   Consonant cluster types occurring above and to the right of the spelling-boundary are represented with plenary spelling, while those falling below and to the left of the spelling-boundary are represented using partial spelling.

The *fricative + fricative* and *liquid + liquid* cells, which represent only geminate clusters, are excepted from the generalization (9), as partial spelling is always utilized for the representation of geminate clusters. No instances of *fricative + liquid* clusters are provided by the data,[12] nor are there examples of the types *glide + stop, glide + fricative,* and *glide + nasal.*[13]

The cluster-type *fricative + nasal* thus stands as the single counterexample to the generalization (9). Of the 142 occurrences of this cluster, a majority (80) is written with partial spelling rather than with plenary spelling as would be expected given the proposed spelling-boundary. This is not, however, so serious a counterexample as it would seem to be, as 79 of the 80 occurrences of partially spelled *fricative + nasal* clusters are found in various forms of the term *ke-ke-me-na,* identified by Ventris and Chadwick as κεκεσμενα ([kekesmena], 'communal'], linking it with the Proto-Indo-European root *k̑es-*, 'to cut'. The correct interpretation of the form *ke-ke-me-na* has been the subject of considerable scholarly debate, with several scholars advocating an etymology which derives this participle from a root that does not end in [-s], in which case there would be no [-sm-] cluster.[14] The deviation of *ke-ke-me-na* from an otherwise quite regular pattern may likely suggest that it has not been properly etymologized by those who would connect it with *k̑es-*.

4.1.3 The Hierarchy of Orthographic Strength

The generalization offered in (9) suggests that the Linear B spelling of consonant clusters is dependent upon what I have called a *hierarchy of orthographic strength*

TABLE 4.1. The Occurence of Consanant Clusters in the Mycejaean Documents

Cluster	Plenary Spelling (<CC>)	Partial Spelling (<ØC>)
Stop + Stop	243[a]	0[b]
Stop + Fricative	44	0[c]
Stop + Nasal	120	0
Stop + Glide	19	0
Stop + Liquid	192	0
Fricative + Stop	0[d]	451
Fricative + Fricative	0	0[e]
Fricative + Nasal	62	80[f]
Fricative + Glide	6	0
Fricative + Liquid	0	0
Nasal + Stop	0	214
Nasal + Fricative	0	75[g]
Nasal + Nasal	24	0[h]
Nasal + Glide	10	0
Nasal + Liquid	1[i]	0
Glide + Stop	0	0
Glide + Fricative	0	0
Glide + Nasal	0	0
Glide + Glide	4[j]	0
Glide + Liquid	19[k]	0
Liquid + Stop	0	186
Liquid + Fricative	0	1
Liquid + Nasal	12[l]	201
Liquid + Glide	4[m]	362
Liquid + Liquid	0	0[n]

[a] Included here are a number of instances in which the first stop of the cluster is spelled by utilizing a symbol which has a vocalic component identical to the vowel which *precedes* the cluster (rather than the one which follows it, as is normally the case with Linear B plenary spelling): for example, *wa-na-ka-te*, ϝανακτει ([wanaktẹ:], 'to the king', five times), with which compare the expected *wa-na-ke-te* (one time); *wa-na-ka-te-ro*, ϝανακτερος ([wanakteros], 'of the king', ten times). Almost certainly to be included here, though not counted for reasons already explained, is the possible genitive *]wa-na-ka-to*, ϝανακτος ([wanaktos]). These spellings will be considered further.

[b] There are thirty-eight instances of geminate stops, and these are, as expected, represented utilizing partial spelling.

[c] Ten instances of word-final *stop + fricative* clusters are found in the Mycenaean data base. One of these occurs in the form *to-ra*, θωραξ ([thọ:raks], 'corslet'), which is cited in the glossary of Ventris and Chadwick 1973 as *pa-ra*. On the corrected reading see J. Killen, 1985, "New Readings in the Linear B Tablets from Knossos," *Kadmos* 24:31. Also included in the database though not occurring in the Ventris and Chadwick glossary, are two instances of the spelling *to-ra-ka* found on Tiryns tablet Si5, published in U. Naumann, L. Godart, and J.-P. Olivier, 1977, "Un cinquième fragment de tablette en linéaire B de Tirynthe," *BCH* 101:229–234; see also J. Melena and J.-P. Olivier, 1991, *TITHEMY*, supplement to *Minos*, no. 12, p. 28. The form *o-nu* is likely to be nominative singular ονυξ ([onüks]) and is included in the database, though Ventris and Chadwick do not commit themselves to this interpretation. The possibility of a nominative singular spelled *o-nu-ka* is discussed later. Additional possible sequences of word-final *stop + fricative* clusters have been proposed, and these will also be considered below.

[d] The form *sa-pa-ka-te-ri-ja* has been interpreted by some scholars as σφακτηρια ([sphaktẹ:ria:], 'victims') (so M. Lejeune, 1960, "Essais de philologie mycénienne v 1," *RP* 34:12). The double anomaly of using plenary spelling to represent a *fricative + stop* cluster and the representation of the sequence [-kte-]

(10)   *stop > fricative > nasal > glide > liquid*

within which orthographic strength progressively decreases from stop to liquid. The following spelling strategy, which makes reference to this hierarchy, appears to be utilized for representing consonant clusters in the Linear B script:

(11)   Within a word, any two successive consonants will be represented with plenary spelling if, and only if, the orthographic strength of the first is greater than or equal to that of the second; otherwise, partial spelling will be used.

Thus, we find plenary spelling of the cluster-types (A) *stop + stop, stop + fricative, stop + nasal, stop + glide, stop + liquid*; (B) *fricative + nasal, fricative + glide;* (C) *nasal + nasal, nasal + glide, nasal + liquid;* and (D)

---

as *-ka-ta-* makes this interpretation quite suspect. See Palmer 1963:185 and note the comment of Ventris and Chadwick 1973:390: "Exceptions to the rule that initial *s* is omitted before a stop are very doubtful."

[e] There are eighteen instances of geminate fricatives; as the only fricative in Mycenaean Greek is [s], any cluster of the type *fricative + fricative* would of course be geminate.

[f] Note, however, that seventy-nine of the eighty instances occur in various forms of a single word: *ke-ke-me-na*, κεκεσμενα ([kekesmena], 'communal'). We will return to this later. I have not included in my count the quite problematic form *to-me*, which has been interpreted by some as a dative personal pronoun το(σ)μει ([to(s)mę:]); compare Sanskrit *tásmai*, on which see, among other sources, *Docs.*:263, 450.

[g] In addition, there are eight such clusters which probably occur word-finally. On word-final [-ns] see chapter 3, n. 123, in the present study.

[h] Six occurrences of *nasal + nasal* geminate clusters are found.

[i] The single example of this cluster occurs in the form *o-mi-ri-jo-i*, Ομριοιhι ([omrioihi], 'for the Rain Spirits'), the interpretation of which has not been accepted by all scholars. See chapter 3, n. 151, in the present study.

[j] In two of these four instances the cluster [-wy-] is written *-u-jV.* Here the spelling strategy is thus plenary (as opposed to partial) but differs in detail from the usual case; on this spelling see C. Ruijgh, 1967, *Études sur la grammaire et le vocabulaire du grec mycénien* (Amsterdam: Adolf Hakkert), pp. 25–26. The four forms referred to are two instances of *di-wi-ja* and two of *di-u-ja*, both for Διϝyας,-α ([diwya:s, -a:(i)], genitive and dative of the name of a goddess *Diwya*). Ruijgh plausibly suggests that the grapheme <u> can here substitute for <wi> (⟨i⟩ used before [y]), since there would be little phonetic difference between [w] and [u] following the vowel [i]. There are several related forms of which some number (and perhaps most) could surely be included as additional examples of the plenary spelling of *glide + glide* clusters, but there is uncertainty expressed by Ventris and Chadwick concerning the identification and/or phonetic structure of these: they include *di-u-ja-jo-*, 'the sanctuary of Diwya'?; *di-wi-jo* and *di-u-jo*, 'the sanctuary of Zeus'?, and the former perhaps a toponym; *di-wi-ja-ta*, a toponym; *di-wi-ja-wo* and *di-u-ja-wo*, a man's name; *di-wi-je-ja*, a woman's name or 'priestess of Zeus'?; *di-wi-je-u*, a man's name or 'priest of Zeus'?; and *di-wi-jo-jo*, the name of a month. For most of these Ruijgh (1967:130–131) proposes a phonetic sequence [-wy-]. The adjectives *me-wi-jo, me-u-jo* etc. ('younger'; Homeric μείων ([mé:o:n])) have been interpreted both as μειϝyo– ([mę:wyo-]) and as μειϝιο– ([mę:wio-]), with the latter perhaps more likely; see, *inter alios*, Ruijgh 1967:26; Viredaz 1983:175. On the possibility that *qo-wi-ja* represents γʷοϝyα ([gʷowya:] with the meaning 'decorated with a cow'), see Ruijgh 1967:131–132 and contrast *Docs.*:288, 463.

[k] In one of these nineteen instances the symbol *u* is used to represent the initial [w] of a cluster: *-u-ru-to*, ϝρυντοι ([wrüntoi], 'they are guarding'). This spelling is necessitated by the fact that Linear B has no symbol *wu;* see Ruijgh 1967:27.

[l] Forms of the participle *a-ra-ro-mo-te-me-na*, αραρμοτμενα, -αι ([ararmotmena:, -ai], 'fitted out') represent the instances of plenary spelling of this cluster-type (see the following note).

[m] These are four occurrences of the neuter perfect participle *a-ra-ru-wo-a*, αραρϝοα ([ararwoa], 'fitted'), of which there are several additional fragmented occurrences. With the uncharacteristic plenary spelling here, compare the apparently related form *a-ra-ro-mo-to-me-na* (see the preceding note); also see later discussion.

[n] There are four instances of geminate liquids.

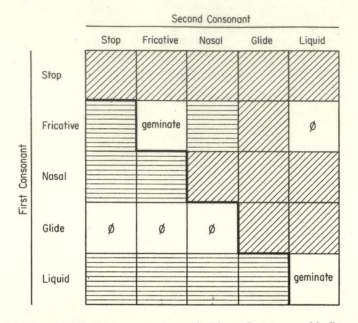

FIGURE 4.1 The spelling of consonant clusters in Linear B: squares with diagonal pattern represent predominant plenary spelling; squares with horizontal pattern represent predominant partial spelling.

glide + glide, glide + liquid. But partial spelling is used in the clusters (E) *fricative + stop;* (F) *nasal + stop, nasal + fricative;* and (G) *liquid + stop, liquid + fricative, liquid + nasal, liquid + glide.* Apart from the problematic *ke-ke-me-na* there are only a very few exceptions to the spelling strategy (11). Of the 213 occurrences of the cluster *liquid + nasal,* 12 are unexpectedly represented with plenary spelling, as are 4 of the 366 instances of the *liquid + glide* cluster-type.

4.1.4   Consonant Clusters in Syllabic Cypriot

The findings from my investigation of the syllabic Cypriot materials[15] are presented in table 4.2. In the column on the left is again listed (in terms of manners of articulation) each of the possible types of two-member consonant clusters. In the middle column is listed the number of occurrences of consonant clusters which are spelled by utilizing progressive spelling ($<V_iCV_jCV_j>$; that type of spelling in which the first member of the cluster is spelled with the CV character that has a vocalic component identical to the vowel which phonetically *follows* the cluster, as in *pa-ti-ri* for πατρι ([patri], 'to (the) father')). The rightmost column contains the number of occurrences of consonant clusters which are represented with regressive spelling ($<V_iCV_iCV_j>$; that type of

spelling in which the first member of the cluster is spelled with the CV character that has a vocalic component identical to the vowel which phonetically
precedes the cluster, as in *a-ra-ku-ro* for αργυρω ([argǘrọ:], 'of silver')).

Several types of clusters have been systematically excluded from table 4.2
because they do not provide evidence for determining those conditions which
motivate the choice of the progressive as opposed to the regressive spelling
strategy and vice versa. As in the case of the Mycenaean data, geminate clusters
are not included (but the number of occurrences is given in the notes to the
table), since it is consistently the case that only one member of such clusters is
actually spelled. In those instances in which the vowel which precedes the
cluster is identical to that one which follows it, as in *a-ka-ra-to-se* for ακρατος
([akratos], 'pure, unmixed'), it is impossible to determine which spelling strategy is being used; consequently, such occurrences are not included in table
4.2 but are footnoted. As I pointed out in chapter 2, the handbooks state that
preconsonantal nasals are not spelled in the syllabic Cypriot script. For this
reason sequences of a nasal followed by some other consonant are also excluded from table 4.2; we will consider such clusters further along in this chapter, however. We have already noted that in the syllabic Cypriot script, unlike
that of the Mycenaeans, *all* word-initial consonant clusters (ninety-six of which
occur in the Cypriot data) are represented. To effect such representation, the
progressive spelling strategy is utilized, regardless of the type of strategy used
for spelling identical clusters occurring word-internally.[16] The Cypriot script
also differs from the Mycenaean, as mentioned in chapter 2, in that word-final
consonants can be written,[17] and, ergo, it should be possible to write word-final
sequences of consonants. Of the various types of word-final consonant clusters
which are allowed in Greek (i.e., [-ps], [-ks], [-ls]) and in certain dialects [-ns]
and [-rs],[18] only one, [-ks], is securely attested in the syllabic Cypriot materials.[19] However, for representing this word-final sequence (as also mentioned in
chapter 2), the Cypriot scribes utilized one of their script's few and anomalous
CCV symbols, the one with the value [kse].[20] Since special strategies are thus
used for representing both word-initial and word-final clusters, the data reported
in table 4.2—upon which our interpretation of the scribes' choice of progressive
spelling or regressive spelling of any given cluster is based—represent only
word-internal clusters; word-initial and word-final clusters are footnoted however.

Utilizing the data reported in table 4.2, the diagram of figure 4.2 can be
constructed. In figure 4.2, which is of the same general form as figure 4.1,
cluster-types for which the use of the progressive spelling strategy predominates are marked by diagonal scoring of the appropriate box while those
cluster-types which are written principally with regressive spelling are marked
by horizontal scoring. Just as with plenary and partial spelling in the Mycenaean script (see figure 4.1), the distribution of progressive and regressive spelling is almost completely complementary in the syllabic Cypriot script. In figure
4.2, as in the earlier figure, cluster-types which are only evidenced by geminate
clusters are so marked, and those cluster-types for which no examples are found

TABLE 4.2.   The Occurrence of Conssonant Clusters in One Syllablic
Cypriot Documents

Cluster	Progressive Spelling ($<V_iCV_jCV_j>$)	Regressive Spelling ($<V_iCV_iCV_j>$)
Stop + Stop[a]	9	1
Stop + Fricative[b]	4	2
Stop + Nasal[c]	14	0
Stop + Glide	0	0
Stop + Liquid[d]	113	3
Fricative + Stop[e]	1[f]	63
Fricative + Fricative[g]	0	0
Fricative + Nasal[h]	0	1
Fricative + Glide	0	0
Fricative + Liquid	4	3[i]
Glide + Stop	0	0
Glide + Fricative	0	0
Glide + Nasal	0	0
Glide + Glide	0	0
Glide + Liquid[j]	1	0
Liquid + Stop	1	38
Liquid + Fricative[k]	0	1
Liquid + Nasal[l]	0	6
Liquid + Glide[m]	0	3
Liquid + Liquid[n]	0	0

[a] There is one example of a geminate *stop + stop* cluster and eight examples of word-initial *stop + stop* clusters.

[b] There are five instances of *stop + fricative* clusters of the type [V_iCCV_i] (i.e., cases in which the vowel which precedes the cluster is identical to that one which follows it). Not included in this row are the occurrences of the special symbols *kse* and *ksa*, used to represent the word-final (and in certain unusual instances word-internal) sequence [ks]; these are treated later.

[c] There are four instances of *stop + nasal* clusters of the type [V_iCCV_i].

[d] There are eleven instances of word-initial *stop + liquid* clusters and two instances of *stop + liquid* clusters of the type [V_iCCV_i].

[e] There are forty-one instances of word-initial *fricative + stop* clusters and seventeen instances of *fricative + stop* clusters of the type [V_iCCV_i].

[f] A second example of the progressive spelling of this cluster-type probably occurs in the inscription *ICS* 92(2): *-e-pẹ-sa-ta-se*, ΕΠΕΣΤΑΣΕ ([epestase], '(s)he set up'), though, as indicated, the reading of the second character is insecure. Similarly, the progressive spelling of this form may occur in the fragmentary inscription *ICS* 93(1): *-e-pe-sa-tạ-sẹ*. Both of these inscriptions were found in the vicinity of Salamiou. Palaima (personal communication) has rightly suggested that such a spelling of this compound verb would only be an apparent exception; that is, στα- ([sta-]) preserves the simplex spelling *sa-ta-*. See my later discussion on morphological interference.

[g] Geminate [-ss-] clusters occur ten times in the database.

[h] There are two instances of *fricative + nasal* clusters of the type [V_iCCV_i].

[i] Each of the seven instances of the cluster-type *fricative + liquid* occurs in proper names which begin with the element 'Εσλο- or 'Εσλα- ([eslo-], [esla-], attested as the variant form 'Εσθλ- ([esth lo-]) in some dialects; see O. Masson, 1962, "Les noms en 'Εσθλ(ο)– et 'Εσλ(ο)– dans les dialectes grecs," *Beiträge zur Namenforschung* 13:75-80). Of these seven, only three occur in sources which I have utilized for the collection of the Cypriot data (specifically, O. Masson 1983 and Traunecker, Le Saout, and Masson 1981; on the sources used see the discussion in section 4.1.1), and in each of these instances the *fricative + liquid* cluster is spelled *regressively*. To include only these forms would be to present a distorted image of the method of spelling

are marked with the null set symbol (∅). Even though clusters which begin with a nasal are not included in table 2, as such clusters are subject to a separate spelling strategy, as I previously stated and discuss later, the articulatory manner *nasal* is included in the left margin of figure 4.2 in order to preserve the symmetry of the diagram; clusters with an initial nasal are marked *na* (not applicable).

The Cypriot data present a less complete picture of the nature of the spelling strategies used for representing consonant clusters than do the Mycenaean data. There are essentially two reasons for this: (1) the Cypriot materials provide attestation of fewer cluster-types; and (2) in these materials fewer examples are found for a number of the cluster-types which are attested. However, if the spelling-boundary which presents itself in figure 4.1 is extrapolated to figure 4.2, the attested cluster-types of Cypriot are found to group together in much the same way as those of Mycenaean:

(12) Those clusters occurring above and to the right of the boundary are represented using one type of spelling strategy (i.e., progressive spelling), and those occurring below and to the left of the boundary are represented by using a different spelling strategy (i.e., regressive spelling).

this cluster-type since a total of four occurrences of the 'Εσλ– formant which are represented by using the *progressive* spelling strategy for the [-sl] cluster are to be found in two other collections of Cypriot inscriptions. Consequently, I have here departed from my usual practice by including data from O. Masson and T. Mitford, 1986, *Les inscriptions syllabiques de Kouklia-Paphos* (Konstanz: Universitätsverlag Konstanz); and T. Mitford and O. Masson, 1983, *The Syllabic Inscriptions of Rantidi-Paphos* (Konstanz: Universitätsverlag Konstanz); the inclusion in the database of other forms from these collections, which contain primarily personal names and are quite fragmentary, would have no critical effect upon my findings concerning other types of Cypriot consonant clusters and their orthographic representation (some of these materials are already to be found in *ICS*). In the former are found the names -*e-so-lo-pa-to*-, Εσλοφαντω ([eslopʰantọ:]; on this form see also Masson 1962:77), and *e-sa-la*, which Masson and Mitford interpret as an abbreviation and restore as Εσλαγοραυ ([eslagorau]; see below on the occurrence of this name at Karnak). From Rantidi come *e-so-lo-te-mi-wo-se*-, Εσλοθεμιϝος ([eslotʰemiwos]), and the abbreviation *e-sa-la-ko*, again interpreted as Εσλαγοραυ (on both of these forms see in addition O. Masson 1962:77). The Kouklia-Paphos materials also provide a form *ẹ-so-lọ*, about which Masson (p. 68) writes, "Lecture plausible de Mitford, mais les s. 1 et surtout 3 sont très partiels. Probablement le début d'un nom en 'Εσλο–." O. Masson (1962:77) also cites the name *ẹ-so-lo-ṭi-[mọ]*, referencing it to a personal communication from Mitford and identifying it as Εσλοτι[μω] ([eslotimọ:]). As indicated above, however, I have eliminated from the database any forms in which the reading of the symbol preceding or following the cluster is uncertain (since the occurrence of a cluster of the type [V$_i$CCV$_i$] could in this way be obscured). Each of the three instances of the use of regressive spelling to represent the sequence [-sl-] is found in O.Masson 1983. The form -*ẹ-se-lạ-ko-ra-se*- (i.e., with the first and third signs marked as uncertain) occurs in *ICS* 435 and is interpreted as the personal name Εσλαγορας ([eslagoras]). In Traunecker, Le Saout, and Masson 1981:269, however, Masson indicates that the reading of the form is secure. *ICS* 327(A) offers both *e-se-lo-[*, Εσλω[ν] ([eslọ:n]), and *e-se-lo-ka-ri-?-[*, Εσλοχαρις ([eslokʰaris]).

[j] There are three instances of word-initial *glide* + *liquid* clusters and one occurrence of a *glide* + *liquid* cluster of the type [V$_i$CCV$_i$].

[k] There are two instances of *liquid* + *fricative* clusters of the type [V$_i$CCV$_i$].

[l] There is a single occurrence of a *liquid* + *nasal* cluster of the type [V$_i$CCV$_i$].

[m] There are two instances of *liquid* + *glide* clusters of the type [V$_i$CCV$_i$].

[n] Geminate liquid clusters are found eighteen times.

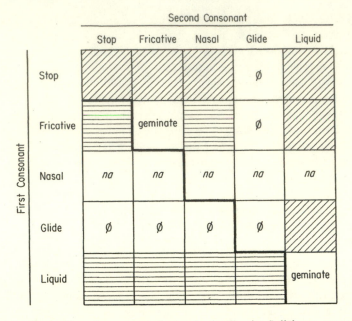

FIGURE 4.2 The spelling of consonant clusters in the Cypriot Syllabary: squares with diagonal pattern represent predominant progressive spelling; squares with horizontal pattern represent predominant regressive spelling.

4.1.4.1 Fricative + Nasal

The cluster-type *fricative + nasal* (specifically the sequence [-sm-]) stands as the only counterexample to the generalization (12). This is the same cluster which provided the single exception to the Linear B spelling strategy (11). As we have seen, however, it is entirely possible that Ventris and Chadwick (and others) have erroneously etymologized *ke-ke-me-na* and, accordingly, that the one cluster-type which appears to behave as an exception to the Mycenaean strategy does not, in fact, do so. In the case of the Cypriot data, the single counterexemplary form is the perfect passive participle *i-na-la-li-si-me-na, ιν–αλαλισμεναν* ([inalalismenan], 'having been written upon', from ιναλινω [inalinọ:]).

There is without doubt, however, a second Cypriot counterexample of the same type, which was excluded from the database in accordance with the principles adopted for the selection of secure data (see section 4.1.1). In inscription *NK* 266b (corresponding to *ICS* 231 and 233), the form *te-ka-[ti]-si-mo-i* occurs, which Mitford (1980:200–202) interprets as δεκατισμωι ([dekatismọ:i], dative object of the preposition απο ([apo]), glossed by Mitford (p.38)[21] as 'tithe'; Masson (1983:415) accepts the reading. The corresponding genitive, δεκατισμου ([dekatismu:]), occurs in alphabetic inscriptions from Kafizin (see, e.g., *NK* 251 and 264).

There is probably still a third example of a Cypriot [-sm-] cluster. The cluster occurs in a form in which, as with *te-ka-[ti]-si-mo-i*, the sign preceding the cluster is illegible and which, consequently, was excluded from the database. This form, also from Kafizin, is the adjective *[a]-se-me-na*, ασμενα ([asmena], 'pleased'), occurring in *NK* 136. Notice that in this instance, however, the *fricative + nasal* cluster is written with *progressive* rather than regressive spelling, and hence the spelling of the cluster conforms to the generalization (12).[22]

4.1.4.1.1 Morphological Interference?

If we should for the moment accept Ventris and Chadwick's interpretation of *ke-ke-me-na* as κεκεσμενα, an interesting observation presents itself. As we have just seen, the only cluster-type which violates either the Linear B or the syllabic Cypriot spelling generalizations (11) and (12) is the type *fricative + nasal*; the specific sequence involved is [-sm-]. In the case of each of the three mentioned forms violating the spelling generalizations (i.e., Mycenaean *ke-ke-me-na* for κεκεσμενα ([kekesmena]), with unexpected partial (rather than plenary) spelling of the cluster; and Cypriot *i-na-la-li-si-me-na* for ιναλαλισμεναν ([inalalismenan]) and *te-ka-[ti]-si-mo-i* for δεκατισμωι ([dekatismo:i]), both with unexpected regressive (rather than progressive) spelling of the [-sm-] sequence), the two members of the cluster are separated by a morpheme-boundary. Mycenaean κεκεσμενα and Cypriot ιναλαλισμεναν are both perfect passive participles in which the [-m-] occurs as the initial segment of the participial suffix *-μεν-* ([-men-]). Regardless of the precise derivation of δεκατισμος,[23] it is clearly a form produced by the addition of the commonly occurring and highly productive nominal suffix *-μος* ([-mos]).[24]

As I noted, there are in the Linear B database eighty occurrences of partially spelled *fricative + nasal* clusters, seventy-nine of which represent various forms of *ke-ke-me-na*. The one remaining form showing unexpected partial spelling of this cluster-type is *ka-ra-ma-to*, κλασματων ([klasmatǫ:n], 'fragments', a genitive plural which appears to have been mistakenly written for a nominative plural[25]). The two members of the [-sm-] cluster are again separated by a synchronically transparent morpheme-boundary. The suffix *-μα*, (genitive) *-ματος* ([-ma-tos]) is used to form nominals that designate the result of some action; this suffix is "one of the most productive types in Greek, the number running to several thousands."[26, 27]

On the other hand, in the one instance of a Cypriot [-sm-] cluster which is spelled as predicted given the observed spelling-boundary (i.e., *[a]-se-me-na* for ασμενα ([asmena], with progressive spelling of the cluster)), there was probably no synchronically recognizable intervening morpheme-boundary between the [s] and [m]. While it is undoubtedly the case that ασμενα was in origin also a middle participle, the formation of the term must be quite archaic (as is suggested by the uncertainty of its etymology[28]), and it appears unlikely that by the first millennium this adjective was still associated with any verb paradigm.

The above cited forms are not the only instances of a claimed spelling irregularity coinciding with a morpheme-boundary. Chadwick has proposed that the Pylos form *pa-wo-ke* be read as nominative plural παν–ϝοργες ([pan-worges], 'maids of all work'; the form also occurs in the genitive plural).[29] A compound-boundary would then separate the two members of a *nasal* + *glide* cluster, and that cluster would be written with partial spelling (not with the expected plenary spelling). The interpretation of the form is uncertain, however, and has not been included in our database.[30] Beyond this, recall that Sextus Empiricus tells us that a morpheme-boundary (created by the attachment of a prefix) can interfere with the normal process of "syllable-division," and that Threatte has observed that in Athenian inscriptional practice word-division must be made after the [-s] of εἰς, πρός, and definite articles ending in [-s].[31]

There is thus perhaps some indication that a synchronically transparent intervening morpheme-boundary may at times abrogate the expected utilization of plenary spelling in Linear B and the corresponding progressive spelling in syllabic Cypriot. There are, of course, instances in which this does not happen; for example, Linear B *e-ra-pe-me-na*, εppαπμενα ([errapmena], 'sewn', a perfect passive participle). If morphological interference is at work here, perhaps relative difference in aperture between the two members of a cluster is also a factor.

4.1.4.2 *The Hierarchy of Orthographic Strength and the Cypriot Syllabary*

The generalization (12) indicates that the orthographic hierarchy (10) which was posited above and repeated here as (13) is also utilized in the spelling of word-internal consonant clusters in the syllabic Cypriot script:

(13)   *stop > fricative > nasal > glide > liquid*

The spelling strategy which appears to be at work is the following:

(14)   If the first of two successive consonants occupies a position on the hierarchy which is higher than or equal to that of the second, then it will be written with the CV symbol whose vocalic component is identical to the vowel which follows the cluster; otherwise it will be written with the CV symbol whose vocalic component is identical to the vowel which precedes the cluster.

This is, *mutatis mutandis,* the same strategy utilized by the Mycenaean scribes (i.e., (11)).

4.1.4.3 *Nasal-First Clusters in Syllabic Cypriot*

As indicated above, it is reported in the handbooks that preconsonantal nasals are not written in the syllabic Cypriot script; hence, the spelling of clusters having a nasal as their initial member would not conform to the general spelling strategy (14). Regarding the representation of such clusters, Buck,[32] Chadwick[33] and Thumb-Scherer,[34] for example, each report simply that a nasal is not written when it occurs before another consonant. Masson, however, states, more narrowly, that nasals are not written when they precede a stop or a fricative.[35] In order to understand better the nature of the spelling of nasal-first clusters in the Cypriot script, let us examine each of the possible two-member clusters which begin with a nasal:[36]

(15) *nasal + stop*   93
      nasal + fricative   2
      nasal + nasal   7
      nasal + glide   0
      nasal + liquid   0

As (15) reveals, the Cypriot data provide examples of nasals preceding stops, fricatives and nasals; however, no sequences of the types *nasal + glide* and *nasal + liquid*[37] occur. In the case of the cluster-types *nasal + stop* and *nasal + fricative,* the inherited nasal is not spelled, just as the handbooks indicate, for example:

(16) *pa-ta,* παντα ([panta], 'all')
      pe-pa-me-ro-ne, πεμπαμερων ([pempamerǫ:n], 'of a period of five days')
      i-o-si, ιωνσι ([iǫ:nsi], 'they should remain')

Further, as we would expect, only a single member of the geminate sequences [-nn-] and [-mm-] is written, in keeping with the regular strategy for spelling geminate clusters. When the *nasal + nasal* cluster is nongeminate (i.e., [-mn-]), however, *both members* of the cluster *are* written. There are four examples of such clusters occurring in the Cypriot database:

(17) A. *ma-na-se-se,* Μνασης ([mnasẹ:s], proper name)
      B. *ma-na-ma,* μναμα ([mnama], 'memorial')
      C. *li-mi-ni-si-o-se,* Λιμνισιος ([limnisios], ethnic adjective)
      D. *me-ma-na-me-no-i,* μεμναμενοι ([memnamenoi], 'having remembered')

Example (17B), *ma-na-ma,* also occurs in the Kouklia inscription *KP* 228 (with the same spelling).[38] As we would expect, the full representation of the cluster [-mn-] is effected by using the progressive spelling strategy when the cluster occurs word-initially, as in (17A) and (17B). The directionality of the spelling (progressive or regressive) of (17C) is ambiguous since the vowel which precedes the cluster is the same as that one which follows. Example (17D) reveals, however, that it is progressive spelling which is utilized for representing word-internal nongeminate *nasal + nasal* clusters, and this is in keeping with the general Cypriot spelling strategy (14).

An examination of those Cypriot clusters having a nasal consonant as their initial member suggests, then, that what has been interpreted as the typical nonrepresentation of preconsonantal nasals in the syllabic Cypriot script is actually a function of two separate phenomena:

(18) A. the accidental absence of the cluster-types *nasal + glide* and *nasal + liquid*
      B. the use of a spelling strategy for representing preconsonantal nasals which is distinct from that one which is otherwise used for spelling consonant sequences in the Cypriot Syllabary (i.e., (14))

With respect to (18B), it would appear that the strategy which is attested in the syllabic Cypriot documents for spelling clusters having an initial nasal is the same as that strategy which is used for representing *all* consonant clusters in the Linear B system (i.e., (11)). Thus, just as in the case of Mycenaean, Cypriot clusters of the form *nasal* + *stop* and *nasal* + *fricative* are written with partial spelling, while nongeminate *nasal* + *nasal* clusters are represented using plenary spelling.[39] This analysis would predict that if Cypriot *nasal* + *glide* and *nasal* + *liquid* clusters were attested (as perhaps at least the former will be eventually), these cluster-types would also be written with plenary spelling.

By the preceding analysis, the strategy of *plenary versus partial* spelling which is characteristic of Linear B has survived as a component of the syllabic Cypriot script and is utilized when the initial member of the cluster is a nasal. Whatever the precise motivation for the preservation of a vestige of Mycenaean *plenary versus partial* spelling may have been, it appears to be bound up with the phonetics or phonology of the nasal consonant itself. This "exceptional" nonrepresentation of preconsonantal nasals in the Cypriot script is paralleled by orthographic tendencies in various other syllabic scripts. For example, in the syllabic writing system of Hittite, as discussed by Justeson and Stephens,[40] there is a relatively high frequency of orthographic omission of nasals which precede either two consonants or a word-final consonant. Similarly, certain preconsonantal nasals are not written in Germanic runic inscriptions.[41]

In contrast, however, to what we have just seen to be the usual mode of representing preconsonantal nasals in the Cypriot script, there are three instances of the uncharacteristic spelling of a *nasal* + *stop* cluster utilizing the general syllabic Cypriot strategy (14). These are various case forms of the noun *Νυμφα* ([nümpʰa] 'nymph'):

(19)   A. *-nu-mu-pa-se-*, *Νυμφας* ([nümpʰas], genitive singular)
       B. *nu-mu-pa-i*, *Νυμφαι* ([nümpʰai], dative singular)
       C. *-nu-mu-pa-i-se-*, *Νυμφαις* ([nümpʰais], dative plural)

Compare these forms with the more common and expected spellings, such as the following:

(20)   *nu-pa-i*, *Νυμφαι* ([nümpʰai])

Forms (19A) and (19B) occur in inscriptions from Kafizin, while that of (19C) is of disputed provenience.[42] The Kafizin materials are late, dating to the third century B.C. The extension of the Cypriot *progressive versus regressive* strategy (14) to the spelling of clusters beginning with a nasal perhaps reveals an evolutionary "regularization" of the representation of nasal-initial clusters, if not simply confusion concerning "proper" syllabic spelling practice at this late date. Often, a single artifact at Kafizin will bear both an alphabetic and a syllabic inscription; this fuller spelling of nasal-first clusters was perhaps motivated in part by the influence of alphabetic spellings, in which, of course, preconsonantal nasals were written. Conversely, on a few occasions the nasal is omitted from the alphabetic spelling of *Νυμφα* (i.e., such spellings as *Νυφηι* are found[43]), and this quite likely occurs under the reverse influence of the syllabic spelling strategy for representing preconsonantal nasals.

We see, then, that there are instances of the spelling of preconsonantal nasals in the syllabic Cypriot script: namely, nongeminate *nasal + nasal* clusters and a few exceptional cases of *nasal + stop* clusters. If these clusters are incorporated into figure 4.2, then the distribution of cluster-types relative to the proposed spelling-boundary shows an even greater similarity to that distribution exhibited within the Linear B system (see figure 4.1). Figure 4.2 is repeated with these modifications as figure 4.3.

4.1.5 The Sonority Hierarchy Again

In my discussion of Tronsky's interpretation of the spelling of consonant clusters in the syllabic scripts of Greek, I introduced the phonetic and phonological notion of sonority and the scale known as the sonority hierarchy (see (1)). According to that scale, consonants are hierarchically arranged in the following sequence, where sonority increases progressively from left to right:

(21)   *stop > fricative > nasal > liquid > glide*

Strictly speaking, the hierarchy as formalized in (21) would perhaps be more accurately termed one of nonsonority, since the consonant with least sonority

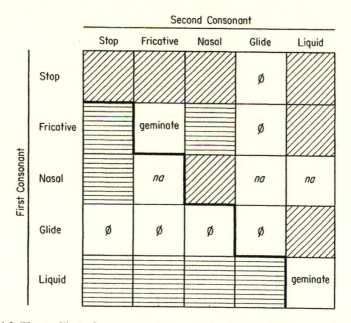

FIGURE 4.3 The spelling of consonant clusters in the Cypriot Syllabary, revised: squares with diagonal pattern represent predominant progressive spelling; squares with horizontal pattern represent predominant regressive spelling.

occurs at the top of the hierarchy. Such a scale has also been interpreted as a *hierarchy of consonantal strength,* in which *stop* is the strongest consonant and *glide* is the weakest.[44]

The *hierarchy of orthographic strength* (10), repeated here as (22),

(22)   *stop > fricative > nasal > glide > liquid*

upon which the Linear B and syllabic Cypriot spelling strategies, (11) and (14) respectively, are dependent is almost identical in form to the consonantal sonority hierarchy (21). The sole difference between the two is plainly that the sound classes *liquid* and *glide* occur in reverse order in the two hierarchies: while the class *glide* outranks *liquid* in the orthographic hierarchy (22), *liquid* outranks *glide* in the sonority hierarchy (21). There is evidence, however, that the structure of the sonority hierarchy shows some language-specific variation—specifically, that in the case of particular languages, glides may occur higher on the sonority hierarchy than liquids; that is, liquids may be more sonorous than glides.

In a study of consonant assimilation in Pali, a Middle Indic language, J. Hankamer and J. Aissen have proposed that the direction of such assimilation is determined by the rank of the consonants involved on the sonority hierarchy. Essentially, they claim that for any given sequence of two consonants, the consonant which occurs lower on the hierarchy will assimilate to the consonant which occurs higher on the hierarchy. If both consonants are of the same rank on the hierarchy, the assimilation will be automatically regressive; that is, the second consonant will assimilate to the first. The sonority hierarchy which they posit for Pali is of the following form:

(23)   *stop > s > nasal > l > w > y > r*

Here, the glides [w] and [y] both occur at a higher position on the hierarchy than the liquid [r].[45] Hankamer and Aissen further propose that assimilation in Hungarian is similarly dependent upon the sonority hierarchy and that in this language the sonority hierarchy has the following structure:[46]

(24)   *stop > fricative > nasal > y > r > l*

Here, the single glide [y] outranks both of the liquids, and so, in terms of major sound classes, this sonority hierarchy is identical in form to hierarchy of orthographic strength proposed in (22). Hankamer and Aissen conclude, then, that the sonority hierarchy is essentially a language universal but that, as a consequence of the articulatory variation which is characteristic of glides and liquids, there is some language-specific variation at the bottom end of the hierarchy.[47]

As in the case of the sonority hierarchy which Hankamer and Aissen have proposed for Pali (i.e., (23)), the sonority hierarchy of Greek is one in which the glide [w] occurs at a higher position than the liquid [r]; that is, it is of the following form:

(25)   *stop > fricative > nasal > glide > liquid*

This is revealed by the occurrence of the word-initial sequence [wrV-], a Proto-Greek cluster which survives in various dialects, for example:[48]

(26)	Mycenaean	*wi-ri-no,* ϝρινοι ([wrinoi], 'ox-hides')
	Cypriot	*we-re-ta-se,* ϝρϝτας ([wrẹ:tas], 'treaty')
	Elean	ϝρᾱτρᾱ ([wra:tra:], 'treaty')
	Arcadian	ϝρησις ([wrẹ:sis], 'declaration')
	Aeolic	ϝρηξις ([wrẹ:ksis], 'bursting')

Similarly, word-initial [wlV-], which like [wrV-] is a Proto-Indo-European sequence, occurred in Greek, though is less well attested. The Mycenaean materials may offer at least one example:

(27)) *wo-ro-ma-ta,* ϝλωματα ([wlọ:mata], 'containers'?)[49]

And from the first millennium, is attested the following:[50]

(28) Elean αϝλανεōς ([awlaneọ:s], 'wholly')[51]

It should be noted that at least one dialect appears not to conform at all points to the sonority hierarchy proposed in (25): namely, the dialect of classical Attic (in which word-initial [wr-] is no longer preserved). This is revealed by the absence of compensatory lengthening of vowels which preceded word-internal *[-rw-] clusters. For example, while Proto-Attic-Ionic *κορϝᾱ (*[korwa:], 'girl') becomes κούρη ([kú:rẹ:]) in Ionic upon loss of ϝ ([w]), in the sister dialect of Attic it becomes κόρη ([kórẹ:]). As discussed by Allen,[52] this divergence indicates a different syllabification of word-internal [-rw-] clusters in the two dialects. In Ionic it must be the case that the [-rw-] cluster is heterosyllabic (i.e., [-r$w-]). With the loss of the glide [-w-], the syllable-boundary was shifted to a position preceding the liquid; this occurred in accordance with the Greek property of syllabification according to which -CVCV-sequences are syllabified as -CV$CV-. To preserve the heavy quantity of the initial syllable of *κορϝᾱ, this repositioning of the syllable-boundary was accompanied by a lengthening of the short vowel of this syllable, in other words

(29) *[kor$wa:] > *[ko$rẹ:] > [ku:$rẹ:]

In contrast, the failure in Attic of the initial vowel to lengthen in response to loss of [-w-] indicates that the quantity of the initial syllable of κόρη ([kórẹ:]) was light prior to deletion of [-w-] and, accordingly, that the syllable boundary *preceded* the [-rw-] cluster rather than dividing it, in other words

(30) *[ko$rwa:] > [ko$rẹ:]

This in turn suggests that in Attic, [r] was *less* sonorous than [w], since it is generally the case, as we have seen, that within a syllable (here [$rwa:]) consonants preceding the vowel of the syllable are arranged in order of increasing sonority.[53] Hence, the sonority hierarchy utilized by the Attic dialect was not one in which [w] outranks [r], as in (25), but was more like that of (21), in which reverse ranking is found. This reversal in the order of the sound classes *liquid* and *glide,* however, is an Attic development which occurred *subsequent* to the separation of the sister Attic and Ionic dialects from their common parent, as is indicated by the disparate treatment of [-rw-] in these two dialects. That Ionic is the conservative dialect is indicated by the agreement of its sonority hierarchy with that one evidenced by the various dialects preserving word-initial [wr-], among which is the oldest attested dialect of Greek, Mycenaean.

4.1.6 The Resolution of Recurring Problems

The theory of the hierarchy of orthographic strength allows us to account for the representation of consonant clusters in the syllabic scripts without having to propose an ad hoc syllable structure for the Mycenaean and Cypriot dialects, such as is required by theories which are syllable-dependent. After all is said and done, it actually does not matter what the syllable structure of the dialects was; though as I have argued, there is no indication that Mycenaean and Cypriot syllable structure differed appreciably from that of other dialects. Quite to the contrary, there is good reason for thinking there was no such difference. Spelling of consonant clusters simply proceeds linearly by the scribes' applying the hierarchically dependent spelling rule whenever a sequence of consonants is encountered in a phonetic string. Whenever consonants and vowels alternate in a phonetic string they are of course rendered orthographically simply by utilizing the appropriate CV symbols (or V symbols in the case of word-initial vowels and diphthongs). Note, in fact, that the CV symbol as a unit itself adheres to the practice of spelling in accordance with the hierarchy of orthographic strength. Vowels as a class are of greater sonority than consonants, and thus, conversely, in our terms, consonants are of greater orthographic strength than vowels. A CV symbol consequently serves to spell by overt expression a sequence in which the first sound (consonant) is of greater orthographic strength than the second (vowel). Perhaps it is even in this relationship that we are to find the germ of the practice of spelling consonantal sequences in accordance with the hierarchy of orthographic strength.

Utilizing the notion of the hierarchy of orthographic strength (i.e., (22)) and the analogous Mycenaean and Cypriot spelling strategies (i.e., (11) and (14), respectively), the representation of any given type of consonant cluster will be correctly predicted. This includes the notoriously problematic *[s] + stop* clusters which we have seen to fell one interpretation after another. The hierarchy (22) and the Linear B strategy (11) effortlessly generate the observed partial spelling of these clusters both word-initially and word-internally in the Mycenaean script. Likewise, regressive spelling of this cluster-type word-internally in the syllabic Cypriot system is the predictable outcome of the application of the Cypriot strategy (14) in combination with the hierarchy (22); as we have seen, word-initially all clusters are spelled progressively in the Cypriot script.

In the same way, we readily account for the observed representation of word-internal clusters which are not of a type that occurs word-initially. Thus, the hierarchy (22) and the Linear B strategy (11) correctly predict that *nasal + glide* clusters are represented in the Mycenaean script using plenary spelling.

We have seen—and will see again—that word-final *stop + [s]* clusters also present themselves as an ever-present stumbling block to the various attempts to account systematically for Linear B and syllabic Cypriot spelling of consonant clusters. In the next chapter we will look carefully at word-final clusters and find that our theory of a hierarchy of orthographic strength (i.e., (22)), coupled with rule (11) for Linear B and rule (14) for syllabic Cypriot, elegantly predicts in a straightforward and natural manner the attested spellings of such clusters. Presently, however, let us consider the remaining two non-syllable-dependent approaches to analyzing Linear B and syllabic Cypriot strategies for representing consonant clusters.

4.2 Stephens and Justeson

A second interpretation of syllabic Greek spelling which is non-syllable-dependent (as far as it was developed) is that one offered by L. Stephens, in part in collaboration with J. Justeson.[54] In an unpublished lecture presented at Yale University in 1979, Stephens proposed that the Linear B strategy for spelling consonant clusters is one which is sensitive to "resonance" (i.e., what we have called "sonority"), and to this extent Stephens's interpretation is like that one offered immediately above for Mycenaean spelling. The text of this lecture is, however, no longer available.[55] Justeson reports Stephens's proposal in his 1988 review of Sampson's book *Writing Systems*. Justeson formulates the proposal as follows:

(31)   No consonant is spelled before a consonant of lesser resonance [i.e., sonority].[56]

This interpretation of Linear B consonant cluster representation is essentially analogous to my proposal (11), though no indication is given as to the form of the scale of sonority upon which (31) is dependent.[57] Justeson further reports:

(32)   In word-final consonant sequences, the hierarchy is reversed . . . ; so, more generally, a consonant is not represented if it is separated from the nucleus of its scribal syllable[58] by a consonant of lower resonance.

This latter formulation is no doubt offered to account for spellings of forms containing a word-final sequence of the type *stop + fricative,* such as those we encountered in the previous chapter, for example,

(33)   *wa-na-ka,* ϝαναξ ([wanaks], 'king')
       a₃-ti-jo-qo, Αιθιοqʷς ([aitʰiokʷs], a man's name)

According to the principle (32), the word-final [-s] is not written in forms of this type, since standing between the fricative and the vowel of its syllable is a sound of less sonority, that is, [k] or [kʷ]. There are at least two problems with this interpretation of the spelling of word-final clusters. According to (32), the nonrepresentation of the [-s] in the word-final sequences [-ks] and [-kʷs] is unrelated to the general nonrepresentation of word-final consonants in Linear

B. That the two phenomena are coincidental, rather than identical, is hardly plausible. The second problem involves the spelling of word-final clusters of the form [-ns].[59] In the case of such sequences, neither of the consonants is spelled:

(34)   *si-a₂-ro*, σιhαλονς ([sihalons], 'fat hogs', accusative plural)
        -pa, πανς ([pans], 'all', nominative singular)

The word-final fricative is not spelled here, contra (32), even though the consonant which separates it from the preceding vowel (i.e., the nasal [-n-]) is one which is of *greater* rather than less sonority than [s]. Again, the orthographic deletion of the word-final [-s] is undoubtedly a result of the general omission of word-final consonants.

What prediction does the proposal in (32) make concerning the representation of the nasal in the word-final sequence [-ns]? Since the strategy for spelling clusters is said to be reversed in word-final positions, the [n], it would appear, should be written out. That is to say, since in the Linear B script the second member of a biconsonantal cluster which is not word-final is always spelled, with the first member being either written or omitted depending upon its sonority, a reversal of the strategy in word-final position should result in the *first* member of the cluster always being spelled, with the *second* member being either written or omitted depending upon its sonority. Thus, the strategy (32) would suggest that the nasal in a word-final sequence [-ns] should be spelled; in other words, for the forms of (34) we would expect the following spellings:

(35)   **si-a₂-ro-no*, σιhαλονς ([sihalons])
        *-pa-na, πανς ([pans])[60]

This is not the case. The spelling of word-final clusters is problematic for Stephens's analysis (as it is presented by Justeson), just as it was for the various non-syllable-dependent analyses of Linear B spelling examined in chapter 3. As I show in chapter 5, the system of analysis which I have proposed, utilizing the notion of a hierarchy of orthographic strength, will properly account for word-final clusters.

Justeson concludes his remarks on syllabic Greek spelling systems by stating:

(36)   A brief comparison of Linear B spelling with the closely related Cypriot syllabary would be useful; the latter spells in accordance with syllable structure.[61]

As we have seen, the underlying basis for consonant cluster representation in the syllabic Cypriot system is the same as that utilized for Linear B spelling, and neither practice is dependent upon syllable structure. Those interpretations of the Cypriot strategy for spelling consonant clusters which hold that spelling is dependent upon syllable structure advocate essentially the same unacceptable analysis of syllable structure as that one utilized by syllable-dependent interpretations of Linear B spelling.[62]

4.3 Viredaz

The final non-syllable-dependent interpretation of consonant cluster spelling in the Greek syllabaries to be considered is that offered by R. Viredaz in *Minos* 18.[63] Viredaz's analysis utilizes a scalar component and spelling rules which make reference to this scale. Superficially, then, this interpretation may appear to be quite similar to my own. As we shall see, however, there are quite significant differences.

4.3.1 Linear B

Viredaz identifies the two basic Linear B strategies for spelling consonant clusters in this way:

> (37) Une consonne suivie d'une autre consonne est tantôt supprimée graphiquement (*«traitement 1»: wastu wa-tu*), tantôt notée (*«traitement 2»*), que ce soit à l'aide d'une voyelle fictive . . . (*agros a-ko-ro*).[64]

Treatment 1 thus corresponds to what I have termed *partial spelling* and *treatment 2* to *plenary spelling.*[65] Viredaz proposes that whether treatment 1 or treatment 2 is utilized by the Mycenaean scribes for representing any given sequence of consonants is determined by the following *escalier,* a hierarchical arrangement of consonant *graphemes:*

> (38) $k, q, z > p > t, d, s > m > n > w > r > y$

Unlike my own hierarchy of orthographic strength, the units of this hierarchy (38) are orthographic symbols rather than consonantal sounds. As discussed in chapter 2, the Linear B grapheme $<k>$ represents the sounds [k, k^h g]; $<p>$ represents [p, $p^{h,}$ b]; $<t>$ represents [t, t^h]; and so on. The symbol z is used to represent two different sounds—one voiceless, the other voiced. As I discuss later, these probably represent affricates or sounds similar thereto. It is curious that Viredaz should assign z such a specific rank in his hierarchy, in light of the fact that it does not occur in clusters with other consonants. If the symbol z does represent types of affricates (voiceless and voiced), it probably should, in fact, be grouped closely with the stops, though it is a rather moot point here because of its failure to cluster with other consonants.[66]

This *escalier* is utilized together with the following spelling formula:

> (39) Le groupe C_1C_2 a le traitement 2 si C_1 précède C_2 dans l'escalier . . . . , le traitement 1 dans le cas contraire.[67]

In other words, if the first member of a cluster occurs higher on the *escalier* than the second member, both consonants will be written; otherwise the first consonant will be deleted from the orthography.

4.3.1.1 Word-Final Consonants

We have seen that the word-final cluster-type *stop* + *fricative* is quite problematic for the various syllable-dependent interpretations and for the non-syllable-dependent analysis of Stephens and Justeson. This same word-final consonant sequence causes trouble for Viredaz.

With regard to single word-final consonants in Linear B, Viredaz simply states that the only three consonants which can occur at the end of a word in Greek ([-r], [-n], and [-s]) are never written in final position. Regarding the word-final cluster [-ks], he indicates that he believes that the Linear B representation of the sequence *cannot* be predicted by his rule of the *escalier,* since, as he says, on this hierarchy *k > s,* yet *k* does not occur in word-final position:

(40)   [C]omme *k > s* et que *k* n'existe (probablement) pas à la finale, la règle
de l'escalier ne permet pas de prévoir la graphie de *-ks.* [68]

His reasoning here is not altogether clear. Perhaps he thinks that the spelling of a final [-ks] cluster as *-kV* (which his rule does, in fact, predict as he has stated it, though the rule does not specify the vowel component of the *kV* grapheme) would be problematic since there is no word-final [-k] spelled *-kV* to serve as an orthographic model. Strictly speaking, the [-k-] of [-ks#] is not word-final and Linear B does provide examples of penultimate [-k-] occurring in word-final [-kV] sequences, which are, of course, spelled *-kV* (e.g., *re-u-ka,* λευκα ([leuka], 'white (things)')).

In a footnote, however, he suggests that the treatment of word-final consonants, including clusters, may be the consequence of an even higher entity, a final word-boundary, occurring on his *escalier:*

(41)   On pourrait représenter la fin de mot par un signe spécial, qui figurerait en
tête de l'«escalier»; on aurait p.ex. *r < #* (omission graphique de *r* final):
le «groupe» *ks#* serait du type ambigu. [69]

By "type ambigu" he is referring to consonant clusters of the form $C_1 > C_2 < C_3$, where $C_1 < C_3$. [70]. A consideration of such a cluster-type arose in his discussion of clusters of more than two consonants. He points out that while clusters of three or more consonants are treated in the same way as biconsonantal clusters, [71] given his rule of the *escalier,* a problem would exist in the case of a triconsonantal cluster having the structure $C_1 > C_2 < C_3$, in which $C_1 < C_3$: here C_1 should be written before C_2, while C_2 should not be written before C_3; Viredaz states that his rule will not predict if C_1 would then be anomalously spelled before the higher ranking C_3. However, this is only a potential problem, he says, in that such clusters do not actually occur in Linear B; that is, of course, unless the word boundary should be treated as occurring as the topmost member of the *escalier,* in which case the sequence *ks#* would constitute just such a cluster.

Additional comments which Viredaz offers concerning the representation of word-final [-ks] require careful attention. It was pointed out in chapters 2 and 3 that [-ks#] and [-k^{w}s#] are usually spelled *-kV* and *-qV* respectively (i.e., with the [-s] deleted from the orthography), as in the following examples (now often repeated):

(42)   *wa-na-ka,* ϝαναξ ([wanaks], 'king')
       a₃-ti-jo-qo, Αιθιοqʷς ([aitʰiokʷs], a man's name)

However, as already mentioned,[72] spelling omission of the [-k-] of word-final [-ks] is also attested, as in the following example:

(43)   *to-ra-ka* beside *to-ra,* θωραξ ([tʰǫːraːks], 'breastplate')[73]

On the one hand, Viredaz appears to suggest that this variation in the representation of word-final [-ks] is to be linked with that "ambiguity" in the spelling of such clusters which he finds inherent in his rule of the *escalier* which we discussed immediately above.[74] On the other hand, he proposes that there appears to be some phonological conditioning which is responsible for this variation: a word-final *-Ks* (where Viredaz uses *K* as a cover symbol for *stop*) is consistently represented as *-KV* when the vowel which precedes *-KV* is *a* or *o* (as in the examples of (42)), but after the vowels *e, i,* and *u,* the *-KV* syllabogram may be optionally deleted. In support of the latter proposal, he offers the following examples:

(44)   A. *o-nu* beside *o-nu-ka* for *onuks* (a textile term, the meaning of which is
          debated)
       B. *to-ro-wi* possibly beside *to-ro-wi-ka* (a man's name)
       C. *we-pe-za* which Viredaz identifies as *hweks-pedya* (perhaps 'having six
          feet')
       D. *e-te-re-ta* beside *e-ka-te-re-ta* which he identifies as "*ekstrēta* (?)" (a
          term describing chariot frames)[75]

Moreover, further along in his discussion Viredaz states, with appropriate tentativeness:

(45)   En fin de mot . . . , il semble que la voyelle morte soit régulièrement *a,*
       indépendamment de la voyelle précédente.[76]

He indicates that this practice would then parallel the syllabic Cypriot use of the empty vowel *e* for representing word-final consonants.[77] The empty vowel is *o*—rather than *a*—in the case of *a₃-ti-jo-qo* ([aitʰiokʷs]), not because the vowel preceding the word-final cluster is written *o* (i.e., not for orthographic reasons) but because the "regular" word-final empty vowel *a* is rounded to *o* either under the phonetic influence of this preceding [-o-] vowel or, perhaps more likely he says, under the influence of the labiovelar [-kʷ-].[78]

We now need to take a careful look at each of the examples of (44).
   A *o-nu / o-nu-ka.* Of the forms cited by Viredaz, it is this one which carries the greatest weight as evidence for the Linear B use of <-ka> to represent word-final [-ks]. As I indicated at (44), the precise meaning of the term (attested only at Knossos) is uncertain. It is affiliated with textiles and comes in at least two colors, white and variegated. Ventris and Chadwick suggest broadly that it

may "be some part of or appendage to textiles."[79] Melena identifies the meaning quite specifically as 'the woollen yarn of the weft.'[80] More recently, Killen has proposed that the meaning of the term is perhaps 'decoration.'[81] Aside from the nominative singular *o-nu*, there occurs nominative plural *o-nu-ke* (four times; possibly dative singular?), ονυχες ([onük^{h}es]), and the compounds *po-ki-ro-nu-ka*, ποικιλονυχα ([poikilonük^{h}a]), and *re-u-ko-nu-ka*, λευκονυχα ([leukonük^{h}a]; multiple occurrences of each)—both nominative neuter plural. The form *o-nu-ka* occurs three times and is perhaps nominative singular, in which case *o-nu-ka* must represent ονυξ ([onüks]), with *-ka* for [-ks]. The identification of the grammatical case is not beyond doubt, however.

B *to-ro-wi / to-ro-wi-ka.* The shorter form, *to-ro-wi*, is a man's name which occurs twice at Pylos—once in a list which contains names of smiths in the nominative case (and an inventory of bronze in the possession of each smith; Jn 601) and once in a catalogue of flocks (Cn 131). On the latter tablet, other names occur in the dative case preceded by the preposition παρο ([paro]); *to-ro-wi*, however, is preceded by a place name, apparently in the locatival-instrumental case. Ventris and Chadwick interpret *to-ro-wi* in Cn 131 as nominative.[82] *To-ro-wi-ko* also appears in a catalogue of flocks from Pylos (Cn 655). Some of the names on this tablet occur in the nominative case and others in the genitive; Ventris and Chadwick identify *to-ro-wi-ko* as genitive.[83] Of course, the alternation of a nominative *to-ro-wi* and a genitive *to-ro-wi-ko* indicates a nominative terminating in −ιξ ([-iks]). The form *to-ro-wi-ka* is found in an inventory of personnel from Pylos (An 5), concerning which Ventris and Chadwick state, "possibly alternative spelling of *to-ro-wi* (nom. *-ix?*)."[84] Chantraine, however, suggests that *to-ro-wi-ko* could perhaps be nominative, and regarding *to-ro-wi-ka* and the suggestion that it is a variant spelling of *to-ro-wi*, he writes,"Mais je ne connais aucun exemple de cette graphie, et l' hypothèse, proposée sans conviction, est arbitraire. Il reste à poser un masculin en *-ā*, type qui n'est pas rare en mycénien et plus tard."[85]

C *we-pe-za.* This problematic (though seemingly semantically transparent) compound occurs on Pylos tablet Ta 713, a document recording an inventory of three tables, two of which are described as *e-ne-wo-pe-za*, 'nine-footed'. The third table is said to be *we-pe-za*, and this surely is to be understood as 'six-footed', that is, as coming from *hweks-ped-* (from Proto-Indo-European *sweks, 'six'). The absence of [-s-] from the orthography is fully expected, but the nonoccurrence of a grapheme for [-k-] is surprising and has led to a variety of interpretations. Viredaz had noted these variant interpretations in an earlier work and rightly pointed out that there are difficulties with each.[86] For example, Ventris and Chadwick propose as possible readings either *(h)weppeza* or *(h)wespeza;*[87] the latter reading is also offered by Vilborg and Palmer.[88] Both of these suggestions call for the postulation of ad hoc sound-change scenarios not otherwise attested in the historical phonology of Greek, though similar to attested developments. The reading *(h)wespeza* requires the loss of the initial stop of a triconsonantal sequence *stop + fricative + stop* (i.e. *[-ksp-] → [-sp]), while *(h)weppeza* is derived by the loss of *[-s-] between two stops, with ensuing complete assimilation of the first stop to the second (i.e.,

*[-ksp-] → *[-kp-] → [-pp-]). Though Greek [-s-] was historically deleted in those instances in which it occurred between a preceding [-k-] or [-p-] and an ensuing stop, this change was accompanied by aspiration of the stop which had preceded the [-s-], not by its assimilation to the following stop. Beyond this, as I show in chapter 5, the evidence suggests that the simplification of *stop + fricative + stop* clusters was post-Mycenaean.[89] With regard to the assumed change *[-ksp-] → [-sp-], it should be pointed out that, in contrast to what we have just seen, the initial consonant in *[k] + fricative + stop* clusters was indeed lost in certain instances, but that this is a dissimilatory change and is limited to those cases in which the final stop of the cluster is also velar (unlike the case of [-**ksp**-]); again, this is discussed in chapter 5.[90] In compounds in various first millennium dialects the final [-ks] cluster of the numeral ἕξ ([héks], 'six'), with which we are concerned in the form *we-pe-za,* may be preserved or restored analogically before a consonant, as in ἑξκαίδεκα ([hekskaídeka], 'sixteen') beside ἑκκαίδεκα ([hekkaídeka]), ἕξπους ([hékspu:s], 'six-footed') beside ἕκπους ([hékpu:s]). Thus, pressure to maintain the morphological integrity of the numeral has allowed some compounds of ἕξ to escape the regular phonological fate of *[-ks-] + stop* (note also the absence of *stop*-aspiration in the ἑκ- forms).

Viredaz follows Doria in reading *we-pe-za* as *hwekspeza.*[91] The nonrepresentation of [ks] in this instance, proposes Viredaz, is a consequence of this sequence occurring immediately before the boundary which separates the two members of the compound (i.e., *hweks-peza*). He contends that the compound-boundary is behaving like a word-boundary for purposes of orthographic processing, and as evidence of this equivalence, he cites the dual spelling of the sister compound meaning 'nine-footed':[92] on tablet Ta 713, for example, it appears (twice) as *e-ne-wo-pe-za;* on Ta 642, however, the two members of the compound are graphically separated by a word-divider (i.e., *e-ne-wo, pe-za* (also occurring twice)).

D *e-te-re-ta / e-ka-te-re-ta.* These two forms occur on Knossos chariot tablets Se 879 and Se 891 respectively and are identified as adjectives which describe chariot frames.[93] In addition, tablet So 894 preserves a form *a-te-re-te-a,* used to describe wheels. Comparison of the three forms suggests that they perhaps represent compounds with variation in the initial member.[94] Viredaz cautiously suggests that *e-ka-te-re-ta* and *e-te-re-ta* may represent *eks-trēta,* which he glosses as possibly 'troués', citing, after Ventris and Chadwick, ἕκ–τρημα ([éktrẹ:ma]), ἕκτρησις ([éktrẹ:sis], 'trepanning hole').[95] These same forms, *e-ka-te-re-ta* and *e-te-re-ta,* were invoked by Householder[96] when he conjectured that word-final [-ks] and [-qs] are perhaps regularly spelled *-ka* and *-qo* respectively, without regard to what vowel precedes the cluster: "The only thing remotely approaching evidence here is this: *if e-ka-te-re-ta* . . . and *e-te-re-ta* . . . are the same word, and *if* that word is **ektrēta* or the like (or was it still **ekstrēta?*), and *if* one or both words are not simple errors, then *ka may* represent final *k* (or *ks* only?)."[97] Beyond Householder's remarks, we should note that even if *e-ka-te-re-ta* were to be read as a compound *eks-trēta* it is by no means the case that *e-te-re-ta* of necessity spells the identical word: the latter could represent a compound beginning with ἐν ([en]) or εἰσ ([ẹ:s], for example; compare the just mentioned *a-te-re-te-a*.[98]

The acceptability of Viredaz's suggestion (45) depends entirely on the correct identification of the examples of (44), since only here do we find a *-ka* syllabogram used after a vowel other than *a* or *o*. The examples of (44) are thus doubly critical: they provide the evidence both for the proposal that the [-k] of [-ks#] may optionally not be written in certain contexts (after *e, i, u,*) and for the proposal that the word-final sequence [-ks] is (otherwise) regularly spelled *-ka,* regardless of what the preceding vowel is.[99] Now it is important to notice that these two claims taken together mean that the "regular" representation of [-ks#] (i.e., *-ka*) occurs *obligatorily* only in a rather limited context: namely, in the case of a word-final sequence [-aks] (as well as [-oks#] if, within the framework of Viredaz's analysis, the empty *o* vowel in the spelling *o-qo* for [-ok^ws#] should be, in fact, a consequence of the labial element of [-o-] or [-k^w-], not of the preceding *o* vowel grapheme).

The most—or perhaps the only—secure example of the nonspelling of [-k-] in a word-final sequence [-ks] is one which Viredaz does not cite, the identification of the form having been published subsequent to Viredaz's article (Killen 1985): namely, the example of (43), which is repeated here as (46):

(46)   *to-ra-ka* / *to-ra*, θωραξ ([tʰọ:ra:ks], 'breastplate')

This means of course that in *to-ra* the [-k-] of a word-final [-ks] sequence is *not* spelled in the one place (or perhaps one of two places) in which its spelling is *obligatory* by Viredaz's analysis, that is, after the vowel [-a-]. This stands as a most serious counterexample to his hypothesis. Beyond that, as I have suggested, each of Viredaz's examples in (44), with the possible exception of (44A), is to some degree questionable; his interpretation of examples (44B) and (44D), and hence his identification of a [-ks] cluster in those forms, must be considered quite tentative.

Viredaz's claim (i) that the "optional" nonspelling of [-k-] in a word-final cluster [-ks] is phonologically conditioned by the quality of the vowel preceding the cluster is, at the very best, highly dubious, as demonstrated by the counterexample *to-ra*. This is not even to mention the fact that the notion that the orthographic deletion of a word-final CV syllabogram could be motivated by the presence of a particular vowel in the ultimate syllable hardly seems to be a likely one. His suggestion (ii) that the "regular" spelling of a word-final sequence *stop* + *s* is <*stop* + *a*> certainly appears to be an overstatement. Almost all of the secure examples which exhibit such a spelling are ones in which [-a-] just happens to precede the stop [-k-], and the exceptional <*stop* + *o*> spelling occurs when [-o-] just happens to precede the stop—the vowel of the final syllable appears clearly to play a crucial role in determining the vocalic component of the word-final CV symbol. At the same time, the idea that *-ka* can at times be used to represent [-ks#] when a vowel other than [-a-] precedes the [-k-] cannot be dismissed altogether and is further considered in chapter 5.

4.3.2 Cypriot Syllabary

Viredaz next turns his attention to the syllabic Cypriot script. He proposes that the spelling of consonant clusters in this writing system likewise utilizes an *escalier* and proceeds according to the following rule:

> (47)   La voyelle morte est identique à la voyelle qui suit le groupe C_1C_2 si C_1 > C_2, à celle qui le précède si $C_1 < C_2$.[100]

He proposes, however, that the Cypriot *escalier* is not identical to that one utilized for Linear B spelling (i.e., (38), repeated here as (48))

> (48) $k, q, z > p > t, d, s > m > n > w > r > y$

but is instead of the following form (which he describes as provisional in nature):

> (49) $k, p > t > m > n > w > r > s, l$[101]

The omission of q from the Cypriot variant of the *escalier* is simply the consequence of the absence of labiovelar stops from the phonemic inventory of the Cypriot dialect; the omission of d is the consequence of the absence of a graphic distinction occurring between voiced and voiceless dental stops in the sign inventory of the Cypriot writing system (recall that Viredaz's *escalier* is constructed as a hierarchy of graphemes, not a hierarchy of sounds, though these graphemes are associated with some phonetic value(s)). While the palatal glide [y] is noted in the Cypriot script, the sound does not occur in consonant clusters, as discussed in chapter 2; accordingly, y is likewise omitted from (49). Conversely, Viredaz includes l in the Cypriot *escalier* since, also as pointed out above, the Cypriot writing system, unlike that of Linear B, graphically distinguishes the two liquids [l] and [r]. Viredaz does not include z in his Cypriot scale, unlike the case of the Linear B *escalier.*[102]

4.3.2.1 The Position of S

The striking difference between the Linear B and Cypriot hierarchies ((48) and (49) respectively) is the shift of s to the bottom end of the Cypriot *escalier.* Viredaz's motivation for this repositioning is, in part, the Cypriot spelling of *fricative + nasal* and *fricative + liquid* clusters. As discussed earlier, the single Cypriot example of the cluster-type *fricative + nasal* is one in which the cluster is (unexpectedly) represented with regressive spelling.[103]

> (50)   *i-na-la-li-si-me-na,* ιναλαλισμεναν ([inalalismenan], 'having been written upon')

Since there is only a single example of this cluster, as Viredaz appropriately points out,[104] the use of regressive spelling for its representation may be of little significance; that is to say, the form could simply be a chance survival of an erroneous spelling. Or, as I mentioned earlier, the use of regressive spelling may be the consequence of a morpheme-boundary separating the two members of the cluster. What seems to be of greater significance to Viredaz are instances of the regressive spelling of the cluster [-sl-]. In my discussion of this cluster,[105] I pointed out that the sequence [-sl-] is found only in the various personal names beginning with the formant 'Εσλ(ο)- ([esl(o)-]). In some instances the cluster is spelled progressively, as in (51A), while in others the representation is regressive, as in (51B):

(51)   A. *e-so-lo-te-mi-wo-se-*, Εσλοθεμιϝος ([eslot^{h}emiwos])
       B. *e-se-la-ko-ra-se-*, Εσλαγορας ([eslagoras])

I have shown that the balance is tipped slightly in favor of the expected progressive spelling of the cluster: four out of seven instances of [-sl-] in my database are spelled in this way. Viredaz, however, in order to accommodate the regressive spelling of [-sm-] and the dual treatment of [-sl-] clusters, assigns *s,* along with *l,* to the lowest tier of his *escalier.* This is straightforwardly problematic, as Viredaz himself is aware, to the extent that the placement of *s* at a position lower than *r* predicts that [-rs-] clusters should be represented with progressive spelling.[106] The spelling of this cluster-type is, in fact, regressive in the Cypriot script (just as, *mutatis mutandis,* the cluster is written with partial spelling in Linear B). There is still an additional problem: given Viredaz's *escalier* (49), the Cypriot spelling of the cluster [-sl-] is not even accounted for by Viredaz's rule (47), since C$_1$ *(s)* is neither greater than nor less than C$_2$ *(l).* His analysis is beginning to break down at this point.

4.3.2.1.1 [s] in Greek.

According to Viredaz, there is an additional motivation for assigning *s* to the bottom end of the Cypriot hierarchy, and this is its "weak" nature, as compared to the *s* of Mycenaean.[107] Proto-Greek *[s] was changed to [h] in most of the Greek dialects in two contexts: (1) at the beginning of a word when the sound which followed was either a vowel, nasal, liquid, or [w]; if the ensuing sound was [m], [n], or [l], the [h] subsequently disappeared:[108]

(52)   A. **sek^w-* → ἕπομαι ([hépomai], 'I follow'); cf. Latin *sequi*
       B. **srew-* → ῥέω ([r^{h}éǫ:], 'I flow'); cf. Sanskrit *srávati*
       C. **sneig^{wh}-* → νείφει ([né:p^{h}ẹ:], 'it snows'); cf. Lithuanian *sniẽga*

The change of *[s] to [h] also occurred (2) in a variety of word-internal contexts, including that of V____V; the resulting intervocalic instances of [h] were likewise subsequently deleted:[109]

(53)   **ĝenH₁esos* → **genehos* → Homeric γένεος ([géneos], 'of race'); cf. Latin *generis* (with *[s] becoming [r] intervocalically in Latin)

However, certain occurrences of *[s] in these contexts were preserved (or restored). The motivation was frequently to maintain morphological integrity, as in, for example, those cases of an *[s] which served as a morphological marker of the future and aorist tenses:

(54)   A. παιδεύσω ([paideúsǫ:], 'I will teach')
       B. ἐπαίδευσα ([epaídeusa], 'I taught')

Here the retention of the *[s] was supported by future and aorist paradigms in which *[s] was preserved as a consequence of occurring in a context which did not promote its deletion (e.g., after a stop):

(55) A. βλέψομαι ([blépsomai], 'I will see')
B. ἔβλεψα (éblepsa], 'I saw')

In addition, as a result of various sound changes, new occurrences of [s] appeared in contexts in which Proto-Greek *[s] had become [h] (or subsequently ø). Thus, the dialect-specific assibilation of [t] to [s] before the vowel [i] produces new instances of intervocalic [s]:[110]

(56) Proto-Greek *didōti → Attic-Ionic δίδωσι ([dídǫ:si], '(s)he gives'); cf. Doric δίδωτι

The survival of these new instances of [s] in contexts in which earlier *[s] had become [h] (or ø) reveals, of course, that the assibilation of *[t] to [s] in such contexts occurred only after the diachronic rule which converted *[s] to [h] had ceased to operate; otherwise the new occurrences of [s] would have likewise been converted to [h].

In a very few dialects, however, the change of [s] to [h] was more thoroughgoing. This is so to the extent that the instances of inherited intervocalic *[s] which had been preserved in most dialects (as discussed above) as well as the newly created occurrences of intervocalic [s] were also affected by a change [s] → [h] between vowels (with, again, later loss of [h]).[111] Thus, in inscriptions written in the Doric dialects of Laconian and Argolic, forms such as the following are found:

(57) A. Laconian
1. εποιἑhε ([epoię:he], '(s)he made', aorist) for ἐποίησε
2. νικαhας ([nikahas], 'the victor', aorist participle) and later νικαας for νικάσας
3. Οναϊτελης ([ona-itelę:s], personal name) for 'Ονασιτέλης

B. Argolic
1. εποιϝhε ([epoiwę:he], '(s)he made', aorist) for ἐποίησε
2. Φραhιαριδας ([pʰrahiaridas], personal name) for Φρασιαρίδας
3. εμπαϊς ([empa-is], 'a tenure of land') for ἔμπασις[112]

However, in some of the early and many of the later Laconian and Argolic inscriptions, forms also occur which agree with most of the other dialects in presenting intervocalic [s] rather than [h] or ø. This variation perhaps represents only orthographic suppression of the local dialect in favor of "standard" forms.[113]

4.3.2.1.2 [s] in Cypriot Greek. Cypriot, it appears, was, like Laconian and Argolic, a dialect characterized by this thoroughgoing mutation of intervocalic [s] to [h] or ø; however, most of the evidence for this is provided by glosses and not by the syllabic inscriptions. Thus, Hesychius offers glosses such as the following:

(58)   A. ἔναυον· ἔνθες ([énauon] : [éntʰes]) for ἔναυσον, 'apply fire'
     B. ἰμίτραον· ὑπόζωσον ([imítraon] : [hüpózdǫ:son]) for *ἰμίτρασον,
      'girt'

In the syllabic Cypriot inscriptions, however, as I have already mentioned, in-tervocalic [s] is usually written.[114] There are, however, a few exceptions which are probably phonetically revealing, such as the following:

(59)   A. *-o-na-a-ko-ra-se-*, Οναἁγορας ([onahagoras], a man's name, *ICS* 231
     (2) and probably 229c) for 'Ονασαγόρας[115]
     B. *-po-e-ko-me-no-ne*, ποέχομενον ([pohekʰomenon], 'attached to', *ICS*
     217 (19, 21) for ποσεχόμενον
     C. *e-pi-si-ta-i-se*, επισταῖς ([epistahis], 'dominion', *ICS* 264 (3)) for ἐπίσ–
     τασις
     D. *po-ro-ne-o-i*, φρονεωί ([pʰroneǫ:hi], 'they would intend', *ICS* 264 (4)
     for φρονέωσι[116]

There is good indication that the consonantal sound which was written with the <sV> set of graphemes in the syllabic Cypriot script could be pronounced as something other than [s]. Thus, in the bilingual Phoenician and Greek in-scription *ICS* 216, the Greek name 'Αλασιώτας ([alasió:tas]), an epithet of Apollo, is rendered in Phoenician as *'lhyts*. The use of Phoenician *h* to tran-scribe Greek ⟨s⟩ suggests of course that ⟨s⟩ here had a phonetic value of [h], or something akin to it, rather than [s]. A similar correspondence occurs in the Phoenician-Greek bilingual *ICS* 215, in which the Phoenician man's name *mnḥm* is matched in the Greek portion of the inscription by the name *ma-na-se-se*. If the latter is to be interpreted as Μνάσης, as appears likely (cf. the commonly occurring Μνασέας),[117] then Cypriot <s> is used to represent a velar fricative (as in German *auch*).

4.3.3 Aperture and the *Escalier*

According to Viredaz, the heightened tendency of [s] to become [h] in Cypriot indicates that Cypriot [s] had an *aperture* greater than that of [s] in Mycenaean and other dialects, and for this reason *s* occurs at the low end of the Cypriot *escalier*.[118] What this means, of course, is that Viredaz is interpreting his ortho-graphic *escalier* as a hierarchy of aperture, with aperture progressively increas-ing from left to right; by the term *aperture,* he is simply referring to the degree of oral opening (or closure) which is characteristic of the articulation of a given type of consonant sound.[119] Concerning these proposals two important issues need to be addressed, both of which are problematic: (1) the form of the *esca-lier* offered by Viredaz, regardless of the nature of its phonetic basis; and (2) his interpretation of aperture as the critical basis for this hierarchy and, thus, for the spelling of consonant clusters in Greek syllabic scripts.

4.3.3.1 The Problem of the Form of the Escalier: Stops

Viredaz's Linear B and Cypriot hierarchies are repeated here as (60) and (61) respectively:

(60) $k, q, z > p > t, d, s > m > n > w > r > y$

(61) $k, p > t > m > n > w > r > s, l$

Here, the hierarchical ranking of certain of the graphemes is based not only upon the type of spelling used for representing a given consonant cluster but also upon the nonoccurrence in the Mycenaean and Cypriot inscriptions—indeed, upon the nonexistence in these dialects—of certain consonant permutations. For example, in the case of the Mycenaean *escalier* of (60), *k* and *p* are assigned a higher rank than *t* since the sequences *velar stop + dental stop* (such as [-kt-]) and *bilabial stop + dental stop* (such as [-pt-]) are represented in the Linear B script using treatment 2 (i.e., plenary spelling) and, *ipso facto*, occur in this dialect. The reverse sequences, [-tk-], [-tʰkʰ-], [-dg-], [-tp-], [-tʰpʰ-] and [-db-],[120] are not attested in the Mycenaean documents or the Cypriot materials, and this is almost certainly because, as Viredaz points out,[121] these clusters did not exist in these dialects.

Certain sequences of the type *dental stop + velar stop* and *dental stop + bilabial stop* did occur at an early stage of Greek but were eliminated by one means or another. Thus, the clusters *[-tk-] and perhaps *[-tp-] were metathesized to [-kt-] and [-pt-] respectively, as in the following examples:[122]

(62)   A. **ti-tk-ō* → τίκτω ([tíktɔ:], 'I engender, beget', a reduplicated present);
           cf. the aorist ἔ–τεκον ([étekon]) without metathesis
        B. **kʷid-pe* → τίπτε ([típte], 'why therefore?'); cf. Latin *quippe*[123]

A second means of eliminating such clusters involves assimilation. When a morpheme-boundary intervened between the two members of a *dental stop + bilabial stop* cluster, the dental was assimilated to the bilabial.[124] For example, in the Mycenaean dialect, clusters of the type *dental stop + [-pʰ-]* arose when the instrumental suffix –φι ([-pʰi]) was attached to nominal stems ending in a stop; the dental was then assimilated to the following [pʰ]:

(63)   A. *e-ka-ma-pi*, εχμαπφι ([ekʰmappʰi], 'with supports') from **ekʰmat-pʰi*
        B. *ko-ru-pi*, κορυπφι ([korüppʰi], 'with helmets') from **korutʰ-pʰi*
        C. *po-pi*, ποπφι ([poppʰi], 'with feet') from **pod-pʰi*[125]

If, on the other hand, the noun stem ended in a velar stop, it appears that the cluster was preserved:

(64)   *po-ni-ki-pi*, φοινιχφι ([pʰoinikʰpʰi], 'with palm trees')[126]

It is, in fact, the survival and plenary spelling of this *velar stop + bilabial stop* cluster which Viredaz adduces as motivation for placement of *k* at a higher level than *p* in his Mycenaean *escalier*.[127]

These treatments of *dental/velar stop + bilabial stop* clusters across a morpheme-boundary in Mycenaean correspond to a set of treatments involving similar clusters which is exhibited in various first-millennium dialects; these clusters developed as a consequence of the attachment of apocopated prepositional prefixes to words beginning with a stop.[128] Thus, when the prepositions κατ– ([kat-]) and ποτ– ([pot-]), which arise by apocopation from κατά ([katá],

'down etc.') and ποτί ([potí], 'at, by etc.') respectively, precede a form beginning with a stop, the final [-t] of the preposition assimilates to that stop: [129]

(65)   A.   Homeric κάπ–πεσε ([káp-pese], '(s)he dropped') from *κάτ–πεσε
             ([kát-pese])
        B.   Homeric κακ–κείοντες ([kak-ké:ontes], 'lying down') from *κατ–
             κείοντες ([kat-ké:ontes])

Such assimilatory changes do not occur, however, when the prefixed preposition ends with a velar stop (i.e., when the preposition is ἐκ):

(66)   A.   ἐκπέμπω ([ekpémpọ:], 'I send forth')
        B.   ἐκτίθημι ([ektíthẹ:mi], 'I set out') [130]

The consequence of the preceding metatheses and assimilatory changes is
that both in the Greek language of the first millennium and apparently in the
Mycenaean dialect as well, the only *stop* + *stop* clusters allowed were (1)
geminate clusters; (2) *bilabial* + *dental* and *velar* + *dental* clusters; and (3)
velar + *bilabial* clusters, with an intervening morpheme-boundary. As indicated immediately above, these phonotactic restrictions on the possible sequences of stops are encoded in Viredaz's Linear B *escalier* (60). In each case,
the first member of a possible (nongeminate) *stop* + *stop* cluster outranks the
second member on this hierarchy; that is, *p (bilabial)* outranks *t (dental)*, and *k
(velar)* outranks both *p* and *t*. Conversely, *stop* + *stop* clusters in which the
first member would occur lower on the Mycenaean *escalier* [131] than the second
member do not exist. [132]

With respect to stop consonant graphemes, Viredaz's Cypriot *escalier* of (61)
is likewise constructed in such a way as to conform to the possible occurrences
of *stop* + *stop* clusters. In the case of the Cypriot hierarchy, however, Viredaz
has placed *k* and *p* in the same tier, [133] since *velar* + *dental* and *bilabial* +
dental stop clusters are attested in the Cypriot inscriptions, but *velar* + *bilabial*
stop clusters are not. [134]

A hierarchically dependent analysis of language (either spoken or written)
which involves constructing statements that make critical reference to the permutations of the linguistic units of which the hierarchy is composed is suscepti-
ble to overspecification (or overpredictability), in that not all possible permutations of these units may actually occur in the language being analyzed. In
Viredaz's hierarchical analysis of Linear B and syllabic Cypriot spelling, this
problem is exacerbated by his decision to differentiate within the hierarchies
the various stop consonant graphemes of these two scripts. At the same time,
in so doing he has rendered his analysis of the spelling of *stop* + *stop* clusters
essentially tautological. As we have seen, the *stop* portion of his hierarchy en-
codes the results of diachronic alterations of combinations of consonants, to the
extent that consonant clusters whose first member is higher on the hierarchy
than the second member exist in the spoken language, while those clusters
which would consist of the reverse sequence do not exist. With respect to stop
consonants, this reduces his spelling rule (39), repeated here as (67),

(67)   Le groupe C_1C_2 a le traitement 2 si C_1 précède C_2 dans l'escalier . . . ,
        le traitement 1 dans le cas contraire

to a formulation which states that a particular spelling strategy (treatment 2, i.e., plenary spelling) will be utilized for spelling a cluster which exists (i.e., a cluster whose first member outranks the second), but that this strategy will not be used if the cluster does not exist (!). To claim that any sequence of stops which occurs in the language will be spelled in full and that a sequence of stops which does not exist in the language will not be spelled in full is merely a highly cumbersome and unnecessarily complicated way of stating that any given stop will be spelled before any other stop.

Viredaz has thus complicated his analysis by not consolidating the various stop graphemes into a single category. He in fact mentions the possibility that these graphemes could be so grouped together, but he indicates that his spelling formula (67) would then need to be modified by specifying that the sequence C_1C_2 is also spelled utilizing treatment 2 (i.e., plenary spelling) if the two consonants belong to the same class. He rejects this modification, suggesting correctly that it would then be necessary to except the treatment of geminate clusters (which are written with treatment 1, i.e., partial spelling) from the strategy (67). To introduce such an exception would undeniably complicate his analysis, and Viredaz appears to interpret this as an unacceptable complication.[135] It is, quite to the contrary, a "complication" which is actually *necessary* for a proper accounting of Greek syllabic spelling.

As we have discussed above, the representation of geminate clusters in syllabic Cypriot spelling agrees with that utilized by the Linear B scribes: in both scripts, only a single member of the cluster is spelled. While no special stipulation is required in order to provide for the partial spelling of geminate clusters in the Mycenaean script, given Viredaz's Linear B spelling rule (67), his Cypriot spelling formula (47), repeated here as (68), will clearly not account for the partial spelling of geminate clusters:

(68)   La voyelle morte est identique à la voyelle qui suit le groupe C_1C_2 si C_1
        $> C_2$, à celle qui le précède si $C_1 < C_2$

Ultimately this is so because the regular spelling option in Cypriot is not the Linear B option of plenary spelling versus partial spelling but one of progressive spelling versus regressive spelling. To indicate that geminate clusters in the Cypriot script are represented not by using either of these regular strategies but by using an exceptional partial spelling instead, it is necessary to introduce the very statement of exception which Viredaz seeks to avoid in his treatment of Linear B consonant cluster spelling.

That only a single member of a geminate cluster should be spelled in the syllabic Greek scripts is not surprising. As I briefly mentioned in chapter 2, this is a common orthographic phenomenon in both syllabic and alphabetic scripts. For example, only one of the consonants of a geminate cluster is spelled in the syllabic writing system of Old Persian;[136] the same is frequently the case with the Akkadian syllabic script.[137] Similarly, the spelling of only one member of a geminate cluster is characteristic of early Germanic runic inscriptions.[138] Single spelling of geminates is the rule in Latin inscriptions prior to the late third century B.C. and is retained in common use until about 115 B.C.[139] In Umbrian inscriptions, only one member of a geminate cluster is written when the Umbrian alphabet is used, and this is also usually the case when Umbrian is written with the Latin alphabet.[140] Finally, and perhaps of greatest relevance for the present discussion, geminate clusters are regularly written singly in the earliest Attic inscriptions[141] and are commonly so written in the inscriptions of various other Greek dialects.[142]

In summary, we have seen that Viredaz's theory of consonant cluster spelling in the syllabic scripts of Greek is problematic because of the way in which he has chosen to elaborate his theory. His analysis is formally unacceptable in that it is tautological and inefficient as a result of his decision not to combine stop graphemes into a single class. This decision was made in order to avoid adding to his analysis a specific statement concerning the spelling of geminate clusters; the inclusion of such a statement would represent a very natural complication, however, as evidenced by the widespread graphic practice of the single spelling of geminate clusters. Moreover, as a consequence of this omission, his analysis is defective to the extent that it will not account for the partial spelling of geminate clusters in the syllabic Cypriot writing system.

4.3.3.2 The Problem of the Form of the Escalier: [s]

A second problem which involves the form of Viredaz's Linear B *escalier* (60) concerns the placement of the fricative grapheme *s* within the same tier as the stop graphemes *t* and *d*. As other investigators have pointed out,[143] the aperture of [s] is greater than that of [t], [d], and the other stops; hence, by Viredaz's criterion for the arrangement of graphemes on this hierarchy, *s* should occur at a lower position than *t, d,* and so on. Viredaz is aware of the problem,[144] but he is compelled to place *s* at this position because of his quite idiosyncratic interpretation of the Mycenaean reflex of the Proto-Greek sequence *[-t$^{(h)}$ + y-] (where + represents a morpheme-boundary).[145]

Proto-Greek *[-t$^{(h)}$ + y-] developed into [-ss-] (a process of palatalization) in most of the Greek dialects of the first millennium, including Arcadian, the dialect (along with its sister Cypriot) to which Mycenaean is most closely related. Attic (but not its sister dialect of Ionic), the Aeolic dialect of Boeotian, and the Doric dialect of Cretan each show [-tt-] instead.[146] Compare the following examples:

(69)   A. Proto-Greek *melit-ya*
　　　　　　1. Attic μέλιττα ([mélitta], 'bee')
　　　　　　2. a. Ionic μέλισσα ([mélissa])
　　　　　　　　 b. Arcadian Μελισσιων ([melissiǫ:n])

　　　　B. Proto-Greek *-wṇt-ya* → –(ϝ)εττα/–(ϝ)εσσα (a feminine noun formant),
　　　　　　as in
　　　　　　1. Attic οἰνοῦττα ([oinû:tta], a type of cake)

2. a. Ionic χαρίεσσα ([kʰaríessa], 'graceful')
   b. Arcadian Παδοεσσα ([padoessa])

The Homeric reflex of *[-t⁽ʰ⁾ + y-] is [-ss-].

A somewhat different outcome is seen if a morpheme-boundary did not separate the dental stop and the glide. In the Attic, Ionic and Arcadian dialects, the Proto-Greek sequence *[-t⁽ʰ⁾y-] (as opposed to *[-t⁽ʰ⁾ + y-]) developed into the nongeminate [-s-]. In the remaining dialects the reflex is the same as that which developed from *[-t⁽ʰ⁾ + y-]—that is, [-tt-] in Boeotian and Cretan and [-ss-] elsewhere (though in all dialects the reflex is [-s-] after a consonant, long vowel, or diphthong; in addition, word-initial *[t⁽ʰ⁾y-] becomes [s-] in all dialects), as is illustrated by the following examples:

(70) A. Proto-Greek *totyo-
   1. a. Attic-Ionic τόσος ([tósos], 'so many', etc.)
      b. Cf. Arcadian ὅσος ([hosos], 'as many', etc.)
   2. Cf. Thessalian ὅσσα ([hossa])
   3. Cf. Cretan οττος ([ottos])

   B. Proto-Greek *metʰyo-
   1. Attic-Ionic and Arcadian μέσος ([mésos], 'middle')
   2. Lesbian μέσσος ([méssos])
   3. Boeotian and Cretan μεττος ([mettos])

It should be pointed out that the reflexes of inherited *[-t⁽ʰ⁾s-], as well as *[-ts-] from still earlier *[-ds-] (by regressive voicing assimilation), are the same as those of *[-t⁽ʰ⁾y-] and follow the same dialectal distribution:

(71) A. Attic ποσί ([posí], 'with feet') from *pod-si
   B. Lesbian ἐδίκασσαν ([edíkassan], 'they judged'), aorist
      indicative of δικάζω ([dikázdọ:]), a derived verb in –αζω, from *-ad-
      yō, aorist *-at-s- (from *-ad-s-)
   C. Boeotian απολογιττασστη ([apologittastẹ:], 'to give an account'), aorist
      infinitive of απολογιζομαι ([apologizdomai]), a derived verb in –ιζω,
      from *-id-yō, aorist *-it-s- (from *-id-s-)

For the reflex of *[-t⁽ʰ⁾y-], as well as that of *[-t⁽ʰ⁾s-], Homer shows both [-ss-] (i.e., τόσσος, μέσσος, ποσσίν) and [-s-] (i.e., τόσος, μέσος, ποσίν), which suggests that the Ionic reflex [-s-], as well as that of Attic and Arcadian, developed from an earlier, intermediate *[-ss-].

The Mycenaean reflex of both Proto-Greek *[-t⁽ʰ⁾ + y-] and *[-t⁽ʰ⁾y-] is represented in the Linear B script simply as *s*. In the case of *[-t⁽ʰ⁾ + y-] the spelling *s* is usually interpreted as representing a geminate cluster (i.e., [-ss-]):

(72) *i-to-we-sa,* ἱστοϝεσσα ([histowessa], 'provided with a mast')
   pe-de-we-sa, πεδϝεσσα ([pedwessa], 'provided with feet')

Lejeune, for example, states concerning this Linear B *s,* "prononciation géminée certaine, mais non démontrable."[147] The interpretation of *s* as [-ss-], rather than [-s-], is bolstered by the Arcadian [-ss-] reflex of Proto-Greek *[-t⁽ʰ⁾ + y-], since, as pointed out above, Arcadian is the dialect most closely related to

Mycenaean Greek.[148] The interpretation of the Linear B spelling *s* for the Mycenaean reflex of Proto-Greek *[-t$^{(h)}$y-] (without the critical intervening morpheme-boundary), as in the following examples, is somewhat less certain:

(73)   *to-so*, τοσ(σ)ος ([tos(s)os], 'so many' etc.) from **to-tyo-*
        me-sa-ta, μεσ(σ)αται ([mes(s)atai], 'of medium size' or 'of medium quality' etc.) from **met^{h}yo-*

Regarding this reflex, Lejeune writes, "prononciation géminée probable, mais non démontrable."[149] It is conceivable that *[-ss-] had already undergone degemination to *[-s-] in the Mycenaean dialect as in Arcadian. The Mycenaean reflex of inherited *[-t$^{(h)}$s-] is also spelled as *s* in the Linear B script:

(74)   *-da-sa-to*, δασ(σ)ατο ([das(s)ato], '(s)he distributed') from **dat-sato*

Again, it is difficult to determine if this represents *[-ss-] or simply *[-s-] (Lejeune's comment is the same as that offered concerning the reflex of *[-t$^{(h)}$y-]: "prononciation géminée probable, mais non démontrable").

Regarding *[-t$^{(h)}$y-], Viredaz agrees that its Mycenaean reflex was either *[-ss-] or *[-s-];[150] however, he believes the reflex of Proto-Greek *[-t$^{(h)}$ + y-] to have been the cluster *[-ts-], rather than *[-ss-], during the Mycenaean era. As a consequence, since the Linear B spelling of this reflex is *s,* he is forced to adopt the untenable position that [t], unlike the other stops, is not written before the fricative [s]. He indicates that his identification of *[-ts-] as the Mycenaean reflex is motivated by the disparate development of *[-t$^{(h)}$ + y-] in the sister dialects of Attic and Ionic: as indicated above, in Attic the development is to *[-tt-], while in Ionic *[-ss-] is the outcome. This variation suggests to Viredaz that the Proto-Attic-Ionic reflex of *[-t$^{(h)}$ + y-] was *[-ts-], and further that, since Achaean (as he identifies the dialectal subgroup to which Mycenaean belonged) was closely related to Attic-Ionic, the Mycenaean reflex must have likewise been *[-ts-].[151]

Viredaz's argument that a Mycenaean reflex *[-ts-]—spelled *s*—is demanded as a consequence of the disparate treatment of *[-t$^{(h)}$ + y-] in Attic and Ionic is not compelling and is a non sequitur. Although Mycenaean shares important features with Attic-Ionic (as well as with Aeolic), it is not likely either that Proto-Attic-Ionic is to be equated with Mycenaean Greek, or that Proto-Attic-Ionic is the immediate descendant of Mycenaean Greek.[152] In fact, Cowgill has argued that, since Mycenaean displays linguistic features not found in any of the first-millennium dialects, it is probable that not even Arcado-Cypriot is to be seen as the direct descendant of Mycenaean Greek[153]. Even if it were the case, then, that Proto-Greek *[-t$^{(h)}$ + y-] had given rise to a Proto-Attic-Ionic *[-ts-], this would not mandate that Mycenaean have the same reflex.[154]

It is completely plausible then, as is usually held, that the Mycenaean reflex of Proto-Greek *[-t$^{(h)}$ + y-] was already *[-ss-] (as in Arcadian). This is indeed clearly indicated by a comparison of the spelling of this Mycenaean reflex with that of the reflex of Proto-Greek *[-k$^{(h)}$y-]. In the various first-millennium dialects the reflex of *[-k$^{(h)}$y-][155] is identical to that of *[-t$^{(h)}$ + y-] (not *[-t$^{(h)}$y-]);

that is, the outcome is [-tt-] in Attic, Boeotian, and Cretan but [-ss-] elsewhere, including Homer:[156]

(75) A. Proto-Greek *p^hulak-$y\bar{o}$
  1. Ionic φυλάσσω ([p^{h}ülásso̧:], 'I guard')
  2. Attic φυλάττω ([p^{h}ülátto̧:])
  3. Boeotian διαφυλαττι ([diap^{h}ülatti], '(s)he watches carefully')

It is generally proposed that the development of *[-k$^{(h)}$y-] to [-ss-] or [-tt-] was one in which affricate and/or nondental fricative stages were intermediate. For example, Rix conjectures that the pathway was that illustrated in (76A) and Ruijgh that of (76B):

(76) A. $ky > k^yy > k^sy > t^sy > t^sy > s^ty > ss^t > ss$ or tt[157]
  B. $ky > ty > t\check{s} > ts > ss$ or tt[158]

It is quite probable that the Linear B spelling of the Mycenaean reflex of *[-k$^{(h)}$y-], which is conventionally transcribed as zV, as in (77) represents just such an intermediate stage:

(77) *ka-zo-e* ('worse') from *kak-yos-es*

Lejeune has argued for some type of a "strong sibilant,"[159] while Chadwick[160] and Heubeck[161] propose an affricate value for this z symbol. Compare Rix's *ss^t* in (76A).[162]

The zV set of signs is, in addition, used for spelling the Mycenaean reflex of *[-gy-],[163] *[-dy-], and instances of *[#y-],[164] each of which has come to have the value [zd] (from an earlier *[dz]), that is, the sound represented by ζ in the first millennium; consider the following examples:

(78) A. *me-zo-e* ('larger') from *meg-yos-es;* cf. Ionic μέζων ([mézdo̧:n])
  B. *to-pe-za* ('table'), from *-ped-ya;* cf. Attic τράπεζα ([trápezda])
  C. *ze-so-me-no* ('to be boiled') from *yes-;* cf. Attic ζέω ([zdéo̧:]), Sanskrit *yásati* 'to boil'

The use of z to spell both sets of reflexes (those of *[-k$^{(h)}$y-], on the one hand, and those of *[-gy-], *[-dy-] and *[#y-], on the other) is simply another example of the Linear B practice of not distinguishing voiceless consonants from their voiced counterparts.

Thus, while the Proto-Greek sequences *[-t$^{(h)}$ + y-] and *[-k$^{(h)}$y-] share the same set of first-millennium reflexes (i.e., [-ss-] and [-tt-]) Linear B orthography indicates that their Mycenaean reflexes are not identical: that of *[-t$^{(h)}$ + y-] is spelled s and that of *[-k$^{(h)}$y-] is written z. In other words, it appears that the evolution of *[-t$^{(h)}$ + y-] and that of *[-k$^{(h)}$y-] must have been at different stages in the Mycenaean period, with that of *[-t$^{(h)}$ + y-] being more advanced. The evidence suggests that the value of this z is, in broad phonetic terms, a voiceless counterpart to the *[dz] reflex (from earlier *[-gy-] and so on) which is metathesized to [zd] and will be spelled as ζ in the alphabet of the first millennium (about which I later say much more). Given this interpretation of z and the fact that, as indicated above, a stop is normally quite regularly spelled in Linear B orthography when it precedes a fricative, the most natural and plausible interpretation of Linear B <-s-> for *[-t$^{(h)}$ + y-] is that it simply represents [-ss-]—not [-ts-], as proposed by Viredaz. There is thus no orthographic or linguistic motivation for including *s* in the same tier of the *escalier* as *t* and *d,* and relative degree of aperture provides considerable phonetic motivation not to do so.

4.3.3.3 *The Problem of Audibility: [s]*

These various difficulties concerning the form of Viredaz's *escalier* are alone sufficient to cause us to question the viability of his analysis; however, far greater problems underlie his entire approach. Viredaz believes it to be unlikely that the Mycenaean scribes were in possession of a theory of consonantal aperture and, consequently, unlikely that they actually utilized a hierarchy of aperture in working out the spelling of consonant clusters.[165] At best, he says, such a hierarchy could have only been formalized as some sort of systematic ordering of syllabogram series, and he regards as improbable even this level of sophistication in the Mycenaean period. Instead, he suggests that the Linear B strategy for representing sequences of consonants was an "implicit" orthographic principle which the novice scribes acquired by learning conventional spellings (thereby internalizing spelling practice) and then, on the basis of such learned spellings, analogically resolving the spelling of consonant clusters in new (or forgotten) forms as they were encountered.

At the same time, Viredaz contends that what was critical for the scribal determination of the type of spelling strategy to be used for representing any given cluster (i.e., regressive or progressive) was most immediately not aperture at all but what he terms *audibility,* by which term he refers to how clearly or distinctly a sound is able to be perceived by the ear,[166] although he indicates that audibility is closely correlated with aperture.[167] This means, of course, that the *escalier*—his hierarchy of aperture—is in effect merely an analytical artifact. By Viredaz's reckoning, then, it is actually the case that, in the instance of Linear B spelling,[168] any given consonant is spelled before any other consonant only if it is (in some sense) aurally perceived more clearly or distinctly, or perhaps one could say more saliently, than the ensuing consonant.[169] For example, in the Mycenaean sequence [-ps-] the stop [-p-] is written. By this analysis, since [-p-] is written the stop must be more audible, more clearly detected by the ear, than the fricative [-s-]. Conversely, in the *fricative + stop* sequence [-sp-] the [-s-] is not spelled, so, by Viredaz's analysis, it is of less "audibility" than the ensuing stop.

Viredaz's notion of "audibility" is in need of careful consideration. It is most unfortunate that this concept is only identified rather imprecisely: "une consonne est notée ou non devant une autre selon qu'elle *s'en détache plus ou moins nettement pour l'oreille.*"[170] Thus, it falls to Viredaz's readers to try to equate this concept with some phonetic property. A reasonable and straightforward interpretation would seem to be that "audibility" corresponds most closely to (or, at the very least, one of its principal components is[171]) that auditory property which is identified by phoneticians as *loudness*.[172] As I discussed in beginning this chapter, loudness is directly correlated with sonority; thus, Ladefoged defines the sonority of a sound as "its loudness relative to that of other sounds with the same length, stress, and pitch."[173] Sonority is that property to which, I have claimed, the strategies devised for representing consonant clusters in the syllabic Greek scripts are ultimately sensitive. It might appear, then, that Viredaz's proposal that audibility is the crucial factor in determining the strategy used for the spelling of consonant clusters in these scripts is completely in keeping with what I have advocated thus far concerning the interaction of such spelling practices and sonority. This is not the case at all.

Let us consider a cluster C_1C_2 in which C_1 is of greater loudness (i.e., of greater sonority) than C_2, as, for example, in the following Mycenaean Greek form:

(79)   αρτεμιτος ([artemitos], 'of Artemis')

Recall that by Viredaz's analysis, C_1 is spelled in a cluster of the form C_1C_2 in which C_1 is of greater "audibility" than C_2; that is, he proposes, it is the greater audibility (or loudness, utilizing our suggested equivalent phonetic property) of C_1 which caused the scribe to note it in the orthography. As the reader is probably already aware, this is the very reverse of actual practice. The Linear B spelling of (79) is not *a-re-te-mi-to*, as Viredaz's interpretation would predict, but *a-te-mi-to*. In other words, directly contrary to Viredaz's claim, it is not when C_1 is of greater audibility (= loudness, i.e., sonority) than C_2 that it is *written*. Instead, this is the very instance in which C_1 is *not written*.

The same reverse, incorrect prediction is made by Viredaz's interpretation in those instances in which C_1 is of less audibility than C_2. He claims that in such cases C_1 is not noted by the scribe. The Linear B representation of, for example,

(80)   αγρος ([agros], 'territory')

in which the first member of the cluster (the stop [-g-]) is of less sonority, and therefore less loud, than the second member (the liquid [-r-]), is not, however, *a-ro*, but *a-ko-ro*, with the first member of the cluster written.

4.4 Concluding Remarks

The theory of the hierarchy of orthographic strength which I have elaborated in this chapter correctly predicts the attested spelling of consonant clusters in the two syllabic scripts in which ancient Greek was written. Tronsky's theory of the Linear B spelling of consonant clusters also correctly predicts the spelling of clusters word-initially but falters word-internally by falling back upon a syllable-dependent analytic framework. The non-syllable-dependent interpretation of Stephens and Justeson can account for the attested spelling of word-initial and word-medial clusters in Linear B but incorrectly predicts that of word-final clusters. Moreover, Justeson advocates that the representation of consonant clusters within the syllabic Cypriot system is syllable-dependent, but as we have seen, such an analysis is as inadequate for syllabic Cypriot as for Linear B. In gross terms, Viredaz's interpretation of consonant cluster spelling in the syllabic scripts is similar to my own theory of the hierarchy of orthographic strength: both consist of a scalar component and a spelling rule which makes critical reference to the former component. In specific terms, however, the two are markedly different. Largely, though not entirely, as a result of the way in which the scalar component is structured (and this structure varies between Linear B and syllabic Cypriot, which is an unnecessary and undesirable complication in itself), Viredaz's theory is found to be wanting, in a significant manner.

In the next chapter we will consider further implications of my theory of the hierarchy of orthographic strength and will find that it not only accounts for additional orthographic phenomena of Linear B and the syllabic Cypriot script but also provides us with insights which go beyond the syllabic writing systems.

Notes

1. I. Tronsky, 1962, "Slogovaja struktura drevnegrečeskogo jazyka i grečeskoe slogovoe pis'mo," in *Drevniĭ mir: Sbornik stateĭ* (Moskow: Izdatel'stvo vostočnoĭ literatury), pp. 620–626. This work is cited by Beekes (1971:342). I wish to acknowledge my debt to the late Professor James W. Poultney, who provided me with an English translation of the entire article, and to express my deepest appreciation to Valentina Apresjan, Andrei Lebedev, and Georg Krotkoff for assisting me with particularly thorny sections of the work, and also to the latter for introducing me to the work of L. V. Shcherba.

2. P. Ladefoged, 1993, *A Course in Phonetics,* 3rd ed. (Fort Worth: Harcourt Brace Jovanovich), p. 245. Not infrequently, sonority is also correlated with the aperture of the articulatory organs during production of a sound, or is described as "vowel-likeness."

3. Tronsky 1962:624. Rather than a translation, this is a paraphrase, though a careful one. Much more literally, what Tronsky says is, corresponding to (4), "the strong-initial part of a syllable . . . is omitted in writing" and, corresponding to (5), "the combination of a series of strong-ending [consonants] arranged in order of nondecreasing sonority with a syllabic vowel is rendered by a series of syllabic signs each of which denotes a combination of a corresponding strong-ending [consonant] with a syllabic vowel." Much of Tronsky's discussion of sonority and syllable structure is presented utilizing the terms *strong-ending consonants* and *strong-initial consonants.* Perhaps somewhat counterintuitively, at least at first glance, strong-ending consonants are consonants which precede the vowel of their syllable, and strong-initial consonants are those which follow the vowel of their syllable. This terminology, as Tronsky indicates, is borrowed from the work of the Russian phonetician L. V. Shcherba. The precise sense of these terms may not be immediately obvious; they refer to the change in sonority which Shcherba perceives as occurring across a consonant or consonant cluster during its articulation. Within a syllable, sonority generally rises throughout the articulation of prevocalic consonants; hence, each prevocalic consonant is "strong-ending" (i.e., sonority at the completion of the articulation of the consonant(s) of the syllable onset is

greater, or stronger, than that at the beginning). Conversely, postvocalic consonants experience falling sonority through the course of their articulation and are thus termed "strong-initial."

4. Tronsky 1962:625.

5. Ibid., p. 623.

6. J. Kuryłowicz, 1948, "Contribution à la théorie de la syllabe," *Bulletin de la société polonaise de linguistique* Fascicle VIII:80–114.

7. Tronsky 1962:625.

8. R. Woodard, 1994, "On the Interaction of Greek Orthography and Phonology: Consonant Clusters in the Syllabic Scripts," in *Writing Systems and Cognition,* ed. W. Watt (Dordrecht: Kluwer Academic), pp. 311–334. Portions of the ensuing discussion are to be found in Woodard 1994, though the discussions have undergone some modification. These ideas (at a less developed stage) were first presented publicly in a lecture that I delivered at Duke University in March 1984 ("The Representation of Consonant Clusters in the Writing System of Mycenaean Greek") during the Thirtieth Meeting of the Southeastern Conference on Linguistics.

9. J.-P. Olivier et al., 1973, *Index généraux du linéaire B* (Rome: Edizioni dell' Ateneo).

10. T. Mitford, 1980, *The Nymphaeum of Kafizin* (Berlin: De Gruyter); 1971, *The Inscriptions of Kourion* (Philadelphia: American Philosophical Society); C. Traunecker, F. Le Saout, and O. Masson, 1981, *La chapelle d'Achôris à Karnak II* (Paris: Editions ADPF), pp. 262–284.

11. In the case of the Cypriot data, however, forms were counted which contain illegible signs or are incomplete as long as the symbols representing a consonant cluster and the vowels which precede and follow the cluster are legible and the editors express no uncertainty regarding the identification of the form. This additional liberty was taken with the Cypriot data for a combination of reasons: correct identification of Cypriot forms is perhaps facilitated somewhat by the fuller representation of words in the syllabic Cypriot system; syllabic Cypriot inscriptions are not uncommonly accompanied by a corresponding alphabetic inscription which serves to confirm the identification of syllabically spelled forms; for pragmatic reasons, as the Cypriot materials simply afford a smaller body of data than the Linear B documents.

12. In Greek the Proto-Indo-European *fricative* + *liquid* clusters were eliminated with accompanying compensatory lengthening of a preceding vowel (or underwent gemination in the case of Aeolic), except in those instances in which the members of the cluster were separated by a morpheme-boundary.

13. In Proto-Indo-European, the palatal glide [y] occurred only before vowels and the labiovelar glide [w] only before vowels, liquids, and [y] (see Lejeune 1982:161–162, 171–173, 181–182). Among the Greek dialects, it is only in Mycenaean that Indo-European [y] is preserved, and here only in particular contexts (see ibid., pp. 162, 165, 167–169, 171). On the other hand, instances of the inherited labiovelar glide [w] are attested in Mycenaean, Cypriot, and certain other first-millennium dialects (see Buck 1955:46–52; Lejeune 1982:162–163, 174–183).

14. See the discussion and references in G. Dunkel, 1981, "Mycenaean *KE-KE-ME-NA, KI-TI-ME-NA,*" *Minos* 17:18–29.

15. For the sources and the method of data evaluation which were utilized, see the above discussion in section 4.1.1.

16. As I indicated above, the utilization of the progressive spelling strategy for writing all word-initial clusters is not a necessary consequence of the Cypriot scribes' propensity for representing consonant clusters in full. The first member of those word-

initial clusters which are written with regressive spelling when they occur word-internally could have, for example, been spelled with the aid of some arbitrary graphic vowel, such as the *e* vowel used for representing word-final consonants.

17. As indicated in chapter 2, however, word-final [-n] and [-s] are frequently not represented. On the nonrepresentation of these final consonants, see n. 41 in chapter 5 below. Also, compare the preceding note on the use of the arbitrary graphic vowel *e*, which is used for spelling word-final consonants.

18. See Allen 1973:208.

19. Since preconsonantal [n] is not written in the syllabic Cypriot script (see below for a clarification of this generalization), a word-final sequence [-ns] would not be fully represented even if it were preserved in the Cypriot dialect, as is sometimes held. On the status of Cypriot [-ns#] and possible evidence for the phonetic loss of [n] before [s] in the Cypriot dialect, see the discussion in O. Masson, 1980, "Une nouvelle inscription de Paphos concernant le roi Nikoklès," *Minos* 19:71–72.

20. There also occurs a CCV symbol with the value [ksa]; in one unusual instance *ksa* is used for representing the word-final sequence [-ks].

21. See also T. Mitford, 1950, "Kafizin and the Cypriot Syllabary," *CQ* 44:103.

22. [α]σμενα is followed by the apparently erroneously spelled imperative *e-su-to*, εσυτω ([esütọ:], 'let her be') for εστω ([estọ:]). For possible dialectal peculiarities in this inscription, see Mitford's discussion (1980:105).

23. Perhaps from a verb *δεκατίζω ([dekatízdọ:]). Note the occurrence of the noun δεκατισταί, the title of a type of cult official (see G. Mendel, 1900, "Inscriptions de Bithynie," *BCH* 24:367–368).

24. See C. Buck and W. Petersen, 1945, *A Reverse Index of Greek Nouns and Adjectives* (Chicago: University of Chicago Press), pp. 184–212.

25. See Palmer 1963:425; *DMic.*:320.

26. Buck 1933:320. See also Buck and Petersen 1945:221.

27. Chantraine (1968, *Dictionnaire étymologique de la langue grecque: Histoire des mots* (Paris: Klincksieck), p. 539) leaves open the possibility that the [-s] occurring at the end of the κλασ- ([klas-]) radical could perhaps be of secondary origin, having been generalized from s-aorist forms. Could *ka-ra-ma-to* represent κλαματων ([klamatọ:n]), without an [-sm-] cluster? A form κλαμα ([klama], 'fragment') survives in a fifth-century B.C. inscription from Aegina (IG 4. 1588. 1, 342).

28. See Chantraine 1984:125.

29. J. Chadwick, 1967, "Mycenaean *pa-wo-ke*," *Minos* 8:115–117.

30. And it is marked as questioned in *Docs.*:569.

31. As reported in table 1, the database includes four occurrences of the exceptional plenary spelling of a *liquid + glide* cluster, found in the perfect active participle *a-ra-ru-wo-a*, αραρϝοα ([ararwoa], 'fitted'). The two members of the cluster showing the unexpected spelling are again separated by a morpheme-boundary, with the second member occurring as the initial consonant of a suffix marking the perfect participle—this time active rather than passive. Similarly, unexpected plenary spelling of a *liquid + nasal* cluster occurs in the case of *a-ra-ro-mo-te-me-na*, αραρμοτμενα ([ararmotmena], 'fitted out', twelve instances occurring in the database). Notice, however, that in these cases the nature of the exceptional spelling is the very opposite of that shown by the *fricative + nasal* clusters; that is, plenary spelling is exhibited where partial spelling is expected. As a number of scholars have suggested (see references cited in Viredaz 1983:147, n. 93), this full spelling of a cluster [-rm-] may well have been motivated by the regular complete representation of the initial reduplicated syllable (i.e., *a-ra-ru-wo-a*, *a-ra-ro-mo-te-me-na*).

32. Buck 1955:210.

33. J. Chadwick, 1990, "Linear B and Related Scripts," in *Reading the Past,* with an Introduction by J. Hooker (Berkeley: University of California Press), p. 186.

34. Thumb-Scherer 1959:153.

35. O. Masson 1983:74.

36. Occurrences of nasal-final proclitics which are followed by consonant-initial tonic forms are not included here.

37. As discussed above, inherited *nasal* + *liquid* clusters were fragmented by the insertion of an epenthetic stop—a process which began in the pre-Mycenaean era. Note that there are ten occurrences of the sequence *nasal* + *glide* occurring in the Linear B materials (see table 1) and that these are represented using plenary spelling. If Mycenaean *pa-wo-ke* were to be read as πανϝοργες ([pan-worges], 'maids of all work'), as Chadwick has tentatively suggested (see *Docs.*:390, 569; 1967:115–117), then this would represent an exceptional partial spelling of a *nasal* + *glide* cluster and offer a superficial parallel to the nonrepresentation of certain preconsonantal nasals in the syllabic Cypriot script. Chadwick suggests that if the form has been correctly identified, the failure to write the nasal may be due to the morpheme-boundary which separates the two members of the cluster (see 4.1.4.1.1). The identification of the form is uncertain.

38. As indicated above, these very fragmentary materials were not included in my database.

39. Recall that in form, Linear B plenary spelling is identical to syllabic Cypriot progressive spelling.

40. J. Justeson and L. Stephens, 1981, "Nasal + Obstruent Clusters in Hittite," *JAOS* 101:367–370.

41. R. Morris, 1919, *Runic and Mediterranean Epigraphy* (Gylling: Odense University Press), pp. 125–127.

42. See Masson 1983:342–343, 420. Note that Masson originally rejected the reading.

43. As *inter alia* in inscriptions *NK* 21 and 58. Note the use of the Koine dialect form in the alphabetic inscriptions (on which see Mitford 1980:264 and 1950:101).

44. For a discussion of the notion of the hierarchy of consonantal strength, see J. Hooper, 1976, *An Introduction to Natural Generative Phonology* (New York: Academic Press), pp. 195–207.

45. J. Hankamer and J. Aissen, 1974, "The Sonority Hierarchy," in *Papers from the Parasession on Natural Phonology* (Chicago: Chicago Linguistic Society), p. 132.

46. Ibid., p. 138.

47. Compare the recent statement of G. Clements (1992, "The Sonority Cycle and Syllable Organization," in *Phonologica 1988*, ed. W. Dressler et al. (Cambridge: Cambridge University Press), p. 65) concerning the "standard" form of the sonority hierarchy (i.e., as in (21)): "I assume that this scale is the sole version of the sonority scale provided by the theory of universal grammar; languages that depart from this scale (e.g. by inverting the rank of certain segments [as in the case of the Pali and Hungarian hierarchies proposed by Hankamer and Aissen], or by making finer distinctions) are viewed as more complex to just that extent."

48. See Buck 1955:51; Lejeune 1982:157.

49. On the interpretation of this form, see *Docs.*:491.

50. Attic and Ionic offer λῆνος [lḗ:nos], 'wool') from *ϝλᾱ–, cf. Old Church Slavic *vlŭna*, Lithuanian *vìlna*, Sanskrit *ū́rṇa-*. Doric λῆν ([lḗ:n], 'to wish') is perhaps from *ϝλέ–; cf. Latin *velle* ('to want'). On these forms, see, *inter alios*, Chantraine 1968:637, 653; and Lejeune 1982:158.

51. The occurrence in Greek of the word-initial clusters [#wr-] and [#wl-] allows equally for the possibility that the sonority hierarchy of Greek was actually of the form *stop > fricative > nasal > [w] > liquid > [y]*, in which the labiovelar glide [w] is less sonorous than the liquids, while the palatal glide [y] is more sonorous than the liquids (cf. Hankamer and Aissen's Pali hierarchy, in which, inversely, the two liquids are separated by the glides: *stop > s > nasal > l > w > y > r*). For that matter, there are several different potential hierarchies, given all of the possible permutations of the sounds [w, y, r, l] along with the sole requirement that [w] must outrank both [r] and [l]. Any such hierarchy would make certain predictions about the possible combinations of glides and liquids in word-initial position (though would not require that such combinations actually occur). For example, the hierarchy *stop > fricative > nasal > [w] > liquid > [y]* would provide for the possibility of word-initial clusters of the type [#wy-]. There is, however, no evidence for the occurrence of any word-initial clusters involving both glides and liquids, aside from [#wr-] and [#wl-], in the Greek language. Consequently, I will propose a sonority hierarchy for Greek, and hence a hierarchy of orthographic strength, which is formulated only in terms of major sound classes and will not attempt to make finer differentiations.

52. Allen 1973:214.

53. The tautosyllabicity of [-rw-] is one expression of the phenomenon of "Attic shortening," mentioned earlier. Note a certain propensity for open syllables in Attic (i.e., *[ko$rwa:], departing from the typical -CV$CV- syllabification).

54. This analysis was apparently limited to Linear B practice. Justeson mentions Cypriot spelling (see below) but surprisingly (and mistakenly) states that consonant cluster representation is, in contrast to Mycenaean practice, dependent upon syllable structure in this script.

55. Personal communication from Stephens.

56. J. Justeson, 1988, review of *Writing Systems,* by G. Sampson, in *Language* 64:423.

57. Justeson and Stephens also relate the omission of consonants in Linear B spelling to a scale of sonority in an unpublished monograph entitled "Syllable and Script: A Typological Study" (I am most appreciative to Laurence Stephens for supplying me with a copy of this work). In their typological discussion of orthographic strategies of consonant deletion, they write (following statements on the orthographic deletion of word-final consonants): "Consonant deletion is also generally disfavored, though not as severely, in representing consonant clusters. This deletion is predictably conditioned by the position of the cluster within the word and syllable, correlatively by its tauto- vs. heterosyllabic status, by the number of segments in the cluster, and by the sonorance and stricture of those segments. . . . Syllable-final consonants in heterosyllabic clusters are deleted in geminate clusters at least to the extent that they are deleted in nasal + consonant clusters, which themselves are deleted at least to the extent they are in liquid + obstruent clusters, which in turn are deleted at least to the extent they are in obstruent + obstruent clusters. . . . This omission hierarchy can be elaborated further in relation to a hierarchy of phonological stricture. Linear B, for instance, omits n, m, l, r, and s regularly before stops, although stops are always spelled before other stops. Furthermore, in tautosyllabic clusters the omission also seems to be governed by the stricture hierarchy; thus s is omitted in tautosyllabic clusters before stops as in #st, while the k of #kt is always spelled. However, there is also in Linear B a tendency to spell liquids before stops and nasals and s before nasals in heterosyllabic clusters" (pp. 32–34). As revealed by the survey of Linear B consonant clusters presented above, the tendency to which reference is made in the last sentence does not actually exist.

58. On the notion of "scribal syllable," see Justeson 1988:423.

59. For a discussion of this word-final sequence see above.

60. To represent the nasal, the symbol with a vocalic component which is identical to the vowel which precedes the final cluster has here been utilized in accordance with the practice for spelling word-final *stop + fricative* clusters.

61. Ibid.

62. And Justeson himself rejects Sampson's syllable-based interpretation of Linear B spelling, stating, "S. provides an interesting, informative discussion of the conventions that determine which consonants are represented, but he does so in terms of an untenable view of Greek syllable structure (e.g., clusters like /kn/ that can occur word-initially are taken as tautosyllabic when medial)" (p. 423).

63. Viredaz 1983:125–207.

64. Ibid., p. 126.

65. Viredaz in fact also speaks of a *notation partielle* and *notation complète* (p. 126), though *traitement 1* and *traitement 2* are his preferred terms.

66. On the idea that affricates are of greater consonantal strength than stops, see Hooper 1976:214.

67. Viredaz 1983:141. He further states, "On peut dire aussi, en termes imagés, que quand la seconde consonne est plus «forte» que la première, elle l'«occulte»."

68. Ibid., p. 158.

69. Ibid., p. 158, n. 168.

70. Ibid., pp. 157–158.

71. I discuss at length in chapter 5 the processing of clusters of more than two consonants in Linear B and the syllabic Cypriot script.

72. See above, n. c to table 4.1.

73. On which, see Killen 1985:31.

74. Viredaz 1983:158.

75. Ibid., p. 159.

76. Ibid., p. 168. One would presume that this proposal does not abrogate that one which he offers concerning the optional spelling of [-ks#] after *e, i, u.*

77. This would not quite represent a parallel usage, however. In the syllabic Cypriot script, in addition to word-final clusters, single consonants occurring finally can be spelled using the *e* empty vowel. Moreover, unlike the case of Linear B, both members of a word-final cluster can be represented in the Cypriot script.

78. This is of course the account of the distribution of *-a* and *-o* in the spelling of word-final *stop + fricative* clusters which was offered by Householder and which we deemed to be less than convincing.

79. *Docs.:*564.

80. J. Melena, 1975, *Studies on Some Mycenaean Inscriptions from Knossos Dealing with Textiles,* supplement to *Minos,* no. 5, p. 113.

81. J. Killen, 1979, "The Knossos Ld(1) Tablets," in *Colloquium Mycenaeum: Actes du sixième Colloque International sur les textes mycéniens et égéens,* ed. E. Risch and H. Mühlestein (Geneva: Université de Neuchâtel), pp. 157–158. Szemerényi (1977, Review of *Dictionnaire étymologique de la langue grecque: Histoire des mots,* vol. 3, by P. Chantraine, *Gnomon* 49:6) conjectures the form to be a borrowing of Hittite *unuwaṣḥa-,* 'ornament, decoration.'

82. *Docs.:*587.

83. Ibid.

84. Ibid.

85. P. Chantraine, 1966, "Finales mycéniennes en *-iko,*" in *Proceedings of the*

Cambridge Colloquium on Mycenaean Studies, ed. L. Palmer and J. Chadwick (Cambridge: Cambridge University Press), p. 174.

86. R. Viredaz, 1982, "*s entre occlusives en mycénien," *SMEA* 23:310–313.

87. *Docs.:*342, 501, 591. Viredaz (1982:310) ascribes only the former of the two to Ventris and Chadwick.

88. Vilborg 1960:102; L. Palmer, 1980, *The Greek Language* (Atlantic Highlands, N.J.: Humanities Press), p. 49. Viredaz (1982:310) cites the reading presented in Palmer 1963 (p. 51), *(h)wekpeza.*

89. As I pointed out in chapter 3, n. 8, Linear B spelling does indicate that certain inherited sequences of the type *stop + [pʰ]* underwent regressive assimilation to yield [-ppʰ-]; the nonassimilation of stops which were juxtaposed after the deletion of an intervening [-s-] would reveal that such an assimilatory process was no longer productive at this later date.

90. When the initial member of a *stop + fricative + stop* cluster was [t], this dental stop was lost, on which see the discussion in the next chapter.

91. M. Doria, 1968, "Strumentali, ablatavi e dativi plurali in miceneo alcune precisazioni," in *Atti e memorie del I° Congresso Internazionale di Micenologie* 2 (Rome: Edizioni dell'Ateneo), p. 777. For additional references, see Viredaz 1982:312, n. 81.

92. Ibid., p. 312–313. Viredaz (p. 312, n. 81) notes that he disagrees with Doria concerning the failure to spell this [-ks-] sequence; for Doria the spelling is a function of the cluster's occurrence in syllable-final position.

93. *Docs.:*369, 542, 546.

94. Ibid., p. 542.

95. Viredaz 1982:313; *Docs.:*369.

96. See the discussion of Householder's ideas in chapter 3, section 3.0.

97. Householder 1964:75.

98. Viredaz (1982:313–314) acknowledges this possibility, on which see also *Docs.:*369.

99. Viredaz's proposal is of course broader than this in that he indicates that any word-final sequence *stop + s* (by which he must mean either [-ps], [-ks], or [-kʷs]) is spelled using the stop consonant syllabogram which has the vocalic component *a* (see p. 159).

100. Ibid., p. 189.

101. Ibid., p. 194.

102. Viredaz indicates (p. 183) that the Cypriot syllabogram *zo* was probably inspired by the Greek alphabetic symbol *zeta* ([zd]). I argue below that this is not the case.

103. This is the term which I have utilized to identify this spelling practice. It is unfortunate that Viredaz uses the term *infection progressive* for the phenomenon which I have called *regressive spelling,* and, conversely, identifies *progressive spelling* as *infection régressive* (ibid., p. 166). As his source for this terminology, he cites C. Gallavotti, 1964, "Le grafie del wau nella scrittura micenea," in *Mycenaean Studies,* ed. E. Bennett (Madison: University of Wisconsin Press), pp. 57–58.

104. Viredaz 1983:194.

105. See table 2, n. i.

106. Viredaz 1983:194: "[O]n ne voit pas bien comment ranger *s* par rapport à *l* et *r* (*l* et *r* devraient avoir le même rang; dans -*rs*- l'infection est progressive [i.e., the spelling is regressive in our terms], dans -*sl*- on a les deux traitements."

107. Ibid.

108. In the case of word-initial *[sw-], *[s] becomes [h], and [w] is subsequently

lost (earlier in some dialects than in others), for example, *sweks → Attic-Ionic ἕξ ([héks]), Delphian Ϝεξ (for [wʰeks], 'six').

109. The evidence for an intermediate stage in which *[h] occurs (as in *genehos), for most of the dialects, is indirect. In some cases the presence of intervocalic *[h] resulted in the aspiration of the vowel preceding the *[h], if this vowel occurred word-initially, as in *eusō → *euhō → εὕω ([heúǫ:], 'I singe'); compare Latin ūrō (see Lejeune 1982:95). However, as we will see below, the intervocalic change of *[s] to [h] was more thoroughgoing in a few dialects, and in these, instances of intervocalic [h] are attested. For a full discussion of word-internal *[s], see, *inter alios,* Lejeune 1982:94–98, 117–138. On the treatment of *[s] between stops, see the discussion in chapter 5 below.

110. It is in the West Greek dialects as well as in the Aeolic dialects of Boeotian and Thessalian (or, if one prefers, in the North Greek dialects, less Lesbian) and in Pamphylian that [t] is generally preserved before [i]. However, even in the assibilating dialects, some sequences of *[-ti-] are maintained, as in ἔτι ([éti], 'yet'), ἀντί ([antí], 'opposite, etc.'). Conversely, other instances of inherited *[-ti-] undergo assibilation in all of the dialects, for example, verbal abstracts formed with the Indo-European suffix *-ti-, such as βάσις ([básis], 'a stepping'). See Buck 1955:57–58; 1933:122–123; Buck and Petersen 1945:574.

111. It is not possible to determine, of course, if the same process by which Proto-Greek *[s] became [h] intervocalically was still operative in these dialects during the period in which *[t] was changed to [s] before [i] or if this rule of [s] → [h] arose subsequently.

112. A. Thumb, 1932, *Handbuch der griechischen Dialekte,* part 1, 2nd ed., ed. E. Kieckers (Heidelberg: Carl Winter), pp. 84–85; Buck 1955:55–56.

113. So Buck (ibid.) interprets this alternation. The occurrence of [h] and ø for intervocalic [s] is also found in certain Elean inscriptions. For a full discussion of these matters, see Buck.

114. For examples, see, *inter alios,* O. Hoffmann, 1891, *Die griechischen Dialekte,* vol. 1, *Der südachäische Dialekt* (Göttingen: Vandenhoeck und Ruprecht), pp. 202–203.

115. *ICS* 231 is the same inscription in which the irregular form *-nu-mu-pa-se-* occurs.

116. Also, the personal name *o-na-i-ti-mo* may represent Οναίτιμος ([onahitimos], *ICS* 195(5)) for Ὀνασίτιμος.

117. For a discussion of these two bilingual texts, see Masson 1983:224–228.

118. Viredaz 1983:194.

119. "On constate en outre que cet ordre de l'escalier correspond à peu près à la notion saussurienne *d'aperture:* une consonne est plus «forte» qu'une autre si elle a moins d'aperture" (ibid., p. 141). Saussure states (F. de Saussure, 1986, *Course in General Linguistics,* trans. R. Harris (La Salle, Ill.: Open Court), p. 44 [70]): "Wherever the point of articulation of a sound may be, it always has a certain *aperture,* which will fall somewhere between the two extremes of complete closure and maximal opening." For Saussure's discussion of consonantal as well as vocalic aperture, see ibid., pp. 44 [70]–49 [76].

120. On the agreement in voicing and aspiration of the two members of *stop* + *stop* clusters, see, *inter alios,* Lejeune 1982:68–69.

121. Viredaz 1983:142.

122. For a discussion of these and related changes see Lejeune 1982:68–72.

123. The change of *[-tp-] to [-pt-] is less than certain, however, as τίπτε ([típte]) could also be analyzed as having arisen from τί ποτε ([tí pote]) by syncopation.

124. A morpheme-boundary also occurs between the [d] and [p] of *k^wid-pe* in (62B). If this should, in fact, be the source of τίπτε ([típte]), then the treatment of *dental stop + bilabial stop* clusters with an intervening morpheme-boundary would show some variation, which is, no doubt, dependent upon some finer conditioning factor(s).

125. The usual mode of writing geminate aspirated stop clusters in alphabetic Greek orthography was πφ, τθ, and κχ. On the phonetic interpretation of such sequences, see Lejeune 1982:71.

126. On the interpretation of the velar as aspirated (i.e., [k^h]) see Ruijgh 1967:43.

127. Viredaz 1983:142. Here he makes the curious and incompatible statement that if the reverse sequence of *labial + velar* existed, one would expect it also to be written with treatment 2 (i.e., plenary spelling).

128. On the dialectal distribution of these apocopated prepositional forms, see the discussion in Buck 1955 (pp. 81–82).

129. If the ensuing form begins with a voiced stop, the final [-t] of the prefix likewise becomes voiced by assimilation. The regressive assimilation of (65) also occurs when the word to which the prefix is attached begins with a nasal, a liquid, or [w-]. In addition, this same set of changes also occurs when the preposition is used not as a prefix but as a proclitic; in other words, this set of assimilatory changes also occurs across a word- (or at least clitic-) boundary. See Buck 1955:83; Lejeune 1982:311–312.

130. In the case of the apocopated prepositions ἀπ– (from ἀπό ([apó], 'from')), ἐπ– (from ἐπί ([epí], 'upon')), and ὑπ– (from ὑπό ([hüpó], 'under')), the final bilabial assimilates in voicing when the preposition is prefixed to a word which begins with [b-], to judge from Homeric ὑβ–βάλλω ([hüb-bállọ:], 'to throw under'). Each of these three apocopated prepositions occurs in the Aeolic dialect of Thessalian. When they precede a word which begins with a dental, regressive assimilation of the final bilabial occurs, as in ατ τας ([at tas], 'from the'), from *απ τας ([ap tas]); ετ τοι ([et toi], 'upon the'), from *επ τοι ([ep toi]); see Buck 1955:81, 83; Lejeune 1982:311–312. Both the Thessalian and Cretan dialects exhibit assimilation of a stop to an immediately following dental stop; on the Thessalian assimilation of [-pt-] to [-tt-] and [-$p^h t^h$-] to [-tt^h-], see Thumb-Scherer 1959:61, 64, and on the similar Cretan change of [-pt-] and [-kt-] to [-tt-], see Thumb-Kieckers 1932:160–161.

131. Concerning the order of stop consonants in the Mycenaean *escalier*, Viredaz remarks (1983:142), "A l'intérieur des occlusives, l'ordre de l'escalier est assez arbitraire." A few lines further down, however, after referring to the nonexistence of certain consonant groups, he states, rather incongruously, "Nous posons donc *k (q) > p > t* pour des raisons purement pratiques."

132. Viredaz apparently includes *q* (i.e., the set of labiovelar graphemes) in the same tier as *k* only upon the basis of phonetic similarity, since, unlike the case of the velars, a labiovelar is attested before a dental stop (*ke-ni-qe-te-we*, χερνιq^{w}τηϝες ([k^hernik^{w}tẹ:wes], 'basin for hand-washing')) but not before a bilabial. It appears to be for similar reasons that he also assigns *z* to this group—a sound which he interprets as a palatal stop in origin (see pp. 144–145; on *z* also see below, n. 162). Concerning the latter grapheme he states (p. 142), "[L]es phonèmes ou groupes notés *z* ne sont pas attestés devant consonne, ni après occlusive, de sorte que nous aurions pu aussi placer *z* avec *p* ou *t*."

133. Labiovelar consonants did not occur in the Cypriot dialect, as mentioned already, hence (61) contains no *q*. For Viredaz's view concerning the Cypriot symbol *zo*, see pp. 183–184. This symbol will be discussed below in chapter 6.

134. With regard to the nonoccurrence of *velar + bilabial* stop clusters, it should

be pointed out that, as will be discussed in the next chapter, in the Cypriot dialect, the preposition cited above as ἐκ ([ek]) takes the form ἐξ ([eks]) when the ensuing form begins with a consonant; hence, the prefixing of this preposition does not give rise to a stop sequence of the type *velar* + *bilabial.*

135. He states (1983:143), "[I]l faudrait alors spécifer que lorsque C_1 et C_2 appartiennent à la même classe, C_1 est noté, sauf si $C_1 = C_2$ (géminées). . . . En l'absence de groupes -*pk*- il était possible, et plus commode, de procéder comme nous l'avons fait."

136. R. Kent, 1953, *Old Persian* (New Haven: American Oriental Society), p. 18.

137. K. Riemschneider, 1969, *Lehrbuch des Akkadischen* (Leipzig: Verlag Enzyklopädie), p. 24.

138. Morris 1919:127–128.

139. E. H. Warmington, 1940, *Remains of Old Latin*, vol. 4: *Archaic Inscriptions* (Cambridge: Harvard University Press), p. xxiii.

140. C. Buck, 1904, *A Grammar of Oscan and Umbrian* (Boston: Ginn and Company), p. 27.

141. Threatte 1980:511–527 (especially pp. 511, 513–514).

142. Buck 1955:76–77.

143. Morpurgo Davies 1987:94, n. 12; and especially Y. Duhoux, 1985, "Mycénien et écriture grecque," in *Linear B: A 1984 Survey*, ed. A. Morpurgo Davies and Y. Duhoux (Louvain-la-Neuve: Cabay), p. 70, n. 103.

144. Viredaz 1983:144. Notice that Viredaz's decision to include *s* in the same tier as *t* and *d* prevents him from grouping all of the stops into a single category. Clusters of [ps] and [ks] occur and are written with progressive spelling; consequently, *s*, and thus *t* and *d*, must be placed lower on the *escalier* than *p* and *k* in order for his spelling rule to predict correctly the spelling of such clusters.

145. Specifically, the sequence arises by the addition of the following suffixes to a form ending in [-t] or [-tʰ]: (1) the present tense suffix -*ye/yo*-; (2) the noun deriving suffix -*ye/yo*-; or (3) the comparative suffix -*yo(s)*-. Perhaps, as H. Rix (1976, *Historische Grammatik des Griechischen* (Darmstadt: Wissenschaftliche Buchgesellschaft), p. 91) suggests, what is critical here is that there be an "erkennbarer Morphemgrenze zwischen /t, tʰ/ und /y/." For discussion of the sequence *[-t$^{(h)}$ + y-], see especially Lejeune 1982:103.

146. The same distribution of dialectal reflexes is found for Proto-Greek *[-tw-] (though without any known Mycenaean occurrences), as well as for *[-k$^{(h)}$y-]; on the latter see below.

147. Lejeune 1982:108.

148. Note also Lejeune's comments at ibid., p. 109.

149. Ibid., p. 108.

150. Viredaz 1983:144.

151. Ibid.

152. Though Risch (1956a, "La position du dialecte mycénien," in *Études mycéniennes*, ed. M. Lejeune (Paris: Centre National de la Recherche Scientifique), p. 170; 1956b, "Caractères et position du dialecte mycénien," in *Études mycéniennes*, pp. 253, 258) proposed that Proto-Attic-Ionic and Proto-Arcado-Cypriot were in the second millennium so closely related as to form essentially a single dialectal subgroup. For a criticism of this idea, see W. Cowgill, 1966, "Ancient Greek Dialectology in the Light of Mycenaean," in *Ancient Indo-European Dialects*, ed. H. Birnbaum and J. Puhvel (Berkeley: University of California Press), pp. 82–83, 89.

153. For example, Mycenaean exhibits: (1) in certain contexts, the reflex [-o-] for

an Indo-European syllabic nasal; and (2) the dissimilation to a labial of the first of two labiovelars occurring within a single word; see Cowgill 1966:93. There is good evidence for the preservation of two distinct Mycenaean dialects within the Linear B tablets, on which see E. Risch, 1966, "Les différences dialectales dans le mycénien," in *Proceedings of the Cambridge Colloquium on Mycenaean Studies,* ed. L. Palmer and J. Chadwick (Cambridge: Cambridge University Press), pp. 150–157; G. Nagy, 1968, "On Dialectal Anomalies in Pylian Texts," in *Atti e memorie del 1° Congresso Internazionale di Micenologie 2* (Rome: Edizioni dell'Ateneo), pp. 663–679; R. Woodard, 1986, "Dialectal Differences at Knossos," *Kadmos* 25:49–74. Cowgill (1966:93) argues for three or possibly four dialects in the second-millennium Mycenaean area. On the advanced development of $*[\text{-t}^{(h)} + \text{y-}]$ to [-ss-] in Mycenaean and the existence of an Ionic dialect in the Mycenaean era, also note the comments in J. Chadwick, 1969, "Greek and Pre-Greek," *TPS,* pp. 92–93.

154. It is possible that the Proto-Attic-Ionic reflex was already *[-ss-] and that this inherited reflex was replaced in Attic by [-tt-], which is almost certainly an areal feature. That Boeotian possessed a reflex [-tt-] and Attic a reflex [-ss-] at the time of the Boeotian influence upon Attic is judged by Allen (1957, "Some Problems of Palatalization in Greek," *Lingua* 7:126) to appear "phonetically less probable" than that both dialects shared an affricate reflex at this period. That the eventual common development to [-tt-] is the result of Boeotian influence rather than Attic is suggested by the Boeotian propensity for stop reflexes: thus, as indicated above, Boeotian displays a [-tt-] reflex for $*[\text{-t}^{(h)}\text{y-}]$, where Attic and Ionic have [-s-]; the same dialectal distribution is attested for the reflexes of the Proto-Greek cluster *[-ts-] (see (70) and (71) above). Compare also Boeotian [-dd-], and [d-] word-initially, corresponding to Attic-Ionic ζ ([zd]); see Buck 1955:70–72.

155. Including those instances which arise from $*[\text{-k}^{w}\text{y-}]$ and $*[\text{-k}^{wh}\text{y-}]$.

156. Word-initially, $*[\text{k}^{(h)}\text{y-}]$ becomes [s-] in those dialects which have [-ss-] as the intervocalic reflex, and develops into [t-] in those which have intervocalic [-tt-].

157. Rix 1976:92, where *ś* apparently represents [š].

158. Ruijgh 1967:49.

159. Lejeune, 1971, *Mémoires de philologie mycénienne,* vol. 2. (Rome: Edizioni dell'Ateneo), pp. 97–139). Note that in Lejeune 1982 (p. 109), he states, in remarking on the difference between the Mycenaean reflex of $*[\text{-t}^{(h)} + \text{y-}]$ and that of $*[\text{-k}^{(h)}\text{y-}]$, "A date mycénienne, *-t(h)y-* a sans doute déjà abouti à une sifflante géminée (notation *s*), *-k(h)y-* en est sans doute encore au stade d'une affriqué (notation *z*)."

160. Chadwick, 1964, Review of *The Interpretation of Mycenaean Greek Texts,* by L. Palmer, in *Gnomon* 36:321. See also *Docs.*:398–399.

161. Heubeck, 1971, "Zur s- und z- Reihe in Linear B," *Kadmos* 10:122.

162. It had been claimed that the Mycenaean reflex of $*[\text{-k}^{(h)}\text{y-}]$ was at times written *s* on the basis of the forms *wa-na-se-wi-ja,* ϝανασσηϝιᾱ ([wanassę:wia:], meaning uncertain) etc., which was taken to be from **wanakyā* (thus Ruijgh 1967:49); however, as Lejeune (see 1982:103, n. 2, 108, n. 4) and others have argued, the form should likely be traced to **wanaktyā.* On the identification of *pa-sa-ro* as ψαλω ([psalǫ:], 'two chains', rather than the Mycenaean equivalent of Attic πάτταλος ([páttalos], 'peg'), Ionic πάσσαλος ([pássalos]), see, *inter alios,* Palmer 1963:358. On the possible alternation of *z* and *k* in Linear B spelling, see *Docs.*:399, with which contrast Lejeune 1982:117, n. 1; Ruijgh 1967:210, n. 558.

163. Including those which develop from $*[\text{-g}^{w}\text{y-}]$.

164. Proto-Greek word-initial *[y-] becomes in some instances [zd-] (ζ) and in some instances [h-]; the critical factors which condition the two different courses of

development have yet to be established conclusively (see, *inter alios,* E. Hamp, 1982, "On Greek ζ: *y-," *JIES* 10:190–191; M. Huld, 1980, "The Oldest Greek Sound-Change," *AJP* 101:324–330; J. van Windekens, 1979, "Once Again on Greek Initial ζ," *JIES* 7:129–132; J.-C. Billigmeier, 1978, "The Origin of the Dual Reflex of Initial Consonantal Indo-European *y in Greek," *JIES* 4:221–231; W. Wyatt, 1976, "Early Greek /y/ and Grassmann's Law," *Glotta* 54:1–11 (and earlier, 1968, "Early Greek /y/," *Glotta* 46:229–237). Mycenaean shows both reflexes: for example, whatever its precise phonetic value, the second-millennium counterpart to first-millennium [zd-] occurs in *ze-so-me-no* (see (78C)), and [h-] in *o-, ὡς* ([hǫ:s], 'thus'), beside *yo-, yως* ([yǫ:s]). This variation suggests that the change of *[#y-] → [#h-] was ongoing during the period in which the Linear B script was in use.

165. Viredaz 1983:141, 200–201. In fact, he contends that the scribes of the Linear B materials had no precise notion "consonant" and speculates that perhaps a CV sequence may have represented a minimal unit for these scribes (p. 200). Contrary to this view, however, it may be the case that spelling variations of the sort $-C_1V-C_2V- \sim -C_1C_2V-$, as in *pe-te-re-wa* ~ *pte-re-wa* (πτελεϝας, ([ptelewa:s], 'of elm wood')) suggest that the scribes were indeed able to conceptually isolate a single consonant.

166. "[N]ous pensons plutôt qu'une consonne était notée ou non devant une autre selon qu'elle s'en détachait plus ou moins nettement pour l'oreille" (Ibid., pp. 141, 202).

167. "Pour les consonnes, l'«audibilité» ou l'«explosivité» de l'une d'elles devant une autre est surtout une question de différence d'aperture, d'où la «règle de l'escalier»" (Ibid., p. 202).

168. Most of Viredaz's interpretative comments at this point are addressed toward the Mycenaean system. Regarding Cypriot, he states, "La raison pour laquelle la «règle de l'escalier», c'est-à-dire en gros l'aperture, joue son rôle dans le choix de la voyelle morte en cypriote est assez obscure" (ibid., p. 203), after which he offers a couple of conjectural ideas.

169. "Si on compare les groupes où $C_1 > C_2$ et ceux où $C_1 < C_2$, on a nettement l'impression que dans les premiers C_1 est «explosif», tandis que dans les seconds il ne l'est pas. . . . [P]ar explosif nous entendons simplement: dont l'explosion se détache, est audible" (ibid., p. 202). On explosivity, see also n. 167.

170. Ibid.; emphasis is mine.

171. Human speech sounds are of course acoustically quite complex and so to equate "audibility" (whatever it may be) solely with the phonetic concept of *loudness* may admittedly be something of an oversimplification; loudness, however, would surely be a (or the) primary aspect of a sound's "audibility" relative to that of another sound.

172. For a discussion of loudness (quantified as sound intensity), see, *inter alios,* Ladefoged 1993:187; 1962, *Elements of Acoustic Phonetics* (Chicago: University of Chicago Press), pp. 13–16; J. Laver, 1994, *Principles of Phonetics* (Cambridge: Cambridge University Press), pp. 500–508; D. Fry, 1979, *The Physics of Speech* (Cambridge: Cambridge University Press), pp. 89–90. Ladefoged writes (1993:187): "In general, the *loudness* of a sound depends on the size of the variations in air pressure that occur. . . . [A]coustic intensity is the appropriate measure corresponding to loudness. The *intensity* is proportional to the average size, or amplitude, of the variations in air pressure."

173. Ladefoged 1993:245.

5

The Hierarchy of Orthographic Strength

In this chapter we will further develop the interpretation of Linear B and syllabic Cypriot consonant cluster spelling as a function of the hierarchy of orthographic strength. We will first consider the representation of clusters which consist of more than two consonants and then turn our attention to what we will see to be a parallel phenomenon, the spelling of word-final clusters.

5.0 Clusters of More Than Two Consonants

5.0.1 Cluster-Types

The discussion of my notion of the hierarchy of orthographic strength and its use in spelling consonant sequences which was offered in chapter 4 dealt only with clusters composed of two consonants; however, the data reported in the tables in chapter 4 actually include biconsonantal clusters which are a component of sequences of three or more consonants. Thus, the Linear B database contains thirty-seven examples of clusters of more than two consonants. Each of the following cluster-types is found and is attested by the designated number of occurrences:

(1) A. *stop + stop + liquid*   14
     B. *stop + fricative + nasal*   1
     C. *fricative + stop + liquid*   3
     D. *nasal + stop + fricative*   2
     E. *nasal + stop + liquid*   7
     F. *liquid + stop + nasal*   7
     G. *nasal + fricative + stop + liquid*   3

The following types of clusters of more than two members occur in the syllabic Cypriot materials:

(2) A. *fricative + stop + liquid*   9 (all word-initial)
     B. *liquid + stop + fricative*   1
     C. *liquid + stop + nasal*   3
     D. *nasal + stop + liquid*   29

5.0.2 The Regular Mode of Spelling

Clusters of more than two consonants are spelled utilizing those very same strategies which I presented in chapter 4 for representing biconsonantal clusters. That is to say, sequences of three or more consonants are treated as overlapping substrings of two contiguous consonants, and spelling proceeds regularly according to the strategy ch. 4, (11) for Linear B, repeated here as (3), and ch. 4, (14) for the Cypriot Syllabary, repeated here as (4):

(3) Within a word, any two successive consonants will be represented with plenary spelling if, and only if, the orthographic strength of the first is greater than or equal to that of the second; otherwise, partial spelling will be used.

(4) If the first of two successive consonants occupies a position on the hierarchy which is higher than or equal to that of the second, then it will be written with the CV symbol whose vocalic component is identical to the vowel which follows the cluster; otherwise it will be written with the CV symbol whose vocalic component is identical to the vowel which precedes the cluster.

For reference purposes, the hierarchy of orthographic strength (ch. 4, (22)), to which the strategies (3) and (4) refer, is here repeated as (5):

(5) *stop > fricative > nasal > glide > liquid*

For example, Mycenaean αρθμος ([art^{h}mos], 'fellowship'), with the three-member cluster [rt^{h}m], is spelled *a-to-mo:* the liquid [r] (ρ) falls lower on the orthographic hierarchy (5) than the dental stop [t^h] (θ) which it immediately precedes; hence, the liquid *is not* written. This stop, however, occupies a higher position on the hierarchy than the bilabial nasal [m] (μ) which it in turn precedes; accordingly, the stop *is* written. The Cypriot form τερχνιγα ([terk^{h}niya], 'trees') likewise contains a cluster of the type *liquid + stop + nasal,* and, again, spelling follows the strategy used for biconsonantal clusters, producing *te-re-ki-ni-ya.* The liquid [r] (ρ) occurs lower on the hierarchy than the stop [k] (κ) and is, accordingly, spelled with the symbol whose vocalic component is identical to the vowel preceding the cluster; in turn, [k] outranks the nasal [n] (ν) on the hierarchy and so is spelled with the symbol whose vocalic component is identical to that vowel which follows the cluster.

5.0.3 A Potential Problem

One could imagine the possibility that clusters of more than two members may exist which would give rise to problematic spellings, given the strategies (3) and (4). Let us consider, for example, a purely hypothetical cluster *fricative + nasal + stop* and attempt to spell such a cluster using the Linear B strategy (3). The fricative should be written before the immediately following nasal (i.e., plenary spelling should be utilized), since *fricative* outranks *nasal* on the orthographic strength hierarchy (5); but this nasal should be deleted before the following stop (i.e., partial spelling should be utilized) since *nasal* occurs at a lower position on the hierarchy than *stop*. Deletion of the nasal would result in an orthographic sequence of the type <*fricative + stop*>. If the application of the strategy (3) were in some sense iterative, one would then expect the fricative to be deleted, since *fricative* is of less orthographic strength than *stop* on the hierarchy (5). If such application were noniterative, however, the aberrant plenary spelling of a *fricative + stop* sequence would result.

Such problematic spelling interactions do not generally occur, however. All clusters of three or more consonants which are attested in the Mycenaean and Cypriot Greek data are found either (A) word-initially or (B) word-internally at syllable junctures. With regard to the former position, the only *word-initial* consonant clusters of more than two members which are allowed in Greek are clusters of the type

(6) *fricative + stop + {liquid, nasal}* [1]

as, for example, in the following:

(7) στρατηγός ([stratẹ:gós], 'general')
στλήν ([splẹ:n], 'spleen')
σκνίψ ([skníps], an insect)

The spelling of such clusters word-initially is not problematic for either Linear B or the syllabic Cypriot script. In the case of Linear B, the initial [s-] is not represented, which is as expected, given the orthographic hierarchy (5) and the Linear B spelling strategy (3). Similarly, the spelling of the remaining portion of the cluster (*stop + {liquid, nasal}*) proceeds predictably; that is, this portion of the cluster is written in full. Thus, we find the spelling

(8) *tu-ru*-pte-ri-ja for στρυπτηριας ([strüptẹ:rias], 'of alum')

in which the fricative [#s-] is not written but the [-tr-] sequence is.

The spelling strategy used for representing word-initial trisyllabic clusters in the case of syllabic Cypriot spelling is simply the regular strategy used for writing all word-initial clusters in this script: namely, each such cluster, regardless of type, is represented in full, and the members of the cluster are spelled by using syllabic symbols whose vocalic component is identical to the phonetic vowel which follows the cluster. Thus, the following syllabic spelling is found in Cypriot:

(9) *so-to-ro*-pi-ki for στροφιγγι ([strophiŋgi], 'on the point')

Consequently, problematic spellings such as that hypothetical case described above do not occur word-initially in either the Mycenaean or the Cypriot syllabic writing systems.

When a consonant cluster of three or more members occurs *word-internally,* a syllable-boundary falls at some point within the cluster. If more than a single consonant precedes the syllable-boundary, those consonants (which are the consonants of the coda of the preceding syllable) decrease in sonority up to the syllable-boundary and, accordingly, increase in orthographic strength. If more than a single consonant follows the syllable-boundary—and this is of course also the case with word-initial clusters—those consonants generally increase in sonority and correspondingly decrease in orthographic strength. The result of this condition is that within a word-internal cluster of three or more consonants, there is some consonant which *peaks* in orthographic strength, while the consonant or consonants on either side of it are of less (or, at most, equal[2]) orthographic strength. Therefore, the type of spelling complexity described above and illustrated by the hypothetical *fricative + nasal + stop* cluster also does not *generally* occur word-internally. The complexity exhibited by this hypothetical *fricative + nasal + stop* cluster is a consequence of a consonant occurring in the middle of the cluster (nasal) which is weaker in orthographic strength than the consonants occurring on either side of it (fricative and stop). Again, as we have just seen, it is generally the case that such a configuration is not possible.

5.0.3.1 Stop + Fricative + Stop

There is, however, a highly significant exception to the preceding generalization about the nonoccurrence of a consonant which is flanked on either side by consonants of greater orthographic strength (i.e., of less sonority). One word-internal trisyllabic cluster of such a form did occur in the history of Greek: namely, the cluster *stop + fricative + stop.* Though no such clusters are attested—at least none unambiguously—in either the Mycenaean or syllabic Cypriot materials, in early Greek the sequences [-ks-] and [-ps-] occurred before stops, as in the following examples:[3]

(10) *τετραπσθαι* (*[tetrapst^hai]) → *τετράφθαι* ([tetráp^ht^hai], 'to have turned')
   πεπλεκσθαι (*[peplekst^hai]) → *πεπλέχθαι* ([*peplék^ht^hai], 'to have twisted')

Somewhat similarly, [-ks-] could precede a nasal, as in (11):[4]

(11) *λυκσνος* ([lüksnos]) → *λύχνος* ([lúk^hnos], 'lamp')

As the examples of (10) and (11) illustrate, the fricative [-s-] was eventually deleted from these clusters, and this deletion was accompanied by aspiration of the initial stop of the cluster. There is, in addition, as I discuss later, a distinct development of [-ks-] clusters which occurred when the ensuing consonant was a velar stop.[5]

With respect to the chronology of these changes, it is known that the deletion of [-s-] from clusters of the type *stop + fricative + nasal* was post-
Mycenaean, as is revealed by the occurrence in Linear B of the following form

(12)   *a₃-ka-sa-ma* for αικσμανς ([ai**ksm**ans], 'points')

Although, as indicated above, no Linear B form is attested which clearly exhibits the sequence *stop + fricative + stop,* there is nothing which would lead us
to believe that a fricative disappeared from the context *stop _____ stop* earlier
than from the context *stop _____ nasal.* Indeed, consider that following a
word-boundary (i.e., in word-initial position, a phonetic context which closely
parallels the post-stop position, about which I will have more to say below),
the sequence *fricative + stop* was stable:

(13)   *σπερ-* → σπέρμα ([spérma], 'seed')

But the sequence *fricative + nasal* was not stable. Before a nasal, as well as
before the liquids and [-w-], a word-initial [s-] became [h-], which in turn was
lost before the nasals and [-l-]:

(14)   *σμερ-* > μείρομαι ([mé:romai], 'I receive my due')
         σρευ- > ρέω ([hré:], 'I flow')[6]

Linear B *ra-pte* for ραπτηρ ([hrapte:r], 'sewing-man') suggests that loss of the
fricative [s-] in this context had in fact occurred by the Mycenaean era.[7]
     It is reasonable to posit that the fricative [-s-] was also preserved between
stops during the Mycenaean era (at least when the initial stop was a velar or a
bilabial[8]). We saw in chapter 4 that Viredaz (following Doria in one instance)
has conjectured that such a triconsonantal cluster lies beneath the Linear B
spellings *we-pe-za* (hwe**ksp**eza) and the pair *e-ka-te-re-ta* and *e-te-re-ta.* The
latter conjecture can be said to be *séduisant,* but nothing more; the former is
perhaps a different matter. *We-pe-za,* if identified correctly, is a word in which
a *stop + fricative + stop* cluster would have occurred at a sufficiently early
period in the history of the Greek language, and the attempts to explain away
the absence of a grapheme for [-k-] by positing unique Mycenaean sound
changes are not satisfying; later in this chapter I will consider this form further.

5.0.3.1.1 Cypriot [ks] + Stop.

We would thus expect that the clusters *[ks] +
stop* and *[ps] + stop* were reduced to two members no earlier than the beginning of the twelfth century B.C. As we have seen, the Cypriot Syllabary was
already in use for writing Greek by at least the middle of the eleventh century
B.C.[9] The relatively brief time-span separating the periods of attestation of the
two syllabic scripts allows for the possibility that the Cypriot Syllabary was
devised for writing Greek at a time which also preceded the general reduction
of clusters of the type *[ks] + stop* and *[ps] + stop.*
     Beyond such considerations of probability, there is quite direct evidence
which indicates that at least *[ks] + stop* clusters were present in the dialect of
the syllabic Cypriot inscriptions. There existed in ancient Greek a preposition
meaning 'out of' which occurred in three variant allomorphic forms:

(15) ἐξ ([eks]), ἐκ ([ek]) and ἐς ([es])

All three forms were used as both proclitic prepositions and prefixes. In most of the dialects, these variants occur in complementary distribution: ἐξ ([eks]) is used when the word which follows begins with a vowel, while either ἐκ ([ek]) or ἐς ([es])—the choice is dialect-specific—occurs when the word which follows begins with a consonant. As an illustration of this distribution, consider the following forms (where ¢ represents a clitic-boundary):[10]

(16) A. Attic-Ionic ἐξ Ἀθηνῶν ([#eks ¢ atʰẹːnộːn#], 'out of Athens')
            ἐξαίρω ([eksaírọ:], 'I lift up')
            ἐκ Πύλου ([#ek ¢ pǔlu:#], 'out of Pylos')
            ἐκπέμπω ([ekpémpọ:], 'I send out')
       B. Arcadian εξελαυνοια ([ekselaunoia], 'I would drive out')
            ες τοι ([#es ¢ toi . . .#], 'out of the . . .', dative)
            εσπερασαι ([esperasai], 'to transgress')
       C. Cretan εξαρχιδιον ([eksarkʰidion], 'initial')
            εξ Ιεραπυντας ([#eks ¢ ierapüntas#], 'out of Hierapytna')
            εκς αδελπιον ([#eks ¢ adelpiọ:n#], 'of the brothers')
            εστεισαντανς ([estẹ:santans], 'having paid back')
            ες τεκνον ([#es ¢ teknọ:n#], 'from children')

The preconsonantal form ἐκ ([ek])—both the proclitic preposition and the prefix—which is found in Attic-Ionic is the product of the regular phonological reduction of *[ksC] clusters which was discussed above,[11] though here there is a conspicuous absence of aspiration on the initial velar stop, apparently as a consequence of the intervening morpheme- or clitic-boundary. Note, on this point, that the identical distribution of proclitic and prefixal forms indicates that this cluster reduction process operated across a clitic-boundary.[12]

It was mentioned earlier that a different course of development is found when a [ks] consonantal sequence (or for that matter [kʰs] or [gs]) is followed by a velar stop. In this case there is no loss of the [s] with accompanying aspiration of the initial velar stop of the cluster; instead, the initial velar is deleted, as in the following examples:[13]

(17) A. *δικσκος (*[dikskos]) → δίσκος ([dískos], 'quoit')
       B. *λεχσκᾶ (*[lekʰska:]) → *λεχσχᾶ (*[lekʰskʰa:]) → λέσχη ([léskʰẹ:], 'lounging area' etc.)
       C. *μιγσκω (*[migskọ:]) → *μιγσγω (*[migsgọ:]) → μίσγω ([mísgọ:], 'I mix')[14]

The ἐς preconsonantal form of the preposition, as seen in the Arcadian and Cretan forms of (16), perhaps arose via the operation of this particular dissimilatory change (i.e., the regular reflex of *ἐξ ([eks]) preceding a velar was generalized to all preconsonantal positions); this is the analysis of Buck.[15] Alternatively, as proposed by Lejeune,[16] the general treatment of word-internal [ksC] clusters (i.e., *[ksC] → [k^{h}C]), differed in dialects such as Arcadian and Cretan from that treatment exhibited when [ks] was followed by a clitic- or morpheme-boundary; in this latter context, just as before velar stops generally, the cluster-initial [k] was dissimilated (i.e., *[ks{¢,+ }C] → [s{¢,+ }C]). Each of these analyses has its merits. Lejeune's interpretation avoids the somewhat counterintuitive notion that the form of the preposition which would arise only before a velar stop by regular sound change should be generalized to all preconsonantal contexts. But if theoretical economy is important to us, Lejeune's interpretation is less preferred, because it requires the postulation not just of an additional sound change but of a sound change which is suspiciously similar to (and, in fact, something of a blend of) the two additional sound changes which are still required by his analysis.

The closely related dialects of Arcadian and Cypriot differ in the preconsonantal form of the preposition ἐξ ([eks]). The type of allomorphic variation in the form of this preposition which is exhibited by the various dialects and illustrated in (16) is not to be found in the dialect of the syllabic Cypriot inscriptions. Instead, in this dialect, the preposition consistently takes the form ἐξ ([eks]), even before an ensuing consonant,[17] as in the following example:

(18)   *e-xe to-i* for εξ τõι ([#eks ¢ tọ:i . . . #], 'out of the . . .')

So, then, while Arcadian has ἐς ([es]) before consonants, Cypriot has ἐξ ([eks]).[18] This difference suggests that the simplification of *[ks]* + *stop* clusters occurred after the split of the parent Arcado-Cypriot dialect into Arcadian and Cypriot, a separation generally held to be post-Mycenaean.[19] The observation that *stop* + *fricative* + *stop* clusters remained intact until some point beyond the separation of Cypriot from its sister dialect of Arcadian may provide further motivation for speculating that the Cypriot syllabic writing system was devised at a time when such clusters were still generally preserved. Nevertheless, the possibility cannot be eliminated that Cypriot analogically leveled an inherited Proto-Arcado-Cypriot prevocalic *ἐξ (*[eks]) allomorph for use before both vowels and consonants.

Regardless of the general status of *stop* + *fricative* + *stop* clusters in early Cypriot Greek, there is excellent and obvious evidence (as the reader has undoubtedly already noted) that at least one such cluster-type existed. As pointed out above, the examples of (16) reveal that when the preposition is used as a prefix in composition it shows the same conditioned variation as that exhibited by the preposition when used as a proclitic; that is, ἐξ ([eks]) occurs before vowels and ἐκ ([ek]) or ἐς ([es]) before consonants. This is not surprising. While there are morpho-syntactic differences between *proclitic preposition* + *tonic noun* combinations, on the one hand, and compounds containing a prefix, on the other, phonetically the two structures must have been almost identical. Allen's summary comments concerning enclitics and proclitics are worth quoting:

(19)   [W]e may note that in Greek, for example, a sequence such as φιλῶ σε, with enclitic pronoun, shows the single accent characteristic of a word like φιλοῦσα; and the phonological adherence of proclitics to the following

word is seen in the accentuation of such forms as πρόπαλαι, διά–πεντε.[20]

Though no examples of the *prefixal use* of the preposition ἐξ before a consonant are yet attested among the syllabic Cypriot materials, the identical distribution of allomorphs in the case of both the prefix and the proclitic in other dialects is a reliable indicator that the Cypriot form of the *prefix* was ἐξ ([eks]) even before consonants.[21] This means that clusters of the form *[ks]* + *stop* occurred word-internally without even an intervening clitic-boundary in the Cypriot dialect,[22] either because otherwise Panhellenic phonological changes failed to occur in at least this one particular context (owing to the relative isolation of the Cypriot dialect) or because of analogical leveling.[23]

5.0.3.1.2 The Spelling of *[ks]* + *Stop.*

In summary, we have seen (i) that clusters exhibiting the sequence *[ks]* + *stop* and *[ps]* + *stop* were likely present in Mycenaean Greek; (ii) that these same clusters may have occurred *generally* in early Cypriot, though the evidence of this, such as it is, is only suggestive in nature and is open to another interpretation; and (iii) that *[ks]* + *stop* clusters are regularly found in the Cypriot dialect.

Now, it would seem that the representation of such clusters would not have been problematic for the Mycenaean scribes: the [s] simply would not have been written. Thus, in a sequence such as

(20)   [-eksth a-]

the cluster could be spelled as

(21)   -ka-ta-

The [s] is not written, since it occurs before a stop, and the initial stop of the cluster ([k]) is represented by using the symbol whose vocalic component is identical to the vowel which phonetically follows the entire cluster ([a]). We will come back to the Linear B spelling of such a cluster later in this chapter.

In the syllabic Cypriot writing system, however, a *[ks]* + *stop* cluster would evoke a cumbersome and patently bizarre representation. Let us again consider the sequence [-eksth a-]. The stop [k] is of greater orthographic strength than the fricative [s] which follows it; given the regular Cypriot spelling strategy (4), we would expect that the [k] would be represented by using the symbol whose vocalic component is identical to the vowel which *follows* the cluster (i.e., *ka*). Since [s], the next member of the cluster, is of less orthographic strength than the consonant which follows it (i.e., the stop [th]), [s] should be represented using the symbol whose vocalic component is identical to the vowel which *precedes* the cluster (i.e., *se*). This procedure produces the extremely odd spelling in (22):

(22)   *-e-ka-se-ta-* for [-eksth a-]

The first consonant of the cluster is spelled progressively (-*e-ka-se-ta*-), while the second is spelled regressively (-*e-ka-se-ta*-), resulting in a bizarre spelling crossover.

Spellings of clusters of the type *[ks]* + *stop* may thus appear to be quite problematic for the interpretation of the consonant cluster spelling strategy for the Cypriot Syllabary which I have proposed above—the interpretation which is based upon the hierarchy of orthographic strength. To the contrary, however, such clusters actually corroborate this interpretation. There appears to have been a special mechanism which was devised by the Cypriot scribes to deal with such clusters: namely, a set of special symbols representing the consonant sequence [-ks-]. As I pointed out in chapter 2, the syllabic Cypriot inscriptions have preserved the CCV characters with the value *kse* and *ksa,* and these, along with the symbols corresponding to alphabetic *zeta,* are the only symbols of the Cypriot Syllabary with a value other than V or CV. These, and no doubt other *ksV* symbols, appear to have been developed to avoid those very problematic spellings such as that one illustrated in (22). Utilizing these CCV symbols, a sequence such as that in (20) could be spelled simply and straightforwardly as in (23):

(23)   *-e-ksa-ta-*[24]

5.0.3.1.3 *[ks#]* = *[ks]* + *Stop.*   As pointed out above, clusters of the type *[ks]* + *stop* are clearly attested in the Cypriot data only in instances of the proclitic ἐξ ([eks]) preceding a stop. Beyond these, the *ksV* symbols are regularly used in word-final position, as in the example of (24):

(24)   *wa-na-kse* for ϝαναξ ([wanaks], royal title)

The occurrence of these characters both before a stop and word-finally suggests that for purposes of orthographic processing, a stop is equivalent to a word-boundary in the syllabic Cypriot system. This interpretation is supported by close parallels from the realm of phonology; there exist various phonological processes in which a word-boundary is also seen to behave like a consonant, and, in certain instances it behaves not like any consonant in general but specifically like a stop or some other obstruent.[25] Consider, for example, the basic rule accounting for the distribution of the syllabic allophones (i.e. those allophones which can function as the nucleus or vowel of a syllable) of the Indo-European sonorants, as formalized by Schindler[26] (where [+son] stands for *sonorant,* [+syll] for *syllabic,* and [-syll] for *nonsyllabic*):

(25)   [+son, -syll] → [+syll]/{[-syll], #} ___ {[-syll], #}

Here, a word-boundary (#) functions just like a consonant ([-syll]) in conditioning the appearance of the "vowel-like" form of the sonorants, that is, [r̥, l̥, m̥, n̥, i, u] for /r, l, m, n, y, w/ respectively.

Two further examples of the phonological equivalence of a consonant and a word-boundary are presented by processes of voicing assimilation in Old English and Modern German, as analyzed by Lass.[27] The fricatives of Old English assimilate in voicing to adjoining segments; Lass generalizes that a fricative is voiced when it occurs between two sonorants (which are voiced sounds) but is voiceless if it is contiguous either to a voiceless obstruent or to a word-boundary. Thus, Lass proposes that a word-boundary is here "in terms of the power to inhibit voicing . . . really a voiceless obstruent."[28] He points out that a word-initial or word-final fricative is voiceless even when it occurs next to a sonorant, as in the Old English forms of (26):

(26) A. *healf* ('half')
       B. *smītan* ('smite')

He interprets this to mean that a word-boundary is stronger than a sonorant in that it can abrogate the sonorant's potential for spreading voicing to the fricative. He thus proposes that *word-boundary* lies higher on a hierarchy of consonant (or segment) strength than does *sonorant*. The hierarchy that he envisions is in form essentially that of the sonority hierarchy, and the position of *word-boundary* is equivalent to that of *voiceless obstruent,* which occurs in the topmost position on the hierarchy.[29]

Lass adduces distributional criteria as evidence of a similar equation of *voiceless obstruent* and *word-boundary* in Modern High German.[30] When occurring in word-final position, obstruents are devoiced. As a consequence, there is a contrast in the voicing feature of word-final and word-internal obstruents in forms such as the following:

(27) A. *Weib* ([vaip], 'woman')
          Weibes ([vaibəs], 'woman's')
       B. *Bund* ([bunt], 'association')
          Bundes ([bundəs], 'association's')

Thus, *[-voice obstruent]#* is a possible sequence, but **[+ voice obstruent]#* is not. In a completely parallel fashion, Lass claims, word-internal clusters of the type *obstruent + obstruent* must be voiceless; in other words, a word-boundary again behaves like a voiceless obstruent.[31]

Just as in these instances a word-boundary is equivalent to an obstruent for the sake of phonological processing, so in the Cypriot Syllabary a word-boundary is equivalent to an obstruent—specifically, to a stop—for the sake of orthographic processing. Here again, orthography is essentially paralleling phonology.[32]

5.0.3.1.4 The Hierarchy of Orthographic Strength and <ksV> Motivation. I would underscore the fact that the motivation for the development of the CCV symbols *kse* and *ksa* in a system which otherwise utilizes almost only V and CV symbols is revealed only by interpreting the spelling of consonant clusters as a function of the orthographic hierarchy (5) and the spelling strategy (4). Notice that no such motivation exists given the conventional interpretations of syllabic Cypriot spelling which are dependent upon syllable structure, such as those we encountered in chapter 3 (and chapter 4). Let us consider again, as an example, Buck's formulation:

(28) For groups of consonants, the first is indicated by the sign containing the vowel of the syllable to which this consonant belongs.[33]

Given any such strategy and the accompanying implicit assumption that a syllable-boundary occurs before a word-internal cluster which is capable of occurring in word-initial position, the representation of a *stop* + *fricative* + *stop* sequence, as in [-eksth a-], would be straightforward and nonproblematic. Assuming the syllabification [-ek\$sth a-] (as [#sth -] is a possible word-initial sequence of Greek, but *[#ksth -] is not), the cluster would simply be spelled as in (29):

(29)   *-e-ke-sa-ta-*

no special *ks*V symbol would be required. The same is true even if it should be claimed that the syllable-boundary here falls before the second stop, that is, [-eks\$th a-] (because [-ks#] is possible word-finally in Greek but *[-k#] is not, or for whatever motivation). In this case the sequence could be spelled straightforwardly as follows:

(30)   *-e-ke-se-ta-*[34]

Compare syllabic Cypriot spellings such as the following:

(31)   A. *se-pe-re-ma-to-se* for σπερματος ([spermatos], 'seed')
       B. *so-to-ro-pi-ki* for στροφιγγι ([strop^{h}iŋgi], 'on the point')

In these examples the fricative is likewise separated from the vowel of its syllable by an intervening stop (as well as a liquid in the case of (31B)).
    Within the framework of each of the various other interpretations of syllabic Cypriot consonant cluster spelling, *ks*V symbols are an unmotivated, unnecessary redundancy. Within the analysis of Cypriot spelling which is based upon the hierarchy of orthographic strength the *ks*V symbols are a necessity.

5.0.3.1.5 The Complementary Distribution of <ksV> and <kVsV>. In addition to being used to spell [-ks] clusters occurring at the end of a word, the *ks*V symbols appear also to be the regular means for representing a word-final sequence [-ksV], where [V] can be short or long, a monophthong or a diphthong.[35] Thus, we find spellings such as the following:

(32)   A. *e-we-kse* for εϝεξε ([ewekse], '(s)he carried')
       B. *o-ru-kse* for (εξ)ορυξη ([orükse̞:], '(s)he should expropriate')[36]
       C. *me-te-kse-i* for μεθεξει ([met^{h}eksei], 'for participation')
       D. *e-we-re-ksa* for εϝερξα ([ewerksa], 'I offered')

As we will see immediately below, other word-internal (i.e., intervocalic) occurrences of the cluster [-ks-] are regularly spelled <-kV-sV->; in other words, the *ks*V symbols usually are not used to represent word-internal [-ks-], except in the spelling of final syllables. The use of the *kse* character to represent a final sequence [-kse] (as in (32A)), not just a word-final cluster [-ks] (recall that the empty vowel used for spelling word-final consonants is *-e*), can reasonably be interpreted as a development based on the dual use of the symbol *se* for both word-final [-s] (as in (33A)) and word-final [-se] (as in (33B)):

(33) A. *po-to-li-se* for πτολις ([ptolis], 'city')

  B. *ka-te-se-ta-se* for κατεστασε ([katestase], '(s)he set up')

That is to say, the scribal "equation" would be something like this: if [-se#] is spelled exactly like [-s#], then [-kse#] should be spelled exactly like [-ks#]. Since vowel length is not distinguished in the syllabic Cypriot script, the symbol *kse* is automatically used also for the long-vowel word-final sequence [-ksẹ:] (as in (32B)). From this starting point, it is likely that the use of the *ksV* symbols was then extended to spell [-ksV#] sequences other than [-kse/ẹ:#], such as [-ksei#] (as in (32C)) and [-ksa#] (as in (32D)).[37]

If we accept the practice of using the *ksV* symbols for spelling word-final [-ksV] sequences as a secondary development, then we find the mode of spelling attested [-ks-] clusters, aside from this secondary development, to be a matter of complementary distribution: <-ksV> is the representation of word-final [-ks], and <-kV-sV-> is that of word-internal (i.e. prevocalic) [-ks-]. Such word-internal sequences are, as would be expected, regularly written by utilizing progressive spelling, as in the following examples:[38]

(34) A. *e-u-ka-sa-me-no-se* for ευξαμενος ([euksamenos], 'having vowed')

  B. *to-ka-sa-to-ro* for Δοξανδρω ([doksandrọ:], 'of Doxandros')

That the *ksV* symbols are regularly used word-finally (and *not* prevocalically) clearly reveals that there is something about word-final position which prohibits the use in that context of the <kV-sV> spelling, the very type of <CVCV> spelling which is otherwise used in this writing system for representing consonant clusters. That "something" is, of course, that the word-boundary is orthographically equivalent to a stop; hence, the pre-stop method of representing [-ks-] clusters must be used.[39]

It has been claimed, or assumed, that the Cypriot Syllabary acquired its *ks* symbols under the influence of the Greek alphabet, which possesses the [ks] character ξ *(xi)*.[40] In other words, such acquisition represents a fairly late development in the history of the syllabic Cypriot script. This is highly unlikely, however, given the complementary distribution of the Cypriot symbols used to represent the sequence [ks] which was discussed and motivated immediately above. If the Cypriot scribes simply borrowed from the Greek alphabet the practice of using *ks* symbols, one would certainly expect that such symbols would be used in all contexts. We shall consider the matter of the relationship between the syllabic Cypriot *ks* symbols and alphabetic ξ in considerable detail in chapter 6.

5.1 Word-Final Clusters in Linear B

5.1.1 Types of Word-Final *Stop* + *[-s]* Representation

We have found the Linear B spelling of *stop* + *[-s]* clusters in word-final position to be heterogeneous. If we accept *o-nu-ka* to be a spelling of ονυξ ([onüks]), then three different types of word-final *stop* + *[-s]* spellings can be identified:

(35) Type 1: as in *to-ra* for θωραξ ([tʰǫ:ra:ks])
      Type 2: as in *to-ra-ka* for θωραξ ([tʰǫ:ra:ks])
      Type 3: as in *o-nu-ka* for ονυξ ([onüks])

In no case is the final [-s] spelled. With type 1 spelling there is also no grapheme for [-k-]; the stop [-k-] is represented by utilizing the regressive spelling strategy in type 2 and by using an arbitrary empty vowel in type 3.

5.1.1.1 Type 1

In the preceding sections of this chapter I argued that just as a word-boundary can behave as a stop in phonological processes, so a word-boundary is equivalent to a stop in the orthographic processing of ancient Greek syllabic writing. Incorporating this find into my hierarchy of orthographic strength results in a hierarchy of the following form:

(36) *{word-boundary, stop} > fricative > nasal > glide > liquid*

We can now see that the Linear B spelling strategy (3), repeated here as (37), correctly predicts that single word-final consonants will not receive overt representation in Mycenaean spelling.

(37) Within a word, any two successive consonants will be represented with plenary spelling if, and only if, the orthographic strength of the first is greater than or equal to that of the second; otherwise, partial spelling will be used.

The only consonants which can occur word-finally in Greek are, as noted earlier, [-r, -s, -n], and each of these falls lower on the hierarchy than the *stop/ word-boundary* term; hence, plenary expression is not used (i.e., the first member of the C# sequence is not spelled).[41]

When a Mycenaean scribe went about the process of applying the strategy formalized in (37) to the spelling of the word-final consonantal sequence in a phonetic string such as [#tʰǫ:raks#], what would be the outcome? Spelling from left to right, phonetically speaking (i.e., from the beginning of the word to the end of the word), [-ks#], like any other three-member sequence, is processed as two overlapping substrings, [-ks-] and [-s#]. In the instance of [-ks-], since [-k-] outranks [-s] on the hierarchy (36), [-k-] is represented with plenary spelling utilizing the *kV* syllabic symbol having a vocalic component which is identical to the vowel which phonetically follows the entire three-member sequence. But the vowel which follows the cluster in this particular case is of course nonexistent—a zero-vowel. The "logical" application of the strategy (37) would then call for the use of a *kV* symbol with an arbitrary zero-vowel component, that is, an empty vowel which arbitrarily marks the nonoccurrence of a phonetic vowel in absolute final position. As we have seen, such symbols exist in the syllabic Cypriot writing system; these are the *Ce* symbols which are used in spelling word-final consonants (as in *ka-re*, γαρ ([gar], 'for')). But such word-final symbols had not been provided within the Linear B system, in which single word-final consonants receive no overt expression, as the regular consequence of strategy (37). In practice then, the only CV symbol with an arbitrary zero-vowel value which is available to the Mycenaean scribe is a "zero-CV symbol," that is, no CV symbol; hence, no grapheme is assigned to [-k-] in the spelling of the sequence [#tʰǫ:raks#]. The next sequence encountered by the scribe in the spelling process is [-s#]. Since [-s] occurs lower on the hierarchy (36) than *word-boundary*, it also is not written, and the sequence [#tʰǫ:raks#] is thus spelled *to-ra*. The same process generates the spelling *o-nu* for ονυξ ([#onüks#]).

5.1.1.2 Type 2

Though the *to-ra* type of spelling of [#tʰǫ:raks#] is generated by the regular, principled application of the Linear B spelling strategy (37), such a spelling is clearly, at the same time, antithetical to the system. A stop [-k-] occurring before the fricative [-s] is represented not by plenary spelling (as it would be had it occurred at any other location within the word) but by partial spelling. This is a violation of a sort which is otherwise strictly avoided. Rigorous application of the spelling strategy leads to a violation of the spelling strategy.

One solution to this Catch-22 which presented itself to some innovative scribe was to alter the direction in which the search is conducted for the phonetic vowel that is to be used as the template for an empty vowel. Linear B is consistently rightward looking in this regard (i.e., it looks ahead in the word), but by looking to the left, a means is found for resolving the dilemma of the partial spelling of a *stop* + *fricative* cluster. In this way—by introducing regressive spelling into the Linear B system—a stop can be represented before a word-final fricative by utilizing plenary spelling, in accordance with (36).[42] A phonetic sequence [#tʰǫ:raks#] can thus be spelled *to-ra-ka*. The same type of innovative spelling occurs in *wa-na-ka* for ϝαναξ ([#wanaks#], 'king') and in *a₃-ti-jo-qo* for Αιθιοqʷς ([#aitʰiokʷs#], a man's name).[43] It is in large measure (though not completely) the substitution of regressive spelling for partial spelling which distinguishes syllabic Cypriot practice from Mycenaean. Perhaps we might even see in the introduction of regressive spelling into the Linear B system in this single context an idea which was exploited in the development of the syllabic Cypriot system.[44]

Type 2 spelling is the predominant mode of Mycenaean word-final *stop* + *[-s]* representation (within the Linear B database, there are seven occurrences of type 2 spelling and two occurrences of type 1). It is of course this plenary spelling of such word-final sequences with which earlier interpretations of Linear B spelling have struggled. Syllable-based analyses holding that the consonants which follow the vowel of their syllable (i.e. the consonants of the syllable coda) are not spelled would predict type 1 representation of word-final *stop* + *[-s]* clusters. As we saw, special mechanisms must then be devised to account for the usual plenary spelling (type 2 representation, in which a stop which follows the vowel of its syllable *is* spelled) of these clusters, and these mechanisms are without motivation.

Such ad hoc measures stand in stark contrast to the tongue-and-groove naturalness of our approach. We discovered immediately above that, as with these syllable-dependent analyses, type 1 representation of word-final *stop + [-s]* clusters also follows from the interpretation of Linear B spelling which is based upon the hierarchy of orthographic strength, though for a different reason— because Linear B consonant cluster spelling is thoroughly rightward looking (i.e., progressive). At the very same time, however, such representation, with its failure to spell a stop occurring before a fricative, manifestly violates the principle of Linear B consonant cluster representation which is dependent upon the hierarchy of orthographic strength; thus, the advent of a means for orthographically rendering word-final *stop + [-s]* in a plenary fashion (type 2 representation) is completely motivated within and is in agreement with the interpretation.

5.1.1.3 Type 3

Still a different solution to the problem of the aberrant partial spelling of a word-final *stop + [-s]* cluster can be seen in the innovative representation *o-nu-ka* for ονυξ ([onüks]), if we accept this interpretation of *o-nu-ka*. In this case the direction in which the scribe searches for the phonetic vowel serving as a template for the empty vowel does not shift; instead, plenary spelling is achieved by introducing the use of an arbitrary empty vowel <-a> into the Linear B system.

The acceptance of the reading *o-nu-ka* for [onüks] would obviously open up the possibility that the final <-a> of *to-ra-ka* and/or *wa-na-ka* is also an arbitrary empty vowel and that these forms do not then display the regressive spelling of a_3-*ti-jo-qo* for Αιθιοq^{w}ς ([ait^{h}iok^{w}s]). It would be impossible to determine which of the strategies is at work. However, the spelling of oblique cases and derivatives of *wa-na-ka* (ϝαναξ ([wanaks], 'king') are worth considering in this regard. The dative of this word appears in our database five times with the spelling *wa-na-ka-te* for ϝανακτει ([wanaktẹ:], attested at both Knossos and Pylos) and only once with the expected spelling *wa-na-ke-te* (at Pylos). Similarly, the occurrences of the derivative formed in *-ter-* are without exception (ten times in the database, at Knossos, Pylos and Thebes) spelled with <-ka-> and not <-ke->: *wa-na-ka-te-ro* for ϝανακτερος ([wanakteros], 'of the king') etc. It has been often suggested that what we find here is a kind of orthographic paradigmatic leveling of the nominative singular spelling *wa-na-ka*.[45] If this is so, perhaps it would be more likely for *wa-na-ka* to have been formalized and generalized as the spelling of a phonetic sequence [wanak-] if the phonetic template for the empty vowel of <-ka-> were encoded within the formalized spelling, as would be the case if *wa-na-ka* is the product of regressive spelling but not if the vocalic component of <-ka-> were only an arbitrary empty vowel used in word-final spellings; this is, however, just speculation.[46]

5.1.1.4 Within the Word

In the discussion of *stop + fricative + stop* clusters earlier in this chapter, I indicated that the spelling of such clusters in Linear B would appear not to be problematic. The [s] should not be written (since it occurs lower on the hierarchy than the following stop). The initial stop could be written with the CV symbol having a vocalic component which is identical to the phonetic vowel which follows the entire cluster; we see a stop looking across two intervening consonants in search of a vocalic template in, for example, a_3-*ka-sa-ma* for αιξμανς ([aiksmans], 'points'). I suggested, therefore, that for a phonetic sequence such as [-ekst^{h}a-], the cluster could be spelled as -*ka-ta-*.

Both in chapter 4 and earlier in this chapter, I mentioned that Viredaz conjectures that a three-member cluster occurs in the Mycenaean word spelled *we-pe-za* ('six-footed')—a cluster of the form *stop + fricative + stop* ([hwekspe-]). If the form does contain such a cluster, as is possible, then the spelling attested is not of that type which we envisioned in the preceding paragraph, in other words, not *we-ke-pe-za, but *we-pe-za*, with no grapheme for the interconsonantal [-s-], but also none for [-k-]. In other words, a *medial stop + fricative* cluster *occurring before a stop* is spelled utilizing one of the canonical representations for a *word-final stop + fricative* cluster: namely, type 1. This does not surprise us at all; since a word-boundary is equivalent to a stop in the orthographic processing of consonant clusters in the Greek syllabic scripts, we would expect that in a word-internal cluster of the type *stop + fricative + stop*, the Linear B scribes could represent the *stop + fricative* sequence in the same manner in which such sequences are spelled word-finally. This particular example is, however, complicated by the fact that the [-ks-] portion of the cluster occurs as the final phonetic sequence of the first element of a compound.[47]

5.2 Concluding Remarks

The interpretation of the spelling of consonant clusters in the two syllabic scripts of ancient Greek which is based upon the hierarchy of orthographic strength has been further explored in this chapter. We have found that this interpretation properly accounts for the spelling of clusters of more than two consonants. Of the utmost crucial significance is the observation that the interpretation predicts that the spelling of *[ks] + stop* clusters in the syllabic Cypriot script (and likewise *[ps] + stop* clusters if their integrity were maintained until the development of the script) would be cumbersome and problematic. Consequent to this difficulty, the interpretation motivates the occurrence of anomalous CCV characters (the *ksV* characters) within the inventory of syllabic Cypriot graphemes. This interpretation of consonant cluster spelling also accounts elegantly for the observed representation of word-final clusters in both the Cypriot Syllabary and Linear B. In the case of the latter, the interpretation predicts the "regular" spelling of such clusters and, at the same time, provides a spelling system within which such a spelling is antithetical, thus motivating the occurrence of a variant (and, in fact, predominant) mode of representing these final clusters.

Notes

1. See Allen 1973:208.

2. It is possible that the segments could be of equal orthographic strength, as two contiguous consonants may have (in gross terms) the same sonority value; that is, two stops, two nasals, and so on, may occur side by side.

3. For further discussion, see Lejeune 1982:74, from which the examples of (10) and (11) were drawn.

4. For possible examples of the clusters *[ksl], *[ksr], and *[psr] (which undergo the same process of reduction), see A. Meillet and J. Vendryes, 1979, *Traité de grammaire comparée des langues classiques*, 5th ed. (Paris: Champion), p. 67.

5. The sequence [-ts-] also occurred preconsonantally at an early period in the history of Greek but was subject to a different treatment; that is, [-ts-], probably via assimilation to [-ss-] and subsequent degemination, was reduced to [-s-] before a consonant, as in *δατσμος (*[datsmos] > δασμός ([dasmós], 'division'). If this process essentially coincided with the change of prevocalic [-ts-] to [-ss-] (in Attic-Ionic and Arcadian; [-s-] in the remaining dialects, though [-tt-] in Boeotian and Cretan), then it would be of pre-Mycenaean date (as this latter change appears to be pre-Mycenaean): for example, Linear B *da-sa-to* for δασ(σ)ατο ([das(s)ato], 'he distributed') from earlier *[datsato]. See Lejeune 1982:74–75, 108, and the discussion of this change which was presented in the preceding chapter.

6. Lejeune 1982:119; on the occasional preservation of *#sm- in Greek, see pp. 120–121.

7. On the preservation of the cluster *stop + fricative + stop* in the Mycenaean dialect, note also the comments and bibliography of Viredaz 1982:302–304.

8. See n. 5 above.

9. See Mitford and Masson 1982:75.

10. See M. Bile, 1988, *Le dialecte crétois ancien* (Athens: École Française), pp. 275, 303, 305; Thumb-Scherer 1959:75, 139; as well as Buck 1955:83–84.

11. It is at least the *regular* outcome when the consonant following the [ks] cluster is a stop or a nasal, and possibly when this ensuing consonant is some other manner of articulation (see above, n. 4). If it should be the case that this change was only regular when [ks] preceded a stop or a nasal, then the occurrence of the ἐξ ([eks]) form of the preposition before consonants generally is the consequence of analogical spread.

12. Alternatively, it could be claimed that the variation in the form of the prefix which arose through the action of the "word-internal" change was extended analogically to the proclitic preposition. The compound containing the prefix ἐξ and the ἐξ + *tonic form* combination are most probably so phonetically similar that recourse to an analogical interpretation is simply not necessary, however.

13. See, among other treatments, the discussion in Lejeune 1982:67 and Rix 1976:78. Some investigators have identified the same type of dissimilation as occurring in the case of the sequence [psp^(h)]; thus, Buck (1933:153) cites *[blapsp^ha:mos] → [blásp^ẹ:mos], 'slanderous, blasphemous' as an example of this change. The etymology of this form is uncertain, however (see Chantraine 1968:178–179). In any event, the above discussed changes involving various sequences of the form [-CsC-] represent a

component of a more general phenomenon, concerning which Rix (1976:78) notes: "zwischen Konsonanten (außer neben /y/ oder /w/) bleibt /s/ erhalten, wenn der Konsonant vor /s/ ein Nasal oder Dental ist oder wenn /s/ zwischen gleichen Konsonanten steht; der Konsonant vor /s/ schwindet. . . . Sonst ist interkonsonantisches /s/ über /h/ geschwunden, wobei benachbarte Tenuis und . . . wortanlautender Vokal aspiriert werden."

14. On the progressive assimilation in (17B–C), see ibid., p. 95.

15. Buck 1933:153.

16. Lejeune 1982:314.

17. See Buck 1955:83, Thumb-Scherer 1959:172.

18. The Greek lexicographer Hesychius in the gloss of a phrase which he identifies as Paphian cites the preconsonantal preposition in the form ἐς ([es]). The discrepancy between the syllabic texts and Hesychius may well be a function of the late date at which he wrote—fifth/sixth century A.D.; see Thumb-Scherer 1959:168.

19. Cowgill (1966:88) argues that the differentiation of Arcadian and Cypriot may have begun in "at least the late days of the Mycenaean empire."

20. Allen 1973:24–25.

21. In the fifth-century Idalion tablet *ICS* 217, there is preserved a prefixed verb form *e-kse* | *o-ru-kse* in which the prefix is separated from the verb by a word-divider. The separation is curious. Regarding this spelling, Morpurgo Davies (1986a:276, n. 15) states, "Compounds are regularly written as single words with the exception of *e-xe o-ru-xe* found four times in the Idalion inscription . . . ; there may be graphic or phonetic reasons for this spelling . . . but we do not understand them." Perhaps what has happened here is that the orthographic treatment of the proclitic preposition (on which see the next note) has simply been extended to the prefix. With regard to this spelling, see also the comments of O. Masson (1983:241) with references to the treatment of this compound by earlier editors (see also p. 70).

22. While proclitics which end in a nasal are, in the Cypriot script, graphically joined to the ensuing tonic form, those ending in [-s] are kept separate by writing the [-s] with the empty *e* vowel which is used in the representation of word-final consonants; proclitics ending in a vowel are likewise kept graphically distinct from the tonic form upon which they lean phonetically. In some instances word-dividers separate proclitics ending in [-s] from the following word and sometimes not. Among the five instances of *e-xe to-i* (or *ta-i*) which occur in *ICS* 217, only once is the preposition separated from the ensuing article by a word-divider. For a full discussion of the spelling of proclitics, see O. Masson 1983:69–70; see also Morpurgo Davies 1986a:269–270; E. Hermann, 1908, "Zur kyprischen Silbenschrift," *IF* 19:241–248. Enclitics are graphically united with the tonic form which precedes them, except for the case of ημι ([ẹ:mi] 'I am'; see O. Masson 1983:70, though note exceptions cited in Morpurgo Davies 1986a:276, n. 13). This proclitic spelling practice is odd and probably has not yet been adequately accounted for. Since the final [-s] of proclitics is treated as a word-final consonant, instances of such proclitics preceding tonic forms beginning with a consonant do not appear in my tabulations of Cypriot *[s] + consonant* clusters which are presented in chapter 4.

23. As I pointed out in the preceding chapter, the final [-ks] cluster of the numeral ἕξ ([héks], 'six'), serving as the first member of a compound, may be preserved (or restored) analogically before a consonant, as in ἑξκαίδεκα ([hekskaídeka], 'sixteen') beside ἑκκαίδεκα ([hekkaídeka]).

24. Or perhaps, though it seems less likely, *-e-kse-ta-*; it is impossible, of course, to predict whether progressive or regressive spelling would have been utilized.

25. *Obstruent* is that class of sounds which consists of stops, fricatives, and affricates.

26. J. Schindler, 1976, "Notizen zum Sieversschen Gesetz," *Die Sprache* 22:56.

27. R. Lass, 1971, "Boundaries as Obstruents: Old English Voicing Assimilation and Universal Strength Hierarchies," *JL* 7:15–30.

28. Ibid., p. 16.

29. Lass (ibid., p. 17) further expands this hierarchy by subdividing the class *voiceless obstruent* as follows: *stop, [-voice] > stop, [+voice] > fricative, [-voice] > fricative, [+voice]*. Recall that the sonority hierarchy as we presented it in section 4.0.1 likewise has *voiceless stop* in the topmost slot.

30. Ibid., pp. 26–27.

31. Labov reports that in Philadelphia English and, even more broadly, in New York City English, tensing of a short vowel [æ] occurs before certain consonants if such consonants are in turn followed by an obstruent, an inflectional morpheme-boundary, or a word-boundary. He indicates that the boundary conditioning is open to an analogical interpretation (W. Labov, 1981, "Resolving the Neo-Grammarian Controversy," *Language* 57:285). For an interpretation of the status of word-boundaries which differs somewhat from that proposed by Lass, see M. Halle, 1971, "Word Boundaries as Environments in Rules," *LI* 2:540–541.

32. I would point out that I am not here advocating the notion that a word-boundary exists as a distinct phonological entity in the sense of a consonant or vowel, only that word-boundaries and stops (or obstruents) are treated in a parallel fashion both phonologically and orthographically.

33. Buck 1955:210.

34. Given the syllable-dependent analyses, perhaps *-e-ke-se-ta-* would even be the expected spelling, since, as we have seen, word-internal *fricative + stop* clusters must be viewed as "exceptionally" heterosyllabic within this interpretation.

35. In my Cypriot database, *ksV* symbols are so used seven times: once for [-kse#] (see (32A)); four times for [-kse̜:#] (see (32B)); once for [-ksei#] (see (32C)); and once for [-ksa#] (see (32D)). There is an additional instance in which word-final [-kse] was undoubtedly intended to be written, but the symbol *to* was erroneously used instead of *kse*.

36. See note 21 above.

37. Note that I have here transcribed Cypriot *e-i* as a diphthong (as it obviously was at the time this syllabic spelling was devised); see my introductory remarks on my transcription practice.

38. There are eight examples of word-internal spellings (excepting occurrences involving final syllables) of [-ks-]. In four of these instances, the cluster is unambiguously spelled progressively (i.e., $<$-V_i-kV_j-sV_j-$>$); in two cases the vowel which precedes the cluster is phonetically identical to that one which follows it (i.e., $<$-V_i-kV_i-sV_i-$>$); once there is an unexpected regressive spelling of the cluster (i.e., $<$-V_i-kV_i-sV_j-$>$); and once the cluster is spelled using the CCV symbol *kse*. The latter form comes from the Kafizin materials, which, as we have seen, are very late and show other spelling peculiarities; compare the comments in chapter 4 concerning the spellings *nu-ma-pa-se,* and so on. There is a second possible example of such a word-internal use of *kse* which occurs at Kafizin: Mitford (1980) restores *te-mi-xe[* as the personal name Θεμιξενω ([tʰemik-senọ:]). Concerning the restoration, see the comments of O. Masson (1981, "À propos des inscriptions chypriotes de Kafizin," *BCH* 105:644), who states, "Cela est assez plausible."

39. Since *ksV* symbols are regularly used in word-final position, one could imagine

that a critic might argue that the *ksV* symbols have their origin merely as word-final spelling variants; in other words, they have nothing to do with the representation of *stop + fricative + stop* clusters, they are simply the characters that one uses for spelling at the end of the word. It would then fall to the critic, however, to identify some motivation for a purely cosmetic prohibition which has the effect of preventing a sequence [-CC#] from being spelled <-CV-CV>; what such a motivation could be is not evident. Why would a word-final sequence [-ks] not be spelled <-ke-se> (using the regular word-final empty vowel *e*) just as easily as a mirror image word-initial sequence [spe-] is spelled <se-pe-> (as in (31A)) or an initial cluster [stro-] is spelled <so-to-ro-> (as in (31B))? In other words, in terms of graphic appearance, how is one side of a word-boundary intrinsically different from the other side?

40. See, for example, O. Masson 1983:56.

41. In the syllabic Cypriot script, word-final consonants are, as we have seen, written by using <-Ce> symbols, where <-e> is an arbitrary empty vowel (we will return to this immediately below). It was pointed out in chapter 2, following O. Masson (1983:73–74), that word-final [-r] is regularly spelled in this way, though word-final [-s] and [-n] are sometimes omitted from the orthography. Morpurgo Davies has examined the geographical and chronological distribution of the syllabic Cypriot spellings of word-final [-s] (1988, "Problems in Cyprian Phonology and Writing," in *The History of the Greek Language in Cyprus,* ed. J. Karageorghis and O. Masson (Nicosia: Zavallis Press), pp. 113–124) and argued cogently that this spelling variation is to be linked with the phonological change of [s] to [h] in word-final position—a change which appears to have preceded the same development intervocalically, and concerning the date of which she states, "[W]e should think in terms of a loss or an alteration of the final sibilant as early as the sixth century (and conceivably earlier)" (p. 119). The case of word-final nasals is in need of elucidation. One should probably be cautious about attributing their occasional nonoccurrence in the orthography to phonetic weakness. Discussing phonological changes which occurred in Greek during the Middle Ages, Browning (1983, *Medieval and Modern Greek,* 2nd ed. (Cambridge: Cambridge University Press), pp. 75–76) states: "A phonological change in the common language which can be dated with some probability to this period is the disappearance of final *-v* [-*n*], except before a vowel or plosive in the following word, where the two words form a single accentual group." However, he goes on to say: "By the fifteenth century final *-v* seems to have disappeared in the central areas of Greek speech, except, as explained above, before a following vowel or plosive. But in many dialects, e.g. *those of Cyprus,* of the Dodecanese, and of southern Italy, it still survives." (emphasis is mine). Such longevity of word-final Cypriot [-n] does not suggest particular "phonetic weakness" of the sound in this context.

42. The spelling of a word-final *stop + fricative* cluster is plenary or partial in that the stop either is overtly written (plenary) or is not (partial). In either case the fricative is not overtly written since it is, in turn, the first member of the "cluster" *[-s] + word-boundary* (and *fricative* occurs lower on the hierarchy than *word-boundary*).

43. An additional occurrence of the type 2 spelling of a word-final *stop + fricative* cluster is perhaps to be found in the man's name *po-ki-ro-qo,* probably Ποικιλοϙʷς ([poikilokʷs]); see *Docs.*:99.

44. If so, this idea was likely transported to Cyprus by Mycenaean émigrés, on which see chapter 7 below; compare n. 46 on the notion of a Mycenaean source for the Cypriot use of an arbitrary empty vowel in spelling word-final clusters.

45. Viredaz (1983:167, n. 224) credits Panagl (1971, "Eine 'Interferenz' von nominaler Stammbildung und Linear B-Schrift," *Kadmos* 10:125–134) with the idea.

46. The spelling *wa-na-ka-te-ro* for ϝανακτερος ([wanakteros], 'of the king'), with its irregular spelling of a consonant cluster which is divided by a highly transparent morpheme-boundary ([-k + t-]), is reminiscent of those instances in which *fricative +* *nasal* clusters that are divided by a transparent morpheme-boundary exhibit exceptional spelling (Cypriot *i-na-la-li-si-me-na,* etc.); see section 4.1.4.1.1. If the use of an arbitrary empty vowel were actually attested in Linear B, one might wonder if this provided the inspiration for the regular Cypriot use of an arbitrary empty vowel <-e> in the spelling of word-final consonants. Morpurgo Davies (1987:103) has remarked on this: "Finally, why *wa-na-ka* etc. and not *wa-na* (we may have both *o-nu* and *o-nu-ka*)? . . . Could it be that this is simply a first attempt made by the scribes to develop a way of indicating a consonant in word final position in anticipation of what will happen later in Cyprus? This suggestion is not original but need not be wrong."

47. It is because of this intervening compound-boundary, as we saw, that Viredaz treats this form as an example of "word-final" [-ks-]. Palaima (personal communication) has suggested that because of such morphemic considerations [weks-] is spelled as it would be when it occurs independently (i.e., [weks#]). Viredaz (1982:314–321) has also conjectured that a *stop + fricative + stop* cluster lies beneath the Linear B forms *a-re-ko-to-re* and *di-pte-ra.* The former is a man's name which is usually read as the well-known anthroponym Ἀλέκτωρ ([aléktǫ:r]); Viredaz's interpretation of the form as Ἀλεκστωρ ([alekstǫ:r]) is difficult to defend (cf. Chantraine's remarks (1968:58) on the etymology of the name). The latter (*di-pte-ra*) is identified with the first-millennium διφθέρα ([dipʰtʰéra], 'piece of leather'). Others have suggested the possibility that there formerly occurred a fricative [-s-] between the two stops, but the etymology of this form is generally treated as ultimately uncertain (see the discussion in Chantraine 1968:287– 288). If it were the case that the Mycenaean form contained the sequence [-pst-], it would be tantalizing to conjecture that the anomalous *stop + stop* syllabogram *pte* came to be utilized as a means of disambiguating the spelling of the sequences [-pst-] and [-pt-] (Viredaz (1982:321) leaves the impression that he views the possible spelling of [-pst-] as <-pt-> to be somewhat worrisome). In the historical phonology of Greek, *[py] developed into [pt], and it is often supposed that in origin the value of the Linear B syllabogram *pte* was *pye*.

6

The Alphabet

In the preceding chapters I have sought to demonstrate by careful and detailed argumentation that the spelling of consonant clusters in the two prealphabetic, syllabic scripts of ancient Greek was carried out by utilizing strategies based upon a hierarchy of orthographic strength. Consequent upon the use of this strategy, a difficulty arises in representing sequences of the type *stop + fricative + stop* in the syllabic Cypriot writing system. In order to resolve this difficulty, the Cypriot scribes devised a series of symbols having the value *ksV.*[1] These observations bring us at last to what is the centerpiece of our inquiry: namely, the origin of the Greek alphabet.

6.0 Phoenician Beginnings

It is unquestionably the case that the Greeks acquired their alphabet from some Semitic-speaking peoples who used a Canaanite writing system in which each character represented an individual consonant sound rather than a syllable, as had been the case with the second-millennium Greek scripts. Herodotus,[2] among other ancient authorities, tells us that it was the Phoenicians from whom the Greek alphabet was acquired: Kadmos, the founder of Thebes, was Phoenician and brought his script with him to Greece when he came in search of his sister Europa. Since the beginning of the scientific study of Greek epigraphy in the nineteenth century, scholars of this endeavor have widely concurred with Herodotus in his identification of the source of the Greek alphabet as Phoenician. McCarter[3] points out that the reasons for this are essentially three: (1) the characters of the most archaic Greek scripts closely match those of the Phoenician script; (2) the sequence of characters is almost the same in the Greek and

Phoenician scripts; and (3) the characters of the two scripts have very similar Semitic (and not Greek) names (see figure 6.1).[4]

While a general consensus on the source of the Greek alphabet then exists, having been reached long ago, there is at present considerable disagreement among scholars who study the spread of the Canaanite script to the Aegean concerning where and when this transmission occurred and at what impetus.

PHOENICIAN		GREEK		
Name	*ca. 900 B.C.E.*	*800–600 Attic (400)*		*Name*
'ālep	K K X	Δ Δ Λ	A	alpha
bēt	9 9	ᗴ Ɓ B	B	bēta
gīmel	ᒋ ᒐ	Γ Γ C	Γ	gamma
dālet	Δ Δ Δ	▷ Δ D	Δ	delta
hē	Ⅎ Ⅎ	Ᏻ Ᏻ E	E	e psilon
wāw	Y Y Y	F F Ϲ		digamma
zayin	I ⱶ I	I ⱶ I	I	zēta
ḥēt	ᗷ ᗷ ᗷ	ᗷ ᕼ ᗷ	H	ēta
ṭēt	⊗ ⊕	⊗ ⊕ ⊙	Θ	thēta
yōd	Z Z ᘐ	⟨ ⟩ l	I	iōta
kap	ᴗ ᴠ Y	K Ƙ ᛕ	K	kappa
lāmed	∠ ∠ ∠	L ᒐ Λ	Λ	lambda
mēm	⟨ ⟩ ᛘ	ᛙ ᛙ M	M	mu
nūn	⟨ ⟩ ᛩ	ᛙ ᛙ N	N	nu
sāmek	‡	‡ ‡ ≣	Ξ	ksi
'ayin	O	O	O	o mikron
pē	⟩ ⟨	ᒋ Γ	Γ	pi
ṣādē	ᛙ ᘐ	M		san
qōp	Φ Φ Φ	Φ Φ		qoppa
rēš	ᒯ 4	P D ᖇ	P	rhō
śin/šin	W	⟨ ⟩ ⟨	Ɛ	sigma
tāw	+ X	T	T	tau
		Ɣ Y V	Y	u psilon
		Φ Φ φ	Φ	phi
		X +	X	chi
		Ψ Ψ	Ψ	psi
		Ω Ω Ω	Ω	ō mega

FIGURE 6.1 Phoenician characters and their Greek equivalents. Adapted from Peter T. Daniels and William Bright, eds., *The World's Writing Systems* (Oxford University Press, 1996). Reprinted by permission of Oxford University Press.

LAMP : Riverside Comm

Home   Help   New Search

Search

Keyword ▾ for [   ] in [All RCCD Libraries/Collections]

or Search by:

- Keywords (Advanced)
- Title (Book, Journal, or Periodical)
- Author
- Subject
- Call Number

Greek writing

PA273.W66bla c.1

Toward proposing an answer to these questions, the following discussion is offered.

6.1 Greek Modifications

6.1.1 The Phonemic Inventories

The Greeks not only adopted the Phoenician consonantal writing system but modified it in a quite fundamental manner. Each of the characters of the Phoenician script had only a consonantal value; vowel sounds were not written. The Semitic language of the Phoenicians contained a number of consonantal sounds which were quite alien to Greek. Consider the consonantal inventory of Phoenician:[5]

(1) Stops   p   t   k   ʔ
       b   d   g
       ṭ   q
   Fricatives   s   š   ħ   h
        z   ʕ
        ṣ
   Nasals   m   n
   Liquids   l
        r
   Glides   y   w

With the inventory in (1) compare the smaller and, in part, quite distinct inventory of consonant phonemes found in early first-millennium Greek:[6]

(2) Stops   p   t   k
       p^h t^h k^h
       b   d   g
   Fricatives   s   h
   Nasals   m   n
   Liquids   l
        r
   Glides   w

Most striking are the differences between the systems of stops and fricatives (that is the obstruent consonants) of the two languages.

6.1.2 The Creation of Vowel Characters

Owing to this variation in the consonantal inventory of the two languages, the Greek adapters had at their disposal a set of Canaanite graphic characters which had no closely matching phonetic value in their own language. As is well known, to certain of these leftover consonant symbols, the Greek scribes assigned vowel values and thus created the first alphabetic writing system to represent systematically both consonant and vowel sounds.[7] In the Phoenician script the symbol *'alep* was used to represent a glottal stop /ʔ/;[8] as Greek had no such consonant phoneme, *'alep* was utilized by the Greek adapters to represent the vowel *a* (both long and short); that is, this symbol was borrowed as the character *alpha*. Phoenician *'ayin* represented a voiced pharyngeal fricative /ʕ/, a commonly occurring consonant among the Semitic languages but grossly unlike any sound which Greek possessed.[9] To *'ayin* the Greek adapters assigned the value *o* (i.e., /ọ:/, /ǫ:/, and /ǒ/), calling the symbol *ou,* later *omicron*. The Phoenician letter *he* represented the sound /h/—a sound which also occurred in Greek (though not in all dialects). However, Phoenician *he* was not utilized by the Greek adapters to spell *h* (for this, Phoenician *ḥet*, /ħ/,[10] was appropriated) but was instead used to represent the vowel *e* (i.e., /ẹ:/, /ę:/ and /ĕ/), and to which was given the name *ei,* later *epsilon*. Phoenician *yod* and *waw,* the symbols for the glides /y/ and /w/, were also adopted by the Greeks as vowel characters and were utilized to spell long and short /i/ *(iota)* and long and short /u/ (called *u,* later *upsilon*)[11] respectively. In summary, then, the Greeks utilized Phoenician consonantal characters for representation of Greek vowel phonemes as follows:

(3)　A. *'alep*; /ʔ/　→　*alpha*; /a:/ and /ă/
　　　B. *he*; /h/　→　*epsilon*; /ę:/, /ẹ:/, and /ĕ/)
　　　C. *'ayin*; /ʕ/　→　*omicron*; /ọ:/, /ǫ:/, and /ŏ/
　　　D. *yod*; /y/　→　*iota*; /i:/ and /ĭ/
　　　E. *waw*; /w/　→　*upsilon*; /u:/ and /ŭ/

In addition to the vowel characters of (3), distinct symbols for /ẹ:/ and /ọ:/ were devised in particular local, or epichoric, Greek alphabets. Certain Greek dialects such as East Ionic and Cretan lacked the sound /h/. In the scripts of these *psilotic* dialects, Phoenician *ḥet* was utilized as a vowel character (i.e., *eta*) in order differentiate /ę:/ from the other mid front vowels.[12] In various alphabets, including that of Ionia, a symbol with the corresponding back value /ǫ:/ was eventually created; this letter, *omega,* was apparently derived from *omicron* by opening up one side of this circular symbol.[13]

6.1.3 Changes in Consonantal Values

The assigning of vowel values to certain consonantal characters was not the only change which the Greek adapters of the Phoenician writing system effected; the value of a number of the Semitic symbols which continued to be used for representing consonants was likewise altered. These adjustments in consonantal value were a consequence of the significant variation in the system of stops and fricatives which we have seen displayed by these two languages. For example, typical of Semitic languages, Phoenician possessed a set of so-called emphatic consonants: namely, those represented by the symbols /ṣ/, /ṭ/, and /q/. Like these symbols, the label *emphatic* is little more than a phonetically nondescriptive cover term.[14] The actual phonetic realization of the emphatic consonants of the modern Semitic languages differs from language to language, and even within a single language; however, the emphatics are generally consonant sounds which are produced while, in one way or another, modifying the shape of the back portion of the vocal tract (a process which involves the production of a "secondary articulation") or while forcefully ejecting air out of or into the mouth by raising or lowering the glottis. Though the precise phonetic nature of the emphatic consonants of Phoenician cannot be determined with precision, it is quite probable that they were similar to corresponding emphatics in the modern languages; we will have more to say concerning these consonants later.[15] The Greek language had no such emphatic consonants, and so these Phoenician symbols were utilized for spelling other kinds of consonantal sounds by the adapting scribes: *ṭet*, /ṭ/, became *theta* (representing a voiceless aspirated dental stop /tʰ/); *qop*, /q/, yielded *qoppa* (the symbol used to spell a /k/ which occurred in the vicinity of a rounded vowel), and *ṣade*, /ṣ/, was adopted as *san*, the character which was used in certain epichoric Greek alphabets to represent /s/.

6.1.3.1 *Phoenician* Samek

Another consonantal letter transformation—one which is strikingly curious— involved the Phoenician character *samek*. Semitic *samek* represented the dental fricative /s/; to this character, however, the Greek adapters ascribed not the value /s/ but that of the sequence /k/ + /s/; that is, *samek* is the source of the Greek letter *xi*. Owing to its position deep within the alphabet (the same position as that occupied by Phoenician *samek*), it is generally held, and reasonably so, that *xi* is a component of the earliest Greek alphabet rather than being some later addition. That provision should have been made in the new alphabetic system of Greek—the first thoroughgoing alphabetic system—for a character with the value /k/ + /s/ seems a manifestly inappropriate measure given the essential alphabetic strategy of "one grapheme = one sound." That is to say, the advantage which an alphabet offers over a syllabary (the other type of phonetic writing system) is one of simplicity: in an alphabetic script, a character is required only for each individual sound, rather than for each possible syllabic combination of consonant(s) and vowel (or some subset of these possible combinations, as is the case with both Linear B and the Cypriot Syllabary). To create a symbol with the value /k/ + /s/ in an alphabetic system in which there is also a symbol with the value /k/ and a symbol with the value /s/ is, hence, to encumber unnecessarily the system—to fail to utilize the very principle that was exploited in the creation of the vowel characters. When a consonantal sequence /ks/ can simply be written with a *k* followed by an *s*, what could possibly have motivated the Greek adapters of the Phoenician script to include in the new alphabetic system a character having the highly idiosyncratic value /k/ + /s/?

Before pursuing the answer to the question raised in the preceding paragraph, I would point out that there of course also occurred in the Greek alphabet a character which represents the consonantal sequence /p/ + /s/, that is, the letter *psi*. As I discuss later, quite fundamental differences between *xi* and *psi* reveal an asymmetric treatment of the sequences /k/ + /s/ and /p/ + /s/. This asymmetry, I believe, will be seen to be of acute significance in our attempt to elucidate the origin of the Greek alphabet.

6.1.3.2 The Phoenician Sibilant Characters

The account of the development of Greek *xi* from Phoenician *samek* which could perhaps be referred to as "standard" is offered by Lillian Jeffery in her masterful and influential work *The Local Scripts of Archaic Greece*. According to Jeffery, in the process of borrowing the Phoenician script, the Greeks confused the names and phonetic values of the four Semitic sibilant[16] characters: *zayin, samek, ṣade,* and *shin.* To each of these Phoenician letters, Jeffery assigns the following values:

(4) A. *zayin* [z] (as in *z*ip)
　　 B. *samek* [s] (as in *s*ip)
　　 C. *ṣade* [ts] (she appears to be indicating a dental affricate,[17] as in German *Z*ipfel, 'tassel')
　　 D. *shin* [š] (as in *sh*ip)[18]

Simply in terms of position within the alphabet (i.e., alphabetic order), these Phoenician sibilant symbols correspond to Greek characters as follows:

(5) A. *zayin* = *zeta*
　　 B. *samek* = *xi*
　　 C. *ṣade* = *san*
　　 D. *shin* = *sigma*

Jeffery identifies the consonantal value of each of the Greek letters in (5) as the following (it appears Jeffery construes these as the "original" values of the Greek characters):

(6) A. *zeta* [ds] or [sd]
　　 B. *xi* [kš]
　　 C. *san* [z]
　　 D. *sigma* [s][19]

6.1.3.2.1 A Case of Confusion? While the linear sequence of letter-shapes which occurred in the Phoenician script was preserved by the Greek adapters, Jeffery contends that the names and phonetic values of *zayin* and *ṣade* were reversed, as were the names and phonetic values of *samek* and *shin:*[20]

(7) A. *zayin*　　*zeta*
　　 B. *samek*　　*xi*
　　 C. *ṣade*　　*san*
　　 D. *shin*　　*sigma*

In other words, *zayin* provided a name and a value for *san* (rather than for *zeta*), likewise *ṣade* for *zeta* (rather than for *san*), *samek* for *sigma* (rather than for *xi*), and *shin* for *xi* (rather than for *sigma*). She bases this conclusion upon the dual similarity which she perceives to exist in the forms of these Semitic[21] and Greek letter-names and in their respective phonetic values:[22]

(8)   A. *zayin,* [z]   ≈   *san,* [z]
      B. *samek,* [s]   ≈   *sigma,* [s]
      C. *ṣade,* [ts]   ≈   *zeta,* [ds] or [sd]
      D. *shin,* [š]   ≈   *xi,* [kš]

How could such a confusion of letter-name and letter-value vis-à-vis letter-shape as described in the preceding paragraph possibly have arisen? Jeffery contends that this is a consequence of the learning of the alphabet being a two-faceted process: the learner must learn both (i) the name (and, following from this, the value, as this is encoded in the name[23]) of the characters in their proper order (which she identifies as an aural memory process) and (ii) the shape of the characters (the corresponding visual memory process). She cites accounts from antiquity (though none of these is concerned with Greek practice specifically) which describe children as first learning the names of the letters of the alphabet and only subsequently acquiring knowledge of letter-shapes.[24] As a consequence of the dual nature of this learning process, Jeffery argues, the Greek adapters of the Phoenician script were able to learn correctly the order of letter-shapes while, at the same time, confusing the sequence of letter-names (and, with that, values). Since this confusion occurred in the aural, rather than the visual, component of the learning process, she proposes that the Greeks learned the Semitic script not primarily by repetition of the character-names in their proper order (as is, in contrast, the case now with preschool children who learn the English alphabet by singing a ditty) but by focusing upon the graphic representations of the Phoenician characters and only upon their names individually (rather than in running sequence): "[T]he first Greeks learnt their alphabet more from concentrating on the written row and applying the names than from continuous oral repetition."[25, 26]

6.1.3.2.2 Problems with the Case for Confusion?

Jeffery's confusion hypothesis is not altogether convincing.[27] To begin with, it is not at all obvious that the way in which children learn the alphabet conventionally used for spelling their language offers a close parallel to that monumental procedure by which adults—probably professional scribes—went about adapting a foreign writing system for use in recording their own language. Beyond that, a hypothesis which must make recourse to a blunder of such a fundamental nature on the part of adapters who so skillfully and elegantly converted a consonantal script into one which represents both consonants and vowels strains for credibility. Later I offer a counterproposal which holds that there was no confusion of the aural vis-à-vis the visual, but that, quite to the contrary, the assignment of Greek values to the Phoenician sibilant graphemes was a deliberate process not unlike the assignment of vowel values to certain Semitic consonant characters. To demonstrate this, we must give careful consideration to each of the Greek letters which is derived from a Phoenician sibilant character, and this examination turns our attention once again to the Greek letter having the CC value of [k] + [s]. However, prior to beginning my discussion of *xi,* I must first say something about how the various local alphabets of the Greeks are classified.

6.2 The Epichoric Alphabets

6.2.1 Blue and Red

The ancient Greek peoples utilized a variety of regional alphabets. These fall into two major families, an eastern group and a western group. Conventionally and conveniently these two divisions have been identified as *blue* and *red* respectively, after the colors utilized by A. Kirchhoff in marking the distribution of alphabet-types on the map appearing in his work *Studien zur Geschichte des griechischen Alphabets*.[28] The blue alphabets are further divided into *dark blue* and *light blue* varieties. This classificatory scheme is based primarily upon the order and value that the various local alphabets assigned to the so-called supplemental letters φ, χ, and ψ, that is, those consonantal characters of the Greek alphabet which were added to the end of the adopted Phoenician script (see figure 6.2). In the blue and red alphabets alike, the character φ represents a voiceless aspirated bilabial stop [p^h]. The dark blue and light blue alphabets further share in common the value of the letter χ, in both of which this is the symbol for [k^h], the voiceless aspirated velar stop. The two blue varieties differ, however, in that while the dark blue alphabets represent the *stop + fricative* combination [ps] by the character ψ, the light blue alphabets use the sequential spelling φσ (and lack the character ψ).[29] This variation is paralleled by the representation of the [ks] sequence: in dark blue alphabets [ks] is represented by the letter ξ, while in light blue alphabets it is written componentially as χσ (and there is no symbol ξ). In the red alphabets χ is the symbol used to designate the sequence [ks] (ξ does not occur),[30] while ψ represents the voiceless aspirated velar stop [k^h].[31] These alphabets share in common with the light blue alphabets the spelling φσ for the sequence [ps].[32]

If we draw upon the treatment of the epichoric alphabets which is found in Jeffery 1990, we can separate those scripts into the three classes of dark blue, light blue, and red. Not surprisingly, for certain regions there is variation in the type of alphabet used or some uncertainty as to type, due to a paucity of inscriptions; see figure 6.3.

	Red	Dark Blue	Light Blue
φ	[p^h]	[p^h]	[p^h]
χ	[k] + [s]	[k^h]	[k^h]
ψ	[k^h]	[p] + [s]	—
ξ	—	[k] + [s]	—
	φσ = [p] + [s]		φσ = [p] + [s]
			χσ = [k] + [s]

FIGURE 6.2 Character values in red, dark blue, and light blue alphabets.

(9) A. Dark blue alphabets: Corinth and Corcyra; Megara; Sicyon; Phlius, Cleo-
nae and Tiryns; Argos and Mycenae; Megara Hyblaia and Selinus; certain of the Ionic islands of the Aegean (e.g., Ceos); the Ionic Dodecapolis and colonies; Cnidus[33] and Halicarnassus; Aeolis;[34] Chalcidice,
Chalcedon and other northern colonial areas.[35] In Aetolia and Syracuse[36]
both blue and red-type alphabets were in use.

B. Light blue alphabets: Attica; Aegina and Cydonia; certain of the Ionic
islands of the Aegean (e.g., Paros and Thasos; Naxos[37] and Amorgos)

C. Red alphabets: Euboea and colonies; Boeotia; Thessaly; Phocis; the Lo-
crides and colonies; the Eastern Argolid; Arcadia; Elis; Laconia, Taras
and Messenia; Ithaca and Cephallania; Achaea and colonies; Gela and
Akragas; Rhodes.[38] In Aetolia and Syracuse[39] both red and blue alphabets were in use.

6.2.2 Green or Primitive

In addition, Kirchhoff marked as *green* the alphabets of Crete, Thera, and
Melos. Of all the Greek alphabets, this group of *primitives,* as they are commonly designated and to which also belong the alphabets of Anaphe and Si-
cinos, bear the greatest similarity to the Phoenician script; this is particularly
so in the case of the Cretan alphabet.[40] Furthermore, the primitives are distinguished from the other alphabets of the Greeks by the regular absence both of
the supplemental letters and of a character having the value [ks]. The latter is
spelled sequentially as κM (the primitives use M, *san,* rather than *sigma* for
[s][41]); similarly, the cluster [ps] is spelled πM, rather than by utilizing the
supplemental character (dark blue) ψ (compare the sequential spelling $\phi\sigma$ in the
light blue and red alphabets). In the same fashion, in the alphabets of Thera
and Melos the aspirated stops [p^h] and [k^h] are spelled sequentially as πh and
κh respectively (rather than by utilizing ϕ and (blue) χ or (red) ψ); h is here a
transcription of the Greek letter *eta,* which in these alphabets represented the
consonant [h] as well as a long mid front vowel.

6.2.2.1 Cretan Aspirated Stops

The treatment of the aspirated stops in the Cretan alphabet requires some attention. In contrast to the spelling of these sounds in the alphabets of Thera and
Melos, in the Cretan script [p^h] and [k^h] are represented simply as π and κ
respectively; that is, no orthographic distinction is made between [p] and [p^h]
or between [k] and [k^h]. The Cretan dialect, like the dialects of East Ionic,
Lesbian, and Elean, lost the fricative [h] which had developed word-initially
from earlier *[s]. Thus, Cretan is a so-called psilotic dialect.[42] As a consequence of having no [h] sound, the Cretan letter *eta* represented only the long
e-vowel and did not have the dual value which it had in the alphabets of Thera
and Melos.

Jeffery suggests that the loss of the aspirate in the Cretan dialect is the
probable reason for the nonoccurrence of characters with the value of [p^h] and
[k^h] in the Cretan alphabet; in other words, she supposes that [p^h] and [k^h] also

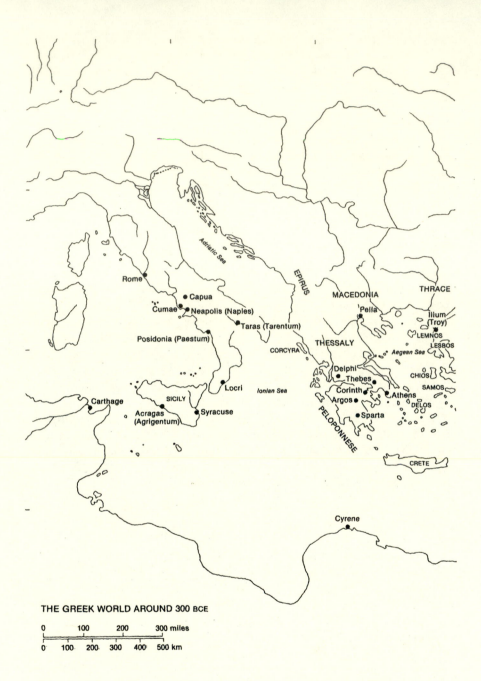

THE GREEK WORLD AROUND 300 BCE

| 0 | 100 | 200 | 300 miles |

| 0 | 100 | 200 | 300 | 400 | 500 km |

FIGURE 6.3 Map of Greece and the Aegean World. Adapted from J. Boardman et al., *The Oxford History of the Classical World* (Oxford University Press, 1986), with the permission of Oxford University Press.

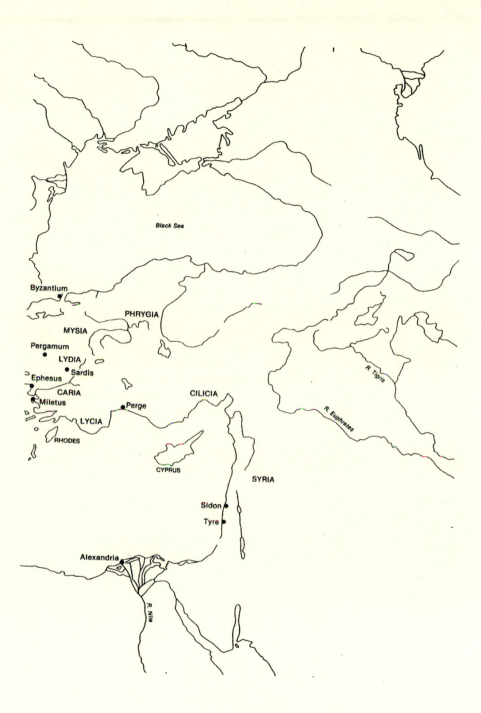

Black Sea

Byzantium

PHRYGIA

MYSIA

Pergamum

LYDIA

Ephesus • Sardis

CARIA

Miletus

LYCIA • Perge

CILICIA

RHODES

CYPRUS

SYRIA

R. Tigris

R. Euphrates

Sidon •

Tyre •

Alexandria •

R. Nile

lost their element of aspiration.[43] However, those dialects in which the consonant [h] was lost do not show a concomitant *deaspiration* of the aspirated stops.
Recall that Proto-Greek *[s] became [h] in two contexts: (i) word-internally
between two vowels; and (ii) at the beginning of a word when the sound which
followed was either a vowel, nasal, liquid, or [w]. In general, the resulting [h]
was eventually lost (i) word-internally and (ii) word-initially except when followed by a vowel or by the liquid [r]. *Psilosis* is simply a dialect-specific
extension of [h]-deletion in word-initial context when a vowel or [r] follows;
psilosis does not affect the aspiration component of the voiceless aspirated
stops.[44]

Cretan is, of course, unlike the other psilotic dialects in that it is characterized by the aforementioned absence of an orthographic recording of the presence of aspiration in [pʰ] and [kʰ]; notice, however, that it does so mark aspiration in the case of [tʰ]; that is, the Cretan alphabet contains both τ ([t]) and θ
([tʰ]). The utilization of this latter spelling distinction speaks loudly for the
existence of voiceless aspirated stops in Cretan, at least at the dental articulation position; but beyond that, there is quite strong evidence for the persistence
of Cretan [pʰ] and [kʰ] as well.[45] We find, for instance, that upon the adoption
of the Attic alphabet (beginning in the fourth century[46]), which contained symbols for both [pʰ] and [kʰ], the Cretans correctly distinguished in their spelling
between π and φ and between κ and χ; in other words, it was known exactly
where the voiced aspirated characters were to be used.

One could perhaps argue that the correct usage of the Attic [pʰ] and [kʰ]
characters was the result of the influence of the Attic dialect upon Cretan speakers who were seeking to spell "properly"; however, there is clear evidence that
the Cretans were actually spelling words as they pronounced them in their own
dialect. Like various other dialects, Cretan is characterized by instances of metathesis of aspiration, as seen, for example, in the following sixth-century
Cretan forms: θροπαν ([**tʰropan**], accusative); cf. Attic τροφήν ([**tropʰ**ế:n],
'subsistence'[47]); θυκαγαθαι ([**tʰükagatʰai**], dative); cf. Attic τύχἀγαθῇ ([**tük**ʰ-
agatʰệ:i] 'by the gods' good favor'). In these cases the *[[-aspirated] . . . [+ as-
pirated]]* stop sequence undergoes metathesis of the aspiration component to
produce the sequence *[[+ aspirated]] . . . [[-aspirated]]*. With the adoption of
the Attic script, instances of metathesis which were previously hidden by the
Cretan alphabetic orthography are revealed. Thus, we find, for example, in
the third century: καυχωι ([kaukʰǫ:i], dative); cf. Attic χαλκός ([kʰalkós],
'copper'); Αχαντω ([akʰantǫ:], genitive of a proper name Ακανθος
([akantʰos])).[48] The first of these examples also demonstrates a peculiar Cretan
phonetic and orthographic trait: the quality of [l] in certain contexts was of a
velar nature, and, accordingly, in these contexts it was at times represented
orthographically as *u*.[49] It is clearly the case that in these instances the Cretans
were not mimicking either Attic orthography or Attic pronunciation (this is
particularly obvious with the first example) but were accurately rendering their
own dialectal pronunciation. In doing so, they reveal a phonological change
which had begun to occur by at least the sixth century and the continued occurrence of voiceless aspirated stops in their dialect.

Regarding Cretan psilosis, it should be pointed out that there is one bit of inscriptional evidence which has been taken to suggest that Cretan word-initial [h] was lost subsequent to the acquisition of the alphabet. As described by Jeffery, in the refuse of the 1900 excavation of the Minoan palace at Phaistos, a sherd dating to the sixth or fifth century was discovered on which was inscribed *Ηερακλες*—the divine name *Heracles*.[50] Guarducci has proposed that the value of *eta (H)* is here [h];[51] this interpretation entails that Cretan *eta* originally represented [h], that [h] was then lost from the Cretan dialect, that in response *eta* was assigned its regularly attested Cretan value of a long *e*, and that this inscription preserves the earlier value. As Bile has pointed out, however, there are alternative interpretations of the spelling which do not contradict the otherwise regular psilotic character of Cretan. For instance, *Ηε*– may be an occurrence of the type of "hyper-spelling" of long *e* which is found in the seventh-century Theran *ηεμι* for [ẹ:mi], 'I am'.[52] Beyond this, it is not even certain that this inscription is written in the Cretan alphabet. Jeffery notes that the archaic alphabet of Phaistos is typical Cretan, but the script of this sherd is like that of Cydonia, which, being a colony of Aigina, uses the blue alphabet of Aigina. Moreover, the inscription appears to have been scratched in the sherd after the pottery of which it was a part had been broken. Consequently, Jeffery speculates that the graffito could possibly have been the handiwork of a Cydoniate tourist in antiquity or, in light of certain oddities, even a modern hoax.[53]

6.2.2.1.1 Powell on the Cretan Aspirated Stops. In his recent work on the origin of the Greek alphabet, Powell has advocated the position that the Cretan dialect did lack aspirated stops.[54] Yet, as demonstrated above, it is almost certain that Cretan possessed both of the sounds [pʰ] and [kʰ] as well as [tʰ]. Powell actually makes brief reference to some of the evidence which reveals this, but he passes over it quickly.[55] Regarding the *τ* verses *θ* opposition, he suggests that the value of the latter character had become either that of a fricative or an affricate;[56] though further along in his discussion, he in fact actually allows that even within such a proposed alphabetic system, there are certain instances in which the character *θ* continues to represent a stop:

(10) [T]he positions of *θ* and *τ* within the series [by which term he is referring to the alphabet exclusive of the supplemental characters] encouraged the continued use of these signs, although to *θ* in *some cases at least* was assigned the value of fricative (or affricate). (emphasis is mine)[57]

Powell's conclusion that the Cretan dialect lacked aspirated stops appears to be demanded by his theory that the Greek alphabet at the stage at which it came to Crete already possessed the supplemental characters *φ* ([pʰ]), *χ* ([kʰ]) and *ψ* ([ps]).[58] He argues that because these letters are not attested in the Cretan script, the dialect of Crete must have lacked aspirated stops such as [pʰ] and [kʰ]; if the dialect had possessed aspirated stops, the supplementals *φ* and *χ* should have been used on Crete. In defense of his position that aspirated stops did not occur in the Cretan dialect, he reasons as follows:

(11)   For had the early Cretan receivers [of the alphabet] clearly heard aspirated
        stops, but never received the supplementals, surely they would have written
        [ph] as πh and [kh] as κh (⁹h) [where *h* represents *eta* with the value [h]],
        as did in fact Melos and Thera, who can only have taken their script from
        Crete at a time when *(h)eta* could still have the value [h].[59]

This claim calls for comment. To begin with, Powell has presumed that the
alphabets of Thera and Melos acquired the practice of using *eta* to represent
both [h] and long *e* from the Cretan alphabetic tradition. This need not be the
case; it is equally possible that this dual function of *eta* was taken over from
the Ionic alphabet of neighboring islands, as Jeffery has pointed out.[60] There is
an even more serious problem with this line of analysis, however. Powell is
claiming that Cretan did not have aspirated bilabial and velar stops since the
spellings πh and κh are not *attested*. But if *eta* ever had the value [h] in the
Cretan alphabet, this condition existed in a prehistoric stage of this script (as
termed by Bile, "un système reconstruit"[61]). Recall that there is only one
Cretan form possibly preserving *eta* with the value [h], and this is quite dubious. The phonological loss of [h] from the Cretan dialect (psilosis) precedes
the attestation of the alphabet. Consequently, if [pʰ] and [kʰ] were ever spelled
by the Cretans as πh and κh respectively, this spelling also belonged to a prehistoric (i.e., unattested) stage of the alphabet and belonged *only* to such a
stage. Once *eta* had ceased to have any value other than long *e* (as a consequence of the loss of the consonant [h]), which is its only value in the attested
stages of the Cretan alphabet, πh and κh could no longer have been used to
represent aspirated stops and so, of course, would not in any event be attested.

6.2.2.2 Supplemental Characters and the Primitive Scripts

The primitive (or green) alphabet-type lacks the supplemental characters φ, χ,
and ψ, as well as the (nonsupplemental) letter ξ. Does the nonoccurrence of the
supplemental characters in the primitive scripts indicate that these letters had
not yet become a part of the Greek alphabet when it first arrived in Crete (and
Thera and Melos)? This interpretation has been generally accepted. Yet, as Jeffery has pointed out,[62] following this line of reasoning would also lead to the
conclusion that the Greek alphabet which made its way to Crete was likewise
without ξ. While this character may not be found in Greek materials from
Crete, it does occur in alphabetic inscriptions from Praisos (in the east of Crete)
which are written in the Eteocretan language.[63] Furthermore, this dark blue *xi*
occurs in the alphabet of Thera, and in Theran inscriptions it is regularly used
in lieu of ζ for spelling the initial consonant of the name **Z**eus;[64] in fact, the
letter *zeta* does not occur in the Theran script.[65]

In the preceding pages we have seen two related attempts to account phonologically for the nonoccurrence of the supplementals φ and χ in the primitive
alphabet-type. Jeffery concludes that the Cretan dialect had no aspirated stops
since it was psilotic, but this is a connection which ought not be made. Powell
seems (at least at one point) to make the proper distinction between psilosis
and deaspiration of stops, but he still goes on to contend, despite weighty evi-

dence to the contrary, that aspirated stops do not occur[66] in the Cretan dialect. As we indicated above, it appears that for Powell the conclusion that Cretan phonology lacked aspirated stops is a necessary one, required by his greater thesis "that the supplementals belonged to the earliest alphabet."[67]

The Cretan dialect, I have argued, did indeed possess aspirated stops; however, the earliest attested form of the Cretan alphabet lacked symbols for [pʰ] and [kʰ], spelling these simply as π and κ respectively. It is possible that this disparity of sound and symbol does in fact indicate that at that time at which the Greek alphabet was acquired by Cretan speakers, it had not yet had appended to it the symbols φ, χ, and ψ; but it does not of necessity indicate this. There are obviously other possible interpretations of the impoverished state of the Cretan alphabet, such as the following: (i) the Cretans acquired a form of the alphabet which possessed the supplementals, but they intentionally chose not to utilize them; or (ii) the Cretans acquired a form of the alphabet which had already been tampered with by some earlier group of innovators who had removed the supplementals. Whatever the motivating force behind the nonoccurrence of φ and χ in the primitive alphabet-type, this condition is likely to be linked with the general absence of characters with the values [ks] and [ps]. These issues are bound up with the greater problem of the early modifications of the alphabet and will be considered further below when we turn our attention to that matter.

6.3 The Greek Letter *Xi*

6.3.1 Greek [kš]?

In terms of the linear arrangement of graphemes, as we have discussed already, the Greek letter which corresponds to the Phoenician character *samek* is *xi* (i.e., that consonantal symbol which has the value [ks]). Again, Jeffery claims that with the adoption of the Phoenician script, the Greeks confused the name and value of *samek* with the name and value of *shin*; so, in other words, Greek *xi* should have the value of Phoenician *shin*. Recall, however, that the value of Phoenician *shin* is [š]. If we imagine for the moment that such a *samek/shin* reversal occurred, the question which then immediately presents itself is, "How did *xi*, the Greek character which inherited the value of *shin* ([š]), come to represent the *stop* + *fricative* sequence [k] + [s]?" To answer this question Jeffery proposes the following scenario.[68] When the Greek adapters of the Semitic script attempted to verbalize the [š] sound of Phoenician *shin*, the best they could do—since Greek had no phoneme /š/—"may have been something like" [kš] (hence the *original* value assigned to *xi* in (8) above). These Greek adapters then passed along to the remainder of the Greeks an alphabet in which there was a character ξ having the approximate value [kš]. For most of the Greek speakers to whom the new alphabet came, she says, this sign was then of no use since they lacked [š] in their dialects. However, she continues, the speakers of those dialects—or some subset of such dialects—which are written with the dark blue alphabet-type (the only type of alphabet that maintains the *xi* character which continues the graphic shape of Phoenician *samek*) must, in fact, have had, "originally at least," an [š] sound.[69]

If there existed a dialect, or dialects, marked by the possession of a fricative [š], it, or they, would surely have constituted only some part of the totality of dialects which utilized the dark blue alphabet, as Jeffery allows. This particular script, as I indicated above, is the Ionic and Corinth-Argos alphabet-type and hence is a writing system used by a dialectally highly heterogeneous group of Ionic, Aeolic, and Doric speakers. If this [š] existed, it was surely not a trait common to all such speakers. Further along in her discussion of Greek *xi,* Jeffery posits that only speakers of Ionic possessed this fricative [š], stating that the sound "was alien to the *purer* Greek dialects, but may have been less so among those of Ionia (which, it will be recalled, differed perceptibly among themselves . . . , and must in some cases, e.g. Miletos, have owed something to their contact with the non-Greek races of Caria and Lydia)"[70] (emphasis is mine).

A number of points in this scenario require comment. Citing work by Carpenter, Jeffery holds that the Greek acquisition of the Phoenician script must have taken place in a bilingual community. This is undoubtedly the case. Recall that the Greek adapters of this script are supposed to be responsible for assigning the value [kš] to the new Greek letter ξ; it is they, in Jeffery's words, who gave "to the Semitic *samek*-sign the name and value of *shin, sh,* as near as their tongue could get to it, which may have been something like *ksh.*"[71] Are we to believe that the Phoenician-speaking Greeks of this community who adapted the Semitic script for Greek use went around speaking a kind of Phoenician in which [kš] was substituted for each occurrence of [š]? For example, did these Greeks pronounce Phoenician [š-r-š] ('root') as [kš-r-kš]? If Greek speakers had difficulty correctly producing the [š] sound of Phoenician *shin,* for these speakers to produce this sound in combination with a preceding velar stop would almost surely have involved considerably greater difficulty still. In the event that they could not manage [š], it is most likely that these speakers would have simply substituted [s] in its place, as did, for example, the Greek physician-herbalist Dioscurides in his transcription of [š-r-š] as συρις[72]—this is the regular Greek transcription. It is quite improbable that these Greek adapters of the Semitic script would have squandered the Phoenician character *samek* by assigning to it a value which was (i) not its value in Phoenician, *and* (ii) a value which it did not have for the Greek adapters as they spoke Phoenician, *and* (iii) a value which would have rendered the symbol of no use to the adapters in recording their own Greek speech. Better uses could have been made of this symbol than putting it into service for representing a nonsense-cluster, such as utilizing it to represent [kʰ] or [pʰ], aspirated stop consonants for which non-Phoenician symbols had to be appropriated. Assigning such values to the Phoenician symbol for [š] would have required a willingness on the part of the adapters to be arbitrary of course. But such arbitrariness is exactly what we see in their appropriation of certain Semitic consonant symbols for the representation of Greek vowels. The character *xi* was not introduced into the Greek alphabet because of lead-tongued Greeks.

6.3.2 Greek [š]?

As we have seen above, Jeffery claims that the *xi* character which has the form
of Phoenician *samek* (i.e., blue *xi* (ξ)) was preserved in the dark blue alphabets,
and only in these, because the dialects of those speakers who wrote with this
form of the alphabet, or some dialectal subset thereof, were actually characterized by the occurrence of a phonetic sequence [kš]—the value which she claims
the Greek adapters of the Phoenician script assigned to Semitic *shin* ([š]) as a
consequence of articulatory inability. We have found the articulatory ineptness
theory to be highly improbable and have rejected it. Something approaching
Jeffery's account of the development of blue *xi* (ξ) could only be maintained
by adding to it the requirement that the Greek adapters of the Semitic script
were themselves speakers of a dialect which contained the fricative [š]. Let us
explore this possibility.

To begin with, the evidence indicates that the single sibilant consonant of
early Greek was simply a dental or alveolar fricative [s].[73] When Greek words
containing *s* are transcribed using the scripts of languages which possess both
/s/ and /š/ fricative phonemes, it is the /s/ phoneme character which is used to
transcribe the Greek sound. For example, on Indic coins Λυσίου ([lüsíu:],
proper name) is transcribed as *Lisikasa*, Διονυσίου ([dionüsíu:], proper name)
as *Dianisiyasa*, and Ἱπποστράτου ([hippostrátu:], proper name) as *Hipastra-
tasa*; similarly, forms occur in Coptic such as *Diomētos* for Διομήδης ([dio-
mę́:dę:s], proper name), *systadikē* for συστατική ([süstatikę́:], 'introductory,
etc.'), and *apoklēsis* for ἀπόκρισις ([apókrisis], 'separation, etc.').[74] The same
is true for Greek words containing the sequence [ks]: for example, Ἀλεξάν–
δρου([aleksándru:], proper name) is attested on a Jewish coin as [ʾl]ksndros[75]
and Φιλοξένου ([pʰiloksénu:], proper name) on Indian coins as *Philasinasa*.[76]

There is, however, at least one allophonic variant of Greek /s/. As was probably already the case in the Indo-European parent language,[77] when /s/ preceded a voiced consonant, it was realized as the voiced fricative [z], that is, it
assimilated in voicing to the following consonant. This is indicated by inscriptional spellings such as Αθεναζε for Ἀθήνασ−δε ('to Athens'), where the
value of ζ is [zd]. In the fourth century B.C., by which time the sequence [zd]
had been reduced to [z], spellings such as Πελαζγικόν ([pelazgikón], 'Pelas-
gian'), rather than Πελασγικόν, begin to be found. At still later periods, that
voicing assimilation has occurred is revealed by transcriptions of Greek words
using scripts which distinguish [s] and [z], as in the case of Gothic *praízbw-
taírei* for πρεσβυτέριον ([presbütérion], 'council of elders').[78]

Is it possible that in the Greek dialect of the adapters of the Phoenician
script, the phoneme /s/ also had an allophonic variant [š], the appearance of
which was conditioned by a preceding velar stop [k]? In other words, in this
dialect, and (adhering generally to Jeffery's scenario) likewise in the dialect of
(at least) that group of Greek speakers who first received the dark blue
alphabet-type, was the phonemic sequence /ks/ realized phonetically as [kš], so
that a word such as ξανθός ('yellow') was pronounced [kšantʰós]? There appears to be no orthographic evidence, such as that presented above, which
would suggest an allophonic relationship of this sort, though if this were an

idiosyncratic and quite localized dialectal phenomenon, the probability of the preservation of such evidence would perhaps be low. However, if this allophonic relationship happened to occur both in the dialect of the adapters and in the dialect of one or more of the recipients of the dark blue alphabet-type, it is not clear that we would actually be faced with a highly localized development.

The realization of /s/ as [š] after /k/ would be a synchronic palatalization process,[79] and, as we saw in chapter 4, palatalization (as in the change of *[-t$^{(h)}$y-] to [-ss-] etc.) is an important phenomenon in the diachronic phonology of Greek, though not one which in any case ultimately gives rise to a fricative phoneme /š/ in antiquity. The palatalization of consonants in Greek, however, is conditioned by a front vowel or a palatal glide [y] following the consonant; this is in fact the precise context which crosslinguistically is most effective in triggering palatalization.[80] Not only does a preceding velar stop not otherwise induce palatalization in Greek, but crosslinguistically such a conditioning context appears to be quite rare.

Excursus 1: A Crosslinguistic Investigation of Palatalization

Excursus 1.1: Type 1 Palatalization.   In order to gauge the naturalness or expectability of palatalization being conditioned by a preceding velar stop, I conducted a typological investigation of synchronic palatalization processes utilizing the Stanford Phonology Archive.[81] Among the 197 languages catalogued in the archive, nineteen[82] possess palato-alveolar consonants (recall that the fricative [š] is palato-alveolar in its place of articulation) which occur as conditioned allophones of some phoneme.[83] Purely for the sake of exposition, I refer to this synchronic allophonic palatalization process as *type 1 palatalization*. In almost every instance these palato-alveolar consonants are allophones of dental/alveolar phonemes, most frequently the fricative /s/ or /z/.[84]

Among the various allophonic processes of this type which are reported for these languages, the most common conditioning environment giving rise to palato-alveolar allophones is that of an *ensuing front vowel*. Allophonic variation of this sort is found in nine languages, and in all nine the front vowel that conditions the change is a high vowel; in addition, in three of these languages, mid front vowels can also induce palatalization, and in one of these three, the conditioning vowel can even be low.[85] The occurrence of a palato-alveolar allophone is induced by an *ensuing consonant* in eight languages, three of which are among those in which the change is also conditioned by a following vowel. In four languages this consonant is the palatal glide [y];[86] and in four others it is a palato-alveolar consonant.[87]

There are far fewer languages in which this type of palatalization is induced by a sound which precedes the target phoneme. In three languages a *preceding front vowel* (a high vowel in two of the languages and either a high or a mid in the third) so effects palatalization, as does a *preceding consonant* in four languages—[y] in two and [n] in two. As in the case of palatalization induced by an ensuing sound, these latter two groups of languages represent partially overlapping subsets: in two languages palatalization is effected by both a preceding front vowel and a preceding palatal glide.[88]

In none of the nineteen languages is it the case that some instances of this type of palatalization are effected by a preceding sound while others are effected by an ensuing sound; that is, the allophonic change is either progressive or regressive for any given language. Notice that in the case of none of these nineteen languages is it reported that the appearance of the palato-alveolar allophone is conditioned by a preceding stop /k/ or, for that matter, by any kind of preceding velar consonant.

Excursus 1.2: Type 2 Palatalization.   In addition to these instances of palatalization processes which give rise to palato-alveolar allophones, the archive catalogues forty-six languages[89] in which certain consonantal phonemes are allophonically palatalized to yield consonants with a secondary palatal articulation, that is, instances in which /C/ becomes [C^y].[90] I refer to this type of allophonic variation as *type 2 palatalization.* The most frequently occurring conditioning factor is again that of an *ensuing front vowel:* for thirty-three of these languages,[91] it is reported that the palatalization of /C/ to [C^y] is so effected. In all but one of the thirty-three, high and/or mid front vowels induce this palatalization;[92] furthermore, in almost one-third of these languages palatalization is also induced by a following low front, central, or high back vowel (in order of decreasing frequency). Palatalization is conditioned by an *ensuing consonant* in fifteen languages: the palatal glide [y] in eleven of these;[93] some other consonant articulated in the palatal (or "prepalatal") region in two languages; and a palato-alveolar affricate [č] or [ǰ] in three languages.[94] Ten of those languages in which palatalization is induced by a following consonant belong to that set of languages in which the change is also conditioned by a following vowel.[95]

The number of languages in which type 2 palatalization is induced by a *preceding vowel or consonant* is on a ratio basis even smaller than in the case of palatalization processes which result in the generation of a palato-alveolar allophone.[96] Among the forty-six languages showing the [C]~[C^y] allophonic variation, a *preceding high front vowel* induces palatalization in five (and in one of these, Sentani, a high back vowel does as well), while only in three languages does palatalization occur under the influence of a *preceding consonant:* in each instance, the consonant is, not surprisingly, the palatal glide [y] (with a preceding [w] also having this effect in Sentani). These three languages in which palatalization is conditioned by a preceding consonant constitute a subset of those in which a preceding vowel induces palatalization.[97] As with type 1 palatalization, in no instance does a preceding velar consonant—[k] or otherwise—induce palatalization.

I pointed out above that for type 1 palatalization, any given language palatalizes either progressively or regressively but not in both directions. In the case of type 2 palatalization this pattern is not adhered to absolutely, but there is a strong tendency toward such complementarity. Only in two of the forty-six languages are consonants palatalized by both preceding and ensuing sounds: Kota appears to be primarily progressive in its palatalizing orientation, though consonants are also palatalized before an ensuing glide [y];[98] and in Sentani the contexts for palatalization are mirror images of one another. Notice, more-

over, that among the sixty-five languages which together comprise the two palatalizing groups considered above, six languages have dual membership; that is,
they are reported as exhibiting both palatalization type 1 and type 2. For five
of these six languages the two types of palatalization are either both progressive
or both regressive.[99] The data thus reveal a strong tendency for palatalization
processes—both type 1 and type 2—to be thoroughly either regressive or progressive for any given language.

Excursus 1.3: Bhat on Palatalization.　In his typological study of palatalization, D. N. S. Bhat considers "about 120 instances of palatalization" which are
drawn from a variety of the world's languages.[100] Among all of the examples
of palatalization which he presents, very few are progressive in direction. Bhat
states, "There are only a limited number of instances in which a front vowel
(or a high back vowel) is reported to have palatalized a following consonant"
(in a number of the examples which he offers, the sound inducing palatalization
is actually [y] or some other consonant, rather than a vowel). He goes on to
define two distinct categories of such progressive palatalization: (i) "instances
in which a language that has undergone extensive palatalization has some limited environments in which the front vowel also palatalizes a *following* consonant" (emphasis is mine); and (ii) "instances in which palatalization appears to
have taken place exclusively as a progressive change."[101] In (i) it is clear from
context that by "extensive palatalization," he means extensive *regressive* palatalization. Taken together these two statements provide independent corrobora-
tion for the observations which I presented above on the basis of my examination of the Stanford Phonology Archive: namely, that (i) in any given language,
palatalization tends to be either consistently progressive or consistently regressive; and (ii) regressive palatalization is substantially more common than progressive palatalization.[102] In addition, among those few instances of progressive
palatalization cited by Bhat, there is only a single example of such palatalization being induced by a preceding velar stop. This is the case of Proto-
Indo-European *[s] being changed to [š] "after i, u (also after k, r . . .)" in
Avestan. The change is in fact common Indo-Iranian,[103] with the Sanskrit
equivalent being the well-known *ruki* rule by which Proto-Indo-European *[s]
becomes retroflex [ṣ] after the long and short high vowels [u] and [i] (including diphthongs which end in these vowels), long and short [r̥], [r] and [k].[104]
What is important to be noted about this Indo-Iranian change is that it is not
induced by [k] alone. In other words, this change occurs after a broad range
of segments, some of which we have seen repeatedly to be highly favorable
for inducing palatalization (i.e., the high vowels, particularly the high front).
On the basis of the evidence presented above from my own investigation and
from Bhat's, it is clear that [k] must be at the low end of any sort of hierarchy
of palatalizing sounds. It is not surprising, then, that if "palatalization" occurs
after [k] in Indo-Iranian, it also occurs after high vowels. It would be highly
surprising if palatalization did not occur after high vowels while it did occur
after [k].

6.3.3 Greek [š]? Continued

The results of my cross linguistic investigation of synchronic palatalization, together with the findings presented by Bhat, indicate that it is quite unlikely that Greek /s/ was palatalized to [š] after [k]. This is so for several reasons. First of all, typological evidence shows that for any given language, there is a strong tendency for palatalization to be consistently either regressive or progressive and, moreover, that progressive palatalization is far less common than regressive. These findings speak against a progressive palatalization of /s/ after [k] in Greek being of high probability; ancient Greek is a language in which palatalization played an important phonological role, but those demonstrable palatalization processes are consistently regressive. Second, and perhaps of much greater significance, is the finding that a preceding velar stop only rarely induces palatalization. The crosslinguistic infrequency of the occurrence of such a palatalizing agent renders its presence in Greek improbable. Beyond that, as we have seen, it would only be expected that such an unlikely palatalizing agent as a preceding [k] could effect the allophonic realization of /s/ as [š] if /s/ were also palatalized after strong inducers of palatalization such as [i] and [e] or [u], and there is no evidence of palatalization occurring after front or high vowels.

6.3.4 The Spelling of a Greek [š]

The last point made leads us to the final matter to be considered with regard to the possible allophonic palatalization of /s/. We have been evaluating the probability, or rather improbability, of the existence of an [š] allophone in ancient Greek. A quite distinct problem which requires attention is that of the orthographic representation of such an allophone, had it existed. Recall that we have here been addressing the possibility of the occurrence of a palatalization process which just happened to characterize both the dialect of the adapters of the Phoenician script and the dialect of the early receivers of the dark blue alphabet-type. I indicated in the preceding paragraph that there is no evidence for the palatalization of /s/ after [i], [e], and so on. But what sort of evidence could we in fact hope to find of such a phonological development? There are no other dialectal phonological phenomena which appear to be triggered by [š] occurring after high or front vowels. Of the Greek words (proper names or loanwords) written in foreign scripts possessing an [š] character, I am not aware of any, from any period, which document a dialectal palatalization of /s/ after a front or high vowel. And there is within the local orthographic traditions of the Greek language no indication of the use of a special character to represent [š] occurring in this context. But, then, would there be? In other words, if [s] were palatalized after [i] or [e] or [u]—or after [k]—would this allophonic variation even be marked orthographically?

It is generally the case that phonographic writing systems[105] do not spell allophonically; that is to say, orthographic representation tends to be phonemic.[106] For example, the voiceless stops of English occur as aspirated allophones in certain contexts (e.g., in word-initial position) and as unaspirated in others (e.g., after tautosyllabic [s]); thus, the /p/ of *pie* is realized as [pʰ] while that of *spy* is [p], without aspiration. This allophonic variation is not registered by English orthography, but in the case of both words the spelling of the bilabial stop reflects its underlying or phonemic value /p/. As here, spelling is usually phonemic; though, as we shall see, there do exist exceptions to this general tendency.

Since alphabetic spelling tends to be phonemic, it is most probable that even if Greek /s/ had an allophone [š] which occurred after front or high vowels, this allophonic variation would not have been represented graphically. That having been said, it must be pointed out, however, that there is one set of allophonic variants which curiously are orthographically distinguished in early, though not in later, Greek alphabets. There occurred in the Phoenician script a character *kap* which represented the voiceless velar stop [k]. In adapting the script for Greek use, the Greek scribes essentially (speaking in broad phonetic terms) preserved the Semitic value of the character; that is, *kap* is the source of the Greek letter *kappa*. The Phoenician language also possessed, as discussed above, an "emphatic" velar stop, which was represented by the letter *qop*. As Greek had no such velarized or pharyngealized consonants, *qop*, or *qoppa* as the Greeks named it, was used to represent an allophone of /k/ which occurred before the high and mid back vowels represented by *upsilon* and *omicron* respectively (a liquid [l] or [r] could optionally intervene between /k/ and the back vowel).[107] *Qoppa*, which must represent a type of backed [k] allophone, had disappeared from all of the Greek alphabets by some period within the fifth century.[108] Like all languages, ancient Greek must have been characterized by a number of allophonic relations, even if only very subtle ones; but with the exception of the *kappa* versus *qoppa* distinction[109] (and possibly one other distinction to be discussed below), these are not marked orthographically.[110]

Bearing all of the preceding in mind, let us now suppose, for the sake of further exploration, that /s/ was indeed palatalized to [š] after [k] in the dialect of the Greek adapters of the Phoenician script, and let us further suppose that this allophonic variation was represented orthographically. If this were so, how would [š] then be written? The Greek adapters had at their disposal a Phoenician character, *shin*, with this very value [š]. For whatever reason, as we saw in (5) above, *shin* was adopted as Greek *sigma*; that is, it was assigned the value [s]. One of the other sibilant characters of Phoenician, such as *samek*, could then have been assigned the value [š] by the Greek adapters. Obviously this did not happen; *samek* is (as we have been discussing) the Semitic letter which was adopted as Greek *xi*—the Greek character having the original value [kš] according to Jeffery's interpretation. We have seen that the Greek adapters of the Phoenician script were able to recognize the difference between [k] and its backed allophonic variant—a difference probably somewhat analogous to that between the initial consonants of English *k*eep and *c*ool. This is a subtle difference, and one whose recognition reveals significant phonetic sophistication on the part of the adapters. Scribes of such sophistication would certainly not have needed to lump together clumsily the allophonic variant [š] and the preceding sound [k], which we are now supposing to have conditioned the occurrence of [š], into a single orthographic unit *kš* in order to record this allophonic variation. These adroit adapters would have been quite capable of segmenting the two sounds and using the Phoenician character to represent [š] alone; they had already made provision for representing [k]. As argued above, [š] would have almost certainly appeared after front and/or high vowels if it occurred after [k], and the adapters would have needed this symbol to represent [š] after those sounds as well; it is highly improbable that the adapters would have chosen to record the allophonic variant in one context but not in others. But of course, there is no symbol which is so used to represent [š] after [i] or [e] or [u].

6.3.5 Conclusions on Greek [š]

Our crosslinguistic investigation of palatalization reveals the hypothesis that [š] was an allophone of /s/ which occurred only after /k/ to be an improbable one. Moreover, our probings and surveyings have uncovered no evidence which would lead us to propose that [š] was an allophonic variant that was orthographically distinguished within the Greek writing system. Jeffery's [kš] hypothesis does not hold up under careful scrutiny. Whatever may have been the motivation for incorporating a [k] + [s] symbol into the newly devised Greek alphabet, it was not done because /s/ was pronounced as [š] after [k].

6.3.5.1 The Cypriot Connection

We have found the conventional, phonetic-based account of the origin of Greek *xi* to be unacceptable. What, in fact, could possibly be the motivation for the incorporation of a letter into the Greek alphabet with the value [k] + [s]? The great advantage of an alphabet is that it combines phonemic precision with economy: it allows writer and reader to record and visually perceive language in a relatively unambiguous manner using a minimal number of symbols. It is clear that the Greeks responsible for expanding the Semitic script into a full-fledged alphabetic system (i.e., one which contained symbols for both consonant and vowel phonemes) were quite capable and skillful. Again, why would these individuals have antithetically complicated this system without increasing its expressive precision by adding to it a [k] + [s] character when the system already possessed both a [k] character and an [s] character? I believe that the alphabet offers no intrinsic motivation for such a decision. That is to say, there is nothing about the use of an alphabetic script for spelling the Greek language which prescribes the incorporation of such a symbol into that script. In bracing contrast, however, there is powerful motivation for the inclusion of *ks* symbols in another orthographic system which was used for spelling the Greek language. As we have seen, the occurrence of *ksV* characters in the syllabic Cypriot script was mandated by a peculiar intersection of Greek phonology and the unique spelling strategies for representing consonant clusters in this writing system. I believe that it must be the case that there is a *ks* character in the

Greek alphabet because it was in essence inherited from the syllabic Cypriot system. In other words, the Greek scribe or, surely more likely, scribal school responsible for adapting the Phoenician script for the alphabetic spelling of Greek was one which wrote Greek utilizing the Cypriot syllabary. Since there were *ks* syllabic symbols in the Cypriot script, a *ks* character was included in (i.e., transferred to) the graphemic inventory of the new alphabetic script. We will have more to say on this matter later, when we consider the [p] + [s] character of Greek scripts.

The Greek adapters' decision to utilize Phoenician *samek*—which we have identified as having the value [s]—for representing the Greek sequence [k] + [s] may have been less arbitrary than it may immediately seem to have been. As McCarter has pointed out, evidence provided by Egyptian transcriptions of Canaanite suggests that the value of *samek* was, at least at an early period, not [s] but that of some sort of palatalized stop such as [k^y] or [t^y] or an affricate such as [č].[111] However, the possibility that the relationship between Semitic *samek* and Greek *xi* is largely arbitrary and is not based upon phonetic similarity at the moment of the Greek acquisition of the alphabet, cannot be eliminated. In any event, as will become obvious as we progress through our investigation, the utilization of *samek* for *xi* is not the consequence of any sort of confused learning of the Phoenician system on the part of the Greek adapters (as Jeffery has suggested) and, hence, has nothing to do with the Semitic character *shin*. In the following pages, I pursue this Cypriot connection with the alphabet and show that it draws together and makes sense of a number of independent phenomena.

6.4 The Greek Letter *Psi*

6.4.1 The Distribution of [k] + [s] and [p] + [s] Symbols in the Alphabet-Types

As noted above in the discussion of the fundamental types of Greek alphabets (as identified according to the traditional scheme of Kirchhoff), there occurs in the dark blue alphabet-type a supplemental character ψ (*psi*) having the value [p] + [s]. This grapheme ψ also occurs in the red alphabets, in which case, however, it has the value of [k^h] rather than [p] + [s]; there is, recall, no [p] + [s] symbol in the red alphabets. In contrast, we have seen that a [k] + [s] symbol occurs in the dark blue and the red scripts alike (ξ in the former and χ in the latter).[112]

There have recently come to light four tablets on which are inscribed in repeating series an abecedarium which does not match precisely any of Kirchhoff's alphabet-types. One of these tablets, the most carefully studied to date, is housed in the Martin-von-Wagner-Museum of the University of Würzburg (the Würzburger Alphabettafel), two are (or were) in the possession of a dealer in antiquities in New York (the Fayum Tablets), and the fourth is in a private collection. These tablets are reported to be of Egyptian provenience and date at the latest to the late ninth or early eighth century; consequently, these very important documents appear to provide us with the earliest examples of a Greek alphabet yet discovered. The script of the tablets is like that of the dark blue alphabet-type to the extent that it contains the character ξ, but it differs from the dark blue, and all other, Greek alphabet-types, in that, precisely like the Phoenician model of the Greek script, this alphabet ends in the letter τ (*tau,* [t]; Semitic *taw*). Hence, the Würzburg-Fayum alphabet lacks *upsilon* ([u] or [ü]), as well as the supplemental characters φ, χ, and ψ, and *omega* ([ǫ:]).[113] Clearly it is impossible to determine the value assigned to ξ in the Würzburg-Fayum alphabet without having access to inscriptions written with this script; for that matter, it is impossible to know the value assigned to α, β, γ, δ, or any other character occurring in the abecedarium in the absence of such inscriptional evidence. The value of the letter ξ is, however, constantly [k] + [s] throughout the Greek world (as well as in its Eteocretan use),[114] with the exception of Thera; in the primitive script of Thera, in which [k] + [s] is written componentially as κM, ξ is used to spell the initial consonantal sound (sequence?) of the divine name Ζεύς (usually pronounced [zdeús]).[115] Owing to the widespread constancy of the value of ξ, the *prima facie* and reasonable interpretation of the value of Würzburg-Fayum ξ is that it likewise represents [k] + [s]. Should its value be demonstrated to be otherwise, its removal from the scheme which follows will have no critical effect upon my analysis.

6.4.1.1 Stop + [s] Asymmetries

The distribution of [k] + [s] and [p] + [s] characters among the Greek alphabets then falls into the following pattern:

	(12)	[k] + [s]	[p] + [s]
	A. Dark blue alphabets	ξ	ψ
	B. Würzburg-Fayum alphabet	ξ	none
	C. Red alphabets	χ	none
	D. Light blue and green alphabets	none	none

There is a quite fundamental difference which exists between the utilization of [k] + [s] symbols and [p] + [s] symbols by the various Greek alphabets; the distribution of *stop + [s]* symbols in the Greek alphabet-types is clearly of an asymmetrical nature:

(13) A. A [k] + [s] character occurs in each script in which a [p] + [s] character occurs.
B. A [k] + [s] character occurs in some scripts which lack a [p] + [s] character.
C. No [p] + [s] character occurs in a script which lacks a [k] + [s] character.

The relationship between [k] + [s] and [p] + [s] graphemes is thus implicational:

(14) The presence of a [p] + [s] character implies the presence of a [k] + [s] character, but not vice versa.

Still a second asymmetrical relationship can be identified. Within the one alphabet-type which possesses both [k] + [s] and [p] + [s] characters (i.e., the dark blue alphabet-type of (12A)), there is an asymmetrical treatment displayed in the selection of graphemes used to represent these *stop* + *[s]* sequences. One of the sequences is represented using a character native to the Phoenician script (namely, ξ), and the other by a novel character, tacked on at the end of the inherited Semitic portion of the alphabet (i.e., ψ); it is, of course, [k] + [s] which is encoded within the Phoenician component of the script. If Powell is accurate in his claim that the supplemental characters were a part of the earliest Greek alphabet, then the Semitic ξ versus non-Semitic ψ asymmetry is significant in its own right. If, on the other hand, ψ and the other supplemental characters represent later additions to the earliest Greek alphabet, then of course the Semitic ξ versus non-Semitic ψ asymmetry is secondary, following upon the first mentioned [k] + [s] versus [p] + [s] character asymmetry.

This asymmetrical treatment is significant and informative. Why should the reverse asymmetry not have occurred? In other words, why is it not the case that some alphabets have a symbol with the value [p] + [s] and no symbol with the value [k] + [s] (we have seen that the occurrence of a [k] + [s] symbol in the Greek alphabet is not a function of the phonetics of the precursor Semitic character)? If both ξ and ψ should belong to the earliest Greek alphabet, then why is it not [p] + [s] which was chosen to be represented by a character of the Phoenician script rather than [k] + [s]?

As I indicated earlier, an identical asymmetry—the occurrence of [k] + [s] symbols, but no [p] + [s] symbols—may have existed in the syllabic Cypriot writing system. This cannot be determined with certainty until documents are recovered which attest instances of the word-final sequence [-ps#]. However, even if it should turn out to be the case that the Cypriot script did have *psV* symbols, this writing system would still be characterized by a fundamental *ksV* versus **psV* character asymmetry. While *ksV* and **psV* symbols may have both occurred word-finally, only *ksV* characters were utilized word-internally; as is attested, word-internal sequences [-ps-] are spelled $-pV_i-sV_i-$. As I discussed above, the use of *ksV* symbols word-internally originated (or persisted, as the case may be) as a consequence of the uniquely Cypriot use of the prepositional prefix ἐξ ([eks]) before morphemes beginning with a stop.[116] I have even suggested that the word-final use of the *ksV* symbols is simply an extension of this word-internal application. The syllabic Cypriot *ksV* versus **psV* character asymmetry is thus, at the very least, one of distribution, and it is perhaps one of existence. The restriction of **psV* symbols, if they existed, to word-final position means that, *ipso facto,* the set of *ksV* symbols was utilized more frequently and broadly and, thus, that these symbols were better integrated into spelling practice.

6.4.1.2 The Cypriot Source

I have argued that the Phoenician alphabet was adapted for Greek use by persons accustomed to spelling Greek with the Cypriot Syllabary. This claim was based initially upon the observation that the presence of *ksV* syllabic symbols is highly motivated within the Cypriot writing system, while the presence of a *ks* symbol in the alphabet appears to be without internal motivation. The observed [k] + [s] versus [p] + [s] asymmetries of the Greek alphabet are consistent with and follow from my hypothesis of a Cypriot Greek adaptation of the Phoenician script: the asymmetry involving *ksV* and *psV* symbols in the Cypriot Syllabary is the likely source of the alphabetic asymmetries involving [k] + [s] and [p] + [s] characters.

The Cypriot scribes who adapted the Phoenician script for Greek use did not have at their disposal a sufficient number of Semitic characters to represent the full range of Greek phonemes. Each of the Phoenician characters which was matched in value (in broad phonetic terms) by a Greek sound was utilized to represent that sound. With the characters which were then left over, it appears that the Greek adapters placed highest priority upon developing symbols to represent vowel sounds. After so doing, only a few Phoenician characters remained untapped. To one of these was assigned the value [k] + [s]. This would appear to be an odd sort of squandering of graphic raw material, since this left one fewer character still with which to represent the *individual* phonemic sounds of Greek. The *prima facie* idiosyncrasy and wantonness of this orthographic extravagance on the part of the adapters offers strong support for the claim that the occurrence of a [k] + [s] alphabetic symbol is an inheritance from the syllabic Cypriot system, in which such symbols are motivated. Notice that [k] + [s] not only took precedence over a [p] + [s] character, for which there was not now a Semitic symbol left, but it took precedence over symbols for the aspirated stops [pʰ] and [kʰ] as well—the representation of both of these sounds was also relegated to supplemental characters. This is doubtless because the Cypriot scribes were trained in the use of a syllabic script in which there were no such symbols; that is, *pV* and *kV* symbols represented both [p] and [pʰ] and both [k] and [kʰ] respectively.

The *stop + [s]* asymmetry of the red alphabets, in which the [k] + [s] character is itself a supplemental and in which no [p] + [s] symbol occurs, mirrors the above described asymmetry of the blue system in which [k] + [s] representation is assigned to the Phoenician component and [p] + [s] to the supplemental layer; in the red system, the asymmetry is essentially displaced to a higher orbit. This again must be an inherited phenomenon. Below we will consider the origin of the asymmetry of the red alphabet-type in detail.

6.4.2 Powell on ψ

As indicated above, the supplemental character ψ has the value of [p] + [s] in the dark blue alphabets and [kʰ] in the red scripts. Powell has argued, as a component of his thesis that the supplementals belong to the earliest Greek alphabet, that the symbol ψ in origin had the value of aspirated *qoppa* (ϙ). Recall that we pointed out above that in various earlier forms of the Greek alphabet, *qoppa* was used instead of *kappa* before the back rounded vowels represented by *o* and *υ* and that this allography suggests the occurrence of a backed allophone of /k/ in this phonetic environment. Powell contends that "*the* adapter" of the Phoenician script,

(15)   perceiving the usefulness of a system of aspirated plosives [i.e., stops] on
the model θ *theta* = [th]/ τ *tau* = [t], . . . created a new sign for the
bilabial aspirated plosive, ϕ *phei* = [ph], and two other aspirated signs to
correspond to the unaspirated velars *kappa* and *qoppa*, namely χ = [kh]
(corresponding to *kappa*) and ψ = [*ʕh] (corresponding to *qoppa*).[117]

He further states:

(16)   The similarity in sound between κ *kappa* and ? *qoppa* led, however, to the
eventual disappearance of *qoppa* while creating a parallel confusion between the letters *khei* and *ʕhei.[118]

Powell proposes the consequences of the loss of the conjectured *[ʕh] value
of ψ to be as follows:

1. In the alphabet of Attica (light blue), χ ([k^h]) is expanded in use to sup-
plant the character ψ having the value *[ʕh] (just as *kappa*, the symbol for the
most widely occurring allophone of unaspirated /k/, in all alphabets eventually
supplants *qoppa*, the symbol for the backed variety of /k/).[119]

2. Conversely, in Euboea (having a red script), the backed variant ψ ([ʕ^h]) is
generalized, acquiring the value [k^h] in spite of the fact that there is already a
character with this value (i.e., χ), "leaving χ with nothing to do."[120] Powell
conjectures that the sequence [ks] was "originally" spelled $\chi\sigma$, and that upon
the aforementioned demise of χ with the value [k^h], "the Euboians reduced
original $\chi\sigma$ = [ks] to χ = [ks].[121]

There are a couple of different aspects of Powell's interpretation of ψ as
originally [ʕ^h] which are curious or bothersome in nature and at least one which
is sufficiently problematic as to render the hypothesis highly improbable.

6.4.2.1 Contra Powell

To begin with, as I mentioned earlier, that the Greek adapters of the Semitic
script should have made provision for representing a backed allophone of the
voiceless unaspirated velar stop phoneme /k/ is in itself quite remarkable. If
this allophonic spelling were extended to the aspirated phoneme /k^h/ as well, it
would be yet more remarkable still; this does not mean that it could not have
happened, but its probability must be open to question. Second, while the creation of a symbol with the value of *[ʕ^h] (along with characters for [p^h] and
[k^h]) may indicate that an adapter has perceived the "usefulness of a system of
aspirated" stops (see (15)), it would appear that this adapter has overlooked the
usefulness of a system of voiced stops. In other words, if the graphic representation of allophones occurring before certain back vowels were deemed significant enough to extend this treatment to the *aspirated* velar /k^h/, it is curious
that the *voiced* velar /g/ was denied the same treatment. It is equally curious
that in Euboea, according to Powell's analysis, it is the graphic symbol for the
marked allophone *[ʕ^h] (i.e., that one which is severely limited in distribution)
which is generalized in use at the expense of that character which is used for
spelling all other instances of /k^h/ (i.e., χ) and which, consequently, occurs
much more frequently and broadly.[122]

The serious problem with Powell's hypothesis concerning the value of ψ is one of chronology. As indicated above, the graphic distinction between [k] and its backed variant occurring before the vowels of *o* and *υ* (i.e., the *kappa/qoppa* distinction) is eventually lost in all of the alphabets, gradually disappearing in the sixth and fifth centuries.[123] It is of course this observable loss of *qoppa* which has suggested to Powell the idea of reconstructing *[ʔʰ] as the "original" value of *ψ*; I repeat here his comment cited above: "The similarity in sound between κ *kappa* and ϙ *qoppa* led, however, to the eventual disappearance of *qoppa* while creating a parallel confusion between the letters *khei* and *ϙhei*."[124] We would then expect that the disappearance of the alphabetic character *qoppa* would approximately coincide with the disappearance of its conjectured aspirated counterpart—that is, Powell's *ψ* with the value of *[ʔʰ]. In other words, *ψ* should only begin to appear with its red value of [kʰ] and its blue value of [ps] at about the same time that *qoppa* disappears from use. This is not what we find at all.

In order to see this difficulty with Powell's theory, let us consider, as an example, the case of *ψ* and ϙ in the Euboean alphabet: the character *ψ* with the value [kʰ] occurs on a quite early sherd from Lefkandi, dating ca. 740;[125] Euboean ϙ occurs alongside *ψ* ([kʰ]) on "Chalcidic" vases which date ca. 550–510;[126] Jeffery cites the use of ϙ in the Chalcidic Euboean alphabet as late as the early fifth century.[127] Thus, we have documented evidence that the [k]/backed [k] allophonic distinction was graphically tolerated for about three hundred years after Euboean *ψ* is attested with the value [kʰ] (originally *[ʔʰ] according to Powell); similar evidence exists for other alphabets. Powell attributes both the loss of the ϙ character and the loss of the *[ʔʰ] value of *ψ* to the blurring of subtle phonetic differences. That these subtle distinctions between allophones of /k/ would continue to be orthographically recorded for three hundred years or more after the purported graphic distinction between allophones of the nearly identical phoneme /kʰ/ had ceased to be functional appears so highly improbable as to render Powell's *[ʔʰ] hypothesis untenable.

6.5 The Greek Letter *Zeta*

We come now to a consideration of the alphabetic Greek character *zeta*. Recall that this symbol is the graphic counterpart to the Semitic character *zayin*, though Jeffery has claimed, as part of her confusion theory, that the Greek name and value of the symbol are derived from Semitic *ṣade*. Before I develop a counterproposal to Jeffery's *zeta* hypothesis, attention needs to be paid to the phonetics of *zeta*.

6.5.1 The Phonetics of *Zeta*

In our discussion of the syllabic Greek scripts in chapter 4, it was pointed out that there are several different historical sources of the sound which is represented by the alphabetic character *zeta*, namely, the following:

(17) A. certain instances of word-initial *y-
      e.g., *yug- ⇒ ζυγόν ([zdügón], 'yoke')

B. the sequence $*g^{(w)}y$

   e.g., $*meg\text{-}yo\text{-} \Rightarrow$ Ionic $\mu\acute{\varepsilon}\zeta\omega\nu$ ([mézdǫ:n], 'greater')

C. the sequence $*dy$

   e.g., $*dy\bar{e}us \Rightarrow Z\varepsilon\acute{\upsilon}\varsigma$ ([zdeús], divine name *Zeus*)

In addition to the Greek reflexes of $*y$- and the consonantal sequences listed in (17), *zeta* is also used to represent the inherited phonetic sequence *[zd]—that is, the phonemic sequence */sd/ in which the initial fricative has been voiced to [z] by the regular phonological process (both Proto-Indo-European and Greek) of regressive voicing assimilation.[128] This is illustrated by the following examples:

(18)   A. Proto-Indo-European $*osdo\text{-} \Rightarrow \check{o}\zeta o\varsigma$ ([ózdos], 'branch')

   B. $*\beta\upsilon\sigma\text{-}\delta\tilde{\alpha}\nu \Rightarrow \beta\acute{\upsilon}\zeta\eta\nu$ ([bǔzdę:n], 'close pressed')

What exactly is the phonetic value of *zeta?* In her discussion of the sibilant characters of the Phoenician script, Jeffery identifies the sound of Greek *zeta* as "*ds, sd*" and states, "Its fundamental value in Greek appears to have been that of *ds,* although it was also used, by metathesis, for *sd.*"[129] Powell, in his treatment of this same problem, similarly marks the value of *zeta* as "[dz], [zd]" and writes, "The Phoenician affricate [ts] (*ṣādē*) became the Greek voiced [dz], soon metathesized to [zd] (*zēta*)."[130] It would appear that the value of *zeta* is somewhat schizophrenic. Let us consider this matter further.

The inherited sequences $*[g^{(w)}y]$ and $*[dy]$ as well as instances of initial $*[y]$ (i.e., those sounds which will evolve into the sound represented by *zeta*) eventually merge in a common phonetic reflex, and it is widely held that this reflex was *[dz]. As Allen points out, a similar sort of development can be seen in, for example, the evolution of Latin *medius* ('middle') into Italian *mezzo.*[131] The reflex *[dz] eventually undergoes some sort of metathesis. The linguistic evidence points persuasively to [zd] as the phonetic value of the alphabetic character *zeta* and reveals, in fact, that the metathesis of *[dz] to [zd] occurred prior to the alphabetic period:[132]

1. As has already been pointed out, from its earliest attestations in the alphabetic period, the inherited sequence $*\sigma\delta$ (i.e., phonemic /sd/, phonetic [zd]) is spelled as ζ (see the examples of (18)).

2. Until the early fourth century *zeta* was used to transcribe the Persian sequence [zd]; for example, Old Persian *Auramazda* appears as $\mathrm{'}\Omega\rho o\mu\alpha\zeta\eta\varsigma$; *Artavazda* as $\mathrm{'}A\rho\tau\alpha\beta\alpha\zeta o\varsigma$ (Herodotus) and $\mathrm{'}A\rho\tau\alpha o\zeta o\varsigma$ (Xenophon). It appears that by the late fourth century the ζ of the Attic Koine script had begun to acquire the fricative value [z] (the value which the character has in Modern Greek); consequently, *zeta* is from that point used to transcribe Persian [z], which had earlier been rendered by Greek σ.

3. In the literary Lesbian of Sappho and Alcaeus, the componential spelling $\sigma\delta$ is used (probably by later editors) in lieu of *zeta*; for example, $\check{\upsilon}\sigma\delta o\varsigma$ ([úzdos], 'branch'; Sappho 4.93) for Attic $\check{o}\zeta o\varsigma$ ([ózdos]; from $*osdo\text{-}$). The same spelling also occurs in certain Lesbian inscriptions.[133] On the other hand, the character ζ is used to represent the reflex of a sequence *[dy] which corresponds to the prevocalic sequence [di] in other dialects; for example, ζα for διά ([diá], 'through'). (The spelling σδ for [zd] suggests that the value of the *zeta* which spells the reflex of this *[dy-] was something other than [zd].)[134]

4. Ancient grammarians such as Dionysius Thrax and Dionysius of Halicarnassus explicitly state that the value of ζ is σ plus δ.[135] As Allen points out, such descriptions likely reflect an earlier and conservative pronunciation and not that which belonged to the vernacular of the day of the grammarians.[136]

5. In certain quite early inscriptions, such as one from sixth-century Argos, a kind of hyperrepresentational spelling σζ (i.e., [zzd], as it were) occurs alongside the parallel spellings σστ for [st] and σσθ for [ssth].[137]

6. There is one additional piece of evidence to be considered, and it is this which most convincingly reveals that the sound of *zeta* was [zd] at a quite early date—*prior to* the introduction of the alphabet. In the case of inherited sequences of the type *[ns] + consonant,* the nasal is lost without compensatory lengthening of a preceding short vowel, as in the following examples:

(19)   A. Proto-Greek *kenstos ⇒ κεστός ([kestós], 'stitched')
       B. Proto-Greek *demspotās ⇒ δεσπότης ([despóte̦:s], 'master;
           despot')
       C. Proto-Greek *sunstasis ⇒ σύστασις ([sústasis], 'composition')[138]

The loss of the nasal likewise occurs when it is followed by the sequence of sounds which would later, in the alphabetic period, be spelled with the letter *zeta*; hence, the sequence following the nasal must here also be *fricative + stop,* that is, [zd]. Note that a nasal is not lost before an ensuing *stop + fricative* cluster[139] (such as [dz]). The deletion of a nasal before [zd] is exemplified by the following:

(20)   A. Proto-Greek *Atʰe̦nanz-de ⇒ * Ἀθήνασ−δε, which is spelled Ἀθή−
           ναζε ([atʰé̦:naz-de], 'to Athens')
       B. Proto-Greek *salping-yō ⇒ *salpinzdō ⇒ σαλπίζω ([salpízdo̦:], 'to
           blow the trumpet')
       C. Proto-Greek *sun-zdugos (from Proto-Indo-European *-yug-) ⇒ σύ−
           ζυγος ([súzdügos], 'yoked-together')

The loss of a nasal before an ensuing *fricative + consonant* cluster is assigned to an early period in the history of the Greek language. Buck, for example, speaks of the change occurring in "proethnic Greek,"[140] and Lejeune states, "Si la sifflante était précédée d'une nasale, il y a, en grec commun, simplification aux dépens de la nasale."[141] Observe that the source of the *zeta* sound before which nasal deletion occurs is not only inherited *[zd] but also *[#y-] and the consonant combinations detailed in (17). If the sequence which would come to be spelled by *zeta* was thus already [zd] at quite an early period, prior to the introduction of the alphabet, and if *zeta* has the demonstrable value [zd] early in the alphabetic period, why has it been claimed that upon the Greek adoption of the Semitic script, Phoenician *zayin* was assigned the Greek value [dz]? This would entail an untenable and dizzying series of switches between [dz] and [zd]:

(21) A. In Common Greek

$*gy$

$*dy$ $\Rightarrow$ $*dz$

$*\#y$ (in certain occurrences)

$*zd$ [142]

B. Still in Common Greek, the product of (A) is "metathesized":

$*dz \Rightarrow *zd$

C. Subsequently, but still prior to the adoption of the alphabet:

$*zd \Rightarrow *dz$

D. And then, very soon after the adoption of the alphabet, once again:

$*dz \Rightarrow zd$

Such a scenario is incredible. What, then, could possibly be the motivation for the proposition that Phoenician *zayin* was assigned the Greek value [dz]?

6.5.1.1 Cretan Zeta

Before further pursuing the question posed at the end of the preceding section, I would point out that it has been argued that at least in one dialect—namely, Cretan—there is evidence that the alphabetic character *zeta* was pronounced [dz]. It has long been known that *zeta* was also used in the earliest inscriptions from central Crete to spell the *voiceless* sound which developed from the historically earlier sequences *[-ts-] and *[-ty-].[143] As I discussed in chapter 4, these sequences eventuate word-internally as [-(s)s-] in most dialects, but as [-tt-] in Boeotian and, by the fifth century, in Cretan[144] (*[t + y] also produces Attic [-tt-]). According to Bile, *zeta* is used three times in Cretan inscriptions of the seventh and sixth centuries to spell the reflexes of *[-ts-] and *[-ty-]: once in the aorist middle infinitive ανδαζαθαι (Attic ἀναδάσασθαι ([anadá-sasthai], 'to redistribute') from *-dat-sasthai); and twice in the nominative plural pronoun οζοι (Attic ὄσοι ([hósoi], 'as many as') from *hotso-).[145] An affricate such as *[tˢ] is often conjectured to have occurred as an intermediate reflex in the evolution of {*[-ts-], *[-ty-]} to {[-(s)s-], [-tt-]}; it could be, and has been, proposed that it is the *[tˢ] stage of this process which is recorded by this Cretan use of *zeta* for spelling the {*[-ts-], *[-ty-]} reflex. One might then assume that the corresponding voiced value of Cretan *zeta* must have been [dz]; that is, the assumption would be that if *zeta* had represented the metathesized [zd] in the Cretan script, the character would not have likely lent itself to the spelling of voiceless [tˢ].[146] Beyond this, Brixhe has proposed that the *zeta* value [dz] is further indicated by the preservation of the nasal in the fourth-century Cretan form σαλπινδε[ν] ([salpinden] 'to blow the trumpet'), cf. Attic σαλπίζειν ([salpízdẹ:n]). As I pointed out above, this verb develops from the stem *salping-yo-. Since the nasal has not been deleted in this Cretan form, then, according to Brixhe's analysis, it must have developed from a Cretan intermediary *salpindzo- with a stop occurring after the nasal (and not with a fricative occurring after the nasal, as in *salpinzdo- ⇒ *salpizdo-; see (20B). By the fifth century the sound of Cretan *zeta* had been replaced by [dd] or [d]—hence the *delta* (rather than *zeta*) of σαλπινδεν.[147]

It is *a priori* possible that the Cretan dialect has conserved a *[-dz-] reflex beyond the time when it had been eliminated by metathesis in the other dialects. That the dialect(s) of Crete and Thera differed from others in this regard may indeed be signaled by the use of *xi* (ξ) to spell the *zeta* sound: we saw above that this is the regular means for spelling the initial sound of *Zeus* in Theran inscriptions; the character is also so used once in a Cretan inscription from Lyttos (sixth century), where we find οξοι rather than οζοι (Attic ὅσοι ([hósoi], 'as many as'; see the discussion immediately above).[148] In other words, one could argue, the scribes responsible for such spellings knew that in their own dialect the pronunciation of that sound which occurs at the beginning of *Zeus* was different from its pronunciation in the dialect of the speakers from whom they acquired the alphabet (Cretan, Theran [dz-] as opposed to [zd-] elsewhere); since the consonantal sequence [k] + [s] was spelled componentially as κM in their own variety of the alphabet, the idle ξ was appropriated by these scribes for spelling their dialectal [-dz-]. Alternatively, rather than innovating in this manner, other scribes chose not to tamper with the spelling of words containing *zeta* which they encountered in the orthographic system that was introduced into Crete; in other words, these Cretan scribes continued to spell *Zeus* as Ζευς after the manner of those whose alphabet was brought to Crete, but for Cretans the pronunciation was by this scenario, [dzeus] rather than [zdeus]. A single orthography can well accommodate phonetic differences across linguistic boundaries; compare, for example, the pronunciation of English and Italian *zucchini* and English and German *zwieback* and *Zurich*.

It is not altogether clear, however, that the evidence compels us, or even leads us, to interpret the value of the central Cretan voiced sound spelled with *zeta* as anything other than [zd]. Two different issues must be addressed here. First, the use of *zeta* to spell the reflex of {*[-ts-], *[-ty-]} almost certainly does indicate that in the central Cretan dialect of the seventh and sixth centuries, the sound of this *zeta* was, or consisted in part of, some sort of sibilant, though this was clearly not the [-(s)s-] reflex of most of the dialects (and obviously not yet the [-tt-] of fifth-century and later Cretan[149]).[150] This does not mean, however, that the sound was of necessity the affricate [t^s] (or alternatively a phonemic sequence [ts]). In his conjectured pathway of the evolution of *[-ty]- and *[-ky-] (which latter we saw in chapter 4 to yield almost the same set of dialectal reflexes as {*[-ts-], *[-ty-]}), Rix proposes a stage in which a sequence of a type *-*t*-*s*- has undergone metathesis to yield *-*s*-*t*-; for Rix the sound developments involved in the common pathway are specifically . . . *t^{s}y ⇒ *s^{t}y ⇒ *ss^t, with further development to *(s)s* in most dialects, but *tt* in Boeotian and Cretan. Among the evidence which Rix adduces for a metathesized stage in which the sibilant component precedes the stop component (**ss^t* by his reckoning) is the Boeotian treatment of inherited *[-st-]; the Boeotian reflex of this *fricative* + *stop* sequence is also [-tt-] (the very same reflex which occurs for the sequences *[-ty-], *[-ky-] as well as *[-ts-]), apparently arising by regressive assimilation. Beyond that, metathesis is of course well attested in the voiced analogue of this reflex, that is, *[-dz-] ⇒ [-zd-]; and in Attic loss of a nasal occurs prior to the [-tt-] reflex of *[-k$^{(h)}$y-], suggesting the existence of a *nasal* + *fricative* sequence at the time of the loss (as nasals are lost before [-s-] but not before stops).[151] The Cretan use of *zeta*—a character which regularly appears to have the value [zd] in the various Greek alphabets—to spell the seventh- and sixth-century voiceless reflexes of {*[-ts-], *[-ty-]} may well indicate that at this period the Cretan reflex was one in which a sibilant component preceded a dental stop component (in gross terms, a voiceless counterpart to [zd]). Unlike the case of Boeotian, a kind of regressive assimilation which transforms such a sequence into the fifth-century [-tt-] reflex appears not to be replicated by the inherited sequence [-st-];[152] however, the treatment of inherited [-st^h-] offers a remarkable parallel. In the earliest documents the sequence is spelled $\sigma\theta$, but later, by the end of the archaic period according to Bile,[153] assimilation has operated to produce a sequence spelled $\theta\theta$ (representing [-t^{h}t^h-] or perhaps [-tt^h-][154]). The inherited sequence *$\sigma\delta$ (i.e., *[-zd-]) likewise experiences regressive assimilation to yield [dd].[155] Assimilation is well attested in Cretan; in his discussion of assimilation in the various Greek dialects, Buck states, "Assimilation is most extensive in Cretan."[156] This Cretan propensity for assimilation is not, however, one which is equilateral in nature. Assimilation in all of Greek is primarily regressive, but this appears to be especially so in Cretan; Thumb-Kieckers records, "Die Neigung zur regressiven Assimilation ist im Kretischen stärker als anderwärts ausgeprägt."[157] Progressive assimilation is hardly attested in Cretan; Bile writes, "Or, l'assimilation progressive est rare en crétois," and cites only a single instance of progressive assimilation: [-mn-] ⇒ [-mm-].[158] The marked disparity between regressive and progressive assimilation in Cretan further diminishes the possibility that the voiceless *zeta* sound of Cretan was [-t^s-] (or the like), as its development to [-tt-] would require an assimilatory change which is progressive in direction. In the very same way, if the voiced value of Cretan *zeta* had been [-dz-] (rather than [-zd-], as elsewhere), its further evolution to [-dd-] would have required an anomalous progressive assimilation. In summary, if the use of *zeta* to spell a voiceless sound in early central Cretan tells us anything about the phonetics of that sound, it probably tells us that it consisted of a sibilant component followed by a stop component; it most likely does not tell us that the sound of voiced *zeta* was [-dz-].[159]

Second, attention needs to be paid to Brixhe's analysis of the fragmentary form $\sigma\alpha\lambda\pi\iota\nu\delta\varepsilon[\nu]$. Not only is Cretan characterized by extensive regressive assimilation word-internally, but it is also the dialect which best preserves orthographic evidence of assimilation occurring across an intervening word-boundary; concerning such sandhi phenomena, Buck writes, "Cretan shows the most extensive and radical series of consonant assimilations."[160] Assimilation is not, however, the only consonantal sandhi phenomenon which is well preserved in Cretan. As I indicated above, at a quite early period in the history of Greek a nasal was lost when it preceded the sequence *fricative* + *consonant*. Such nasal-deletion also took place when the ensuing fricative and consonant were separated by a word-boundary, that is, in the context *[n][fricative] # [consonant]*. For example, the accusative plural of the thematic nouns (second declension) had terminated in *−ovs (*[-ons#]) and that of the *-ā-* feminines (first declension) in *−αvs (*[-ans#]). When the word which followed began with a consonant, nasal-deletion applied to produce accusative plurals in $-o\varsigma$ and $-\alpha\varsigma$; when the ensuing word began with a vowel, $-ov\varsigma$ and $-\alpha v\varsigma$ were preserved (with nasal intact). In the various dialects either the nasal-less formant was generalized at the expense of the formant preserving the nasal or vice versa; in certain of those dialects which generalized the formant with the nasal, this nasal was then subsequently deleted with compensatory lengthening of the preceding vowel. Thus, regardless of whether the word which follows begins with a consonant or a vowel, we find, for example, the accusative plurals $-o\varsigma$, $-\alpha\varsigma$ in Thessalian, Arcadian, and probably Cyprian; $-ov\varsigma$, $-\alpha v\varsigma$ in Argolic; $-ol\varsigma$, $-\alpha l\varsigma$ in Lesbian; and so forth.[161] In the central Cretan dialect of Gortyn, however, both of the variant sets are uniquely preserved, with $-ov\varsigma$ occurring alongside $-o\varsigma$ and $-\alpha v\varsigma$ beside $-\alpha\varsigma$; the survival of the variants is not limited to thematic and $-\bar{a}$- accusative plural nouns but occurs in the case of other original word-final *[-ns] sequences as well.[162]

Now, what in all of this is of significance for our present concerns is the following: the variation exhibited by the accusative plural forms of the $-\bar{a}$-stems (i.e., $-\alpha v\varsigma$ beside $-\alpha\varsigma$) is analogically extended to the accusative plurals of consonant stems (third declension). The accusative plural of consonant stem nouns should terminate in $-\alpha\varsigma$ (from earlier *[-Cn̥s]); however, a variant terminating sequence $-\alpha v\varsigma$ is created by analogically introducing a nasal from the $\bar{a}$-stem formant $-\alpha v\varsigma$. Thus, there occur accusative plurals of consonant stems such as $\theta v\gamma\alpha\tau\epsilon\rho\alpha v\varsigma$ ([tʰügaterans], 'daughters') and $\kappa v v\alpha v\varsigma$ ([künans], 'dogs').[163] The nasal which occurs in the fourth-century present infinitive $\sigma\alpha\lambda-\pi\iota v\delta\epsilon[v]$ is likewise in all probability analogically introduced from the many stem-forms in which it is regularly preserved, such as the aorist $\dot{\epsilon}\sigma\dot{\alpha}\lambda\pi\iota\gamma\xi\alpha$ ([esálpiŋksa]) and the nouns $\sigma\dot{\alpha}\lambda\pi\iota\gamma\xi$ ([sálpiŋks], 'war trumpet') and $\sigma\alpha\lambda-\pi\iota\gamma\kappa\tau\dot{\eta}\varsigma$ ([salpiŋkté:s], 'trumpeter') It is likely that the form $\sigma\alpha\lambda\pi\iota v\delta\epsilon[v]$ simply arises by the common analogical process of leveling and ought not be offered as evidence that the Cretan reflex of *[-dz-] was not metathesized [-zd-].

6.5.2 The Phonetic Motivation

Now let us return to an examination of the proposition that, in contradiction to what is indicated by the linguistic evidence, upon the adoption of the Semitic script, Phoenician *zayin* was assigned the Greek value [dz]. At least two distinct motivations for this proposal can be identified, one of which could be termed *phonetic* and the other *structural*. The phonetic motivation is encountered as a component of Jeffery's confusion hypothesis. Recall that Jeffery has argued that while the graphic shape of *zeta* was taken from *zayin*, its name and its value were actually derived from the Phoenician character *ṣade*. Thus, she states concerning *zeta* (and *sigma*):

(22) I think there can be little doubt that *ṣade/zeta* must be paired, and likewise *samek/sigma*; in both cases the names are very similar, and (even more important) the acrophonic principle holds good, i.e. the sound-values which the Phoenicians gave to *ṣade* (*ts*) and *samek* (*s*) are the sounds given by the Greeks to *zeta* (*ds, sd*) and *sigma* (*s*).[164]

Further along she adds, apparently for the sake of clarification:

(23)   *Zeta*, then, has the correct Semitic sign which followed that of *waw*, but
the name + sound of another sibilant, *ṣade*. Its fundamental value in Greek
appears to have been that of *ds*.[165]

Concerning the name of *zeta*, we will have more to say below; however, for
the present I would just point out that its name is probably based upon that of
the two characters which follow it in the Greek alphabet: *eta* and *theta* (from
Semitic *ḥet* and *ṭet*). It appears that it is Jeffery's acrophonic principle which
leads her to embrace the view (perhaps more automatically than deliberately,
or more implicitly than explicitly) that the value of *zeta* was—at least fundamentally—[dz]. In other words, Phoenician *ṣade* had the value of [ts]; Greek
zeta was similar in sound to *ṣade*; therefore, the value of *zeta* must be [dz].
There is more than one problematic term in this equation: beyond the dubious
[dz] value of *zeta*, the value of Phoenician *ṣade* was not simply [ts].[166]

6.5.2.1 The Phonetics of Ṣade

As I mentioned earlier, both ancient and modern Semitic languages—or, more
broadly speaking, Afro-Asiatic languages[167]—are phonetically characterized by
possessing a set of consonants which have traditionally been designated by
scholars of Semitic grammar as *emphatic*. This term actually denotes several
different phonetic realities. In Modern Arabic and Berber,[168] the emphatics are
those consonants which are produced while constricting the back portion of the
oral cavity, either by raising the back of the tongue (i.e., velarized consonants)
or by narrowing the pharynx (i.e. pharyngealized consonants).[169] Ladefoged
describes the process of *velarization* as the articulation of a consonant while
the tongue is held in the position that it would occupy when producing the
vowel [u] (though without the rounding of the lips which occurs in the production of this vowel). *Pharyngealization* is similarly effected, but with the back
of the oral cavity in the position associated with the production of the vowel
[*a*].[170]

The emphatic consonants of other Afro-Asiatic languages are characterized
by *glottalization*.[171] In South Arabian, Ethiopian, and Cushitic the emphatics
are reported to be explosive glottalized consonants, or ejectives. Such sounds
are produced by closing the glottis (the opening between the vocal cords in the
larynx) and then forcefully ejecting air out of the mouth by raising the larynx.
In Chadic the emphatics take the form of either explosive or implosive glottalized consonants. Implosives are phonetically more complex than ejectives but
are essentially sounds produced by lowering the larynx while the glottis is (partially) closed, so that air is pulled rapidly into the oral cavity through the
lips.[172]

The Phoenician language possessed three emphatic consonants. Of these
three, two are stops: an emphatic voiceless dental stop (traditionally transcribed
as *ṭ*) and an emphatic voiceless velar stop (*ḳ*, *q*). The former sound is represented in the Phoenician script by the character *ṭet* and the latter by the symbol
qop. The Greek adapters of the Phoenician writing system utilized *ṭet* to repre-

sent the voiceless aspirated dental stop [t^h]; that is, this is the source of the Greek character *theta* (θ). *Qop* was utilized, as we indicated above in the discussion of the Greek grapheme *qoppa* ($?$), to spell a variant of [k] which occurred before high and mid back vowels. If the emphatic sound of Phoenician *qop* was a velarized [k] (i.e., [k] articulated with the tongue held in the position for producing the vowel [u]), it is not difficult to see how the Greeks could have been seduced into straying from the path of phonemic spelling.

The third emphatic consonant of Phoenician was a voiceless dental fricative, and it is this sound which was represented by the character *ṣade* (transcribed by Semitists as *ṣ*)—the Phoenician letter which Jeffery claims matches the sound value of Greek *zeta*. We must keep in mind of course, as has already been mentioned, that it is not possible to identify with certainty the precise phonetic quality of Phoenician *ṣade* or of any of the emphatic consonants in the ancient Semitic languages; however, these are usually and reasonably interpreted to be similar to the surviving emphatics. Perhaps especially noteworthy in this regard are the emphatics of the phonologically quite conservative Modern South Arabian and Arabic, about which latter it has been said, "Arabic preserves Proto-Semitic phonology almost perfectly."[173] Concerning the emphatic consonants of Phoenician, Segert, for example, states, "For the so-called emphatic consonants, /q/, /ṣ/ and /ṭ/, a pronunciation with the constriction of the expiration stream below the velum may be supposed."[174] What Segert is referring to of course is the sort of modification which we described above, that is, pharyngealization and so on. Currently, a glottalized value appears to be most favored among Semitists for the ancient emphatics. If, then, Phoenician *ṣade* represented a voiceless glottalized (or pharyngealized or velarized) dental fricative [s], just how phonetically similar would it have been to the voiced sequence [dz], Jeffery's "fundamental" value of Greek *zeta?*

Rather than pursuing the answer to this question, however, let us consider another possibility. Could the sound of Phoenician *ṣade* have been both an "emphatic" consonant and, as Jeffery supposes, an affricate [ts] (or, more carefully, [t^s])? In other words, could this symbol have represented an emphatic affricate? In a recent work, Steiner[175] has argued that a glottalized affricate represented by the character *ṣade* occurred in several Semitic languages at various periods.[176] Steiner contends that such an affricate pronunciation was a characteristic of Punic, the dialect of Phoenician which was spoken in the Western Mediterranean colonies of Phoenicia (the earliest Punic materials date to the fifth century B.C.; from 146 B.C. (the date of the fall of Carthage) until its disappearance in the sixth century A.D., the language is identified as Late Punic or Neo-Punic).[177] The principal evidence which Steiner advances for this value of Punic *ṣade* is the variation exhibited in Greek transcriptions of this sound. Dioscurides, the Greek physician-herbalist of the first century A.D., transcribes *ṣade* in the Punic word **ḥṣr* ('grass, plant') as σ, τ, or $\sigma\tau$.[178] Steiner cites instances of the Greek practice of transcribing the affricate [t^s] (as in *church*), occurring in Greek transcriptions of forms from various languages, as σ at times and τ at others, and argues that the same variation in the transcription of Punic *ṣade* reveals that the value of that sound was likewise an affricate, though with the value [t^s'].[179]

Steiner goes on to argue that in Phoenician proper the character *ṣade* also had the value of a glottalized affricate [tˢ'].[180] The evidence which he offers in this case, however, is, as he acknowledges, open to other interpretations, and his argument is less compelling. Acceptance of an affricate value of Punic *ṣade* does not require projecting that value back into earlier phases of Phoenician. It is well known that in the Punic period, especially in Late Punic, there were significant phonological changes in the language (as well as considerable orthographic confusion). During this era, we observe, for example, a breakdown in the (at least orthographic) distinction of emphatic and nonemphatic consonants and confusion in the representation of the fricative sounds of Punic.[181] Concerning Punic, Harris states:

(24)   In this transplanted form of Phoenician many linguistic developments which had begun in Phoenician continue their course unabated. The greatest changes, especially in pronunciation, took place among the mixed Phoenician-Berbers of North Africa, particularly outside Carthage. In Neo-Punic, in which the conservative influence of Carthage and the mother country was no longer felt, the new developments at times betray non-Semitic local influence.[182]

Nevertheless, if we should give Steiner (and Jeffery) the benefit of the doubt and accept the value of early Phoenician *ṣade* as a glottalized [tˢ'], would we then be compelled to identify the value of *zeta* as [dz] at the time of the adoption of the alphabet, in contradiction to linguistic evidence which indicates that its value was [zd]? The answer to this question is clearly no. Many of the consonant sounds of Phoenician do, in gross phonetic terms, correspond to equivalent sounds in the Greek language: both languages have voiceless and voiced bilabial, dental and velar stops; both have bilabial and dental nasals; both have the liquids [l] and [r] and so forth (though even here there are undoubtedly *at least* slight phonetic differences). In the case of such "equivalent" sounds, the Greek adapters of the Phoenician script in essence permitted the acquired Semitic characters to retain their native value; thus, the value of Phoenician *bet* is essentially that of Greek *beta* (*b*), the value of Phoenician *lamed* is that of Greek *lambda* (*l*), and so on. On the other hand, there are Phoenician consonants which do not have such close correspondences in the Greek language. In the case of Phoenician characters representing such sounds, the Greek adapters either (i) gave the characters a somewhat close phonetic Greek fit or (ii) were more or less arbitrary in the Greek values assigned to the characters. We have seen that the arbitrary strategy is employed, to a greater or lesser degree, in the development of the Greek vowel characters and perhaps in the assignment of the Greek value [ks] to Phoenician *samek,* while the "close-fit" strategy is used, for example, in the assigning of the Greek value [h] to the Phoenician character *ḥet,* which represents a voiceless velar fricative [x] in Semitic (as in German *auch*).[183] The latter strategy is also displayed in the Greek adapters' use of the Phoenician symbols for the emphatic dental and emphatic velar stops to represent the Greek aspirated dental stop [tʰ] and a backed allophonic variant of [k] respectively.

Now, we have discussed at length the value, of Phoenician *ṣade* and have found that it was likely a glottalized (or in some way "emphatic") fricative— we have even allowed the possibility that it was a glottalized affricate [tˢ']. The Greek language has no consonant which corresponds at all closely to either an emphatic [s] or an emphatic [tˢ] (whether glottalized [tˢ'] or whatever). At the very best, the relationship between the value of *ṣade* and that of *zeta* (regardless of the value of the latter) would be one of a "close fit" and could be a quite arbitrary one. Consequently, the phonetics of *ṣade* would tell us little about the precise phonetics of *zeta* and do not compel us to posit a value [dz] for this character. Beyond this, and conversely, as we shall see, the value of Greek *zeta* does not compel us, or even induce us, to identify *ṣade* as its phonetic analogue in the parent Phoenician script.[184]

6.5.2.2 A Greek Confusion of Ṣade and Zayin?

The final remark of the preceding paragraph leads us to a consideration of a different problem. I have argued that the value of Phoenician *ṣade* does not motivate the identification of the phonetic value of *zeta* as [dz], as opposed to [zd], at the time that the Greeks acquired the Semitic script. I have not as yet, however, *directly* addressed Jeffery's claim that it is the value of *ṣade*, rather than the value of *zayin*, which suggested to the Greek adapters a value for their new alphabetic character *zeta*; this is of course a component of her confusion hypothesis. I have done so *indirectly*, however, to the extent that I have contested the phonetic similarity which Jeffery supposes to have existed between Phoenician *ṣade* and Greek *zeta* (a similarity which is integral to her confusion hypothesis in that the more arbitrary the purported phonetic relationship between *ṣade* and *zeta* becomes, the less motivation there is for the notion of a switch in the values of *zayin* and *ṣade*). Let us take a more direct look.

As I discussed earlier, the graphic form of the character *zeta* clearly comes from that of *zayin*, and *zeta* occupies a position in the Greek alphabet which corresponds to the position of *zayin* in the Phoenician script. If the *value* of Greek *zeta* did not also come from *zayin* but is instead to be traced back to the value of Phoenician *ṣade*, then it would surely be expected, within the framework of Jeffery's hypothesis, that *ṣade* would be normally transcribed (in the case of Phoenician loanwords, Phoenician place-names etc.) by the Greek character *zeta*; recall Jeffery's statement cited above, "[T]he sound-values which the Phoenicians gave to *ṣade* (*ts*) and *samek* (*s*) are the sounds given by the Greeks to *zeta* (*ds*, *sd*) and *sigma* (*s*)."[185] Such transcription practice, however, is not what we find. It was pointed out above that Punic *ṣade* is transcribed by Greek *τ*, by *σ* and by *στ* (most frequently by the first-named in the case of the examples cited by Steiner). Phoenician *ṣade*, however, is usually transcribed by Greek *sigma* ([s]),[186] as in *Σιδῶν* ([sidọ:n], a place-name; Herodotus 2.161).[187] This observation alone should make us somewhat suspicious of the claim that the value of *zeta* corresponds to that of *ṣade* and, hence, of the hypothesis that an exchange occurred in the values of *ṣade* and *zayin*.

Is it necessary to resort to the confusion hypothesis to find an appropriate and sufficient phonetic analogue for Greek *zeta* in the Phoenician script? It is not. Recall that the value of Phoenician *zayin* is [z]; if the value of Greek *zeta* at the time of the adoption of the alphabet were [zd], as the linguistic evidence indicates, then the phonetic similarity which exists between the two symbols is patently obvious: the sound of Phoenician *zayin* is identical (speaking in broad phonetic terms) to the onset of the sound of Greek *zeta*. *Zeta* not only matches *zayin* in graphic form and position within their respective scripts but bears a phonetic value which is much more suggestive of *zayin,* the voiced fricative, than of *ṣade,* the glottalized (or in some manner "emphatic") voiceless fricative (or affricate?).

6.5.2.3 Zayin *in Cypriot Phoenician*

We have seen important and crucial connections begin to unfold between the Greeks of Cyprus (or, at the least, practitioners of the syllabic Cypriot script) and the process of adapting the Phoenician script for Greek use. Cyprus was inhabited in the early first millennium not only by Greeks but by Phoenicians as well. There is evidence that in the Cypriot dialect of Phoenician the sound of the character *zayin* was unlike that which it had in other Phoenician dialects.[188] In Phoenician, a prothetic vowel is sometimes added before a word-initial cluster of two consonants, thus effectively parceling the consonants into two different syllables.[189] As distinct vowel characters do not occur in the Phoenician script, the presence of this prothetic vowel is graphically marked by the addition of the character *'alep* to the beginning of the word. This vowel insertion process occurs particularly often in Cypriot Phoenician; thus, the Phoenician word for 'two', *šnm* ([šnVm]), appears in the Cypriot dialect as *'šnm* ([VšnVm]). The same prothetic vowel regularly occurs before the demonstrative pronoun *z* ([zV]) in Cypriot Phoenician, as is indicated by the spelling *'z* ([VzV]). Consequently, it appears that in the Cypriot dialect the character *zayin* did not represent simply [z] but a sequence of two consonants, or something phonetically quite similar to such a sequence. In other words, *zayin* represented a sort of double consonant—like *zeta*. If "ordinary" Phoenician *zayin* suggested itself as a candidate for representing Greek [zd] (and it would appear to have been the most likely candidate) to the scribes who had undertaken the task of adapting the Phoenician script for use in writing their own language, then Cypriot *zayin* may well have presented itself as a grapheme with particular phonetic characteristics that made such a choice even more compelling. Cyprus again raises its hand in response to the question, "Whence the alphabet?"

6.5.3 The Structural Motivation

The second or, as I we termed it, structural motivation for the view that the original value of the letter *zeta* was [dz] (rather than [zd]) is well summarized by Allen. In discussing the "metathesis" of Greek *[dz] to [zd], he states:

(25)   A sequence [dz] would in any case have been peculiarly isolated in Greek when it possessed neither any other affricates such as [ts] nor an indepen-

dent /z/ phoneme; in the sequence [zd], on the other hand, the [z] element would be a normal voiced variant of the /s/ phoneme as in, for example, Λέσβος [([lésbos], a place-name)].[190]

Allen then continues:

(26) [I]t nevertheless remains probable that at the time when the Semitic alphabet was adopted by Greek, the "*zayin*" symbol was at first applied to a still existing affricate type of combination; for it is difficult to see why a sequence [zd] should not have been represented by σδ instead of by a special sign; whereas, since voice-assimilation in Greek is normally regressive rather than progressive, δσ would not be a satisfactory representation of [dz].

In other words, Greek has not only [zd] sequences but also *fricative + voiced stop* clusters of the type [zb] and [zg]. The latter named cluster-types are simply spelled as σβ and σγ respectively as in, for example, πρέσβυς ([prézbüs], 'elder') and μίσγω ([mízgo̧:], 'I mix'). The phoneme /s/ is realized as a voiced allophone [z] before a voiced stop, but since, as was pointed out above, spelling is normally phonemic and not allophonic, this pre-stop [z] is simply spelled σ. That being the case, what would be the need for a distinct character *zeta* if that character represented the *fricative + voiced stop* sequence [zd], as such a sequence could be readily represented as σδ? Since, however, a distinct character *zeta* was created, it is reasoned, the value of *zeta* at the time of the adoption of the Phoenician script must have been [dz].

   In order to see why a *zeta* character which in fact had the value [zd] was included in the alphabet by the Greek adapters of the Semitic writing system, we must once again direct our attention to the historical development of the sound represented by this symbol *zeta*. By the period of Mycenaean Greek, earlier *[gy], *[dy], and the relevant occurrences of word-initial *[y] had already merged as some common reflex, as is demonstrated by the Linear B spelling of each of these reflexes with the one syllabic symbol *zV* (the exact value of this reflex is uncertain at this stage of the language; to avoid speculating on this value, I have arbitrarily used the cover symbol [Z] to represent this sound in the phonetic transcriptions of the following Linear B forms):[191]

(27) A. instances of word-initial *y-
         e.g., *yeug- ⇒ ze-u-ke-si; ζευγεσσι ([Zeugessi], 'for pairs')
      B. the sequence *gy
         e.g., *meg-yo- ⇒ me-zo; μεζως ([meZo̧:s], 'greater')
      C. the sequence *dy
         e.g., *-ped-ya- ⇒ to-pe-za; τορπεζα ([torpeZa], 'table')

Whatever the value of the consonantal component of the *zV* symbols at this early stage of the language (a palatalized stop, an affricate, or whatever[192]), the value must have been such that, *at the time the syllabary was devised,* the sound was perceived as a single sound-unit (i.e., as a unitary phoneme), rather than as some sequence of sounds.

   The Cypriot Syllabary likewise possesses *CV* symbols which correspond to alphabetic *zeta*.[193] The character *zo* is well attested and occurs in forms such as the following proper names (in the phonetic transcriptions, [Z] is again used merely as a phonetically noncommittal cover symbol):

(28)   A. Ζωϝαγορας ([Ẓọ:wagoras])
       B. Ζωϝαλιος ([Ẓọ:walios])
       C. Ζωϝης ([Ẓọ:wẹ:s])

It is possible that the syllabary also preserves a character with the value *za*, though there is uncertainty concerning this.[194] Furthermore, as Masson explicitly states, the syllabary surely contained other *zV* symbols, such as *ze* (which would be needed to spell, for example, ζεῦγος ([zeûgos], 'a yoke of animals'), a word attested in Cypriot's sister dialect of Arcadian) and *zu* (as would be needed, for example, for writing the common term ζυγόν ([zügón], 'yoke')); but these are not attested in the inscriptions recovered thus far.[195]

In the case of the Cypriot *zV* characters, the practice of using a single symbol to represent the "*zeta*-sound" could have come about, in theory, by way of either of two different routes. As with the Mycenaean script, one could argue that this sound was still perceived as a unitary phoneme at the time that the Cypriot syllabary was appropriated for the spelling of Greek (by at least the mid-eleventh century, with some prehistory of experimentation likely). This, however, is not a likely scenario. As argued above (see 6.5.1), the [zd] reflex developed quite early. Consequently, as the "*zeta*-sound" had acquired a value which could have been readily and reasonably represented by a sequence of two syllabic symbols, the use of *zV* characters in the Cypriot Syllabary appears to be still another instance of the fine-tuning of an earlier Cypro-Minoan script by transplanted Mycenaean Greek scribes under the influence of the Linear B syllabary of their homeland: since the "*zeta*-sound" had been spelled with a symbol *zV* in their own Mycenaean script, such a symbol was deemed desirable for and was incorporated into the Cypriot script.

The process of transferring from one writing system to another the practice of using a single symbol to represent the "*zeta*-sound" then occurred yet again upon the adoption of the Phoenician script. The Cypriot Greek scribes were now accustomed to utilizing a syllabic writing system containing *zV* symbols which had the value [zd]. Given the Cypriot adapters' conservatism, which is revealed by their inclusion of a *ks* alphabetic character in the new writing system, it does not surprise us that the tradition of spelling with a [zd] character should also have been extended to the alphabetic script; Phoenician *zayin* presented itself as an attractive candidate, having the value [z] or, in Cyprus, perhaps a value even perceptually closer to the [zd] of the *zV* syllabic symbols. Structural considerations of the type described by Allen lose their significance.

Proposing a Cypriot origin of the Greek alphabet at the hands of scribes accustomed to writing with the syllabic Greek script of Cyprus thus once again brings order to the process of the Greek acquisition of the Semitic script. It does so in this case by attractively and reasonably accounting for a superficially incoherent state of affairs: the [zd] value of *zeta* at an early alphabetic period (as evidenced by linguistic factors) and the representation of the [zd] *sound sequence* by means of a single character rather than by means of a σδ *spelling sequence.*

6.6 The Greek Letters *Sigma* and *San*

In the preceding pages, I have argued against that portion of the confusion hypothesis, advanced by Jeffery, according to which *xi* and *zeta* derive their values (and names) from *shin* and *ṣade* respectively (illustrated in (29)):

(29) A. *zayin*   *zeta*
     B. *samek*   *xi*
     C. *ṣade*   *san*
     D. *shin*   *sigma*

I have contended for the position that Greek *xi* and *zeta* have as their respective Phoenician precursors, regarding value (and therefrom name), the characters *samek* and *zayin*, with which they undeniably share alphabetic position and graphic shape. Most reasonably then, *shin* and *ṣade* are the Phoenician analogues of Greek *sigma* and *san,* not only in terms of position and shape, but in terms of value (and name) as well:

(30) A. *zayin*   *zeta*
     B. *samek*   *xi*
     C. *ṣade*   →   *san*
     D. *shin*   →   *sigma*

The occurrence of the Greek letters *sigma* and *san* in inscriptions written in the various epichoric alphabets is one of almost complete complementary distribution. In other words, the two graphemes occur practically to the exclusion of one another: the fricative [s] is represented by *sigma* in inscriptions from, for example, Attica, Boeotia, Thessaly, Locris, Aegina, Megara, Arcadia, the Doric colonies of Sicily, the Ionic Islands, the Ionic Dodecapolis, and Rhodes; it is spelled with *san* in inscriptions from, for example, Corinth, Sicyon, Ithaca, Achaea, and Crete. By the late fifth century, however, *sigma* has supplanted *san* in all of the alphabets except, as Jeffery indicates, that of Crete, yet another revelation of the Cretan alphabet's pronounced conservatism.[196]

6.6.1 The Background of *San*

Although *san* has the value [s] in all of the alphabets of which it is a part, it is commonly held that its earliest Greek value must have been something other than that: it is manifestly unlikely that the Greeks assigned the identical value of [s] to two of the characters which they adopted from the Phoenician script, and it is *sigma* which is commonly identified as the "original" [s] character. Consequent to her confusion hypothesis, Jeffery suggests that *san* had the value [z] (*ṣade* ([s']) and *zayin* ([z]) having exchanged values), stating:

(31) Perhaps this . . . sound, the voiced sibilant, was used in the Doric dialect
     of Crete and Corinth (which used *san*), but not in the Ionic (which there-

fore used the sign of the harder [i.e., voiceless] sibilant, *sigma*), nor in the
Doric of Rhodes and Lakonia.[197]

There is no *a priori* reason why the early value of Greek *san* could not have
been [z]; if such were the case, however, it is not likely to have been so for the
reason offered by Jeffery. To begin with, I have argued above that the Greeks
did not confuse the values of *ṣade* and *zayin*. The value of the Phoenician
character upon which *san* is formally based was not, then, [z] (the value of
zayin); instead, the value of this *(ṣade)* character was that of some sort of
glottalized (or in some way "emphatic") voiceless fricative (or perhaps even
affricate). Beyond that, there is no indication that Cretan and Corinthian Doric
were characterized by [z] in contradistinction to Rhodian Doric, Lakonian
Doric and Ionic (with [s]). In fact, it is not clear in what sense Jeffery is proposing that this difference existed. Is the former set of dialects supposed to
have possessed a phonemic /z/ as opposed to a phonemic /s/ occurring in the
latter? Or is it meant that the former set of dialects exhibit [z] allophones of
/s/ while the latter group does not? As discussed above, regressive assimilation
of voicing was already a characteristic of Proto-Indo-European; hence, the occurrence of a [z] allophone of an /s/ which preceded a voiced consonant was
surely a Proto-Greek feature and common to all dialects.

While evidence does exist of a somewhat more widespread occurrence of an
allophone [z] in certain dialects, the dialectal subset displaying this characteristic does not coincide with that one advanced by Jeffery, but in fact contradicts
it. In both Elean and late Laconian, word-final *[s] has been changed to [r]; that
is, *[s] has been rhotacized. Rhotacism of [s] is a fairly common phonological
development which usually exhibits an intermediate reflex [z] (i.e., [s] ⇒
[z]⇒[r]). Consequently, it is quite probable that a word-final *[z] occurred at
an earlier phase in the history of these dialects. In the same way, intervocalic
*[s] is frequently rhotacized in Eretrian and thus probably passed thorough a
*[z] stage prior to becoming [r].[198]

We thus see that the linguistic evidence contradicts Jeffery's scheme. Jeffery
has suggested that since the alphabet of Laconian was *sigma*-using rather than
san-using, the sound [z] did not occur in the Laconian dialect. Yet Laconian
speech actually has a particular propensity for [z]: this dialect not only voiced
/s/ to [z] when it preceded voiced consonants, as did all dialects, but possessed
word-final *[-z] as well.[199] Elean, which has the same configuration of [s]/[z]
as Laconian (though rhotacism appears to have begun somewhat earlier in
Elean), and Eretrian, having an intervocalic *[z], are likewise dialects written
with *sigma*-using alphabets. Conversely, the Doric dialects of Corinth and
Crete, written with *san*-using alphabets, show no evidence of possessing [z]
beyond its predictable (pandialectal) occurrence before voiced stops.

Others have proposed that in the earliest period of the alphabet *san* represented some type of voiceless sibilant which was distinct from [s]. Lejeune, for
example, suggests that *san* may have been utilized to represent the sound which
he terms "la sifflante forte."[200] The evidence for suggesting such a value for
san lies in the occurrence of special characters in two of the epichoric alphabets
which have been interpreted as being variant or altered forms of *san*. One of

these characters serves to represent the "palatalized" reflex of the voiceless labiovelar [kʷ], and the other is utilized to spell the reflex of the earlier sequences *[k⁽ʰ⁾y], *[t⁽ʰ⁾y], and *[tw].²⁰¹ Let us consider, in turn, each of these graphemes and their uses.

6.6.1.1 Arcadian Ͷ

In the sister dialects of Cypriot and Arcadian, the voiceless labiovelar of an earlier period of Greek has given rise to a reflex which appears to be unique to this dialectal subgroup; while *[kʷ] regularly becomes [t] before the high front and mid front vowels in the other non-Aeolic dialects,²⁰² in Arcado-Cypriot the outcome is clearly somewhat different. In the syllabic Cypriot script, the Greek indefinite pronoun τις ([tis] < *[kʷis]) is spelled *si-se,* that is, [Cis] (here I use C as a phonetically noncommittal cover symbol for representing this Cypriot reflex of *[kʷ]).²⁰³ In addition, Hesychius (a Greek lexicographer of the fifth and sixth centuries A.D.) cites σί ([sí]) as the Cypriot equivalent of the Greek interrogative pronoun τί ([tí] < *[kʷi]). In a fifth-century Arcadian inscription from Mantinea, one of the special *san*-like symbols referred to above is found—the character Ͷ—and is utilized to represent the Arcadian reflex of *[kʷ]: Ͷινα ([Cina]; cf. Attic τινα ([tina], 'someone')); oͷεοι ([oCeoi]; cf. Attic ὅτῳ ([hótọːi], 'to whomever')), and ειͶε ([eːCe]; cf. Attic εἴτε ([éːte], 'either')).²⁰⁴

The sound ultimately spelled *sV* in the syllabic Cypriot script and represented by the character Ͷ in the Arcadian alphabet was almost certainly some type of sibilant—quite possibly an affricate (or something similar thereto); an affricate such as [č] or [tˢ] would be a likely intermediate reflex in the palatalization of *[kʷ] to [t] before front vowels.²⁰⁵ This is to say, of course, that Arcado-Cypriot preserves an intermediate phase of a phonological process which had already run to completion in contemporary non-Aeolic dialects. Beyond that, however, there is additional orthographic evidence for an affricate or affricate-like pronunciation of Arcadian labiovelar reflexes:²⁰⁶

1. In an early Arcadian legal text (from Cleitor or Lusoi, perhaps sixth century) the character *zeta* is used to represent the reflex of *[kʷ]: οζις (cf. Homeric ὅτις ([hótis], 'whoever', from *[-kʷis])).²⁰⁷

2. The second piece of evidence is provided by an inscription which was actually written in the Doric dialect of Laconian but which displays several Arcadian features by virtue of its being the handiwork of an Arcadian engraver at Tegea.²⁰⁸ One such Arcadianism which crept into the document is the spelling τζετρακατιαι for τετρακάτιαι ([tetrakátiai], 'four hundred', from *[kʷetwr̥-]).

3. There are glosses which record Arcadian forms in which *zeta* is used to spell the reflex of the voiced labiovelar *[gʷ]: Hesychius offers ζέλλω· βάλλω ([bállọː], 'I throw'), cf. inscriptional Arcadian –δελλω ([dellọː]); Strabo (a first-century travel writer) records ζέρεθρα· βάραθρα ([bárathra], 'pits'), cf. here Arcadian inscriptional δερεθρον ([deretʰron]).²⁰⁹ The inscriptional spellings with *d* are probably the result of the influence of other dialects upon Arcadian; as Buck points out with respect to the use of the Ͷ character,

spellings which suggest a sibilant pronunciation are found, not surprisingly, only in early inscriptions.[210] The ζ which occurs in the glosses of (3) reveals a sibilant pronunciation of the Arcadian reflex of palatalized *[kʷ], though its value is perhaps to be understood as simply [z]—the regular value of *zeta* at the late date of the recording of these glosses. Regardless of the value of *zeta* in (3), it is clear that in the case of the early inscriptional spellings of (1) and (2), in which *zeta* is utilized to represent a *voiceless* sound, the scribes are not using the character with its normal value but are adapting it to render the closest possible fit. The spelling with τζ- in (2) is particularly suggestive of an attempt to represent an affricate.[211]

6.6.1.2 Ionic ᛏ

The second of the special orthographic characters which some scholars have speculated to be a modification of *san* is the symbol ᛏ.[212] This character occurs in sixth- and fifth-century alphabets of several of the Ionian cities of Asia Minor[213] and is used to represent an Ionic reflex of the earlier consonantal clusters *[k⁽ʰ⁾y], *[t⁽ʰ⁾y], and *[tw]: for example, τεᛏαρας for τέσσαρας ([téssaras], 'four', accusative).[214] As illustrated by this example, the usual Ionic reflex of these clusters is [ss] (corresponding to Attic [tt], as in τέτταρες ([téttares])); it is probable, much as in the case of ᛉ, that ᛏ represents a reflex which is antecedent to and distinct from the ultimate reflex [ss]. Also as with ᛉ, it is almost certain that ᛏ represents some type of sibilant.[215] These points of similarity between ᛉ and ᛏ are not noted to suggest, however, that the sounds represented by the two symbols are phonetically identical. The two phonological processes which give rise to the intermediate reflexes which these two characters represent have quite distinct ultimate reflexes. This has been revealed already by our above cited example of the numeral four; consider the contrast between the word-initial consonant (from *[kʷ] occurring before a front vowel) and the word-internal cluster (from *[tw]; in the Aeolic dialects of Lesbian and Boeotian the labiovelar has not been palatalized before the mid front vowel, as I discuss later):

> (32) From *kʷetw(V)r- (depending upon the vowel of the second syllable):
> A. Attic τέτταρες ([téttares])
> B. Ionic τέσσερες ([tésseres], more common than τέσσαρες)
> C. Lesbian πεσσυρες ([pessúres]
> D. Boeotian πετταρες ([pettares])

Or contrast Attic σε ([se], 'you'; from *[twe]) with τε ([te], 'and', from *[kʷe]).

6.6.1.3 ᛉ, ᛏ, *and* San

Are these two characters ᛉ and ᛏ to be linked with *san*? In the case of the former (ᛉ), the symbol for the palatalized labiovelar reflex of Arcadian, this affiliation is highly probable and widely accepted.[216] There is an obvious graphic similarity between ᛉ and *san,* and on phonetic grounds Phoenician ṣade appears to present itself readily as the source for a character with such a sibilant (probably affricate) value. Beyond this and of weighty significance, however, as Larfeld points out, the character Ͷ also occurs in the Etruscan abecedarium from Caere, in which it occupies the position of *san*.[217] The case for linking Ͳ with *san* is somewhat less certain. It appears that the symbol was introduced into the Ionic alphabets most immediately from the Carian script of Asia Minor[218] and is probably to be identified with that Greek character which would later be called by Byzantine grammarians *sampi* (ϡ)—so called because it is shaped 'like pi' (ὡς ἂν πῖ ([hǫ:s àn pî]).[219] The character *sampi* occurs at least as early as the sixth century in the Milesian numbering system,[220] in which alphabetic characters are assigned numerical values: in this system *sampi* occurs at the very end of the alphabet and bears the value 900. Because of this positioning, Jeffery contests the identification of *sampi* with *san,* arguing that if the former were derived from the latter, they should both occupy the same alphabetic position—the position of *san* (and *ṣade*)—but they do not.

6.6.1.4 A Further Cypriot Connection

I have argued that the adaptation of the Phoenician script for Greek use was the work of scribes accustomed to writing with the syllabic Cypriot script. Such a hypothesis offers a reasonable and compelling account not only for the presence of a [ks] character in the Greek alphabet but also for the presence of a symbol with the value [zd]—both idiosyncratic and anomalous features of an alphabetic system. This same hypothesis provides an attractive and sensible motivation for the occurrence in the Greek alphabet of the character *san* alongside *sigma*. To see this, let us further consider the Cypriot reflex of the palatalized labiovelar *[kʷ].

As we have seen, there is good evidence that the Arcado-Cypriot reflex of *[kʷ] which occurs before front vowels is a sibilant and quite probably an affricate. This is likely the very value of the Arcadian alphabetic character Ͷ; but how are we to interpret the phonetics of the syllabic Cypriot *sV* spelling of this *[kʷ] reflex? On the one hand, it could be that orthographic <s-> here simply represents the fricative [s] and that this dental fricative is a further development of the Arcado-Cypriot affricate reflex. This is the position of Lejeune, who proposes a value [tˢ] for the affricate reflex, with subsequent Cypriot evolution to [s].[221] On the other hand, it is also possible that the Cypriot scribes utilized the *sV* symbols to represent not only [s] but also a phonetically distinct sibilant reflex of *[kʷ], and that <s-> still had this ambiguous, dual value in the fifth century, when spellings such as *si-se* are attested. This appears to be what Jeffery envisions when she states, "The Arkadian sound was a kind of palatal sibilant, such as is attested for the kindred dialect of Cyprus."[222] The same set of possibilities can be transferred to the later period of the glosses attributed to Hesychius; thus, in the Cypriot gloss σί·τί, σ may represent [s], though it does not necessarily do so, and in the event that it does, the sound need not have had this value in that early period in which the Cypriot scribes engineered the use of the syllabic spelling *sV* to represent the reflex of *[kʷ] (and in fact the above cited remark of Jeffery is offered with reference to Hesychius's gloss).

Regardless of the phonetic value of the Cypriot *sV* syllabograms which are used to represent the palatalized reflex of *[kʷ], it is almost certain that at the time at which the syllabic Cypriot script was adapted for spelling Greek, the Cypriot reflex of this sound was quite similar to the affricate value which is indicated by the more phonetically revealing Arcadian spellings. The unique sibilant reflex of *[kʷ] occurring before front vowels is an Arcado-Cypriot feature; in other words, such a sibilant (probably an affricate) reflex had likely developed prior to the separation of these two dialects. This separation occurred with the extensive migration of Arcado-Cypriot speakers to Cyprus about 1200 B.C. As I pointed out earlier, the syllabic Cypriot script was already being used for writing Greek at least by the middle of the eleventh century; the probability that Cypriot still possessed a distinct sibilant reflex of *[kʷ] when the spelling system was acquired appears to be high. I would hesitate to speculate on how this sibilant may have been expressed orthographically at such an early period in the history of the Cypriot script, though it is probable that the nature of such expression was dependent, at least in part, upon the phonemic status of this sound, about which something should be said.

6.6.1.4.1 Labiovelar Developments.

The labiovelar consonants of Proto-Greek (i.e., *[kʷ], *[gʷ], *[kʷʰ]), generally remain intact in the second-millennium dialect of Mycenaean Greek, though unrounding of the labiovelar has already occurred in immediate contact with the vowel [u], as in the following examples:[223]

(33)   A. *qo-u-ko-ro* for γʷουκόλος, later βουκόλος ([bu:kólos], 'cowherd'), from *[gʷou-kʷol-]

B. *e-u-ke-to* for ευχετοι ([eukʰetoi], '(s)he proclaims'), from *[wegʷʰ-]

In addition, as indicated above, the labiovelars appear to undergo the same pre-Mycenaean development before [y] which is exhibited by velars in this context.[224] Subsequent to the Mycenaean era the labiovelars palatalize before front vowels according to the following scheme: in the non-Aeolic dialects all three labiovelars (*[kʷ], *[gʷ], *[kʷʰ]) palatalize before the mid front vowels; and in all dialects the voiceless unaspirated labiovelar (*[kʷ]) palatalizes before the high front vowel [i]:[225]

(34)   A. Proto-Indo-European *kʷetwr̥- ⇒ Attic τέτταρες ([téttares], 'four'); cf. Aeolic (Thessalian, Boeotian) πετταρες ([pettares])

B. Proto-Indo-European *gʷelbʰ- ⇒ Attic δελφίς ([delpʰís]), 'dolphin'); cf. Aeolic (Lesbian) βελφίς ([belpʰís])

C. Proto-Indo-European *gʷʰer-mo- ⇒ *kʷʰer-mo- ⇒ Attic θερμός ([tʰermós], 'hot')

D. Proto-Indo-European *kʷi-m- ⇒ Attic τίμη ([tí:mę:], 'honor')

As we have seen the Arcado-Cypriot reflex in this context is a sibilant rather than a dental stop. The remaining occurrences of labiovelars (i.e., those which were not eliminated in the pre-Mycenaean period or later palatalized as in (34), are then labialized (i.e., *[kʷ] ⇒ [p], *[gʷ] ⇒ [b], *[kʷʰ] ⇒ [pʰ]).[226] That is to say, in Aeolic *[kʷ, gʷ, kʷʰ] become bilabials before mid front vowels, as illustrated in (34A and B); and in all dialects bilabials develop from *[kʷ, gʷ, kʷʰ] before nonfront vowels (other than [u]) and before consonants, and from *[gʷ, kʷʰ] before high front vowels, as in the following examples:

(35)   A. Proto-Indo-European *pekʷ-to- ⇒ πεπτός ([peptós], 'cooked')
       B. Proto-Indo-European *snigʷʰm ⇒ *snikʷʰa ⇒ νίφα ([nípʰa], 'snow')
       C. Proto-Indo-European *gʷiy- ⇒ βίος ([bíos], 'life')

The palatalization (as in (34)) and labialization (as in (35)) of the labiovelars resulted in phonemic split and merger in all dialects, but in Arcadian and Cypriot this dual phonemic process was accompanied by the addition of a new consonant to the phonemic inventories of the Arcado-Cypriot dialectal subgroup. When the voiceless labiovelar phoneme */kʷ/ palatalized before front vowels in Arcadian, it developed a sibilant allophone, which, for the sake of exposition, I arbitrarily identify as [tˢ]. This means that the Arcadian phoneme */kʷ/ now had two allophones, *[tˢ] occurring before front vowels and *[kʷ] occurring elsewhere. With the subsequent labialization of the *[kʷ] allophone to *[p], however, hand-in-hand processes of phonemic split and merger occur: the *[p] phone which had arisen from *[kʷ] by labialization merged with the preexisting */p/ phoneme and concomitantly split away from its previous labiovelar phonemic membership. Once this had happened, *[tˢ] was left phonemically isolated as */tˢ/—the only phonemically distinct remnant of the earlier labiovelar phoneme */kʷ/. As spelling tends to be phonemic, the Arcadian alphabet utilizes a distinct symbol, the character *san,* to represent this phoneme /tˢ/. The same phonemic processes of split, merger and creation of a new phoneme appear to have occurred in the case of the Arcadian voiced labiovelar */gʷ/, judging from the above cited glosses (and presumably similar phonemic processes occurred involving the voiceless aspirated */kʷʰ/ as well, but orthographic evidence is lacking). In the instance of */gʷ/, however, a unique alphabetic character was not devised for representing the new voiced phoneme which arose by palatalization, or at least there is no evidence of such a character. This orthographic asymmetry may in itself be of considerable significance.

6.6.1.4.2 Arcado-Cypriot Labiovelar Palatalization and the Raison d'Etre for *San.* We have seen that Arcadian displays graphically attested, phonemically distinct sibilant reflexes of the palatalized labiovelars; in the case of the voiceless labiovelar *[kʷ], this reflex is represented by a distinct alphabetic character. Furthermore, I have posited that Arcadian's sister dialect of Cypriot was also characterized by a sibilant reflex of *[kʷ] which was at least phonetically distinct from other consonants of the dialect at the time at which the syllabic Cypriot script was devised for spelling Greek. This position leads us to a reasonable account for the occurrence in the Greek alphabet of the character *san* alongside the character *sigma,* as we shall now see.

While Arcadian and Cypriot do share in common a sibilant reflex for palatalized *[kʷ], it appears that labiovelar evolution in these sister dialects was not identical at all points. There is evidence that in Cypriot, as in the Aeolic dialects, the labiovelars gave rise to bilabial reflexes before the mid front vowels. From three different districts of the island of Cyprus come inscriptions, dating at least as early as the sixth century,[227] which preserve forms of a verb *πει- ([pei-]) from *k^wei-, cf. Attic τί–νω ([tíno̜:], 'I pay') from zero-grade*k^wi-. Both future and aorist subjunctive verbs occur: *pe-i-se-i* (πεισει, [pe̜:se̜:]) and *pe-i-se* (πειση, [pe̜:se̜:]), respectively. With this, contrast the Arcadian aorist -τεισατω ([te̜:sato̜:]), with a dental reflex of the labiovelar as in Attic and elsewhere.[228] In addition, a fourth-century Phoenician-Cypriot Greek bilingual inscription from Idalion (a site providing one of the inscriptions containing *pe-i-se-i*) presents the form -*pe-pa-me-ro-ne,* that is πεμπαμερων ([pempam-ero̜:n], 'a period of five days', genitive plural), which would seem to suggest a Cypriot numeral *πεμπε ([pempe], 'five', from *penk^we) as in Aeolic;[229] con-trast πέντε ([pénte]) in Arcadian, Attic, and so on.

It is probable, then, as Lejeune and others have advocated,[230] that the Cyp-riot development of the labiovelars before the mid front vowels is the same as that which is well known from the Aeolic dialects (i.e., a bilabial reflex is regular in this context). If this is so, then Cypriot obviously departs from the Arcadian sibilant treatment of labiovelars before front vowels to the extent that the sibilant reflex would be far more restricted in distribution in Cypriot than in Arcadian. This view is completely consistent with the actual occurrences of the sibilant reflexes which are attested by these two sister dialects. For Arcadian we have attestation of a sibilant reflex of *[k^w] occurring before [i] and of *[k^w] and *[g^w] before [e]; in Cypriot a sibilant reflex is attested only for *[k^w] and only when it precedes [i]. We see immediately, then, that (i) the occurrence of the sibilant labiovelar reflex in Arcadian appears to be identical in distribu-tion to the occurrence of the dental stop reflex in the other non-Aeolic dialects (aside from Cypriot), while (ii) the occurrence of the sibilant labiovelar reflex in Cypriot shows itself to be of the same distribution as the occurrence of the dental stop reflex in the Aeolic dialects.

The variant distribution of the sibilant labiovelar reflexes in Arcadian and Cypriot is readily accounted for. On the basis of an extensive examination of both philological and typological evidence, Stephens and Woodard argued that the palatalization of the Greek labiovelars occurred in two separate and to some extent independent phases, spreading in wavelike fashion from an innovating center.[231] In the first phase, palatalization occurred only before the high front vowels and affected only the voiceless labiovelar *[k^w], though *[g^w] was also palatalized when followed by a high front vowel *and* preceded by a front vowel. The second phase of the process was areally more restricted, not being thoroughly extended through the Aeolic speech area, but phonetically more pervasive to the extent that all three labiovelars were palatalized; this second phase of palatalization affected labiovelars occurring before the mid front vowels.[232] The initial phase of palatalization must have been accomplished at a time prior to the separation of the Arcado-Cypriot speech community, so that palatalization of *[k^w] before [i], producing a sibilant reflex, affected the entire community. However, the divergence in treatment of the labiovelars before mid front vowels in these two very closely related dialects must signal that the proto-Cypriot speakers had departed from the parent speech community before the arrival in that community of the second wave of labiovelar palatalization.

It appears, then, that when Arcado-Cypriot speakers arrived in Cyprus, their speech was characterized by two allophones of the labiovelar phoneme */kʷ/: a sibilant allophone occurring only before high front vowels and an allophone *[kʷ] occurring elsewhere. The other two labiovelar phonemes, */gʷ/ and */kʷʰ/, appear to have exhibited no allophonic variation (unlike the case of Arcadian). Upon labialization of the remaining labiovelar phones (by which process *[kʷ], *[gʷ], *[kʷʰ] became [p], [b], [pʰ] respectively) and phonemic merger of the resulting bilabial reflexes with the preexisting bilabial phonemes /p/, /b/, and /pʰ/, the sibilant allophone of earlier */kʷ/ was left phonemically stranded, just as occurred in Arcadian, though in Cypriot the sibilant's distribution was much more limited than in Arcadian. If the Phoenician script was acquired subsequent to the labialization of the labiovelars, then, given that spelling tends to be phonemic, we would expect that an alphabetic character would have been provided for the graphic representation of the now phonemic sibilant which was in origin the palatalized labiovelar *[kʷ]. However, the phonetic distinction between the sibilant allophone (perhaps *[tˢ] or *[tˢ]) occurring before [i] and the allophone *[kʷ] occurring elsewhere is so great that a separate alphabetic character probably would have been appropriated for representing this sibilant sound even if labialization of the labiovelars had not yet occurred and thus the sibilant was not yet a distinct phoneme. In this case, however, we would expect that alphabetic symbols for the three labiovelar phonemes would have also been devised, and for this no evidence is forthcoming.

To represent the newly evolved sibilant phoneme of Cypriot, the Phoenician character *ṣade* (Greek *san*) was utilized by the Cypriot adapters of the Semitic script. Since *ṣade* was itself some sort of dental sibilant ("emphatic" in nature), it must have readily presented itself as a natural candidate for this purpose. The only other dialect of Greek which possessed such a distinct sibilant phoneme was, as we have made excruciatingly clear, Arcadian, and it is hardly a coincidence that it is the Arcadian alphabet alone which preserves the productive use of both *san* and *sigma*[233] and that in this alphabet *san* is used to represent the sibilant phoneme which developed from the palatalized labiovelar *[kʷ]. Arcadian also apparently possessed palatalized reflexes of the other labiovelars, occurring before the mid front vowels, but for these it appears there was no distinct alphabetic symbol, as we have seen. This is a consequence of the fact that Cypriot possessed only a sibilant reflex of the voiceless labiovelar *[kʷ] and so passed to Arcadian an alphabet with only one such character.

The other early Greek speech communities which received an alphabet having both *san* and *sigma* possessed dialects without such a sibilant phoneme. We could speculate that perhaps in these communities *sigma* was generally used to represent [s] but *san* was utilized for [s] occurring in certain phonetic environments (or vice versa). If so, this would be somewhat similar to the use of *qoppa* for representing a backed allophone of /k/, though such a *san/sigma* distinction, if it existed, would not necessarily have been allophonic. In any event, the use of either *san* or *sigma* was generalized at the expense of the other for represent-ing [s] in the various epichoric alphabets.[234] This is precisely the condition which exists in the local Etruscan alphabets (acquired from the Greeks). Of the Etruscan reflexes of the three Phoenician characters *samek*, *ṣade*, and *shin*, only two are normally used in any given locale to represent the two sibilant conso-nants which Etruscan is conjectured to have possessed.[235]

6.6.2 The Case of *Sigma*

Greek *sigma* occupies the alphabetic position which corresponds to Phoenician *shin*. We have now disputed and rejected each of the three equations of Jef-fery's confusion hypothesis considered thus far; *ipso facto*, the fourth equation (which holds that the value and name of *sigma* are acquired from *samek*) is eliminated in favor of the straightforward proposition that *shin*, and *shin* alone, is the Phoenician precursor of Greek *sigma*. Of course, the value of Phoenician *shin* is [š] (as in *ship*), while that of *sigma* is [s] (as in *sip*). However, as discussed above, the evidence indicates that Canaanite *samek* represented not [s] but an affricate such as [tˢ] or perhaps even a palatalized stop. Phoenician *ṣade* represented a glottalized (or velarized etc.) fricative or even affricate, and *zayin* had the value of a voiced fricative in most Phoenician dialects but proba-bly represented some type of voiced double consonant in Cypriot Phoenician. Thus, while Phoenician *shin* was not identical in value to Greek *sigma*, its value may nevertheless have been auditorially less *unlike* Greek [s] than that of any of the other Phoenician sibilant characters.

Perhaps, however, the motivation for adopting *shin* to represent Greek [s] was not only negative in character. As Harris points out, another of the distinc-tive characteristics of at least one of the *Cypriot* dialects of Phoenician may have been that *shin* was pronounced as [s].[236] Such a pronunciation is suggested by certain spelling irregularities which occur in materials written in the dialect of Lapethos; for example, the proper name Πτολεμαῖος ([ptolemaîos]) is regu-larly spelled *ptlmyś*, that is, with *shin* for the final [s]. It is interesting, in light of the Cypriot connection with the origin of the Greek alphabet which we see unfolding, that an [s] value of *shin* is suggested for an area of Cyprus, though it may be rash to make too much of this given the fourth/third-century date of these materials.

6.6.3 The Names of *Sigma* and *San*

Jeffery links the name of *sigma* with that of Phoenician *samek*, stating (as quoted earlier), "the names are very similar."[237] Following Jeffery's confusion hypothesis, Powell seeks to account for the differences in these imagined cor-responding Phoenician and Greek letter-names (*samek* and *sigma* respectively) by invoking a process of metathesis. As his starting point, Powell uses the Phoenician letter-name **semk*, after the early Semitic letter-name reconstruction by Nöldeke.[238] Powell writes:

(36) The deviation of the name σίγμα from *semk* is not obvious. We would
expect something like *σέμκα, and the evolution could have gone *σεμκ
> *σεμκα > *σεμγα > *σεγμα > *σιγμα.[239]

We have seen that Jeffery's confusion hypothesis is beset with problems and is
an unnecessary encumbrance. Beyond that, Powell's derivation of the name
sigma from the Phoenician term *semk* presents multiple difficulties.

1. To begin with, it should be noted that Nöldeke shows some hesitation
between *semk,* and *samk* in his reconstruction of the early Semitic character-
name.[240]

2. The proposed incremental change of *σεμκα > *σεμγα (*[semka] >
*[semga]) requires a progressive voicing change which is completely unattested
in ancient Greek. Voicing assimilation in Greek is regressive, not progressive.

3. Concerning the sequence [-mk-] (as in conjectured *σεμκ), Powell states,
"A cluster -mk- is odd for Greek and can be expected to decompose in some
way."[241] This is fair enough, but there is, in fact, a regular treatment of the
cluster *[mk] and it is not one of progressive voicing assimilation (*σεμκα >
σεμγα ([semka] > *[semga])) followed by metathesis (*σεμγα > *σεγμα
(*[semga] > *[segma])). As with all sequences of the type *nasal + velar stop,*
the cluster *[mk] becomes [ŋk], with the nasal undergoing regressive assimilation to the velar place of articulation, as in *συμ−καλεω (*[süm-kaleọ:]) ⇒
συγ−καλέω ([süŋ-kaléọ:], 'I convene').[242]

4. Powell further states that "a metathesis to *σεγμα would be catalyzed
by the fairly large class of Greek neuter nouns in −μα. The form of the name
may well have received support from the onomatopoeic verb σίζω, 'to
hiss'."[243] As I discuss later, it is not necessary to make recourse to an ad hoc
process of metathesis in order to associate the term σίγμα with either the class
of neuter nouns in −μα ([-ma]) or the verb root of σίζω ([sízdọ:]).

5. Concerning the first vowel of σίγμα, Powell remarks, "The unexpected
vowel may be contamination from *shin,* if we could be sure what the vowel
was really like in Phoenician."[244] This hybridization of the proposed Greek
letter-name *segma and the Semitic letter-name *shin* only heightens the ad hoc
nature of this scenario, especially since, as Powell suggests, the vowel of the
Phoenician letter-name was not necessarily *i.*

My fifth objection to Powell's derivation of *sigma* from *samek* brings us to
the next matter to be considered: the Phoenician letter-name for the Semitic
character *shin.* As McCarter has argued, it appears that the early form of the
Canaanite letter-name was *shan* rather than *shin.* This pronunciation is indicated by the Akkadian transcription *sha* of the abbreviation of the name of
the Ugaritic character which corresponds to the Phoenician symbol. McCarter
contends that Phoenician *shan* was borrowed into Greek as *san* and that *san*
was thus the earliest name of the Greek character eventually called *sigma.*[245]
The Phoenician *shan*/Greek *san* match is phonetically straightforward and involves only the minimal modifications which would be required by the borrowing process. There is well-known literary support for such a position, as
McCarter points out. In the first book of his histories, Herodotus (1.139) comments that the names of the Persians all end in the *same letter* (by which

remark he is referring to the transcription of the sound [s]), stating that this is the letter (γράμμα ([grámma])),

(37)   τὸ Δωριέες μὲν σὰν καλέουσι, Ἴωνες δὲ σίγμα·
[which the Dorians call *san,* and the Ionians *sigma*][246]

In addition, *san* remained in common use as the name of *sigma* in poetry. This means of course that we do not actually know the earliest name of the Greek letter (*M*) which was based upon Phoenician *ṣade.*

It would appear, then, that with respect to the Greek alphabetic symbol Σ, that symbol which is counterpart to Phoenician *shan* (Hebrew *shin*), Greek alphabetic traditions fall into three different categories: (i) in some instances the earliest Greek name of the letter—*san*—continued to be used for this character (as with Herodotus's Dorians and in poetry); (ii) in others the Greek name of this symbol was changed to *sigma*; (iii) and in still another group the name *san* was preserved but was used to identify the Greek alphabetic character which had developed from *ṣade.* These are mutually exclusive strategies, and a productively utilized vestige of both *ṣade* and *shan* appears not to occur in any single epichoric alphabet of Greece, with the exception of that of Arcadia[247] (in which case we do not know the names attached to the two letters).

It is not difficult to imagine how such a state of affairs could have arisen if we bear in mind that in each of those early alphabets which in some way actually participated in the process of opting for the *ṣade* analogue at the expense of the *shan* analogue, or vice versa, the (at least phonemic) value of these two symbols was most probably the same, that is, /s/. The two symbols not only shared the same value, but were also graphically quite similar: Greek-*ṣade* and Greek-*shan*, as I will refer to them (i.e., *san* and *sigma*), have the respective (stylized) shapes *M* and Σ.[248] These two [s] characters could easily be interpreted synchronically as redundant variants of one another. It appears that the term *san* was generalized as the name attached to the surviving symbol, regardless of which of the two shapes (i.e., that of Greek-*ṣade* or Greek-*shan*) was eliminated from use. In some subset of those alphabets which retained Greek-*shan* (eliminating Greek-*ṣade*), however, a new name, *sigma*, was coined and assigned to this character. It is quite conceivable that this newly coined term could have also been applied to Greek-*ṣade* in some of the alphabets which retained this character as the [s] symbol and that attestation of this name has simply not survived. Powell indicates that the earliest preserved instance of the recording of a Greek letter-name appears to be in a fragment of Pindar (70b3)—in other words, not until the early fifth century.[249] As McCarter and others have pointed out, *sigma*, the new name for Greek-*shan*, must certainly be derived from the root of σίζω ([sízdǫ:]), from earlier **sig-yo-,* meaning 'I hiss.'[250]

6.7 Concluding Remarks

We are compelled to posit that the Greek acquisition of an alphabetic writing system was the work of scribes who were accustomed to spelling the Greek language with the Cypriot syllabic script. The initial motivation for this hypothesis was supplied by the observation that a symbol with the value [k] + [s] is a redundant, awkward, and nonsensical feature of an alphabetic system—but a necessary feature of the syllabic spelling system of the Cypriot Greeks, given the spelling strategies (based upon a hierarchy of orthographic strength) which I have proposed for the representation of consonant clusters in the Cypriot Syllabary. Operating with the hypothesis of a Cypriot origin of the Greek alphabet, we have found that the Greek adaptation of the Phoenician sibilant characters is straightforward and that positing an implausible confusion of names and values of such characters (à la Jeffery) is unnecessary. Here I summarize my conclusions.

The Phoenician character *zayin* was utilized by the Greek adapters to represent the sound sequence [zd] (the sound of *zeta*). Syllabic characters with the consonantal value [zd-] existed in the Cypriot script (probably ultimately a feature inherited from the Mycenaean syllabary); consequently, provision was made by these Cypriot adapters for expressing such a sequence with an alphabetic symbol. Semitic *zayin* represented a voiced fricative [z], but in Cypriot Phoenician this sound appears to have been some sort of "double consonant," thus rendering *zayin* particularly suggestive for representing the Greek sequence [zd]. Without positing such a syllabic Cypriot background for the alphabetic character *zeta*, the use of a single alphabetic symbol to represent [z] + [d] (the value consistent with linguistic evidence) is enigmatic. The name of the Greek character, *zeta*, is doubtless based upon the letter-names *eta* and *theta* (from Semitic *ḥet* and *ṭet*), which follow *zeta* alphabetically.

Hebrew *samek* represents the fricative [s], but there is evidence that in an early period Canaanite *samek* had the value of a palatalized stop or an affricate. The Greek adapters assigned to *samek* the alphabetic value [ks]. As with *zeta*, this process involved transferring a consonantal value which occurred in the graphemic inventory of the syllabic Cypriot script to that of the new alphabetic script. The assigning of the value [ks] to *samek*, it appears, was to a degree an arbitrary process (not unlike assigning vowel values to certain Phoenician consonant characters), though there may have been at least partial phonetic motivation, especially if the value of Phoenician *samek* was something like [k^y]. The name of the Greek symbol, *xi*, also appears likely to have been a creation *de novo*, simply being constructed from the value of the character ([ks]) followed by a single vowel sound. The choice of the vowel was most probably determined by the letter-name of the next consonantal symbol occurring after *xi* in the alphabet: namely, *pi*.

The Phoenician character *ṣade* represented an emphatic voiceless fricative or, perhaps less likely, an emphatic affricate. The "emphatic" aspect of the consonant was probably realized phonetically as glottalization, velarization or pharyngealization. *Ṣade* was utilized by the Cypriot Greek adapters to devise a grapheme for representing a sibilant reflex of the voiceless labiovelar *[k^w] (either fricative or affricate) which the existing evidence indicates survived only in the closely related sister dialects of Cypriot and Arcadian (in Cypriot, unlike Arcadian, only the voiceless *[k^w] (not *[g^w] or *[k^{wh}]) is so palatalized to produce a sibilant reflex). The earliest Greek name of this character has not survived. In most of the epichoric alphabets it competed with *sigma* for representing the voiceless dental fricative [s]. In these alphabets either this Greek-*ṣade* character or *sigma* was eventually eliminated and the "original" name of *sigma* (i.e., *san*), was applied to the surviving [s] symbol.

The fourth Semitic sibilant character, *shin*, had the value of a voiceless palato-alveolar fricative [š]. This symbol was utilized by the Greek adapters, perhaps by default, to represent the dental fricative [s] (though there is evidence that the Phoenician character had this value in certain dialects of Cypriot Phoenician). The name of the symbol in Phoenician was probably *shan*, which was taken over directly by the Greeks as *san*. In certain epichoric alphabets the symbol acquired the secondary name *sigma*.

Notes

1. And probably *psV* symbols if the script was acquired at a time when *stop + fricative + stop* clusters still remained generally intact.

2. Herodotus 5.58–61.

3. P. McCarter, 1975, *The Antiquity of the Greek Alphabet and the Early Phoenician Scripts* (Missoula, Mont: Scholars Press), p. 2. For a discussion of the history of the scholarship of Greek alphabetic study, see pp. 1–27.

4. It has been alternatively proposed that the Aramaic script was the source writing system. McCarter convincingly demonstrates that this is unlikely, however; see McCarter 1975:125, n. 1, and the discussion at relevant sections in his chapter 3.

5. The consonantal phonemic system of Phoenician was quite similar, though not identical, to that of early Hebrew; see Z. Harris, 1936, *A Grammar of the Phoenician Language* (New Haven: American Oriental Society), pp. 20–21; S. Moscati, 1964, *An Introduction to the Comparative Grammar of the Semitic Languages* (Wiesbaden: Harrassowitz), pp. 22–46. Hebrew differs from Phoenician in distinguishing an additional fricative, transcribed as ś (see Moscati 1964:35). The symbols ṣ, ṭ, and q represent "emphatic" consonants and will be discussed at length further below.

6. This is in essence the consonantal inventory of the classical Attic dialect with the addition of /w/, that is, digamma. As will be discussed below, slight dialectal differences are of course found. Not included in this inventory is the velar nasal of Greek, on which see the discussion below.

7. On the Greek adaptation of Phoenician characters, see, among other works, L. Jeffery, 1990, *The Local Scripts of Archaic Greece*, rev. ed., supplement by A. Johnston (Oxford: Oxford University Press), pp. 1–42. On the Semitic practice of representing certain vowel sounds using consonantal characters, the *matres lectionis,* and the differences between this practice and the spelling of vowels in the Greek alphabetic system, see McCarter 1975:125, n. 1.

8. The sound which is found, for example, as the second consonant in the Cockney pronunciation of the word *bottle* and at the beginning of each syllable in American English *uh-uh* (meaning 'no').

9. Also quite unlike any sound of English, for that matter. Toward familiarizing the reader with such sounds, I quote from Ladefoged's (1975, *A Course in Phonetics* (New York: Harcourt Brace Jovanovich), p. 143) instructions for producing pharyngeal fricatives : "Pharyngeal sounds are produced by pulling the root of the tongue back towards the back wall of the pharynx. . . . The [fricative] sounds [ħ, ʕ] are fairly diffi-

cult to learn to pronounce. Try pulling the root of your tongue as far back as possible, and producing the voiceless sound [ħ]. Now, if you can, produce this sound before a vowel. Next try to make the voiced sound [ʕ], not worrying if it turns out to have creaky voice" (*creaky voice* "is a very low pitched sound that occurs at the ends of falling intonations for some speakers of English. You can probably learn to produce it by singing the lowest note that you can—and then trying to go even lower" (p. 123)). The voiceless pharyngeal fricative [ħ] is, then, somewhat like the sound a person produces when blowing breath vapor onto a camera or eyeglass lens in order to clean it; the voiced fricative [ʕ] is the same but with the vocal cords vibrating.

10. On the phonetic quality of Phoenician *ḥet* /ħ/, see the preceding note.

11. The Greek alphabetic symbol for /w/ (i.e., *wau* or *digamma*) was apparently derived also from Semitic *waw*; for a discussion of this process see Jeffery 1990:24–25, 35. On the date of /ẹ:, ọ:/ see Lejeune 1982:232.

12. For a discussion of the Greek uses of Phoenician *ḥet*, see Jeffery 1990:28–29.

13. See ibid., pp. 37–38.

14. These symbols are cover terms in that they do not utilize diacritics which are designed to indicate precisely the phonetic value of the emphatic consonants.

15. On emphatics as characterized by a secondary articulation (velarization or pharyngealization), see Ladefoged 1993:231–232; in addition, see pp. 131–135, on ejectives and implosives.

16. Sibilants are fricatives which are characterized by high pitch and high acoustic energy, or affricates (on which see directly below) whose fricative component is of this sort; see Ladefoged 1993:167–168.

17. An affricate is a consonantal sound which consists of a stop followed immediately by a (near) homorganic fricative (i.e., a fricative produced at essentially the same position in the oral tract as the stop which it follows). English has two affricate phonemes: a voiceless affricate /tš/ (as in *church*) and a voiced affricate /dž/ (as in *judge*). On affricates see Ladefoged 1993:11, 63.

18. Jeffery 1990:26.

19. Ibid., 26–27.

20. The reversals envisioned by Jeffery involve a shift of "names and values" rather than one of "sign + value," as stated by Powell (1991, *Homer and the Origin of the Greek Alphabet* (Cambridge: Cambridge University Press), pp. 47–48), though earlier on p. 47, Powell correctly speaks of a "switching of the names."

21. The Semitic letter-names listed here are, of course, Hebrew rather than Phoenician, as is customary. On the reconstruction of the various Phoenician letter-names, see the discussions in chapter 3 of McCarter 1975.

22. Jeffery 1990:26–27.

23. Jeffery refers to the inclusion of the value of a symbol in its name as the "acrophonic principle." In introductory comments about the acquisition of the Semitic writing system by Greeks, she states, "The vital fact to which they held was the acrophonic principle—i.e. that the initial sound of each barbarous name which they had to repeat was the actual sound which the sign represented" (ibid., p. 22).

24. Ibid., pp. 25–26. And it is of course still the case that, at least in the United States, children learn to recite the alphabet in full at a considerably earlier age than that at which they begin to read and write alphabetic characters.

25. Ibid., p. 27.

26. Powell (1991:46) adheres to this confusion theory, though his perception of the nature of the learning process which led to the confusion seems to be somewhat different; he writes: "The dislocation was apparently encouraged by the adapter's method of

learning separately the names of the signs and the graphic order of the signs, rather than learning individual names for individual signs." He further states (p. 48): "The switchings of name and value here described must have come about in the memorized spoken oral series of names, learned independently of the physically transmitted series of signs. The switchings could not have taken place if the adapter had learned the names and value of each sign independently."

27. Note, in addition to my comments here, the objections to this theory offered recently by R. Wachter, 1989, "Zur Vorgeschichte des griechischen Alphabets," *Kadmos* 28:50–51, n. 67.

28. The most recent printing is A. Kirchhoff, 1970, *Studien zur Geschichte des griechischen Alphabets,* 4th ed. (Amsterdam: J. C. Gieben).

29. In the light blue script of Amorgos, the sequence is spelled $\pi\sigma$.

30. The spelling $\chi\sigma$ for [ks] occurs in the red alphabets of Laconia, Rhodes, and Boiotia.

31. In the red alphabet of Boeotia, [ks] is also represented by the sequence $\psi\sigma$, as is also the case with the red scripts of Opountian and Cephallenia (though in the latter [s] is spelled with *san,* rather than *sigma,* on which see below).

32. There is a special symbol having the value [ps] which is found in a few of these alphabets and which will be discussed below.

33. The alphabet of Cnidus exhibits an unusual *xi* character which is also found in the Pamphylian script; see Jeffery 1990:346, 348, n. 3.

34. The Aeolic alphabet preserves blue *chi* and dark blue *psi*; see ibid., pp. 359–361.

35. Elements of other alphabet-types also occur in these regions; see ibid., pp. 363–369.

36. Jeffery (1990:264) proposes that Syracuse is likely to have been blue.

37. In the alphabet of Naxos, *xi* is written sequentially, as in other light blue scripts; however, the initial character is not χ but a symbol which is similar in shape to *eta*. In the alphabet of Amorgos, the spelling *eta - sigma* is attested for [ks]. See ibid., pp. 291, 293.

38. On dark blue elements in the Rhodian script, see ibid., pp. 345–350.

39. See n. 36 above.

40. See the discussion in ibid., pp. 8–9, 310. If characters are abstracted from the various local alphabets of Crete, an abecedarium can be constructed which reveals this greatest similarity. As will be discussed below, however, there was recently discovered an early Phoenician inscription in Crete, the script of which is quite *unlike* the Cretan alphabet.

41. In a Theran graffito on a sherd from Taucheira (second half of the sixth century (?)), $\kappa\sigma$ occurs; see ibid., p. 470.

42. On the change of *[s] to [h], see the discussion in section 4.3.2.1.1. The syllabic Cypriot script contains no *hV* characters and, presumably for this reason, has been sometimes called "psilotic" (so Buck 1955:53). It is widely held, however, that this is simply an orthographic omission and not psilosis; see O. Masson 1983:69, 91; Thumb-Scherer 1959:164. Beyond this, as we have seen (4.3.2.1.2), Cypriot is characterized by the presence of word-internal and probably word-final [h]; in these positions [h] can be spelled by *sV* characters.

43. Jeffery 1990:310.

44. On the occasional variation between voiceless stops and voiceless aspirated stops in a variety of dialects, see Buck 1955:60–61.

45. For data and discussion of Cretan aspirated stops, see Bile 1988:139–142. Cer-

tain of Bile's remarks are based upon W. Krause, 1920, "Zum Aussprache des θ im gortynischen," *KZ* 49:121–126, and Lejeune 1982:59–61 (see especially p. 59 with n. 5). See also Buck 1955:59–60.

46. Bile 1988:76.

47. On which form, see L. Jeffery and A. Morpurgo Davies, 1970, "ΠΟΙΝΙΚΑΣ–ΤΑΣ and ΠΟΙΝΙΚΑΖΕΝ: BM 1969. 4—2. 1, A New Archaic Inscription from Crete," *Kadmos* 9:130.

48. Bile 1988:139.

49. Bile (1988:120) indicates that the velar variant of /l/ may occur when the liquid is found between a preceding vowel (either [a], [a:], [e], or [e:]) and an ensuing consonant of one of the following types: (i) a voiceless unaspirated velar stop; (ii) any voiceless aspirated stop; (iii) an interdental fricative [θ], on which see below; or (iv) a nasal.

50. Jeffery 1990:314.

51. M. Guarducci, 1967, *Epigraphia greca, I* (Rome: Istituto Poligrafico dello Stato), p. 70, n. 2.; 1952–54, "Iscrizioni vascolari arcaiche da Phaistos," *Annuario Scuola Atene* 30–32:168–169.

52. Bile 1988:102.

53. Jeffery 1990:314. On the last-made point, see her n. 2.

54. Or something like this: his actual wording is, "[T]he early Cretan receivers of the alphabet heard the aspirate faintly or not at all" (1991:56). Here, by the term *aspiration* he appears to be referring to both the word-initial consonant [h-] and the element of aspiration which accompanies the stops [pʰ], [tʰ], and [kʰ]. In other words, he is continuing the confusion introduced by Jeffery of psilosis and deaspiration of the stops. This is so even though he had stated earlier: "Terminology is important here, and in spite of Jeffery's usage 'psilosis' ought to mean 'the loss of the *spiritus asper*' (the loss of initial /h/), in contrast to 'deaspiration of stops' " (p. 55).

55. He intimates that the evidence can be dismissed upon the basis of the nonuniformity of the Cretan dialect, stating: "A basic difficulty with the epigraphical (and much linguistic) literature on the problem of aspiration in the Cretan dialect is the assumption of a uniform dialect for all of Crete. My own view is that there was considerable variation, both geographical and chronological, that is masked by a uniform alphabet" (ibid., p. 56) The great part of the Cretan materials come from Gortyn in the central portion of the island. One would fully expect there to have been regional and diachronic variations in Cretan Greek; see the discussion of this matter in Bile 1988:10–15, 365–370 and note especially her comment: "«Le» crétois reste, pour l'instant, une entité informe. Il est vraisemblable que des différences dialectales ont existé dans l'Antiquité, tout comme elles existent dans les parlers néo-crétois. . . . Mais c'est une hypothèse indémontrable pour l'instant, qui ne donnera lieu ici à aucun débat" (p. 12). Consider also Buck's comments (1955:171): "[T]here is no sufficient ground for the belief that the East, West and Central Cretan are fundamental divisions of the dialect, or that they reflect to any degree the various constituent elements in the population. The East and West Cretan inscriptions, the latter very meager, are comparatively late, and show a large degree of obvious *koine* influence, partly Attic, partly Doric *koine* of the other islands." The evidence rehearsed by Bile for the presence of aspirated stops in Cretan, a portion of which I cited above, comes from Gortyn principally, but from other sites as well (see Bile, pp. 139–140). The evidence does not lead us to propose (or suspect) variant forms of Cretan which lacked aspirated stops, and variation ought not simply be invoked as a hypothetic panacea.

56. Powell 1991:56. He proposes that an instance of the use of θ*h* in a Theran inscription to represent [tʰ], normally spelled τ*h,* "also suggests that θ was not of itself

marked for aspiration in the alphabet that Thera took from Crete; or at least that some Therans assumed one had to put in [h], even redundantly, to indicate aspiration." Two points need to be made. First of all, this evidence quite obviously does not argue for a fricative or affricate value of Cretan θ; rather, it indicates that the character represented a stop. Second, if θ had been used in the Theran inscription to represent [t] (rather than [t^h]), then perhaps it might suggest to us that the sound of Cretan θ was unaspirated. This is not the case, however; θ is used exactly where it should be used if it had the value [t^h]. The use of *h* likely just reflects normal Theran practice of utilizing this grapheme in the spelling of aspirated stops; in other words, θh is probably a hybridized spelling of [t^h], as Powell himself seems to come close to suggesting in the second clause of the above quoted statement ("or at least that some Therans assumed one had to put in [h], *even redundantly*, to indicate aspiration" (emphasis is mine)).

57. Ibid., p. 57. The question of the value of θ in the *later* Cretan documents (i.e., fourth century and following) is a complex one. In the Attic Koine dialect, which of course supplanted all of the other Greek dialects (with the exception of Tsaconian), the aspirated stops eventually developed into fricatives (i.e., [p^h], [t^h], and [k^h] became [f] (labiodental), [θ] (interdental), and [x] (velar) respectively), and they remain such in Modern Greek (for a full discussion of this development see, among others, Browning 1983:26–27; Allen 1974:20–24; E. Sturtevant, 1940, *The Pronunciation of Greek and Latin*, 2nd ed. (Baltimore: Linguistic Society of America), pp. 83–85). The earliest firm evidence for a fricative pronunciation of one of these sounds in Koine is provided by Pompeian graffiti from the first century A.D. In certain dialects, however, this development occurred at an earlier period, as, for example, in Laconian; this is evidenced by the use on the part of Aristophanes and Thucydides (fifth-century authors writing in the Attic dialect) of σ, perhaps an approximation of [θ], to represent the Laconian sound corresponding to Attic [t^h]. The same substitution occurs in Spartan inscriptions of the fourth century. One encounters statements in certain of the handbooks which indicate that some sort of an early fricative development of [t^h] also took place in the Cretan dialect (e.g., Rix 1976:85). It is probably accurate to say, however, that the majority of investigators have contended that in the Cretan alphabet, the character θ represents only an aspirated stop [t^h] prior to later periods; see, for example, Sturtevant 1940:84; Thumb-Kiekers 1932:157; Lejeune 1982:59, 118 (though compare Lejeune's comments on p. 107 concerning the value of the orthographic sequence $\theta\theta$ which in fourth- and second-century texts represents clusters that are reflexes of earlier consonant groups such as *[-ss-], *[-ts-], and *[-t$^{(h)}$y]). Evidence for θ having the value [t^h] as late as the second century is provided by instances of dissimilation whereby the sequence [#...C^h...C^h...#] becomes [#...C...C^h...#]; compare, for example, the Cretan genitive of the proper name $T\varepsilon\upsilon\phi\iota\lambda\omega$ ([teup^{h}ilọ:]) with its Attic equivalent $\Theta\varepsilon o\phi\iota\lambda o\upsilon$ ([t^{h}eop^{h}ílu:]) (see Bile 1988:139 for this dissimilation process; also Thumb-Kiekers 1932:157, in which is cited additional evidence for second-century [t^h]). Brixhe has argued that in the dialect of the Gortyn Law Code (fifth century), a fricative sound [θ] existed in complementary distribution with the aspirated stop [t^h]. This fricative is spelled with the character θ, while both [t^h] and [t] are spelled τ; that is, τ here functions just like π and κ in the Cretan alphabet generally, representing both aspirated and unaspirated voiceless stops (C. Brixhe, 1976, *Le dialecte grec de Pamphylie* (Paris: A. Maisonneuve), pp. 89–91).

58. Powell 1991:57.

59. Ibid., p. 56.

60. Jeffery 1990:317. It is commonly held that of the locales exhibiting a "primitive" alphabet, it is Crete which is likely to have first received the script and that from

there it was passed on to Thera and Melos (for discussion, see Jeffery 1990:8–9, 316–317). However, Jeffery points out (p. 317) that there are a number of ways in which the scripts of Thera and Melos differ from that of Crete, including, of course, the dual value of *eta* in the former two, and that, as I have just indicated, certain of these differences may be due to the influence of the alphabets of the Ionic Cyclades (on the dual value of *eta* in the central Ionic scripts, see Jeffery 1990:289 and the appropriate pages in her discussion following thereupon).

61. Bile 1988:76.

62. Jeffery 1990:35, 310.

63. Eteocretan is a heretofore undeciphered language of Crete which is written with the Greek alphabet.

64. The character ξ does occur in a Greek inscription from Lyttos (ca. 500?), though here *xi* has been analyzed as a possible mistake for *zeta* (Jeffery 1990:309; Jeffery and Morpurgo Davies 1970:134). However, other investigators (C. Brixhe, 1982, "Palatalisations en grec et en phrygien," *BSL* 77:213; Y. Duhoux, 1982, *L' Etéocrétois* (Amsterdam: J. C. Gieben), p. 165) have argued that this is not an error at all and connect this occurrence of *xi* with the regular Theran practice of using *xi* to represent the sound elsewhere spelled by *zeta*.

65. In addition, there occurs in a single quite fragmentary archaic Eteocretan inscription (sixth century, from Praisos) one instance (or perhaps two) of the supplemental character ϕ, though it is possible that the character is *qoppa* instead (see Jeffery 1990:309; Duhoux 1982:83, 171–176); ϕ occurs in later Eteocretan inscriptions—fourth and third centuries (ibid., p. 137). *Phi* also occurs in a Greek graffito (second half of the sixth century, from Itanos) which, according to Guarducci (1967:192), is perhaps of Rhodian origin (see Bile 1988:74, n. 7). In the alphabets of both Thera and Melos, ψ occurs in inscriptions of the sixth and fifth centuries having the value [ks] (not [ps] as in the blue alphabets or [kʰ] as in the red); for discussion, see Jeffery 1990:308–310, 317, 320–322.

66. Or he contends for the diminished salience of aspiration on stops; recall again his wording: "[T]he early Cretan receivers of the alphabet heard the aspirate faintly or not at all" (Powell 1991:56)

67. Ibid., 57.

68. Jeffery 1990:27.

69. In the event that only a subset of dark blue alphabet users possessed [š], she states, that subset passed the script on to the various other groups who are attested as using this alphabet-type; ibid.

70. Ibid., p. 32.

71. Ibid., p. 27.

72. *Dioscorides de Materia Medica* 2.193; first century A.D.

73. On Greek *s*, see, *inter alios*, Allen 1974:43–44; Buck 1955:55–57; Lejeune 1982:85–91; Sturtevant 1940:73–76.

74. See Sturtenant 1940:74.

75. Y. Meshorer, 1967, *Jewish Coins of the Second Temple Period*, trans. I. Levine (Tel Aviv: Am Hassefer), pp. 118–119.

76. P. Gardner, 1966, *The Coins of the Greek and Scythian Kings of Bactria and India in the British Museum*, ed. R. Poole (Chicago: Argonaut), pp. 56–57; A. Cunningham, 1969, *Coins of Alexander's Successors in the East* (Chicago: Argonaut; reprint of 1884 edition), p. 195.

77. On which, see, among other sources, W. Cowgill and M. Mayrhofer, 1986, *Indogermanische Grammatik*, vol. 1 (Heidelberg: Carl Winter Universitätsverlag),

p. 119; Lejeune 1982:86; A. Meillet, 1964, *Introduction à l' étude comparative des langues indo-européennes* (University: University of Alabama Press), pp. 97–98; W. Lehman, 1955, *Proto-Indo-European Phonology* (Austin: University of Texas Press), p. 9.

78. Allen 1974:43–44; Sturtevant 1940:75. Sturtevant also proposes that in those Greek dialects which show the change of *[s] to [r] in particular contexts, there may have been an intermediate [z] stage. On the dialects exhibiting this rhotacism, see Buck 1955:56–57.

79. On defining *palatalization,* see D. Bhat, 1978, "A General Study of Palatalization," in *Universals of Human Language,* vol. 2, ed. J. Greenberg (Stanford: Stanford University Press), pp. 47–92. On palatalization in Greek, see Allen 1957; Lejeune 1982:50–51, 62–66, 170–171; L. Stephens and R. Woodard, 1986, "The Palatalization of the Labiovelars in Greek: A Reassessment in Typological Perspective," *IF* 91:129–154.

80. Bhat 1978:30.

81. As presented in J. Crothers, et al., comps. and eds., 1979, "Handbook of Phonological Data from a Sample of the World's Languages: A Report of the Stanford Phonology Archive," 2 vols. (Stanford: Stanford University Department of Linguistics), abbreviated hereafter as SPA.

82. Tigre, Ewe, Igbo, Songhai, Spanish, Ainu, Korean, Ket, Georgian, Hakka, Atayal, Kaliai, Selepet, Oneida, Karok, Southeastern Pomo, Mazateco, Wapishana, Carib.

83. In the case of several of these nineteen, the appearance of the palato-alveolar allophone is phonetically conditioned, but in the conditioning environment this allophone appears as a free variant; that is, its occurrence is limited to particular contexts but is variable (or optional) within those contexts. In addition, there are eight languages, not included in this group of nineteen, in which palato-alveolar allophones occur as free variants of the phonemic form, apparently without any phonetic conditioning.

84. The total number of phonemes involved in such allophonic relations is twenty-eight, twenty-five of which are dental/alveolar: in eleven instances the phoneme is /s/, in three it is the voiced counterpart /z/.

85. In Stephens and Woodard 1986 (pp. 139–141), evidence is presented which indicates that in the case of allophonic palatalization of velar stops which results in the stop acquiring a secondary palatal articulation, there exists an implicational relation of the following form: if a velar stop palatalizes before a mid front vowel to some extent, it will palatalize before a high front vowel to the same extent, but not vice versa. The findings presented above may suggest that this implicational relation can be extended to other types of palatalization processes and that palatalization is subject to an implicational hierarchy such as the following : high front > mid front > low front. The appropriate implicational relation would then be: if a consonant palatalizes before (or after) any segment on the hierarchy, it will palatalize before (or after) every segment which is located higher on the hierarchy (i.e., to the left) but not vice versa. Bhat, in his study of palatalization, has argued that tongue height of an ensuing vowel (or glide) is the factor which is most critical for the palatalization of apical consonants while tongue frontness of an ensuing front vowel is that one which is most critical for the palatalization of velar consonants (see Bhat 1978:21–25). Thus, there may be an implicational relation involving tongue frontness which intersects with that one involving tongue height and produces apparent "exceptional" cases in which a mid front vowel exerts a greater palatalizing effect on a preceding consonant than does a high front vowel, as is the case in the diachronic palatalization of labiovelars in early Greek.

86. In the case of Ewe (SPA:55) and Korean (SPA:211), it is reported that palatalization occurs before the sequence [y + vowel].

87. In other words, in the case of these latter four, the allophonic process is a matter of regressive assimilation in place of articulation.

88. For one of these two languages, Carib, it is reported that the preceding [y] is the second element of a diphthong. It is unclear if sequences of the type [vowel + y] which are not diphthongal occur prior to consonants (SPA:492). In addition, it appears that in Carib this palatalization only occurs when the segment following the palatalized consonant is a vowel (which, in addition, must be a vowel other than [i]). On the importance of intervocalic position (especially contexts in which both the preceding and ensuing vowels are front) for certain palatalization processes, see Stephens and Woodard 1986:141–142.

89. Shilha, Hausa, Akan, Zulu, Luo, Breton, Brazilian Portuguese, Russian, Bulgarian, Lithuanian, Modern Greek, Kashmiri, Persian, Cheremis, Yurak, Kirghiz, Chuvash, Yakut, Even, Gilyak, Ainu, Japanese, Korean, Ket, Kota, Hakka, Cantonese, Dafla, Lahu, Cham, Malagasy, Tagalog, Maori, Sentani, Asmat, Kunimaipa, Aleut, Ojibwa, Wichita, Nez Perce, Zoque, Tiwa, Hopi, Wapishana, Carib, Amahuaca. As with the former group of languages, it is reported that palatalization is exhibited optionally in the case of certain of these languages.

90. It appears to be the case that a secondary palatalization is what is intended by the editors of the archive handbook, though it is possible that in some instances a palatal offglide has simply been added to the palatalized consonant. On palatalization as a secondary articulation, see Ladefoged 1993:230–231.

91. The status of Amahuaca, a language of Peru, is somewhat unclear. It is stated that palatalization of the voiceless velar fricative occurs in syllable-initial position and in syllable-final position if the following syllable begins with a vowel. It appears that this may mean simply that palatalization occurs preceding a vowel; if so, this would bring the total to thirty-four. See H. Osborn, 1948, "Amahuaca Phonemes," *IJAL* 14:188–190.

92. In the case of this type of palatalization, unlike that discussed above in which a palato-alveolar allophone is generated (i.e., type 1 palatalization), those languages in which palatalization is induced by a mid front vowel are not simply a subset of those in which it is induced by a high front vowel. In Kirghiz, palatalization of /p/, /s/, and /m/ is reported as occurring before mid front but not before high front vowels (on the similar palatalization of [k], see R. Herbert and N. Poppe, 1963, *Kirghiz Manual*, Indiana University Uralic and Altaic Series, no. 33 (Bloomington: Indiana University Press), pp. 3–6); and palatalization of /pʰ/, /b/, /f/, and /w/ in Akan, and /k/ and /k:/ in Ojibwa is said to be more pronounced before mid front than before high front vowels. These languages would then stand as exceptions to the implicational relationship suggested above in n. 85.

93. For Korean it is reported that palatalization occurs before the sequence [y + vowel] (SPA:211).

94. In Russian the voiceless palato-alveolar affricate which conditions the change is itself palatalized (SPA:130–131). It is further reported that palatalization is induced by any following consonant for some speakers of Persian (SPA:144) and before [w] in Sentani (SPA:333). For a few languages, it is reported that palatalization is conditioned by a neighboring boundary—either word or syllable; for example, palatalization is said to occur word-finally in Ket (SPA:214) and Cham (SPA:287) and syllable-initially in Hopi (SPA:445).

95. Among the languages exhibiting type 2 palatalization, there are four for which it is reported that palatalization is induced intervocalically. On intervocalic palatalization, see n. 88.

96. The ratio of progressively palatalizing (induced by a preceding sound) to re-

gressively palatalizing (induced by an ensuing sound) languages is 8:48 for the type 2 group and 7:17 for the type 1 group.

97. In the case of Carib, one of the progressively palatalizing languages, for which it is reported that palatalization of each consonantal phoneme generally occurs when the consonant is preceded by [i] or [vowel + y] and followed by a vowel other than [i], what may actually be critical is intervocalic position. In fact, /s/, unlike the other consonants, is said to be palatalized "between high front vowels" (SPA:494). The required presence, in the case of the other consonants, of an ensuing vowel which is "other than [i]" may be a consequence of the palatal quality of an earlier [i] having been absorbed by the palatalized allophone. On such absorption, see Bhat 1978:42–46.

98. Crothers et al. report that "consonants are palatalized following /i/ or /i:/ or vowel + /y/" (SPA:236) and that "consonants are *slightly* palatalized before /y/ and after consonant plus /y/" (SPA:235); emphasis is mine.

99. The sole exception is Ket, in which type 1 palatalization occurs (progressively) after [n] but type 2 is effected (regressively) by an ensuing word-boundary. This is of course only an exception if we consider allophonic changes conditioned by boundaries (word-boundary, syllable-boundary, etc.) to be equivalent to such processes conditioned by consonant and vowel segments; see n. 94.

100. Bhat 1978:19.

101. Ibid., pp. 31–32.

102. However, my findings offer no support for the claim which Bhat implicitly makes in his statement (i) that when a language shows both progressive and regressive palatalization, it is the case that the language is one which exhibits regressive palatalization extensively.

103. On the development in Old Persian, see Kent 1953:40.

104. W. Whitney, 1960, *Sanskrit Grammar,* 2nd ed. (Cambridge: Harvard University Press), pp. 61–62.

105. In other words, those systems which actually attempt to represent the pronunciation of the words which they are used to write. These are syllabic and alphabetic systems as opposed to pictographic or logographic systems.

106. Sampson (1985:43–45) suggests that orthographic systems, such as the English alphabet, in fact tend to be spell at an even "deeper" than phonemic level, approaching *morphophonemic* spelling.

107. See Buck 1955:17–18.

108. Thus Jeffery 1990:33–34. She indicates that *qoppa* was last attested in the scripts of the Doric dialects of Argos, Corinth, Crete, and Rhodes (pp. 116, 152, 307, 346).

109. The allophonic distinction recorded by the use of both *kappa* and *qoppa* appears so out of place that one cannot help but wonder if the value *originally* assigned to *qoppa* by the Greek adapters of the Semitic script was not something other than that value which is attested. I shall refrain from further speculation on this matter.

110. The use of *gamma* (the character which normally represents a voiced velar stop [g]) to represent a velar nasal [ŋ] (as in ἄγκυρα ([áŋküra], 'anchor')) is a more complex case. *Gamma* so used was said to be designated by the Greeks as the letter *agma* (thus report the Latin grammarians Priscian and Varro). The velar nasal exists in an *allophone-like* relationship with both the dental nasal phoneme /n/ (before a velar stop [k], [g], or [kʰ]) and the velar stop phoneme /g/ (before the bilabial nasal [m]). I use the term *allophone-like* because [ŋ] would probably not be identified strictly as an allophone of either of these phonemes according to traditional phonemic practice. In postphonemic linguistics, however, [ŋ] could be said to have /n/ or /g/ as its underlying

representation. It appears that the earliest practice was to use the letter *nu* (the symbol for the dental nasal [n]) to represent the velar nasal occurring before a velar stop. The use of *gamma* to represent [ŋ] may have spread from sequences of /gm/ which were pronounced [ŋm] and spelled γμ. The same pronunciation of the velar perhaps occurs in the sequence /gn/. See Allen 1974:33–37; Sturtevant 1940:64–65.

111. McCarter 1975:98, n. 83.

112. We saw that there is neither a [k] + [s] nor a [p] + [s] character in either the light blue or the green alphabet-types.

113. A. Heubeck, 1986, "Die Würzburger Alphabettafel," *Würzburger Jahrbücher für die Altertumswissenschaft Neue Folge* 12:7–8.

114. See above, nn. 63–64.

115. Jeffery 1990:317; McCarter 1975:98, n. 83. Powell (1991:31, n. 83) disparages the early dating of the Würzburg-Fayum tablets and even expresses reluctance to accept the script as Greek. We have seen that the presence of the supplementals (which are not present in the Würzburg-Fayum abecedaria) in the "earliest alphabet" (ibid., p. 57) is crucial for Powell.

116. As we discussed in chapter 5, it is possible that the general reduction of *stop + fricative + stop* clusters did not occur until after the syllabic Cypriot script was devised for writing Greek. If that were the case, *psV* characters probably occurred word-internally in the spelling of *[ps]* + *stop* clusters. With the reduction of such clusters, the word-internal use of *psV* symbols would have passed.

117. Powell 1991:58. He further states (pp. 58, 60), "The names of these signs, on the model of '*pei*' from the Phoenician name *pe* that he ["the adapter"] seems to have used for the supplementals, must have been *khei* and *⁹hei*." That the name of a character which represented aspirated *qoppa* could have been *⁹hei* with a front vowel following the proposed aspirated *qoppa* sound is manifestly inordinately improbable—recall again that *qoppa* designates a sound which is limited to a phonetic position preceding *back* vowels.

118. Ibid., p. 60.

119. Powell (p. 61) further proposes that the script of Attica was modified by an Ionian reformer: "moribund ψ =[⁹h] and ξ = [*sh]" were respectively assigned the values [p] + [s] and [k] + [s] by analogy with ζ, to which Powell assigns the *stop + fricative* value of [dz] or [ts] (though he allows that "the metathesized forms thereof" may have been the analogical base; regarding this, it is unclear how a *fricative + stop* ("metathesized") character could be interpreted as having brought about the analogical creation of *stop + fricative* characters).

120. Ibid., p. 60.

121. Χσ for [ks] is of course not attested as the earliest spelling of [ks] in the Euboean alphabet; Jeffery (1990:79–80) states that χσ for [ks] occurs only in the fifth century B.C. and then is limited to "two inscriptions which may be in Attic."

122. Powell's hypothesis concerning developments within the Euboean alphabet also illustrates with particular clarity a common problem with interpretations of the development of the Greek alphabet. If upon the assignment of the value [kʰ] to the symbol ψ, "the Euboians reduced original χσ = [ks] to χ = [ks]," then this implies that χ coexisted alongside ψ with the value [kʰ] for at least some time (recall that in the Greek alphabets which spell out the sequences [ks] and [ps] the stop is usually written with the symbol for the aspirated stop). This in itself is not necessarily problematic; we would likely expect such dual usage in a transitional system. Why, however, is the character χ so intimately bound up with the spelling of the phonetic sequence [ks] that χ alone came to be assigned the value [ks]? Why was χ not abstracted from the spelling

sequence χν and preserved with the value [k$^{(h)}$n] or from sequence χρ and assigned the value [k$^{(h)}$r]? Within such a system of interpretation no motivation for the assigning of the value [ks] to an alphabetic character is obvious.

123. Jeffery 1990:33–34.

124. Powell 1991:60.

125. Ibid., pp. 57, 123.

126. Jeffery 1990:80, plate 5.

127. Ibid., pp. 80, 248. On the basis of Cymean coin legends, she sets a *terminus ante quem* for the disappearance of *qoppa* from this Euboean script at some point in the early fifth century.

128. On the possibility of the Proto-Indo-European sequence **sd* being attested in the Linear B materials, see Lejeune 1982:112, n. 4. On the voicing of */s/* before a voiced consonant in Proto-Indo-European, see n. 77 above.

129. Jeffery 1990:26–28. On p. 26 she also writes that the value of zeta "= *ds* or by metathesis *-sd-*."

130. Powell 1991:48 (see pp. 46–48). In contrast to Jeffery's remarks cited in the immediately preceding text and in the preceding note, Powell states (p. 47, n. a to Fig. 3), "Jeffery gives the value of *zēta* as a voiced *s* [z], but it seems not to have acquired this value until the fourth century B.C." The point made in the latter clause is correct, on which see further below.

131. Allen 1974:54.

132. For discussion of the evidence, see, *inter alios,* Allen 1974:53–56; Buck 1955:71; Lejeune 1982:113–115; Sturtevant 1940:91–93.

133. See, *inter alios,* Thumb-Scherer 1959:96–97.

134. Though Lejeune (1982:114), for example, interprets the value of this *zeta* to be also [zd].

135. DT 632.7; *Comp.* 14.

136. Allen 1974:56.

137. See Buck 1955:75; Lejeune 1982:114.

138. As Buck (1955:67), among others, points out, the nasal "might be restored by analogy."

139. The sequence *nasal + stop + fricative* occurs, for example, in σάλπιγξ ([sálpiŋks], 'war trumpet'), with which compare σαλπίζω in (20B).

140. Buck 1955:67.

141. Lejeune 1982:138.

142. It is, of course, not necessarily the case that the inherited cluster *[zd] would have to be included as a participant in this initial stage of metathesis. One could imagine that it was preserved as [zd] all the way through stage (D), in which case it would be necessary to claim—one would presume—that in the earliest alphabetic writings this sequence was spelled *σδ and only subsequently, upon the metathesis of *[dz] to [zd], also came to be represented by the single character ζ. As there is no evidence for such an early spelling of inherited *[zd], I have included it in stage (A).

143. It is quite possible that early Central Cretan reflexes of *[-t^{h}y], *[-tw-], and *[-k$^{(h)}$y-] (on which see the discussion in chapter 4) could have been spelled in the same manner, but these are not attested; Lejeune 1982:107; Bile 1988:144, 145, n. 291.

144. Though [s] in all dialects after a consonant, long vowel, or diphthong, as well as word-initially.

145. Bile 1988:145

146. See, for example, ibid., p. 146.

147. C. Brixhe 1982:210–215; 1975 [1977], review of *Note linguistiche a proposito delle tavole di Eraclea,* by Renato Arena, *Kratylos* 20:60–61.

148. Though Jeffery (1990:309) suggests that this Cretan form may be a spelling error; see the comments in n. 64 above.

149. Though Bile (1988:145, n. 292) cites the spelling οτοι (alongside οζοι) as occurring once in an inscription of this early period from Gortyn.

150. The seventh- and sixth-century Doric dialect of Cretan thus preserved an intermediate reflex which, as we saw in chapter 4, had already been eliminated in the second-millennium south Greek dialect of Mycenaean.

151. Rix 1976:92–93.

152. Though there is one instance in which such a Cretan regressive assimilation of *[-st-] may be attested. The preposition μεστα ([mesta], 'until') appears once in the Gortyn Law Code as μεττ' ([mett-]); see Buck 1955:73. The form occurs in the phrase μεττ' ες ([mett- es]) and has been also analyzed as arising via regressive dissimilation at a distance (i.e., μεστ' ες ⇒ μεττ' ες); see Bile 1988:156, n. 354; Lejeune 1982:118, n. 7. Given that the sounds involved are obstruents, dissimilation seems less likely than assimilation.

153. Bile 1988:159.

154. Ibid., p. 141.

155. Ibid., pp. 152–153.

156. Buck 1955:73.

157. Thumb-Kieckers 1932:160.

158. Bile 1988:152.

159. That earlier *[-dz-] never underwent metathesis to [-zd-] in certain remote dialects or dialects on the linguistic frontier is quite conceivable. On the possible [dz] value of *zeta* in Greek dialects of south Italy and various island locations, see the illuminating summary and discussion in G. Nagy, 1970, *Greek Dialects and the Transformation of an Indo-European Process* (Cambridge: Harvard University Press), pp. 126–135. Concerning these matters, note also Sturtevant 1940:176. In the case of the Greek of south Italy, the phonology of the native languages may play some role.

160. Buck 1955:78.

161. Ibid., 1955:68–69, 86.

162. Ibid.; on the distribution of such forms within the materials from Gortyn, see Bile 1988:128–129. Outside of Gortyn, Bile reports, the nasal-less forms have been generalized.

163. Buck 1955:90; Bile 1988:194–196.

164. Jeffery 1990:26.

165. Ibid., pp. 27–28.

166. Powell (1991:46) follows Jeffery in identifying the value of *ṣade* as an affricate [ts].

167. The next greater linguistic group of which Semitic is a part.

168. R. Hetzron, 1987a, "Afroasiatic Languages," in B. Comrie, ed. *The World's Major Languages* (New York: Oxford University Press), p. 650. Hetzron points out that the only branch of Afro-Asiatic which lacks "emphatic" consonants is Egyptian.

169. Though he adopts Jeffery's value of Semitic *ṣade,* Powell (1990:39, n. 112) speaks to the phonetics of the Semitic "emphatic" consonants, stating, "'Emphatic' is a wholly arbitrary term used in Semitic grammars for what phonetically are apical consonants articulated with the tongue placed high and to the back of the mouth." The term *apical* is normally used to denote sounds which are made with the tip of the tongue (see, for example, Ladefoged 1993:161). Neither within nor without Semitic is this type of back-of-the-throat constriction limited to apical consonants.

170. Ladefoged 1993:230–232. Since both processes in effect involve the "superimposition" of a vowel articulation on a consonant articulation, velarization and pharyngealization are termed *secondary articulations.*

171. Hetzron 1987a:650.

172. For discussion of such glottalic airstream mechanisms, see Ladefoged 1993:130–135.

173. A. Kaye, 1987, "Arabic," in Comrie 1987:665.

174. S. Segert, 1976, *A Grammar of Phoenician and Punic* (Munich: Verlag C. H. Beck), p. 60.

175. R. Steiner, 1982, *Affricated Ṣade in the Semitic Languages* (New York: American Academy for Jewish Research).

176. Or perhaps even in Proto-Semitic, see ibid., pp. 84–89.

177. The affricate interpretation of Punic *ṣade* was earlier offered by K. Meister (1905–1906, "Arkadische Formen in der Xuthiasinschrift," *IF* 18:77–83).

178. Steiner (1982:61) offers a "complete list" of the forms of the Greek transcription, though he indicates (p. 61, n. 108) that he does not include in this list variant readings, which he identifies as "mostly insignificant or inferior." In his list, the σ transcription occurs one time, τ occurs eight times, and στ occurs twice.

179. Ibid., pp. 60–63, 88. He states explicitly that Phoenician *ṣade* had the value of a glottalized affricate [tˢ']; I am presuming that he would hold that the Punic affricate of which he speaks continued the glottalic articulation which he has identified as Phoenician. For additional evidence which he adduces for an affricate pronunciation of Punic *ṣade,* see pp. 63–65. There are also instances of *zeta* being used to transcribe *ṣade* in Greek forms from the period of Late Punic (see Harris 1936:23, 142; Steiner 1982:66–67). At this time, the value of *zeta* was of course [z].

180. Steiner 1982:65–68. Steiner, in fact, argues for an affricate value for Canaanite *ṣade* as well as for *samek* and *zayin* in the second millennium B.C. The evidence for this interpretation takes the form of Egyptian transcriptions of Canaanite words. Here, as in many instances of transcriptions of *ṣade* reported by Steiner as evidencing an affricate value, one wonders if the transcriptions are a consequence of *ṣade* being an emphatic—glottalized or whatever—sound rather than a consequence of being any sort of affricate. The Egyptian transcriptions of the *nonemphatic* sounds of *samek* and *zayin* may reveal much more about their manner of articulation at this early phase of Northwest Semitic than does the transcription of *ṣade,* with its "interfering" emphatic element.

181. Segert 1976:63–65.

182. Harris 1936:9.

183. We have seen that this is so in spite of the fact that Phoenician has a character with the value [h].

184. Jeffery's phonetic identification of Phoenician *ṣade* as [ts] is adopted by Powell, as I mentioned above. Upon specifying this value, Powell notes that "*ṣade* is usually said to have had the value of a voiceless affricate [ts], but in Protosemitic it may have been an 'emphatic' dental fricative" (1991:46) and cites as his authority Moscati 1980:33. We have seen that there are difficulties involved in pressing the claim that the value of Phoenician *ṣade* was [tˢ']; but, beyond this, it is important to look at exactly what Moscati says: "Proto-Semitic has two non-emphatic dental fricatives, voiceless *s* and voiced *z*. It also possesses an emphatic dental fricative *ṣ,* which, unlike some other emphatics, is always voiceless. It has more than once been maintained that this consonant was originally an affricate (of the type [ts]), largely on the basis of the pronunciation of *ṣ* over a wide sector of the Jewish tradition, but this pronunciation is probably secondary." (On this largely, though not exclusively, nineteenth-century interpretation of *ṣade* as an affricate, see Steiner 1982:1–6.) Powell has shifted the emphasis of Moscati's remarks. Moscati is not forging the claim that in Proto-Semitic the sound of *ṣade* "*may have been* an 'emphatic' dental fricative." To the contrary, he is rebutting any notion

that it may have been something *other than* an 'emphatic' dental fricative. In Modern Hebrew, the sound of *ṣade* is the affricate [tˢ]; *ṣade,* like all of the emphatic consonants, has lost the "emphatic" quality which it once had in Hebrew. Hetzron (1987b, "Hebrew," in Comrie 1987:693–694) states: "The emphatic consonants of Biblical Hebrew: *ṭ, ṣ, q* (or *ḳ*) may have been pronounced glottalised (though there is no explicit proof of this). Today, there is no feature 'emphasis' and the three consonants are realised respectively /t/, /c/ (= *ts*) and /k/."

185. Jeffery 1990:26.

186. Harris 1936:23.

187. On Greek Τυρος ([türos]) beside Phoenician *ṣr* for the place-name Tyre, see Harris 1936:23, n. 14; also p. 20, n. 3.

188. With the possible exception of a dialect used in cities of northern Phoenicia, on which see Segert 1976:29.

189. On the following discussion and examples cited therein, see Harris 1936:23–24, 33.

190. Allen 1974:54–55.

191. It is also unclear if there are instances of the earlier sequence *[zd] (*/sd/) attested in the Mycenaean materials; see Lejeune 1982:112, n. 4.

192. Concerning the possible value of the *zV* symbols, see especially Heubeck 1971 for discussion and references.

193. These symbols, like the *ksV* characters, appear not to be found in the Eteocypriot syllabary (O. Masson 1983:55).

194. For discussion of *za?,* see O. Masson 1983:54–55.

195. Ibid., p. 55. Lejeune (1954, "Observations sur le cypriote," *BSL* 50:68–75) proposed that the *ksV* symbols and the *zV* symbols belong to a single set. This appears highly improbable. Note, *inter alios,* O. Masson's comments concerning this idea (1983:55–56).

196. Jeffery 1990:33. She also notes that *san* continued in use "as an emblem on the coins of Sikyon, and also as a brand for the breed of horses called σαμφόραι [sampʰórai]."

197. Ibid.

198. For discussion, see Buck 1955:56–57; Lejeune 1982:305–306. In contrast to the Eretrian condition, as we have seen already, intervocalic *[s] had become [h] in Laconian by the time of the earliest inscriptions; Elean inscriptions show instances of intervocalic [h] for earlier [s] by at least the fourth century. Consequently, [s] between vowels was certainly not voiced in these dialects.

199. It could be argued, of course, that the voicing of word-final *[-s] to *[-z] in Laconian postdated the loss of *san* from the Laconian alphabet, though such a scenario would be quite an uncertain one. While Laconian rhotacism may not be attested until the second century A.D. (Thumb-Kiekers 1932:91), the process of voicing word-final [-s] must have occurred rather earlier. In the case of the Elean dialect, in which rhotacism is already attested in the earliest inscriptions, such an argument would be highly dubious. The voicing of word-final [-s] to [-z] in certain specific contexts (without further development to [-r]) may actually have been a widespread phenomenon; see ibid.

200. Lejeune 1982:89.

201. Ibid., pp. 89, n. 3; 101, n. 6. Compare Lejeune's comment on his p. 106, n. 1.

202. As we will discuss below, in non-Aeolic dialects all three labiovelars (*[kʷ], *[gʷ], *[kʰʷ]) are palatalized to dental stops before mid front vowels and *[kʷ] also becomes a dental stop before the high front vowels. In the Aeolic dialects, in contrast, each of the labiovelars develops into a *bilabial* stop before mid front vowels. In the case

of labiovelars occurring within enclitics, however, the dental development is observed before mid front vowels even in Aeolic dialects. For an examination of these and still other contextually determined reflexes of the labiovelars, see Stephens and Woodard 1986.

203. In the Idalion bronze tablet *ICS* 217, ll. 10, 23 (probably fifth century). On the form *o-pi-si-si-ke* in l. 29, which may provide an additional example, perhaps representing οπι σις κε ([opi sis ke], 'and whenever anyone' (?)), see O. Masson 1983:243–244; Buck 1955:103, 213; Thumb-Scherer 1959:160.

204. See, *inter alios,* Buck 1955:62; Lejeune 1982:51, 89; Thumb-Scherer 1959:124–125. The symbol is also used in the place of δ ([d]) in Arcadian απυ𝐌εδο–μιν[ος] ([apüCedominos], 'ones having been restored'); as Buck discusses (pp. 62–63) the symbol is probably here used to represent not [d] but a dissimilated reflex of *[d]. Buck also notes that, not surprisingly, 𝐌 is only used to represent the Arcadian reflex of *[kʷ] in early inscriptions (see below).

205. Note the comments of Allen 1957:115; see also Lejeune 1982:50–51; Rix 1976:87.

206. See Meister 1905/06 for an early summary of the evidence; more recently see, among others, Buck 1955:62–63; Lejeune 1982:51.

207. Perhaps also ζε for τε ([te], 'and'). See Buck 1955:62, 196–197; Thumb-Scherer 1959:125.

208. On these Arcadian features, see K. Meister 1905/06.

209. Buck 1955:62; Lejeune 1982:51; Thumb-Scherer 1959:124–125. Compare the use of *zeta* for *[d] in very early Elean inscriptions (Buck 1955:58–59).

210. Ibid., pp. 62–63; see also pp. 174–175.

211. It is interesting that in the inscription of (1), there may be preserved an attempt to distinguish graphically between the reflex of the palatalized labiovelar, here spelled ζ, and that sound sequence which is normally represented by the character *zeta,* that is, [zd]. The first line of the inscription offers the form ζτεραιον, which, as Buck (1955:197) indicates, may well be related to ζειρόν ([zdẹ:rón], 'robe'). If this identification is correct, [zd] is, naturally enough, spelled ζτ, apparently owing to the use of ζ to represent the reflex of *[kʷ] before a front vowel. The identification of this form is by no means certain, however.

212. See, for example, Buck 1955:18.

213. Jeffery 1990:38–39.

214. See, *inter alios,* Lejeune 1982:89, n. 3; 101, n. 6; Thumb-Scherer 1959:264–265. The character also occurs in certain names and words of non-Greek origin, on which see the last-cited reference.

215. See the discussion in Rix 1976:92.

216. This is not to say that this affiliation is universally accepted. Jeffery (1990:213) states concerning this character: "The letter-form has been interpreted, from its appearance and value, as a form of *ṣade,* presumably handed on automatically in its place in the abecedarium. The theory is attractive, but why then should it not have been used instead of *zeta* in the other Arkadian inscriptions?" Her hesitations appear again to be consequent upon her confusion hypothesis, according to which *zeta* continues the value of *ṣade.*

217. W. Larfeld, 1914, *Griechische Epigraphik,* 3rd. ed. (Munich: C. H. Beck'sche Verlagsbuchhandlung), pp. 218, 220–221.

218. The Carian script also provides the symbol Ⴘ which occurs in the alphabet of speakers of the Pamphylian dialect of Greek in the place of σσ (as with 𝐌); see Lejeune 1982:101, n. 6; Thumb-Scherer 1959:187.

219. Allen 1974:57–58.

220. The numbering system is dated as early as the eighth century by some scholars, such as Larfeld (1914:294); compare Jeffery 1990:327.

221. Lejeune 1982:51.

222. Jeffery 1990:213.

223. On the phonetic processes involved, see Stephens and Woodard 1986:129–131; also see Lejeune 1982:46–47.

224. On the Mycenaean dissimilation of the first of two labiovelars within a word, see *Docs.*:399–400; Lejeune 1982:47, n. 34–3.

225. For an investigation of this pattern of palatalization, see Stephens and Woodard 1986:131–153.

226. Though it is not critical for the analysis presented here, it is quite probable that the relative chronological order of these developments was palatalization followed by labialization. A claim that the opposite chronological ordering holds would be highly suspect, as such would require positing that all labiovelars first underwent labialization *except* for certain of those occurring before front vowels. While an ensuing front vowel is a well-known conditioner of consonant palatalization, it is not a context which would be likely to inhibit the broadly occurring "labialization" of *[kʷ] ⇒ [p] and so on. This course of development (i.e. palatalization followed by labialization) entails that it was *[kʷ] and so on rather than [p] and so on which was palatalized to produce a dental stop (or a sibilant in Arcado-Cypriot), and this is surely the case. See the discussion in Lejeune 1972:51–53.

227. *ICS* 241, 307, 328.

228. Thumb-Scherer 1959:124.

229. Lejeune 1982:48, n. 2; Thumb-Scherer 1959:160. A bilabial reflex of *[kʷ] would be regular before the vowel [a] (as in πεμπαμερων ([pempamerọ:n])), in all dialects, of course. However, as Lejeune points out, compounds in which the numeral five terminates in the [a] vowel (a construction which is perhaps based upon compounds formed from τετρα- ([tetra-], 'four') usually display the reflex of *[kʷ] which is regular before the mid vowel, as in Homeric πεντά-ετες ([pentá-etes], 'lasting five years') after πέντε

230. See Lejeune 1982:47, 52. Thumb-Scherer 1959:160 disparages any notion that the bilabial of Cypriot *pe-i-se-i* and so on. may be extended analogically from the etymologically related ποινά ([poiná], 'a price paid').

231. Stephens and Woodard 1986:151–153.

232. The study also revealed clitic contexts to be more effectively palatalizing. For additional conclusions, see ibid.

233. Unless the *sampi* of the east Ionic scripts discussed above is also derived from *san*. The value of this sign would also be quite close, though perhaps not identical, to the sibilant reflex of *[kʷ] which characterized Cypriot.

234. Compare the use of three different graphemes in the Etruscan alphabet for the representation of /k/. Upon acquiring the alphabet from the Greeks, the Etruscans used *gamma* for *k* occurring before *e* and *i*; *kappa* for *k* before *a*; and *qoppa* for *k* before *u* (Etruscan had neither /g/ nor any other voiced stop). Some allophonic variation is perhaps involved. This trifold scheme of representation was continued in early Latin orthography, with *C* (the *gamma* character) being used to spell both /k/ and /g/ until the third, or perhaps fourth, century B.C., when a variant character *G* was created for representing the voiced stop. The use of *K* (the *kappa* character) became restricted to a very few forms. See L. Bonfante, 1990, "Etruscan," in *Reading the Past,* with an introduction by J. Hooker (Berkeley: University of California Press), p. 336; G. Bonfante and L. Bon-

fante, 1983, *The Etruscan Language* (New York: New York University Press), p. 63; W. Allen, 1978, *Vox Latina,* 2nd ed. (Cambridge: Cambridge University Press), pp. 15–16; Sturtevant 1940:165–166.

235. Etruscan possessed a fourth sibilant character as well; for full discussion, see Bonfante and Bonfante 1983:65–66. I am indebted to Laurence Stephens for kindly reminding me of this Etruscan parallel.

236. Harris 1936:24.

237. Jeffery 1990:26.

238. T. Nöldeke, 1904, *Beiträge zur semitischen Sprachwissenschaft* (Strassburg: Karl J. Trübner), p. 134.

239. Powell 1991:48. Phonetically, then, the path is: *[semk] > *[semka] > *[semga] > *[segma]> *[sigma]. On the possibility that the sequence -γμ- was pronounced [-ŋm-], see Lejeune 1982:77–78.

240. Nöldeke 1904:134.

241. Powell 1991:48

242. See Lejeune 1982:145–146. This regressive assimilation in place of articulation occurs with all sequences of *nasal + stop,* without regard to the place of articulation of the stop.

243. Powell 1991:48.

244. Ibid.

245. McCarter 1975:100–101, n. 88.

246. [tò dọ:riées mèn sàn kaléu:si íọ:nes sígma]

247. And perhaps both also occurred in the alphabets of the Ionic cities showing the *sampi*-like symbol ⲦⲦ, which we discussed above.

248. It has been suggested that both Greek *san* and *sigma* are derived from Phoenician *shan*; this, however, is unlikely. See McCarter's rebuttal of this idea (1975:100, n. 86).

249. Powell 1991:35, n. 98. Interestingly, this letter-name happens to be *san.*

250. See, *inter alios,* McCarter 1975:99, n. 85; Chantraine 1968:1002–1003.

Cyprus and Beyond

7.0 More Syllabic Cypriot Influence

In chapter 6 I argued that disparate aspects of the Greek treatment of the Semitic sibilant characters are reasonably accounted for when the origin of the Greek alphabet is viewed as the work of adapters who were accustomed to writing with the syllabic Cypriot script and who incorporated features of this script into the alphabet which they were devising. This hypothesis not only makes sense of the use of the Phoenician sibilant graphemes but also has crucial consequences for interpreting other aspects of the Greek alphabetic writing system.

7.0.1 Stop Consonant Graphemes

As I have discussed, the system of stop phonemes of ancient Greek is quite unlike that of Phoenician; the two systems in effect represent partially overlapping sets. Greek possessed voiceless unaspirated, voiceless aspirated, and voiced stop phonemes produced at the bilabial, dental, and velar places of articulation, that is, /p, pʰ, b/; /t, tʰ, d/; and /k, kʰ, g/.[1] Phoenician possessed both voiced and voiceless stops at these same articulatory positions, though this language does not phonemically distinguish voiceless unaspirated and voiceless aspirated stops. In addition, the consonantal inventory of Phoenician includes glottalized, pharyngealized, or in some manner "emphatic" voiceless dental and velar stop phonemes; thus, Phoenician displays the following set of stop phonemes: /p, b/; /t, d, t'/; and /k, g, k'/.[2] In the development of the Greek alphabet, the orthographic treatment of those stop phonemes shared by the two languages, /p, b, t, d, k, g/, is straightforward. For representing each of these sounds, the Greek adapters simply appropriated the Phoenician grapheme with its phonemic value intact; thus, Phoenician *pe* = /p/ was acquired as Greek *pi* = /p/, Phoenician *bet* = /b/ as Greek *beta* = /b/, Phoenician *taw* = /t/ as Greek *tau* = /t/, and so forth. Such direct acquisition of "symbol + value" was not possible in the case of the Greek voiceless aspirated stop phonemes, as such do not occur in Semitic.

The matter of the representation of the Greek voiceless aspirated stops in the newly devised Greek alphabet brings us back to a consideration of the supplemental characters ϕ, χ, and ψ. Though the origin and source of these symbols, which have no obvious counterparts in the Phoenician script,[3] is quite uncertain, it has been generally held that they are in some sense—as their designation indicates—*supplemental*; in other words, these symbols were added to the Greek alphabet subsequent to its initial creation.[4] There are several pieces of evidence which indicate the secondary nature of these symbols:

1. While all three supplemental characters occur in both the blue and red Greek alphabet-types, of the three, only one (ϕ) has the same phonetic value ([p^h]) in both groups.

2. In addition, the order in which the supplementals occur differs in the blue and red abecedaria: blue shows the sequence ϕ, χ, ψ, with the respective values [p^h], [k^h], [ps] (though the light blue alphabets lack ψ, as discussed above); on the other hand, the order is χ, ϕ, ψ, with the respective values [ks], [p^h], [k^h], in the red.[5]

3. The supplemental characters are absent from the conservative script of Crete, and this is not, as we have discussed in some detail, because the Cretan dialect lacked aspirated stops.

4. That ϕ, χ, and ψ represent secondary additions to the Greek script is also strongly suggested by the nonoccurrence of these characters in the recently discovered Würzburg alphabet-table, which, as pointed out above, appears to be the earliest example of the Greek alphabet recovered thus far; this alphabet ends in *tau*.[6]

Now let us refocus our attention on the representation of voiceless aspirated stops (/p^h/, /t^h/, /k^h/) in the newly created Greek alphabet. To represent the aspirated dental /t^h/, the Greek adapters utilized the Phoenician symbol for the emphatic dental stop, *ṭet*. Obviously, the adapters' choice of symbols for Greek /t^h/ was phonetically motivated to the extent that the Phoenician character chosen represented a type of voiceless dental stop. Now, Phoenician had no phonemic aspiration as Greek did, but a language without phonemic aspiration can still possess consonants which are characterized by *phonetic* aspiration. As we saw in an earlier discussion, this is the case with English: voiceless stops are aspirated in certain phonetic contexts, but aspiration of stops can never effect a meaning difference in English; that is, aspiration is not phonemic in this language, unlike in ancient Greek. It is possible that certain types of Phoenician stop consonants could have been characterized by the presence of phonetic aspiration, at least in certain contexts, and this in fact appears to be the case. However, Greek and Latin transcriptions of the Semitic emphatic consonants indicate that it is *not* the emphatics which are so characterized by the presence of aspiration, or at least such transcriptions suggest that the emphatics have less aspiration than the *unemphatic* voiceless stops of Semitic.[7] To the extent that the sound of Phoenician *ṭet* appears to have been less characterized by phonetic aspiration than was the sound of *taw*, the use of *ṭet* to represent Greek /tʰ/ is somewhat arbitrary.[8]

While a Phoenician character was adapted to represent the aspirated dental phoneme /tʰ/, the other two aspirated stop phonemes of Greek are expressed only by the supplemental characters of the red and blue alphabets. In other words, if the supplemental characters are secondary in origin (as it appears), then the Greek adapters of the Phoenician script made no provision for graphically distinguishing /pʰ/ from /p/ and /kʰ/ from /k/. The decision not to do so is surely highly significant for the present investigation. In the Phoenician script the character *qop* represented the emphatic velar stop /k'/. Just as *ṭet*, the symbol for the emphatic dental, was utilized by the Greek adapters to represent /tʰ/, so, in a completely parallel fashion, *qop* could have been taken over as the symbol for the aspirated velar stop /kʰ/. Instead, however, as we have seen, Greek *qoppa* (from *qop*) was used (almost whimsically) to represent a backed allophonic variant of the unaspirated velar stop /k/.[9] There is no emphatic bilabial stop in Phoenician and, hence, no symbol for such a sound which, in keeping with the Greek use of *ṭet*, might be appropriated for representing /pʰ/. We have seen that at times the adaptation of Phoenician symbols for Greek alphabetic use involved an element of arbitrariness—most recently in the use of *ṭet* (/ṭ/) as a symbol for denoting Greek /tʰ/. Phoenician *zayin* could have been arbitrarily assigned the Greek value /pʰ/; instead, it was used to represent the consonantal sequence [z] + [d]. Phoenician *samek* might have been arbitrarily utilized to represent Greek /pʰ/; instead, it was assigned the cluster value [k] + [s]. The use of either of these Semitic symbols to represent /pʰ/ would have involved arbitrariness of an appreciable degree, but no more than is displayed by the adapters in assigning vowel values to Phoenician consonantal characters.

What is of most acute significance in the foregoing observations is that for the Greek adapters of the Phoenician writing system, it was more critical that the new alphabetic script include symbols with the value [z] + [d] and [k] + [s]—which could have simply been written σδ and κσ (!!)—than that there should be symbols for the aspirated stop phonemes /pʰ/ and /kʰ/. These adapters were quite willing to tolerate the lack of a graphic distinction between voiceless unaspirated consonants and voiceless aspirated consonants; it is a small step to infer that the adapters were scribes who were already accustomed to spelling with a system in which such phonemically crucial distinctions were treated as moot. This again brings us back to the syllabic Cypriot script.

As we have seen, one of the peculiar, characteristic features of the syllabic Cypriot writing system is its failure to distinguish between the three types of stops produced at any given place of articulation: voiceless unaspirated, voiceless aspirated, and voiced. Given the evidence which we have already uncovered for positing that the Greek adapters of the Phoenician writing system were practitioners of the syllabic Cypriot script, it is only reasonable to interpret the absence of characters for the voiceless aspirated stop phonemes /pʰ/ and /kʰ/

from the early alphabet as yet another instance in which a structural feature of the syllabic Cypriot script was transferred to the alphabet. The Cypriot Greek adapters of the Semitic script accepted the graphic distinction of voiced verses voiceless stops which was provided by the Phoenician script, but were only motivated to make provision for further distinguishing the voiceless aspirated stops in the case of the dental /t^h/. This fuller graphic differentiation of the various dental stop phonemes than of the bilabial and velar stop phonemes in the early alphabet is hauntingly reminiscent of the practice which we observed in the Linear B script. The Mycenaean scribes, like the scribes of the syllabic Cypriot script, used a single set of symbols to represent the voiceless unaspirated, voiceless aspirated, and voiced stops occurring at a given place of articulation, with the exception of the dentals in Linear B spelling: the voiced dental stops were represented by *dV* symbols, while the voiceless unaspirated and aspirated stops were both spelled *tV.* Whether the higher (though not identical) level of differentiation among dental stops which is observed in the Linear B script and in the early alphabet is in some way the consequence of a continuity of scribal tradition, however labyrinthine the pathway might be, or is a phenomenon which is essentially cognitive in nature is unclear.

7.1 Early Alphabetic Traditions in Cyprus

7.1.1 [ks] and [ps] Across the Alphabets

As I discussed in chapter 6, among the various epichoric alphabets of Greece, there are three different ways in which the consonantal sequence [k] + [s] is represented: in the dark blue scripts, the character ξ, based upon Phoenician *samek,* is utilized; the red alphabets assign the [k] + [s] value to the supplemental character χ, and both the light blue alphabets and the "primitive," or green, scripts spell the cluster sequentially as χσ (or κM etc.). I argued that the graphic representation in these alphabets of the sequences [k] + [s] on the one hand, and [p] + [s], on the other, exist in an asymmetric fashion. My previous summary of the aspects of this asymmetrical relationship is repeated here as (1):

(1)   A. A [ks] character occurs in each script in which a [ps] character occurs.
       B. A [ks] character occurs in some scripts which lack a [ps] character.
       C. No [ps] character occurs in a script which lacks a [ks] character.

As I pointed out, [ks] and [ps] graphemes thus exist in an implicational relationship: the presence of a [ps] character implies the presence of a [ks] character, but not vice versa. I further noted that in the dark blue alphabets— the only scripts to have both a [ks] and a [ps] character—there is a further asymmetry to the extent that [ks] is represented by a symbol taken directly from the Phoenician script, while [ps] is represented by one of the secondary, supplemental characters. The asymmetrical nature of [ks] vis-à-vis [ps] representation in the Greek alphabets, I concluded, is anchored in and proceeds from spelling practices of the Greek scribes who utilized the syllabic Cypriot script and who adapted the Phoenician script for writing Greek. Now, what I did not address in detail earlier is a certain implication of this conclusion: namely, that if the [ks]/[ps] asymmetries of *both* the blue and red alphabetic traditions follow from syllabic Cypriot spelling practice, then *both* of these alphabetic traditions (blue and red) probably have their origin at the hands of the Cypriot adapters of the Phoenician writing system. To this matter we will now turn our attention.

In the dark blue alphabet-type [k] + [s] is represented by the Greek character (ξ) which is derived from Phoenician *samek,* standing in the alphabetic position of *samek.* In the red alphabet-type this character is conspicuously absent; in fact, from *alpha* through *upsilon* (i.e., up to the supplementals) the dark blue and red alphabets are identical in occurrence and order of characters except for this absence of ξ in the latter. In the red script it is as though a hole had opened between *nu* and *omicron* and simply swallowed the ξ symbol which separated the two. However, immediately following *upsilon* in the red type, there stands a different (supplemental) character (χ) which has been given the very same value [k] + [s]! Thus, we have the following prototypic alphabetic configurations at an early phase:

(2) A. Dark blue: $\alpha\beta\gamma\delta\epsilon\digamma\zeta\eta\theta\iota\kappa\lambda\mu\nu\xi\omicron\pi M \rho\rho\sigma\tau\upsilon$ . . .
B. Red: $\alpha\beta\gamma\delta\epsilon\digamma\zeta\eta\theta\iota\kappa\lambda\mu\nu-\omicron\pi M \rho\rho\sigma\tau\upsilon\chi$. . .

What sense is to be made of this? This is a *prima facie* absurdity. Why would a symbol be extracted from the very heart of the alphabet only to be replaced by another symbol having the exact same idiosyncratic value, tacked on to the end of the "nonsupplemental" portion of the alphabet? If both the blue and red alphabetic traditions arose at the hands of the Cypriot scribes, as I have now suggested, then excising ξ and replacing it with χ is the alphabetic equivalent of robbing Peter to pay Paul.

Excursus 2: An Interpretative Essay

In an effort to provide a reasoned answer to the questions raised in the preceding paragraph, I present in this excursus a scenario of the earliest phases of the development of the Greek alphabet. While the ensuing scenario is dependent upon the positions and arguments which I have advanced in the preceding chapters, the reverse is not true. Therefore, the ideas that I have presented and developed thus far concerning the Cypriot source of the alphabet should be judged independently of the reconstruction of episodes in the early life of the alphabet which follows.

Before proceeding, I must remind my readers of two points. First, in addition to blue ξ and red χ there was a third alphabetic means for representing the consonantal sequence [k] + [s]: in the light blue and green traditions this cluster is spelled sequentially as $\chi\sigma$ (or κM, etc.). Second, in the syllabic Cypriot writing system there were two means of representing the sequence [k] + [s]: word-finally, and word-internally before a stop, the cluster is represented using the *ksV* syllabic symbols; word-internally before a vowel, [k] + [s] is spelled sequentially as *kV-sV.*

When Cypriot scribes accustomed to spelling syllabically encountered the Phoenician consonantal script and set about adapting this script for Greek use, they devised an alphabetic system which matched the Phoenician script symbol for symbol: as the Phoenician script ran from *'alep* to *taw,* the new Greek script ran from *alpha* to *tau,* with every Semitic character utilized. In the creation of this new alphabetic script, the Cypriot scribes made provision not only for representing consonants, as in the Phoenician script, but for spelling vowels as well. In addition, two of the Phoenician symbols were adapted for representing consonantal sequences for which individual syllabic symbols also existed in the Cypriot Syllabary: *zayin* was assigned the value [z] + [d] and *samek* the value [k] + [s]. This appears to be essentially the abecedarium which is preserved on the Würzburg tablet. Within this alphabetic system ϝ must have served to represent not only [w] but [u] as well.[10] Soon afterward, though not necessarily prior to the stage described in the ensuing paragraph, a distinct character, *upsilon,* was created for representing [u] and was attached to the end of the now evolving alphabetic script.[11]

Subsequent to the creation of the *alpha* through *tau* (or *upsilon*) alphabet, it appears that some set of Cypriot scribes introduced a modification into this new writing system. The syllabic Cypriot script used both *ksV* and *kV-sV* spellings to represent [ks] clusters. Recall that it was the peculiar empty-vowel spelling strategy based upon the sonority hierarchy that had motivated the inclusion of *ksV* symbols in the Cypriot Syllabary. The considerations of sonority which were responsible for the presence of these *ksV* symbols and which had determined their distribution in syllabic spelling practice did not obtain in the new alphabetic script. Every sound occurring in a word could be represented (though not uniquely at this stage of development, prior to the introduction of characters with the value [pʰ] and [kʰ]), and to do so it was not necessary to utilize graphemic components which had no phonetic reality, that is, empty vowels. The orthographic motivation for *ksV* characters no longer existed. Hence, in keeping with the genius of the alphabet, the [ks] symbol ξ was deleted from the new script by early scribal reformers, and the practice of sequentially spelling [ks] as κσ was introduced (again, the sequential spelling of [ks] clusters, at least in certain contexts, was a practice with which the scribes of the syllabic Cypriot script were completely familiar). Owing either, as I proposed above, to the nonoccurrence of *psV* syllabograms in the Cypriot script or to the lower functional yield of such symbols if they did exist, no Phoenician character had been assigned the value [ps]; instead, such clusters had been from the start spelled sequentially as πσ in the newly devised alphabet. This sequential spelling of [ps] clusters in the alphabetic system undoubtedly encouraged the "regularization" of the representation of [ks] clusters as κσ.

The other CC alphabetic character, *zeta,* escaped this early reform of the alphabet, and the reasons it did are not difficult to perceive. The [zd] symbol and the [ks] symbol of the new alphabet were fundamentally quite different. In the syllabic Cypriot script *zV* was the only regular spelling of [zd]; in other words, unlike the case of the cluster [ks], there was no contextually variant, sequential spelling of [zd] (which would presumably have been *sV-tV*). There was thus no precedent in the syllabic system for a sequential alphabetic spelling of [zd], and hence, one of the principal motivating factors which led to a resolution of ξ into $\kappa\sigma$ did not exist for *zeta*.

A primitive alphabetic system such as that described in the preceding paragraph, with a hole where ξ should have been and a concomitant reformed spelling of [k] + [s] as $\kappa\sigma$, as well as with *upsilon* appended, is essentially the alphabet which was transported to Crete and there preserved in a conservative orthographic tradition (though in Crete *san* will be selected to bear the value [s]). This early variant alphabet, which arose as an adjustment made by certain Cypriot scribes of a new writing system devised by (some other) Cypriot scribes, is thus the source of the alphabetic tradition we have identified as the green script.

The *alpha*-to-*upsilon* alphabetic system from which ξ has been selectively excised and which is progenitor of the Cretan alphabetic script may also be the link which ties the early alphabet-type of (2A), in which ξ = [ks], to that of (2B), in which [ks] is expressed by χ. We questioned above why a Semitic character which had been given the Greek value [ks] would have been removed from deep within the alphabet only to be replaced by a supplemental character tacked on at the tail, having the same value. It seems most unlikely that this process would have occurred as a simple exchange of ξ for χ—at least it is difficult to imagine a convincing motivation for such a swap. However, once ξ had been removed in the process of regularizing the spelling of *consonant* + *[s]* clusters, a kind of vacuum would have been created into which a new [ks] symbol could have been introduced.

Let us elaborate on a possible process of this sort. Cypriot scribes had assigned the value of [ks] to ξ when the Greek alphabetic script was initially developed; other scribes then, in effect, devised a competing alphabet by modifying the representation of [ks] to $\kappa\sigma$, getting rid of ξ. These two nascent alphabetic traditions began to spread among Cypriot scribes, as technological advances do so spread. Some set of these scribes encountered the form of the alphabet from which the [ks] symbol ξ had been removed, and, accustomed to writing with their own syllabic Cypriot script which contained *ksV* symbols and perceiving these as a utilitarian feature of that writing system, they devised and appended to the end of the alphabet (after *upsilon*) a different character (χ) with the value [ks] (presumably unaware that ξ = [ks] had ever been a part of the alphabet). In this way a [ks] character was reintroduced into the alphabet (through a kind of counterreformation) and another variant alphabet was created (that in (2B), running from α through χ, with no ξ and with χ = [ks]) which became the germ of the red alphabets.

It would appear that this group of scribal counterreformers, like the adapters of the Phoenician script, also made no provision for representing the sequence [ps] with a single character. In the case of the process of adapting the Phoenician script (in which only Phoenician characters were used), I proposed that the failure to provide for a [ps] character suggests either that *psV* symbols did not occur in the syllabic Cypriot script or that if they did, they simply carried less of a functional load than *ksV* characters, so that in either case, the limited resource of Semitic characters was not tapped for a [ps] symbol. In the present case, however, in which a supplemental character is devised and attached to the end of the Phoenician portion of the alphabet, the apparent failure to create a [ps] supplemental (recall that no character with the value [ps] occurs in the red scripts) may weigh in favor of the *nonoccurrence* of Cypriot *psV* syllabograms.

The preceding scheme suggests that there was a period of Cypriot experimentation with the Greek alphabet subsequent to its initial creation. This is not unexpected, and, in fact, McCarter has argued for some experimental phase on epigraphical grounds.[12] The fundamental gross structural characteristics which distinguish the various Greek *alphabet-types* may thus be traced to this experimental period, though the particular Phoenician *letter-forms* utilized in the attested Greek scripts may, in some measure, have their origin in a somewhat later period. If this is so, then continued contact between the users of the early Greek alphabet and the Phoenician script would be required. Cyprus would be an ideal location for such interaction.

In our scenario we have thus far seen generated three slightly variant types of the Greek alphabet. These are (3A) the original adaptation of the Semitic script with *upsilon* appended; (3B) a variant which arose when ξ was removed from (3A) and κσ was introduced as the spelling of [ks]; and (3C) an additional variant spawned by the decision to introduce a [ks] symbol into (3B), presumably (though not necessarily) made without knowledge that a symbol with this value had been previously present:

(3)   A. $αβγδεϝζηθικλμνξοπ Ϻϙρστυ$
       B. $αβγδεϝζηθικλμν_οπ Ϻϙρστυ$
       C. $αβγδεϝζηθικλμν_οπ Ϻϙρστυχ$

I have proposed that (3B) and (3C) are the ultimate source of the primitive (green) and red alphabet-types respectively. The alphabet of (3A) would be the source of the dark blue type; to (3A) will of course ultimately be added the three supplemental consonantal characters, one of which (χ) we see already appearing in the alphabet of (3C). Whether it was at the hand of Cypriot innovators that the additional two supplementals φ and ψ were added to (3C) and that the full complement of dark blue supplementals, φ, χ, and ψ, were appended to (3A) is unclear. Jeffery, however, has argued that the three supplemental characters have their origin in the Cypriot Syllabary.[13] Her proposal is a most welcome contribution to the thesis developed in the present work. Beyond that, however, if her interpretation is correct, then the Cypriot scribes were probably also responsible for finishing out the consonantal component of the blue and red alphabets.

Regardless of precisely who was responsible for extending the blue and red alphabets by appending various supplemental characters, this process appears to have been rather uniform across the two alphabet-types, despite formal differences. Metaphorically, the evolutionary structure of the alphabet which has begun to present itself could be called the *onion model* (a descriptively appropriate, if not altogether, complimentary, term). At the core is the adapted *'alep-through-taw* Phoenician script; the alphabet then grows in layers as additional characters are suffixed. Thus, the initial structure, (4A), is enlarged as (4B). Another layer is added in (4C), as the red alphabet begins to take shape:

(4) A. *[αβγδεϝζηθικλμνξοπ M ϙρστ]*
     B. *[[αβγδεϝζηθικλμνξοπ M ϙρστ] υ]*
     C. *[[[αβγδεϝζηθικλμν‿οπ M ϙρστ] υ] χ]*

The next step in the evolution of both the blue and red scripts involved making provision for graphically distinguishing the voiceless aspirated stops [pʰ] and [kʰ] from their unaspirated counterparts [p] and [k]. To this end two additional (supplemental) characters are appended to each of the alphabets (4B) and (4C). Within this new layer the value of the symbols added is the same for both scripts, and in both the order is the same, in that the bilabial character precedes the velar; however, the grapheme which is used to represent [kʰ] differs in the two alphabets:

(5) A. *[[[αβγδεϝζηθικλμνξοπ M ϙρστ] υ] φ (pʰ) χ (kʰ)]*
     B. *[[[[αβγδεϝζηθικλμν‿οπ M ϙρστ] υ] χ] φ (pʰ) ψ (kʰ)]*

With the addition of this new layer, the protoform of the blue script, (4B), is transformed into (5A), and the red (4C) is changed into (5B). The addition to these two alphabetic systems of symbols with the same values, in the same order, but with variation in the form of the [kʰ] character (χ in the blue script and ψ in the red) suggests that this latest modification of the two scripts was the work of independent hands but that the editors involved, in some fashion or another, interacted with one another or had common access to ideas of others.

The preceding analysis of the evolution of the red alphabet suggests that the addition of the χ layer and that of the layer containing φ and ψ were separate processes. It is also possible of course that the [ks] layer and the aspirated stop layer were both appended by the same set of scribal editors at essentially the same time. The attested red alphabets which contain χ = [ks] do also possess φ and ψ. Thus, if the addition of these three supplemental characters occurred in two distinct phases, the intermediate stage (i.e., that one with χ but without φ and ψ) did not survive as a historical alphabetic system. As we shall see below, however, there is evidence for a red system of the converse type (i.e., one with φ and ψ but without χ).

It has been argued by some, as I discussed in chapter 6, that red χ, with the value [ks], arose as an abbreviation of the sequential spelling of this cluster as χσ. We rejected this interpretation as implausible. If there were actually any phonetic link between the [kʰ] blue value of χ (as in (5A)) and the [ks] red value (as in (5B)), it is likely to have been forged in the opposite direction. In other words, the scribes who were responsible for adding the layer containing symbols for voiceless aspirated stops to the evolving blue alphabet may have been led to adopt red χ for representing [kʰ] simply because the initial portion of the value of the character in the red alphabet ([ks]) was that of a voiceless velar stop (perhaps with some aspiration, if the light blue spelling of [ks] as χσ is phonetically revealing). This decision may have been further encouraged by red alphabet hyperspellings of [ks] as $\chi\sigma$ (i.e., *kss*; an English spelling equivalent would occur in something like *exsit* for *exit*). This is a fairly common type of hyperspelling in Greek inscriptions.[14] Alternatively, χ may have suggested itself as a symbol for representing both [ks] and [k^h] in these two alphabetic traditions because of the value attached to the parent symbol in the source script. Then again, the use of the symbol which had the value [ks] in the red script to represent [k^h] in the blue alphabet may have simply been in large measure arbitrary. Such arbitrariness appears to be exhibited in the ensuing phase of blue-alphabet development.

Next, the consonantal component of the blue alphabet (5A) is filled out by the addition to the script of a second CC symbol, namely, ψ for [ps]:

(6)　$[\ [\ [\ [\alpha\beta\gamma\delta\varepsilon\digamma\zeta\eta\theta\iota\kappa\lambda\mu\nu\xi o\pi M\varphi\rho\sigma\tau]\ \upsilon]\ \phi\chi]\ \psi]$

The symbol chosen for this purpose is the same one used in the red alphabet to represent [k^h]. This utilization of a single character to represent the consonantal sequence [ps] in one alphabet and the aspirated stop [k^h] in another poignantly betrays a lack of inhibition regarding the arbitrary association of sound and symbol on the part of either blue or red editors or both.[15]

Still to be addressed in our interpretative essay is the evolution of the light blue variety of the alphabet. Recall that the light blue script shares with the dark blue the supplemental characters for the aspirated stops [p^h] and [k^h] (i.e., ϕ and χ), but differs from the dark blue in that it lacks CC characters for the clusters [ks] and [ps]. At least two possible derivations of this alphabetic system immediately suggest themselves, given the evolutionary model developed above; in either case the genesis of the characters for [p^h] and [k^h] which appear in the dark blue alphabet is prerequisite. On the one hand, the starting point for this script could have been the dark blue system of (5A), repeated here as (7):

(7)　$[\ [\ [\alpha\beta\gamma\delta\varepsilon\digamma\zeta\eta\theta\iota\kappa\lambda\mu\nu\xi o\pi M\varphi\rho\sigma\tau]\ \upsilon]\ \phi\chi]$

If this were so, then the light blue system would have arisen by means of the same sort of reform effort which I proposed was responsible for the development of the alphabetic system which is preserved in the primitive script of Crete. In other words, the [k] + [s] symbol ξ was perceived as redundant given the occurrence of symbols for each of its two components and the nonoccurrence of a [p] + [s] symbol.[16] This character was thus extracted from the alphabet and in its stead the sequential spelling $\chi\sigma$ was introduced, utilizing the "new" supplemental character for the aspirated stop [k^h]. Concomitantly, the representation of [p] + [s] would have been modified from $\pi\sigma$ to $\phi\sigma$.[17] On the other hand, the light blue system could have been built directly from the earlier reformed system which gave rise to the Cretan alphabet—that which had the form of (3B), repeated here as (8), and which utilized the sequential spelling $\kappa\sigma$ for [ks]:

(8)　$\alpha\beta\gamma\delta\varepsilon\digamma\zeta\eta\theta\iota\kappa\lambda\mu\nu\_o\pi M\varphi\rho\sigma\tau\upsilon$

Upon introduction of the symbols for the voiceless aspirated bilabial and velar stops (ϕ and χ respectively), the sequential spelling of the [p] + [s] and [k] +

[s] clusters would have been phonetically adjusted from $\pi\sigma$ and $\kappa\sigma$ to $\phi\sigma$ and $\chi\sigma$.

Beyond Kirchoff's basic alphabetic types, perhaps certain of the red scripts should be interpreted as preserving a vestige of still a different alphabetic system, one which has the expected red supplemental characters for $[p^h]$ and $[k^h]$ but which spells sequentially the cluster $[k] + [s]$ (as well as $[p] + [s]$, as do all red scripts). In other words, this appears to be a system with an abecedarium of the form (9), in which χ ($= [k] + [s]$) is lacking, so that $[k] + [s]$ is represented as $\psi\sigma$ (and $[p] + [s]$ as $\phi\sigma$):

(9) $[\ [\ [\alpha\beta\gamma\delta\epsilon \digamma\zeta\eta\theta\iota\kappa\lambda\mu\nu\_o\pi M \mathit{?}\rho\sigma\tau] \ \upsilon] \ \phi \ (p^h) \ \psi \ (k^h)]$

This alphabetic system would then be the red equivalent of the light blue script. Jeffery cites the red alphabet of Boeotian as one in which the spelling of $[k] + [s]$ as $\psi\sigma$ "is normal"; she further states that the customary red $[k] + [s]$ symbol χ "is not common, but may be found sometimes."[18] The spelling of $[k] + [s]$ as $\psi\sigma$ also occurs in the alphabet of Opountian Lokris, which alphabet Jeffery identifies as "the same as those of its neighbors Boiotia and (as far as it is known) Chalkis."[19] Finally, the poorly attested red alphabet of the Ionian island of Cephallenia shows the spelling ψM for $[k] + [s]$.[20]

An alphabetic system of this type, which could be designated as *light red*, would have, *mutatis mutandis*, the same possible derivations as the light blue system. It could have arisen from the red alphabet by reforming the spelling of $[k] + [s]$, that is, by deleting the character χ and instituting the sequential representation $\psi\sigma$; in the light red system, unlike the light blue, the cluster [ps] was already spelled sequentially and so could have served as additional incentive for the reform. Alternatively, the light red system could have been constructed from the proto-Cretan system of (8), by the addition of the red supplemental characters for $[p^h]$ and $[k^h]$, with an adjustment in the sequential spelling of [ps] and [ks] through the use of the new symbols.[21]

Of the two possible courses of derivation of the parallel light blue and light red systems which is outlined above, that which derives them from an early green system appears to be the preferred. It would seem more likely that once devised, the two competing sets of $[p^h]$ and $[k^h]$ characters (ϕ, χ and ϕ, ψ) were circulated and adapted to existing alphabetic systems, rather than that the spelling reform of $[k] + [s]$ occurred on three separate occasions, coupled once (in the case of the light blue system) with a parallel reform of the spelling of $[p] + [s]$ after a $[p] + [s]$ supplemental character had already been introduced into the system. Purely in terms of theoretical economy, the former analysis is clearly preferable.

In summary, it appears that the various epichoric alphabets of ancient Greece developed from three variant alphabetic systems that were devised by Cypriot scribes in a period of alphabetic experimentation. These three systems, presented above as (3A–C) , are repeated here as (10A–C):

(10) A. $\alpha\beta\gamma\delta\epsilon \digamma\zeta\eta\theta\iota\kappa\lambda\mu\nu\xi o\pi M\mathit{?}\rho\sigma\tau\upsilon$
      B. $\alpha\beta\gamma\delta\epsilon \digamma\zeta\eta\theta\iota\kappa\lambda\mu\nu\_o\pi M\mathit{?}\rho\sigma\tau\upsilon$
      C. $\alpha\beta\gamma\delta\epsilon \digamma\zeta\eta\theta\iota\kappa\lambda\mu\nu\_o\pi M\mathit{?}\rho\sigma\tau\upsilon\chi$

The system (10B) is the germ of the green script exported to Crete. These systems were further developed by the appending of supplemental characters which represent the voiceless aspirated stops [p^h] and [k^h]. With the introduction of this early modification, the complete array of Greek consonant phonemes could be graphically distinguished. The creation of the supplemental characters also probably occurred at the hands of Cypriot scribes if the supplemental symbols have their origin in the syllabic Cypriot script, though it is not necessarily the case that all possible attested permutations of (i) the supplemental characters and (ii) the systems of (10) were produced by Cypriot scribes. The germ of the red scripts was generated by the attachment of [p^h] and [k^h] symbols (ϕ and ψ) to the system of (10C), and that of the dark blue scripts was generated by the addition of characters with these values (ϕ and χ) along with a [ps] symbol (ψ) to the system of (10A). The light blue scripts developed from a system that was devised when the aspirated stop characters ϕ and χ were added to the system of (10B). There is perhaps vestigial evidence of what could be identified as a distinct light red system which was engendered by the addition of the other set of [p^h] and [k^h] supplemental characters (i.e., ϕ and ψ) to the end of the system of (10B).

The preceding scheme of early alphabetic evolution is undoubtedly oversimplified, but in gross terms it accounts reasonably and systematically for the attested alphabetic structures. Of course, as the earliest alphabetic systems were disseminated, various local modifications occurred. Beneath the heading of local alterations lie such items as: (i) the adoption of particular letter-shapes; (ii) the choice of *san* or *sigma* as the [s] character; (iii) early disposal of *qoppa*; (iv) assigning of a vowel value to *eta*; and so forth. And in fact, the addition of supplemental characters representing [p^h] and [k^h] to the system of (10B) should perhaps be placed beneath this rubric. We could imagine, for example, that a primitive system of the type (10B) was exported to Attica and to adjacent Boeotia, perhaps by way of the islands of the southeast Aegean. Under the ultimate influence of a script of the dark blue type, probably one of those neighboring to the southwest, Attica acquired the use of the supplementals ϕ and χ for representing [p^h] and [k^h] and thus acquired a system of the light blue type. Boeotia also acquired the aspirated stop supplementals but took them from one of the neighboring red alphabets, probably that of Euboea, thus procuring the set ϕ, ψ and undergoing the transformation to a light red system. Various letter-shapes in the Boeotian script also appear to have been greatly influenced by the Euboean alphabet of Chalcis.[22]

The addition of the final character of the Greek alphabet, *omega*, is by all accounts relatively late, as one would fully expect by its position in the outermost layer. Jeffery suggests a date of no later than about 600 B.C. and gives southwest Asia Minor as a likely geographical starting point.[23] *Omega* was probably constructed from the character *omicron* by the opening of a gap on the underside of the latter.

7.2 Date of the Origin of the Alphabet

7.2.1 The Mycenaean Exodus

If the origin of the Greek alphabet is to be traced to Cyprus, as we are claiming, then the date at which this event occurred is bound up with the matter of the Greek settlement of Cyprus and the ensuing development of the Cypriot Syllabary by the Greeks.[24] When the Mycenaean centers of the Greek mainland were destroyed at the close of the thirteenth century B.C., there appears to have occurred a massive influx of refugees into Cyprus from the Aegean. These Mycenaean or "Achaean" refugees settled in several locales, including Enkomi, Sinda, Kition, and Maa-*Palaeokastro* (from which site the Achaeans moved to Palaepaphos after some short time; see fig. 7.1).[25] Important evidence provided by recent excavations at Maa-*Palaeokastro* and Pyla-*Kokkinokremos* is consistent with dating the arrival of the wave of Achaean refugees populating the aforementioned locales at around 1200 B.C. or shortly thereafter.[26] Other Eastern Mediterranean sites may have likewise been populated by Mycenaean refugees, but unlike these, Cyprus underwent a process of hellenization—a consequence at least in part of the continued arrival of waves of Greek settlers for some time.[27]

The scribal contingent of the Greek refugee community would not perpetuate the use of the Mycenaean Linear B script but would instead adapt one of the syllabic scripts which they discovered to be already in use in Cyprus. Possibly the motivation for making this orthographic shift was a greater expressability of consonants (in clusters and word-finally) afforded by the Cypriot script. Though such a feature of Cypriot orthography could simply have been integrated into the existing Linear B system (i.e., the Linear B characters could

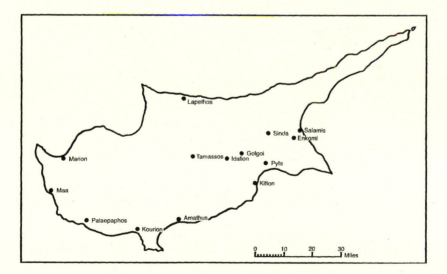

FIGURE 7.1 Map of Cyprus. Used by permission of Roland D. Woodard.

have been preserved), the Greek scribal community of Cyprus "chose" to incorporate certain features of Linear B spelling into a Cypriot writing system—a process which Palaima,[28] following E. Masson,[29] suggests may have occurred in the district of Paphos, owing to certain graphic similarities which the Paphian Cypriot Syllabary, to the exclusion of other regional variations of the syllabary, shares with the Bronze Age Aegean scripts. This is, in effect, exactly what other members of the Cypriot Greek scribal community would do a few hundred years later with the Phoenician script: alphabetic values like those encountered in the Semitic writing system could have been assigned to the familiar characters of the Cypriot Syllabary, but instead the Phoenician script was taken over and certain features of the syllabic Cypriot system were incorporated into it.

7.2.2 The Cypro-Minoan Scripts

The scripts which preceded the Mycenaean refugees in Cyprus were themselves of Aegean origin. Because of the obvious similarity which they show to the writing systems of Minoan Crete, these scripts are termed *Cypro-Minoan,* and their primary source was probably the Cretan script Linear A.[30] The earliest of the Cypro-Minoan scripts—which shows particular similarities to Linear A—occurs on a broken clay tablet unearthed at Enkomi and dated to the late sixteenth century B.C.[31] This tablet along with a very few other artifacts from Enkomi and Katydhata bear an early form of that script identified as Cypro-Minoan 1, remains of which are distributed widely across Cyprus and dated as late as the twelfth or eleventh century B.C. Distinct from Cypro-Minoan 1 is the variant script Cypro-Minoan 2, which occurs only on large clay tablets found at Enkomi and dated to the late thirteenth century. It has been conjectured that the two scripts record two different languages, neither of which has been identified.[32] An additional variant script, Cypro-Minoan 3, has been recovered not in Cyprus but at the site of ancient Ugarit on the Syrian coast and is also dated to the thirteenth century B.C.

7.2.3 Greeks and Phoenicians in Cyprus

According to the preceding analysis, the development and utilization of the Cypriot Syllabary by the displaced Mycenaeans was prerequisite to the acquisition of the alphabet. As I have already indicated, the Greek syllabic script is first attested in the middle of the eleventh century, so, given the limitations imposed by the available evidence, the transmission of the Phoenician script to the Greeks could not be confidently dated earlier than about 1050–1000 B.C. There is of course a second prerequisite to this transmission process: namely, the establishment of close contact between the Greek and Phoenician communities of Cyprus, as the origin of the Greek alphabet must have occurred in a Greek-Phoenician bilingual setting. This requirement will push the date of acquisition forward almost two centuries. There was a building presence of Phoenicians in Cyprus from perhaps the early ninth century.[33] Prior to 800 B.C., probably about 850, there appeared a significant Phoenician settlement in Cyprus at Kition; moreover, at Kition survives evidence which may suggest Phoenician occupation of other parts of the island at the same period. The Phoenicians had constructed a large temple to Astarte in Kition which was destroyed by fire about 800 B.C.; at the destruction level was recovered a fragment of a bowl bearing a Phoenician offertory inscription which has been interpreted as naming a Phoenician resident of Tamassus, a copper-mining center deep within the interior of Cyprus.[34] It is probable, then, that a *terminus post quem* for the acquisition of the Phoenician script by the Cypriot Greeks is to be established at approximately 850 B.C. or perhaps slightly earlier.

The Cypriot Syllabary remained in widespread use in Cyprus well after the creation of the Greek alphabet. The two earliest Cypriot alphabetic texts occur as components of digraphic inscriptions (i.e., documents in which an alphabetic text is accompanied by the corresponding inscription written in the syllabic script); these are short funerary inscriptions—one from Marion, the other from Golgoi—and both are dated to the sixth century B.C. Alphabetic inscriptions surviving from the fifth century and the first half of the fourth are few, but they begin to increase in frequency somewhat in the second half of the fourth century.[35] If Cypriot Greeks were responsible for adapting the Phoenician script for Greek use (perhaps in the ninth century), why is the alphabet so meagerly attested in Cyprus prior to the Hellenistic era? The answer to this question is to be found in the pervasive conservatism of Cypriot Greek culture.

7.2.4 A Mycenaean Renaissance

The tombs of the early Cypro-Geometric I era (beginning ca. 1050 B.C.) indicate a Cypriot preservation of Mycenaean civilization into the Iron Age.[36] At Kourion, Salamis, Lapethos, and especially Palaepaphos-*Skales,* tombs of Mycenaean type dating from this period have been unearthed, and, at least in the case of the last three sites, among the grave-goods recovered have been items of considerable value, including gold jewelry and various bronze and iron implements. It was in one such tomb at Palaepaphos-*Skales* that the bronze spit was discovered on which was inscribed the eleventh-century syllabic Greek text of which we have made mention. Karageorghis observes:

(11)   The material from the Palaepaphos-*Skales* tombs throws much light on the period usually known as the Dark Ages. But considering the wealth of the gifts in other tombs of the same period in Cyprus, and the fact that the script had not been forgotten, it appears that, unlike in the Aegean, this period in Cyprus was one of prosperity, and it was not at all "dark."[37]

The Mycenaean quality of Cypriot culture is in fact preserved long beyond that point which I have identified as a *terminus post quem* for the Greek acquisition of the Phoenician script. Though the "royal" tombs of Salamis of the Cypro-Archaic period (beginning about 750 B.C.) display certain elements of

Near Eastern architectural influence, their contents and the funerary customs which they evidence have been aptly described as "Homeric."

Consider Homer's depiction of the cremation ritual of Patroclus (*Iliad* 23.163–177):

(12)   [B]ut the close mourners stayed by the place and piled up the timber,
and built a pyre a hundred feet long this way and that way,
and on the peak of the pyre they laid the body, sorrowful
at heart; and in front of it skinned and set in order numbers
of fat sheep and shambling horn-curved cattle; and from all
great-hearted Achilleus took the fat and wrapped the corpse in it
from head to foot, and piled up the skinned bodies about it.
Then he set beside him two-handled jars of oil and honey
leaning them against the bier, and drove four horses with strong necks
swiftly aloft the pyre with loud lamentation. And there were
nine dogs of the table that had belonged to the lord Patroklos.
Of these he cut the throats of two, and set them on the pyre;
and so also killed twelve noble sons of the great-hearted Trojans
with the stroke of bronze, and evil were the thoughts in his heart against
them, and let loose the iron fury of the fire to feed on them.[38]

Homer tells us further (23.233–248, 252–255):

(13)   But now they who were with the son of Atreus assembled together
and the sound and murmur of their oncoming wakened Achilleus,
who straightened himself and sat upright and spoke a word to him:
"Son of Atreus, and you other greatest of all Achaians,
first put out with gleaming wine the pyre that is burning,
all that still has on it the fury of fire; and afterwards
we shall gather up the bones of Patroklos, the son of Menoitios,
which we shall easily tell apart, since they are conspicuous
where he lay in the middle of the pyre and the others far from him
at the edge burned, the men indiscriminately with the horses.
And let us lay his bones in a golden jar and a double
fold of fat, until I myself enfold him in Hades.
And I would have you build a grave mound which is not very great
but such as will be fitting, for now; afterwards, the Achaians
can make it broad and high—such of you Achaians as may be
left to survive me here by the benched ships, after I am gone."
. . . .
Then they gathered up the white bones of their gentle companion,
weeping, and put them into a golden jar with a double
fold of fat, and laid it away in his shelter, and covered it
with a thin veil.

Karageorghis notes that multiple elements of this epic funerary tradition recur in the "royal" tombs of Salamis.[39]

1. For example, pairs of horses or asses were commonly sacrificed upon the dromoi leading to the burial chambers; frequently the vehicle which the animals had drawn behind them down the dromos, either a chariot or a hearse, was also left in the tomb.

2. As in the case of the twelve Trojans of *Iliad* 23, there are instances of human sacrifices being offered upon the dromoi as part of the funerary rites at Salamis, the bodies of the victims being left outside of the burial chamber (Tomb 2 preserves the remains of multiple human offerings, Tomb 83 of a single such victim).[40] The practice occurred elsewhere in Cyprus,[41] and there exists evidence of similar human sacrificial victims being offered and interred in the dromoi of Mycenaean tombs.[42] Furthermore, recent archaeological finds from the area of Minoan Knossos have been interpreted as evidencing a rite of human sacrifice[43] and cannibalism of children.[44]

3. Homer tells us that Achilles placed jars of honey and oil on the pyre by Patroclus. Amphorae are common grave-goods in the "royal" tombs at Salamis. In Tomb 3 (which contained a war chariot and several pieces of weaponry, see below) was found an amphora on which was inscribed in the syllabic Cypriot script *e-la-i-wo* (ελαιϝω [elaiwọ:], 'of olive oil');[45] Karageorghis reports that amphorae in Tomb 2 preserved "a spongy substance in the bottom, the remnants of their organic contents."[46] These latter amphorae were tin-plated, as were vessels in Tombs 47, 79, and 105; Mycenaean pottery with such tin-plating is also known.[47] Linear B tablets from Knossos and from Khania record offerings of amphorae of honey made to various deities.[48]

4. While the regular means of corpse disposal at Salamis is inhumation,[49] cremation is also attested. In Tomb 1, a pyre was constructed on the dromos and, in a style quite reminiscent of Homer's description, the ashes of the deceased were wrapped in a cloth and placed in a bronze cauldron.[50] Quite similarly, Tomb 31 surrendered cremated remains which had been placed in an amphora; cremation had again occurred on the dromos.[51] The previously mentioned Tomb 3 (with its inscribed olive oil amphora, war chariot, etc.) also preserved traces of a pyre in the dromos, but, as the chamber had been completely looted in the nineteenth century (the surviving artifacts coming from the dromos), the cremated remains were not recovered.[52] An additional instance of cremation is attested by Tomb 19, where the cremated bones of the occupant were found in a pit within the chamber.[53]

As indicated above, on the dromos of Tomb 3 were found several military implements: two quivers, iron arrowheads, the apparent impression of a bow on the floor of the dromos, an iron spearhead (with the impression of its shaft remaining in the soil), a bronze shield and an iron sword. The pommel of the sword had been attached by means of bronze rivets, the heads of which were silver-plated—a type of sword which has been recovered at other sites in Cyprus.[54] Karageorghis points out that Homer of course knows just such a sword, the ξίφος ἀργυρόηλον or φάσγανον ἀργυρόηλον ([ksíphos / phásganon argüróẹ:lon]) as in:[55]

> (14)　Across his shoulders he slung the *sword with the nails of silver,*
> a bronze sword, and above it the great shield, huge and heavy.
> (*Iliad* 3.335–336; emphasis is mine)

> Afterward he girt on about his chest the corselet,
> and across his shoulders slung the *sword with the nails of silver,*
> a bronze sword, and caught up the great shield, huge and heavy.
>
> (*Iliad* 19.371–373; emphasis is mine)

In addition, Tomb 3 was distinguished by an earthen tumulus mounded upon it. This tumulus was capped by a mud-brick beehive structure. Such beehive tomb structures are quite well known from Mycenaean Greece, and it appears to be the case, as suggested by Karageorghis, that the occurrence of such a construction in seventh-century Cyprus is simply a preservation of the Mycenaean practice.[56]

Associated with the second burial of Tomb 47 was a sacrifice of six horses. Karageorghis reports that the blinkers and headbands of two of the horses were of ivory.[57] Likewise, one of the Mycenaean Linear B chariot tablets from Knossos (Sd0403) refers to ivory blinkers,[58] and Homer makes reference to bridles ornamented with ivory cheek pieces (*Iliad* 4.141–142):

(15)   As when some Maionian woman or Karian with purple
        colours ivory, to make it a cheek piece for horses . . .

The most opulent store of findings at Salamis was provided by Tomb 79. Among its contents were several pieces of furniture, including three wooden thrones.[59] The surface of one of these thrones was completely covered with plaques of ivory. On the backrest some of the plaques were engraved with a guilloche pattern and a sheet of gold stretched across its upper portion. To either side of the throne were mounted exquisite cutout ivory plaques, one in the shape of a lotus flower and the other a sphinx. The latter plaques were decorated with gold and with blue and brown paste. Another throne was covered with plaques of silver and perhaps also with ivory plaques inlaid with blue glass (suggested by the occurrence of such on the floor of the tomb, close by the throne). The silver throne was decorated on the backrest and stretcher with silver rivets having gilded heads; with this throne was found a stool which was likewise covered with silver plaques and studded across its front portion with rivets like those decorating the throne. The third throne, though badly decomposed upon excavation, could be seen to have been decorated with ivory disks and plaques; this throne was also accompanied by a stool to which ivory disks were attached.

In book nineteen of the *Odyssey,* as the disguised Odysseus, now returned to his home, contemplates how he might dispose of his wife's suitors, Penelope enters the hall:

(16)   [A]nd for her they set by the fire, where she was wont to sit, a chair
        inlaid with spirals of ivory and silver, which of old the craftsman
        Icmalius had made, and had set beneath it a foot-stool for the feet, that
        was part of the chair.

(*Odyssey* 19.55–58)[60]

The throne of Homer's description, with its ivory, silver and footstool, is clearly quite similar to those recovered from the "royal" tombs of Salamis. Karageorghis points particularly to the spirals on Penelope's throne and the guilloche engraving on the ivory throne from Salamis.[61] Beyond this, Homer often makes formulaic reference to thrones which, like the second of those from Salamis described above, are "silver-nailed" ($\dot\alpha\rho\gamma\upsilon\rho\dot o\eta\lambda o\varsigma$ ([argüróę:los])), as in the following:

(17) [A]nd [she] made Thetis sit down in a chair that was wrought elaborately
and splendid with silver nails, and under it was a footstool.

(Iliad 18.389–390)

But come, raise the stranger up and seat him on a silver-studded
chair.

(Odyssey 7:162–163)

She made me sit down in a chair that was wrought elaborately
and splendid with silver nails, and under my feet was a footstool.

(Odyssey 10:314–315)[62]

Thrones similar to those depicted by Homer and those recovered from the eighth-century Tomb 79 of Salamis are also described in the Mycenaean Linear B tablets. Among the furniture listed in the Ta series of tablets from Pylos are wooden chairs and footstools, probably of ebony; there are chairs adorned with gold and with ivory and chairs with inlaid ivory figures of various sorts. Tablet Ta714 describes a throne and footstool decorated with *kyanos* (probably either lapis lazuli or blue paste[63]), gold, and silver.[64] Another item of furniture recovered from Tomb 79 at Salamis is a wooden bed which is decorated with ivory plaques, gold, and blue paste.[65]

The tombs of Cyprus, in which are preserved elements of Mycenaean and Homeric culture well into the first millennium, speak to the conservative nature of Cypriot Greek society;[66] and there is still other evidence of this, such as the continued use in Cyprus of the ancient sovereign title *wa-na-kse,* $\digamma\alpha\nu\alpha\xi$ ([wanaks]). In the Linear B tablets, the *wanax* is the king, and this sense of the word still occurs in Homer ($\dot\alpha\nu\alpha\xi$), though the epic usage is somewhat broader than that attested in the Mycenaean materials. In the first millennium, the king is the $\beta\alpha\sigma\iota\lambda\varepsilon\dot\upsilon\varsigma$ ([basileús]); $\dot\alpha\nu\alpha\xi$ is used as a divine epithet and, in tragedy, as an archaizing feature.[67] In Cyprus, however, *wa-na-kse* remains in force as a royal title, being used to designate the king's sons and brothers.[68] Invoking the tradition of the lost epic poem the *Cypria* (by the Cypriot poet Stasinus), Karageorghis has suggested that, as would be expected, bardic activity played a part in sustaining elements of Mycenaean society in Cyprus:

(18) [O]ral tradition must have played an important role in preserving the Mycenaean Greek character, language and culture in general, which was to
experience a remarkable revival during the Cypro-Archaic period.[69]

This prolongation of Mycenaean life was no doubt augmented by the abutment of Greek and Near Eastern (as well as native Cypriot) cultures in Cyprus, a configuration which would have served to focus the attention of these most eastern of Greeks on their own Greekness. Concerning the Assyrian domination of Cyprus in the eighth century, Karageorghis observes:

(19)   The Cypriotes often reacted against this oriental influence, and one way of
        their reaction was the conservation or the revival of cultural elements
        which had their roots in their Mycenaean past. This hostile reaction which
        is often observed on the part of the Cypriotes against the oriental despotism
        and in favour of their hellenic traditions becomes also a familiar pattern in
        their political life, which culminated during the 5th and 4th cent. under the
        inspired leadership of the King of Salamis Evagoras I.[70]

The preservation of a Mycenaean culture into the first millennium in a Hel-
lenic society located on the frontier of the Greek world is strikingly reminiscent
of the well-known conservatism of the Indo-European cultures located on the
eastern and western fringes of the Indo-European world: namely, Vedic and
Iranian society in the east, and Irish and Italic in the west. Both eastern and
western sets preserve institutions of the parent Indo-European culture which
were eliminated from the more interior daughter societies. Hand-in-hand with
this institutional conservatism went linguistic conservatism, at least to the extent that the languages of these fringe cultures preserve Indo-European vocabulary and formulae affiliated with the institutions which did not survive elsewhere.[71] Similarly, the language of the Cypriot dialect of Greek displays a
conservatism which mirrors that of Cypriot culture (consider the matter of
ϝαναξ discussed above). Of the various first-millennium dialects, Cypriot,
along with its sister dialect of Arcadian, is most like the second-millennium
Mycenaean dialect.

Mycenaean culture on the Greek mainland had been destroyed, and Greece
was swallowed up in an age of darkness. However, far away, on the remote
eastern fringe of the Greek map, the conservative Cypriot Greeks continued a
Mycenaean civilization in exile. In all of the Greek world, literacy was preserved only in Cyprus; elsewhere the Greeks had forgotten how to read and
write. It was Cypriot Greek scribes, trained in the profession of writing, aware
of their orthographic surroundings, and perceptive of the advantage offered by
an alphabetic script, who adapted the Phoenician writing system and created
the Greek alphabet. But Cypriot culture, in its hellenocentric conservatism, rejected the new Phoenician-like alphabetic script and embraced its Mycenaean-
like syllabic script. Knowledge of Linear B had long since disappeared from
the collective memory of the Cypriot Greeks, but the Cypriot Syllabary had
become the script of the Mycenaean tradition of Cyprus. The alphabet was
exported westward to the core of the Greek world and was there accepted, but
not so in Cyprus.

7.2.5 Carpenter

From the latter half of the nineteenth century until the appearance of Rhys
Carpenter's 1933 article "The Antiquity of the Greek Alphabet,"[72] most scholars of classical antiquity had positioned the advent of the Greek alphabet at
some point between the last quarter of the second millennium and the end of
the ninth century B.C.[73] Carpenter argued tenaciously, however, that the existing
evidence permits postulating a date of borrowing no earlier than about 700 B.C.

His conclusion was reached after conducting a careful comparative examination of the earliest form of the Greek alphabet (which he dated at ca. 680 B.C.) and Semitic scripts preserved on various artifacts such as the Moabite Stone, the Cyprus Bowl, Aramaic inscriptions from Zincirli, and so on.[74] Such comparison revealed, he asserted, that the Semitic characters most like their earliest Greek counterparts are those from the end of the eighth century B.C.—not those found either earlier or later—and that the acquisition of the Greek alphabet is thus to be assigned a date of ca. 700 B.C. Carpenter attempted to buttress his conclusion with archaeological and historical argumentation; perhaps his most effective supporting argument, however, or at least that one to which subsequent investigators seem to make reference most readily, is his argument based upon the silence of Greek testimony earlier than the eighth century: "The *argumentum a silentio* grows every year more formidable and more conclusive. A negative argument is not valueless if the negative is universal."[75]

An eighth-century date for the origin of the Greek alphabet is now widely accepted among classical scholars, though the date has receded somewhat from Carpenter's proposed 700. Jeffery, who accepts Carpenter's argumentation with some modification, suggests a date of ca. 750 B.C.;[76] and Johnston, in the supplement to Jeffery's work, states, "[A] consensus on the earlier part of the eighth century seems to have been reached."[77] This is not to say that there is no alternative view expressed among classicists. A glance at Jeffery's survey of proposed dates[78] reveals numerous studies authored subsequent to Carpenter 1933 which call for an earlier date; for example, Buck contends that a ninth-century date is most probable.[79] Particularly to be noted is the work of M. Guarducci, who argues for a date of transmission in the latter half of the ninth century.[80]

7.2.6 Naveh

Until fairly recently, leading Semitists were generally in agreement with the classical consensus, assigning the Greek acquisition of the Phoenician script to the eighth or the ninth century B.C. (e.g., Albright, Driver, Lambdin, *inter alios*).[81] In 1973, however, J. Naveh published an influential paper in which he proposed, like certain classicists of an earlier generation, that the Phoenician to Greek script transmission occurred about 1100 B.C.[82] Naveh's arguments are based upon the stance and form of certain Greek letters and upon the variation in directionality of early Greek writing—left-to-right, right-to-left, and boustrophedon.[83] According to Naveh, the corresponding Semitic forms and practice are not to be found in the ninth- and eighth-century Phoenician scripts but in the eleventh-century Proto-Canaanite script. Naveh has been supported in his efforts by a number of his fellow Semitists.[84]

7.2.7 McCarter

A highly significant and well-balanced reexamination of the problem of the date of the origin of the Greek alphabet in the light of Naveh's claims is McCarter's 1975 work *The Antiquity of the Greek Alphabet and the Early*

Phoenician Scripts (to which I have already made numerous references). As suggested by the book's title, McCarter closely follows Carpenter's methodology of script comparison.[85] The conclusions to which this methodological path leads McCarter are not, however, those of Carpenter. As McCarter points out, this divergence is consequent upon the sophisticated development of the discipline of Northwest Semitic epigraphy which has occurred since the 1930s—a' development which is less a result of the discovery of new evidence than of a more accurate redating of existing evidence. Owing to the efforts of scholars such as W. F. Albright and Frank Moore Cross, the course of morphological evolution of the Canaanite scripts has been mapped out in great detail; McCarter in fact states:

(20)   [O]n the basis of palaeography alone a Phoenician inscription can now be dated by a competent epigrapher to within a generation of its execution at any point in the first millennium B.C.[86]

So McCarter's dating of the transmission of the Phoenician script to the Greeks is not that of Carpenter—but neither is it that of Naveh. After carefully comparing the earliest Greek scripts with the various Phoenician types, McCarter concludes:

(21)   The so-called archaisms in the Greek scripts will not sustain an unqualified hypothesis of an origin for the Greek alphabet c. 1100. The earliest Greek alphabets we know most closely resemble a Phoenician prototype of the late ninth or early eighth century. This is the conclusion to which the majority of the oldest forms of the Greek letters forces us.[87]

He continues:

(22)   A reconstructed "Proto-Greek" alphabet, as it must have appeared at the beginning of the independent history of the Greek scripts, could be interpolated into the developing Phoenician sequence at a point not much later than and certainly no earlier than 800 B.C.[88]

Because of the variable direction of the first Greek writing (left-to-right, right-to-left, boustrophedon)—a characteristic of earlier Canaanite, but not ninth-century Phoenician, orthography—and because of the particular stance and form of a few Greek characters which are also not typical of ninth-century Phoenician, McCarter allows the possibility of some earlier period of Greek experimentation with Phoenician writing.[89]

McCarter's conclusions concerning the origin of the Greek alphabet mesh smoothly with my own claims of a Cypriot transmission of the Phoenician script to the Greeks. My *terminus post quem* of about 850 B.C. or slightly earlier allows for the formation in approximately 800 of the earliest attested type of Greek script and for a preceding period of Greek "experimentation" with the Semitic writing system. Recall that we in fact proposed above that early experimentation with the alphabet in Cyprus is suggested by variation in the type of characters used to represent [k] + [s] and by variation in the supplemental characters in general (though this particular kind of experimentation would not necessarily have to precede the formation of the alphabet of 800). McCarter, however, indicates that this period of experimentation could perhaps have begun in the early eleventh century B.C.; my analysis of the origin of the Greek alphabet does not appear to tolerate such a lengthy prehistory.

7.2.8 Directionality in the Early Alphabet and Cypriot Tradition

Recall that McCarter will allow for a period of experimentation prior to 800 B.C. primarily because the variation in direction of early Greek writing and the stance of particular letters—*alpha, beta, lambda,* and *sigma*—find equivalents in early Canaanite script but not in ninth-century Phoenician writing. It is not, however, necessary to look to early Canaanite to account reasonably for the Greek practice. In the ninth century the Phoenicians consistently wrote their script from right to left. The great majority of the Cypriot Greek inscriptions written in the Common syllabic script are likewise right-to-left in orientation (i.e., *sinistroverse*), as are the Eteocypriot inscriptions (though among these Greek materials there do occur a few left-to-right (i.e., *dextroverse*) inscriptions, particularly on coins).[90] However, in the west of Cyprus, in the district of Paphos, a very different tradition obtains. The earliest syllabic Cypriot inscription (middle of the eleventh century), found at Palaepaphos-*Skales,* is *dextroverse,* as were Cypro-Minoan and Mycenaean Linear B. The corpus of materials written in the Old Paphian signary, dated to the seventh and sixth centuries B.C., shows a diversity of script directionality: Mitford and Masson report that 73 percent of these materials are, like the eleventh-century inscription, dextroverse;[91] in the case of the Paphian documents from Rantidi, 60 percent are dextroverse and three of the inscriptions are boustrophedon.[92] The inscriptions written in the New Paphian signary are regularly dextroverse, though fifth- and fourth-century Paphian coins occur which display both dextroverse and sinistroverse legends (on a single coin).[93]

Whatever the origin of this tradition of disparate directionality, it is obvious that such variation is of considerable significance for our hypothesis of a Cypriot origin of the alphabet. Certain of the Cypriot scribes practiced a native orthographic tradition characterized by a high degree of variability in direction of writing—sinistroverse, dextroverse, and boustrophedon. This variation was simply continued when the Cypriot scribes began writing with the adapted Phoenician script. The variable direction of writing attested for the Old Paphian syllabary might be taken to suggest that a scribal community of the Paphos region was responsible for adapting the Phoenician script for Greek use. This is clearly not a necessary conclusion, however; other scenarios can easily be imagined. Perhaps variable direction of writing was common in other parts of the island in the early first millennium but was regularized in favor of sinistroverse writing, in a process not unlike the generalization of dextroverse writing in later Paphos. It should be noted, however, that there is an emerging body of evidence for a Phoenician presence in Paphos;[94] and recall that there is some indication that the Mycenaean scribal community of Paphos may have been responsible for adapting the Cypro-Minoan script and producing the Greek Cypriot Syllabary. Moreover, as we have seen already, Paphos, in the words of

Mitford and Masson, "had enjoyed an opulent Mycenaean civilization"[95]—in other words, this region would have possessed just the sort of traditionalist social climate in which, as I have claimed, the new alphabet was conceived but then rejected.

7.2.9　Letter-Stance and the Cypriot Literacy Factor

With regard to the stance of *alpha, beta, lambda,* and *sigma,* it is again not necessary to appeal to Proto-Canaanite letter-forms in order to offer a reasonable account of their Greek orientation. That certain of the new Greek graphemes would depart from the stance of their Phoenician source is not odd, and such phenomena are not otherwise unknown. A highly pertinent example is provided by Chadwick in his attempt to match the symbols of the syllabic Cypriot script with their respective predecessor Linear A characters; given his equations, a number of Cypriot symbols show a reorientation in stance. As McCarter, among others, has pointed out, the change in stance exhibited by the afore mentioned Greek letters could well be analyzed as a consequence of the variation in direction of writing which characterized early Greek inscriptions. McCarter, however, rejects this analysis, arguing (in favor of a pre-ninth-century acquisition of these particular letter-forms):

(23)　[C]ertain Greek letter-forms show different "normal" stances from those of their Phoenician counterparts. For such a stance to arise and become accepted, it would have to correspond to a Phoenician stance which was established by regular usage. Otherwise, sporadic variations would have been corrected against the standard forms. This follows from our observation in Chapter III that the Greek alphabet was not simply copied from a single Phoenician abecedary but was instead the product of a thorough acquaintance with the Phoenician tradition in all its facets. It would hardly have been possible, therefore, for an error in stance to be preserved in later use unless it had some claim to authenticity. A similar argument could be made against the preservation of an error in stance which was made after the independence of the Greek scripts: it ought to have been corrected against standard forms.[96]

I would embrace without reservation McCarter's premise that the Greek adapters of the Phoenician script were thoroughly familiar with its application. If, however, the ninth-century adapters were controlling the morphology of the new alphabetic script and were intolerant of "nonstandard" letter orientations, would not *alpha, beta, lambda,* and *sigma* have been reoriented and brought into conformity with the existing ninth-century "standard forms"? That is to say, if the stance of *alpha, beta, lambda,* and *sigma* were in some sense standard for the eleventh century, they clearly were not such in the ninth century. There apparently was extensively widespread variation in letter-stance in the Canaanite script of ca. 1100 B.C.; why should the out-of-kilter (from the ninth-century perspective) stances of just these particular letters have had a greater claim to authenticity than such stances of other letters encountered by the Greeks during the hypothesized eleventh-century period of experimentation?

Beyond that, however, it appears that there existed some "regular" stance of letters already in the early eleventh century;[97] if the process of adapting the Phoenician script for Greek use had begun in the eleventh century, why would the adapters, thoroughly familiar with the Semitic tradition at that period, have been any more willing to accept letter-forms which deviated from regular spatial orientation than were their ninth-century counterparts?

To frame the problem of the altered stance of the deviant Greek characters in terms of "error" and "correctness" is perhaps not altogether appropriate. The cognitive aspect of the process of adapting the Phoenician script is not to be overlooked. Divergence from Phoenician letter-stance should not surprise us if, as I have claimed, the Greek alphabet was devised by persons who were already literate in a different orthographic tradition; the Cypriot scribes did not come to the task of adapting the Semitic script for their own use with a blank slate but with an established cognitive apparatus for processing written language. We would expect that they approached this objective with preconceived notions (perhaps completely subconscious) of what a grapheme should look like—what its spatial orientation should be—notions which the scribes acquired through the long-term use of their own native script. This is much the same as when a speaker of some language sets out to acquire a speaking knowledge of some different language. The speaker enters upon the task with a well-developed phonological apparatus constructed for her or his own language, and the phonology of the new language is processed by this apparatus. The result is that the newly acquired language is spoken "with an accent." The reorientation of the stance of certain Phoenician characters could likely have been the outcome of filtering the new script through an existing orthographic conceptual structure.

With regard to the matter of the period subsequent to "the independence of the Greek scripts," it cannot be denied that much heterogeneity did indeed arise among the various letters of the Greek alphabet as it spread. We obviously do not possess a copy of the "original" Greek alphabet; some graphic modification during the very earliest phases of transmission of the alphabet is entirely possible. If the initial diffusion of the alphabet were the work of previously illiterate persons completely unfamiliar with Phoenician standards, perhaps merchants conveying the new script along trade routes,[98] we might expect (for reasons completely different from those invoked above) some perturbation in the graphic system. That this was the sole or even principal means of transmission, however, is doubtful (see 8.3.1).

7.3 Other Investigators on Cyprus as the Place of Origin

7.3.1 Carpenter

The present work does not mark the first occasion on which the origin of the Greek alphabet has been mentioned in the same breath as Cyprus and the Cypriot Syllabary. In "The Antiquity of the Greek Alphabet," in fact, Carpenter mentions Cyprus in his discussion of possible sites of transmission, only to immediately dismiss it as an option. Carpenter argues, quite reasonably, that a highly probable locale for the earliest Greek encounter with the expanding sphere of Phoenician influence would be at the eastward extremity of the Greek regions; it is of course Cyprus which occupies this apical position on the eastern edge of the Greek world. However, he rejects Cyprus as the place at which the Phoenician script was acquired in favor of its neighbor to the west, Rhodes, stating:

> (24)   [T]he Cypriote Greeks were immune as far as the alphabet was concerned, because they still preserved their ancient Achaean mode of writing.[99]

In other words, in Carpenter's view, the scribes of Cyprus were already utilizing a syllabic writing system and, hence, would have had no interest in experimenting with some other mode of orthographic expression (the same opinion is advanced by Jeffery[100]). So, according to Carpenter, it was left to the (presumably) illiterate Rhodians to devise humankind's first thoroughgoing alphabetic writing system.

Such a hypothesis strains for plausibility. Who would be more likely to investigate a new writing system than professional scribes? We have seen that the Mycenaean scribes (or their professional descendents) who arrived in Cyprus with other refugees from the Greek mainland did this very deed: the Greek scribal community of Cyprus eventually relinquished the use of their own Linear B script and adapted a Cypriot orthographic system for spelling Greek, transferring to the Cypriot script certain features of their Mycenaean system of writing, such as the idiosyncratic utilization of a strategy for representing consonant clusters which is based specifically upon the sonority hierarchy of the Greek language, the use of a single symbol for representing the "*zeta*-sound," and so on. When certain of the scribes of a slightly later period in the history of Cypriot Greek society encountered the Phoenician script, they, like their scribal ancestors, set their hands to the task of exploiting a foreign writing system in order to develop a more precise means of graphically recording their language. If anyone on the eastern edge of the Greek world (or in any other part of the Greek world, for that matter) had the interest, motivation and orthographic wherewithal to adapt the Semitic script for Greek use, it was surely the scribes of Cyprus.

In his article which appeared in 1938, entitled "The Greek Alphabet Again"—the sequel article to his 1933 work—Carpenter, in complete contrast to his earlier position, embraces the idea that the Greek adapters of the Phoenician script were people familiar with the use of the Cypriot Syllabary.

> (25)   Nilsson and Hammarström have given us the clue that the Greek alphabet must have arisen out of a knowledge of *both* the Semitic consonantal script and the Cypriote syllabary, and hence could have been created only in a bilingual environment.[101]

The "clue" to which Carpenter refers is one which concerns the representation of vowels in the Cypriot Syllabary and in the Greek alphabet. In both scripts provision is made for distinguishing orthographically only a subset of the complete set of Greek vowel phonemes—the same subset in each script. Carpenter observes:

(26) [W]hoever adapted the Semitic alphabet to vocalic as well as consonantal notation chose precisely the five vowels used in the Cypriote syllabary, in spite of the fact that a Greek ear heard at least seven vowels in the language.[102]

The Greek ear actually heard several more vowels than seven. In addition to the diphthongs, ancient Greek possessed the following sets of short and long vowel phonemes (with dialectal variation):

(27) A. high front   /i, i:/
     B. high back   /u, u:/   (eventually fronted to /ü, ü:/)
     C. mid front   /e, ẹ:, ę:/
     D. mid back   /o, ọ:, ǫ:/ (/ǫ:/ eventually raised to /u:/)
     E. low central /a, a:/

No orthographic distinction was made between the short and long vowels in any given set (A)–(E) in either the Cypriot Syllabary or in the early alphabet; in other words, /i, i:/ were both spelled with the same symbol, /o, ọ:, ǫ:/ were all three represented with the same symbol, and so on. In fact, the short-versus-long vowel distinction was never introduced into the Greek alphabet, with the exception of the distinctions effected by the addition of *eta* (/ę:/) and *omega* (/ǫ:/) and the eventual use of the digraphs ει and ου for /ẹ:/ and /ọ:/ respectively. As I discussed earlier, Ionic speakers utilized *eta* (which they did not need for representing /h/, as Ionic lacked this consonantal phoneme) to spell /ę:/ and introduced *omega* in order to make a parallel graphic distinction among the mid back vowels.

It is the failure to distinguish the long and short vowel phonemes at any single position of tongue height/frontness in both the syllabic Cypriot and early alphabetic systems to which Carpenter is referring. If, as he suggests, this is a feature which the alphabet inherited from the Cypriot Syllabary, it would be a welcome piece of evidence which could be marshaled in yet further support of the claim being advanced in the present work. Unfortunately, however, the indifference of these scripts toward vowel length probably does not constitute such evidence. As reported by Justeson[103] and by Sampson,[104] it appears to be the case that writing systems commonly do not record phonemic distinctions of length—either vowel length or consonant length. The failure of both the Cypriot Syllabary and the alphabet to indicate vowel length is thus not distinctive for these two scripts and, consequently, may be less a matter of the inheritance of an orthographic feature than the expression of a "universal tendency" of writing systems. This is further suggested by the fact that consonantal length (i.e., consonant gemination) is in fact recorded in the alphabetic system, while distinctions of consonant length are not made in the case of either the Cypriot Syllabary or the Phoenician script.

Carpenter adds to his observations on vowel representation in the syllabic Cypriot and early alphabetic scripts a second, "new" argument, concerned with the form of *beta* in certain epichoric alphabets.[105] Of all the letters of the Greek alphabet, *beta* shows the greatest number of variant forms; its evolution is somewhat enigmatic. McCarter conjectures that the earliest form of *beta* is that preserved in the primitive script of Thera, being the *beta* variant most like Phoenician *bet,* though inverted.[106] But certain forms of *beta* appear to be unrelated to the Theran type, and of these there is a subset which, its members bearing some resemblance to the letter *pi,* has been analyzed as stemming from an intentional modification of *pi.* Carpenter interprets the *pi*-like *beta* to reveal the origin of the alphabet's second letter and traces its roots to the syllabic Cypriot practice of not distinguishing between voiced, voiceless unaspirated, and voiceless aspirated stops. In other words, the alphabetic symbol which was assigned the value /p/ (i.e., *pi*), was also pressed into service for graphically representing this phoneme's voiced counterpart /b/. This dual use of *pi,* claims Carpenter, was catalyzed by the similarity in form which existed between Phoenician characters *bet* (/b/) and *resh* (/r/), rendering these two letters, in his opinion, so ambiguous as to make *bet* "something worse than useless" for the Greeks.[107] In contrast, a single character was not utilized for representing both /t/ and /d/ and both /k/ and /g/, because no corresponding ambiguity existed in the Phoenician prototypes of *tau, delta, kappa,* and *gamma.*

We have already seen that in the earliest alphabet *pi* was used not only for /p/ but for /pʰ/ as well, in the same way that both /k/ and /kʰ/ were represented by *kappa.* Carpenter's suggestion that *pi* was also first used for the voiced bilabial /b/ appears, therefore, somewhat alluring; recall that in the syllabic Cypriot system, a single symbol had served to spell /pV/, /pʰV/, and /bV/. There is, however, much in Carpenter's hypothesis which is unclear. Is it the case that *pi* occurred at two positions in the early Greek alphabet (i.e., both after *alpha* and after *omicron*), or was there an altered form of *pi* placed in second position (so that *pi* itself was not actually used for /b/), or was there at first a gap left between *alpha* and *gamma,* which was later filled in with a character that was somehow assigned the approximate name and value of Phoenician *bet?* Beyond these matters, it is certainly the case that not all epigraphers accept the proposition that some subset of the epichoric alphabets displays a *beta* which is derived from *pi*; Jeffery, for example, rejects this hypothesis.[108] Recall that McCarter has advocated the position that the *beta* of the primitive alphabet of Thera closely matches Phoenician *bet.* For the present, Carpenter's 1938 proposal of the origin of *beta* is probably best viewed only as an interesting possibility.

Carpenter does not, however, completely forsake his Rhodian thesis of five years prior. He advances the possibility that a Rhodian resident of some Cypriot city encountered the syllabic Greek and Phoenician writing systems and, weighing their respective advantages and disadvantages, arrived at a compromise script, the Greek alphabet. The particular ethnic affiliations of the adapters, I think, cannot be determined in any absolute sense. What can be said with some confidence, however, is that the adapters were, as I have argued above, individuals—trained scribes—accustomed to writing Greek with the Cypriot Syllabary. One would think that this requirement would make it likely that the adapters were Cypriot Greeks.

Before leaving Carpenter, we should point out that Jeffery reports that Carpenter informed her in a private communication that he had abdicated his theory of a Cypriot connection with the origin of the alphabet in favor of the idea that Al Mina was the spot at which the Phoenician script was transmitted to the Greeks.[109] I return to the matter of Al Mina directly below.

7.3.2 Robb, Heubeck, Johnston, and Burkert

There are still other scholars who have advocated Cyprus as the birthplace of the Greek alphabet, though none have developed the theory in any sort of detail. Robb has suggested the possibility of a Cypriot origin primarily on the basis of the existence of well-established Greek and Phoenician bilingual communities on the island;[110] he also makes reference to the fact that within syllabic Cypriot practice, a means exists for representing vowels (a feature which does not belong to the Phoenician system), and he states that this "might be developed into an argument for the Cypriote origin (by stimulus diffusion) of the alphabet."[111] Heubeck somewhat similarly espouses the idea that close contact between Greeks and Phoenicians in Cyprus and a tradition of Greek literacy on the island conspire to render Cyprus an especially likely candidate for the place of origin of the Greek alphabet. He suggests that Rhodes, however, occupied a more central position along the trade routes passing between Greece and the eastern Mediterranean than did Cyprus, and he thus suggests that a Cypriot-born alphabetic system may have been disseminated out of Rhodes.[112] Recently, Johnston has added his voice to those advocating a Cypriot origin: "I would gladly develop the theory of Robb and Heubeck that a natural catalyst existed in the eastern Mediterranean in the shape of the Cypriot syllabary."[113] Curiously, Johnston thinks that it was Greek visitors to the island who, observing the use of both the syllabic Cypriot and Phoenician scripts, were responsible for the development of the Greek alphabet.[114] As we have seen, this is unlikely, since the adapters were practitioners of syllabic Cypriot writing. To the list can now be added Burkert, who observes:

(28) There is much to substantiate the idea that Cyprus had a role to play as an intermediary station in the transmission of writing: The distinctive designation of the Greek letters as *Phoinikeïa* seems to presuppose that other "scribblings" (*grammata*) were known from which the Phoenician were different. This was the case only in Cyprus, where a linear script of Mycenaean type had been adapted to the Greek and persisted to Hellenistic times.[115]

7.4 Other Proposed Sites of Origin

7.4.1 Al Mina

We noted above that Al Mina has been mentioned as a possible place of transmission of the Semitic script to the Greeks. Al Mina was the site of a Greek trading center on the northern Syrian coast, excavated by Sir Leonard Woolley in 1936–1937 (see figure 7.2).[116] The earliest Greek pottery at Al Mina dates to about 800 B.C.; throughout most of the eighth century it appears that its Greek residents perhaps constituted a minority population.[117] While it is probably accurate to say that there has been no consensus as to the place of the transmission of the Phoenician writing system, Al Mina has enjoyed considerable popularity as a candidate; this is so even though no early Greek or Semitic inscriptions have been recovered at Al Mina with the exception of a Greek graffito on a sherd dated 725–700 B.C.[118]

Other than being a Greek/Semitic bilingual area, Al Mina has little to offer as a potential location for the Greek acquisition of the Semitic script. It is true, as revealed by the large proportion of Euboean pottery found at the site, that early Al Mina appears to have had close connections with Euboea—perhaps was established by Euboeans.[119] This is significant for the history of the alphabet in that it is at Euboea that among the earliest of known alphabetic Greek inscriptions have been found.[120] The site of the Euboean colony of Pithekoussai in the south of Italy has likewise produced early inscriptions, dating to the late eighth century.[121] However, there is an important intermediate term in the Euboea–Al Mina equation: namely, Cyprus. Boardman notes, writing of the eighth century, "The Greek pottery found in Cyprus itself . . . is of much the same sources and in much the same proportions as that at Al Mina."[122] He further

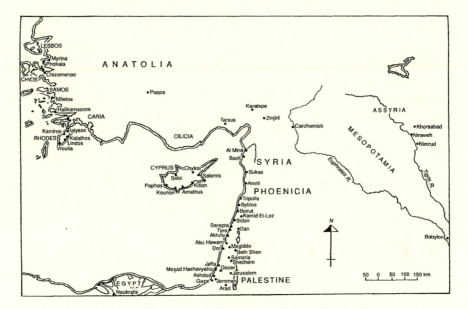

FIGURE 7.2 Map of the Eastern Mediterranean. From A. T. Reyes, *Archaic Cyprus: A Study of the Textual and Archaeological Evidence* (Oxford University Press, 1994). Reprinted by permission of Oxford University Press.

suggests that it may have been the Cypriots that led the Euboeans to Cyprus and that there were Cypriots among the residents of Euboea.[123] Coldstream adds, "Advocates for a Greek presence at Al Mina have also acknowledged that a similar claim could be made there for resident Cypriot traders, on the basis of a considerably larger body of Bichrome and White Painted pottery made in the Cypriot manner. . . . The most recent research . . . has tended to emphasise the Cypriot element at Al Mina at the expense of the Greek."[124] Because of its position on the trade routes, many of the goods which passed between Al Mina and Euboea were certainly transshipped through Cyprus.[125] Reyes surmises, "It seems likely . . . that Paphos, Amathus, Kition, and Salamis acted as the principal staging posts for the Euboians as they travelled eastwards to Al Mina and elsewhere."[126] Karageorghis points out that there was much direct contact between Cyprus and the Aegean in the eighth century ("There must have been strong links between Cyprus and Euboia").[127] Evidence for Cypriot-Euboean trade relations similarly occurs for the tenth and ninth centuries, and even earlier.[128] Ridgway notes, "The first known vase imported to Greece from Cyprus since Mycenaean times is a typical bichrome jug in an exceptionally rich Late Protogeometric (before c. 900) grave in the Palia Perivolia cemetery at Lefkandi."[129] Euboea may indeed have played an important role in the spread of the Greek alphabet to the mainland (and certainly to points farther west); the archaeological evidence allows Euboea's source of the new script to have been Cyprus just as easily as Al Mina, and it is in Cyprus—not Al Mina—that the linguistic, orthographic, and cultural evidence converges.

7.4.2 Crete

Crete and Rhodes are two other locations which have been entertained as probable sites of transmission, both of which we have encountered already in this regard. Crete has been so considered primarily because of its position along the trade routes from the Eastern Mediterranean and its possession of a "primitive script." The alphabet quite possibly did make its way to Crete by way of trade routes from the east, but this does not mean of necessity that it was received there in the form of the Phoenician script. In fact, as others have pointed out, the discovery of a bronze bowl at Knossos bearing a Phoenician inscription, dated to the early ninth century and showing a script which *deviates* from the alphabet of Crete, weakens the case for a Cretan adaptation of the Phoenician script.[130] Introduction from Cyprus, however, is an attractive possibility. Strong trade relations between Crete and Cyprus continued from the eleventh through the eighth centuries B.C.[131] Boardman's words are instructive:

(29)   Cyprus provided the intermediary between Crete and the east, and all the "orientalizing" objects or ideas which Crete accepted during the Dark Ages are either derived directly from Cyprus, or involve the type of object which was as much at home in Cyprus as on the eastern mainland. Even in the depressed period following the end of the Bronze Age, when bronze was scarce, iron was still a novelty (its use perhaps introduced from Cyprus)

and Cretan artists were still working in a Minoan-Mycenaean tradition, there are signs of continued relations between these two islands, which had been among the most important centres of the Late Mycenaean world.[132]

Crete preserves a primitive form of the alphabet which was probably introduced from Cyprus, along with other "ideas oriental." Recall that I have proposed that, though the letter-forms of the Cretan alphabet are those which are closest to the Phoenician characters, the alphabet-type which Crete displays is nonetheless an already slightly altered form of the earliest Cypriot version.[133]

7.4.3 Rhodes

Carpenter early advocated a Rhodian origin for the Greek alphabet, as I have already indicated. The location of Rhodes toward the eastern edge of the Greek world; its position as a hub on the east-west trade route and the northern trade route into Anatolia; the tradition of Cadmeans at Ialysos, attested by Diodorus (5.58); and the occurrence of some evidence for a small Phoenician contingent at Ialysos from the middle of the eighth century have been cited as factors allowing for the identification of Rhodes as a possible place of transmission.[134] Thus the setting is right, but there is not much in the way of persuasive evidence. Johnston notes that "the rather meagre evidence for Rhodian overseas expansion in the earlier eighth century is particularly discouraging,"[135] and he contends that the Euboean finds now undermine a Rhodian origin.[136] Recall that Heubeck suggested that a Cypriot alphabet may have been passed to Rhodes, whence it was disseminated to other locations. In remarking on the considerable differences which exist between the early alphabet of Crete and that of Rhodes, Jeffery states, ". . . [I]t seems to me to be more likely on the whole that Crete and Rhodes each drew its alphabet separately from some earlier source than that Rhodes, for example, was the originator."[137]

The picture which we see emerging is one of the conveying of Cypriot alphabetic traditions to Euboea, Crete, and Rhodes, and elsewhere as well. From these sites there is a further spreading of the script to other locations.

7.5 Concluding Remarks

The scale continues to be tipped ever more in favor of a Cypriot origin of the Greek alphabet. Positing that practitioners of the syllabic Cypriot writing system were responsible for adapting the Phoenician script for Greek use and that they, in the process, transferred various structural features of their own syllabic script to the new alphabetic system immediately reveals to us the reason for the curious absence of symbols for the bilabial and velar aspirated stop phonemes in the earliest alphabet-type. The *terminus post quem* (ca. 850 B.C.) for a Cypriot adoption of the Phoenician script harmonizes well with the date proposed by McCarter, which is based upon a careful epigraphical comparison of the Phoenician and the earliest attested Greek scripts. The early Greek variation in direction of writing and in letter-stance which has been cited by certain

Semitists as evidence for a late second-millennium date for the Greek acquisition of the Semitic script can now be seen as yet another consequence of Greek adapters bringing a tradition of literacy to the task of designing an alphabetic script for their own language. The major variant types of Greek alphabets can be systematically and efficiently accounted for as the products of reforming and counterreforming Cypriot efforts. The society in which the Cypriot acquisition and development of the alphabetic script occurred was a vibrant and vigorous prolongation of Mycenaean civilization—a kind of Homeric eschaton—which contrasted starkly with the greater part of the Greek world, cloaked in darkness. But this superb technological advance, with its Semitic lines and angles, was to fall victim to the hellenocentrism of the latter-day Mycenaeans. Its efficacy would only be fully realized elsewhere, among those who knew not how to write already, those with no competing orthographic tradition.[138]

Notes

1. At an early period, labiovelar stop phonemes also occurred, as we have discussed.

2. Here the emphatic dental and velar stops are arbitrarily transcribed as glottalized.

3. This is not to say that Phoenician precursors of the supplemental characters have not been proposed; they indeed have been. See the discussions in, *inter alios,* Jeffery 1990:36–37; Powell 1987:3, n. 8.

4. See Jeffery 1990:35–37. For a sampling of the extensive bibliography, see Powell, 1987, "The Origin of the Puzzling Supplementals *Φ X Ψ," TAPA* 117:2–3, n. 8. Powell, as pointed out above, argues that the supplementals were a part of the very first Greek alphabet.

5. Jeffery 1990:37 points out the existence of a still different sequence, stating, "In an Achaian fifth-century abecedarium from Metapontion . . . it is *Φ Ψ X X*—i.e. 'blue' chi and 'red' xi together." Powell surely underestimates the significance of this difference in alphabetic order when he states, "About [this variation] I shall not be concerned; I take the minor confusion in abecedaric order to reflect the major confusion in [the value of the supplementals *X* and *Ψ*]" (Powell 1987:3).

6. See Heubeck 1986:16–17.

7. See, *inter alios,* Harris 1936:22 and Steiner 1982:88–89, n. 151, the latter of whom also argues for absence of aspiration in Semitic emphatics on phonetic grounds.

8. And conversely, the use of *taw* to represent Greek unaspirated /t/ is less "natural" than at first appears. On the arbitrariness of using Phoenician *ṭet* for Greek /tʰ/, see McCarter 1975:95, n. 77: "The Greek assignment of the value *th* to the Phoenician *ṭet* sign was somewhat arbitrary."

9. Though, as I indicated earlier, I do think that it is well within the realm of possibility that the earliest value of Greek *qoppa* may have been something different from that which is attested in the epichoric alphabets.

10. Heubeck 1986:16.

11. On *ϝ* as the source of *upsilon,* see Jeffery 1990:35.

12. McCarter 1975:124–126.

13. Jeffery 1990:36–37

14. See Buck 1955:75. Perhaps this is also the origin of the practice of spelling

[ks] as χσ (rather than simply χ) in the Rhodian script, a red alphabet. The same spelling is attested once in the red alphabet of Boeotia and once in that of Laconia; concerning the latter Jeffery (1990:183) suggests that the person who produced it may not have been Laconian. Boeotian χσ, which occurs in an early inscription (probably early seventh century), is perhaps to be linked to the light blue tradition of Attica.

15. Jeffery (1990:37) suggests that red ψ ([kʰ]) and blue ψ ([ps]) were acquired from two distinct scripts. This seems a cumbersome and unlikely hypothesis, apparently motivated by the difference in phonetic value associated with the symbol in the red and blue alphabets.

16. One could propose that the starting point of the light blue alphabet, given the particular route being considered here, was the dark blue system of (6) with both *ks* and *ps* symbols. However, this hypothesis would involve positing a slightly more complicated protosystem for the light blue system, would remove the impetus of the sequential spelling of the [p] + [s] cluster, and does not appear to be required by the evidence.

17. Among those light blue scripts which were in use on the Aegean Islands, the representation of the sequence [ps] is attested only for the alphabet of Amorgos, which uses πσ rather than φσ. The [ks] spelling χσ is attested for Paros and Thasos; on Naxos, the first element of the sequence was represented by a character which is apparently a variant form of *eta* (= [h] or something similar); see Jeffery 1990:290–293.

18. Ibid., p. 89. As pointed out above, the [k] + [s] spelling χσ occurs in an early Boeotian inscription.

19. Ibid., p. 107; also see p. 104.

20. Ibid., pp. 230–231.

21. There are also several red scripts into which have been introduced a character having the value [ps]. This symbol, ⴲ, occurs in alphabets of Achaea (ibid., pp. 249, 259, 458), Arcadia (pp. 207, 213), Ozolian Lokris (p. 105), Thessaly (pp. 96, 436–437) and perhaps in a Doric script from Megara Hyblaia (pp. 262, 462). Jeffery tentatively suggests that its origin was in Achaea and was fashioned after ψ, the dark blue *psi* (see p. 249; subsequent to her penning of these remarks, a more secure example of the character came to light, concerning which see Johnston's remarks on p. 458). With the introduction of a [ps] character, these red alphabets were rendered structurally equivalent to the dark blue system.

22. Ibid., p. 90.

23. Ibid., p. 38.

24. See also my discussion of these issues in Woodard forthcoming.

25. H. Catling, 1975, "Cyprus in the Late Bronze Age," in *CAH*, 3rd ed., ed. I. Edwards et al. (Cambridge: Cambridge University Press), vol. 2, part 2, pp. 198–201; 207–209; V. Karageorghis, 1982a, *Cyprus: From the Stone Age to the Romans* (London: Thames and Hudson), pp. 86–91. There is some indication that Greeks may have been present in Cyprus in appreciable numbers by as early as the beginning of the fourteenth century B.C. (see Catling 1975:199 with references). For a bibliography of recent works on the Mycenaean presence in Cyprus, see Palaima 1989a:38, n. 21.

26. Karageorghis, 1987, "Western Cyprus at the Close of the Late Bronze Age," in *Western Cyprus: Connections,* ed. D. Rupp (Göteborg: Paul Åströms Förlag), pp. 117–118; 1984, "New Light on Late Bronze Age Cyprus," in *Cyprus at the Close of the Late Bronze Age,* ed. V. Karageorghis and J. Muhly (Nicosia: A. G. Leventis Foundation), p. 22. Among other articles in this collection, see J. Muhly, "The Role of the Sea Peoples in Cyprus during the LC III Period," pp. 39–55. Compare C. Baurain, 1984, *Chypre et la Méditerranée orientale au Bronze Récent* (Athens: École Française).

27. Karageorghis 1987:118. Coldstream (1989, "Early Greek Visitors to Cyprus

and the Eastern Mediterranean," in *Cyprus and the East Mediterranean in the Iron Age,* ed. V. Tatton-Brown (London: British Museum), p. 90) writes: "At the beginning of the Iron Age in the eleventh century BC, Aegean Greeks must have been aware of Cyprus in two different ways. First, Cyprus had received, and was continuing to receive, large numbers of their own kinsmen who came as refugees from the collapse of Mycenaean palatial civilisation, to found the settlements which were to grow into the historic Greek kingdoms of Cyprus."

28. Palaima 1989a:54.

29. E. Masson, 1973, "La diffusion de l'écriture à la fin de l'âge du Bronze," in *Acts of the International Archaeological Symposium "The Mycenaeans in the Eastern Mediterranean"* (Nicosia: Zavallis Press), pp. 89–90.

30. See Palaima 1989a; Chadwick 1979. For an overview of the Cypriot scripts, see Chadwick 1990:183–194; *Docs.:*60–66; Chadwick 1967:20–25; Karageorghis 1982a:63–66; Mitford and Masson 1982.

31. On the Cypro-Minoan scripts, see, *inter alios,* Palaima 1989b and E. Masson 1974. Palaima finds the threefold division of the scripts into Cypro-Minoan 1, 2, and 3 (see immediately below) troublesome.

32. E. Masson has argued that the language of Cypro-Minoan 2 is Hurrian; see E. Masson, 1977, "Présence éventuelle de la langue hourrite sur les tablettes chypro-minoennes d'Enkomi," *Revue roumaine de linguistique* 22:483–488.

33. Karageorghis 1982a:123–127; 1982b, "Cyprus," in *CAH,* 2nd ed., ed. J. Boardman et al. (Cambridge: Cambridge University Press), vol. 3, part 1, pp. 523–526.

34. For this interpretation, see A. Dupont-Sommer, 1970, "Une inscription phénicienne archaique récemment trouvé à Kition," *Mémoires de l'Académie des Inscriptions et Belles Lettres* 44:15–28. For discussion and further references, see Karageorghis 1982a:124; also 1982b:526–527.

35. See O. Masson 1983:78–80; T. Palaima, 1991, "The Advent of the Greek Alphabet on Cyprus: A Competition of Scripts," in *Phoinikeia grammata: Lire et écrire en Méditerranée,* ed. C. Baurain, C. Bonnet, and V. Krings (Liège: Société des Études Classiques), pp. 449–471.

36. Karageorghis (1982a:114) states, "Political life during early Cypro-Geometric I must have been centered round the king and the Mycenaean aristocrats who ruled the large cities."

37. Ibid., p. 121.

38. The translation in (12) is that of R. Lattimore, 1951, *The Iliad of Homer* (Chicago: University of Chicago Press), as are all translated selections from the *Iliad* appearing below.

39. See the discussions throughout Karageorghis, 1969, *Salamis in Cyprus: Homeric, Hellenistic and Roman* (London: Thames and Hudson) and additional bibliography.

40. Ibid., pp. 30–31, 130, 132.

41. Ibid., p. 31. See also D. Hughes, 1991, *Human Sacrifice in Ancient Greece* (London: Routledge), pp. 35–42.

42. As in the case of as many as six human skeletons found buried in the dromos of Tomb 15 at Mycenae; see C. Tsountas, 1888, " Ἀνασκαφαὶ τάφων ἐν Μυκήναις," Ἀρχαιολογικὴ Ἐφημερίς, pp. 130–131; C. Tsountas and J. Manatt, 1969, *The Mycenaean Age: A Study of the Monuments and Culture of Pre-Homeric Greece* (Chicago: Argonaut; reprint of 1897 edition), p. 151. For other possible instances of the remains of sacrificed humans found in Mycenaean chamber and tholos tombs, see the summary and discussion with bibliography in Hughes 1991:26–35, 47–48. Hughes's attitude toward many of these reported sacrifices is one of skepticism, though he finds the case

for human sacrifice at Salamis (and also in Cyprus at Lapethos) "convincing" (p. 48). Linear B tablet Tn 316 (Pylos) has been interpreted as possibly recording human sacrifices; if so, they were apparently offered in an attempt to stave off some impending catastrophic event; for discussion and bibliography see Hughes (pp. 199–202), who is again quite skeptical.

43. Y. Sakellarakis and E. Sakellaraki, 1979, " 'Ανασκαφὴ 'Αρχανῶν," Πρακτικὰ τῆς ἐν 'Αθήναις 'Αρχαιολογικῆς, pp. 347–392.

44. S. Wall, J. Musgrave, and P. Warren, 1986, "Human Bones from a Late Minoan IB House at Knossos," *Annual of the British School at Athens* 81:333–388. For discussion and further bibliography, see Hughes 1991:13–24.

45. Karageorghis 1969:71; O. Masson 1983:418.

46. Karageorghis 1969:32.

47. Ibid.

48. *Docs.*:309–310; Hallager, Vlasakis, and Hallager 1992:75–81.

49. Karageorghis 1982a:135.

50. Karageorghis 1969:26.

51. Ibid., p. 72.

52. Ibid., pp. 67, 71.

53. Ibid., p. 73. Tombs 19 and 31 were somewhat smaller than the "royal" tombs, and Karageorghis suggests that they may have belonged to an intermediate class of well-to-do Salamians.

54. Karageorghis 1969:69–70; 1967, "Homerica from Salamis (Cyprus)," in *Europa: Festschrift Ernst Grumach,* ed. W. Brice (Berlin: DeGruyter), p. 167.

55. See the discussion in ibid., pp. 167–168.

56. Karageorghis 1969:71–72.

57. Ibid., p. 54.

58. *Docs.*:365–366; 516. In addition, tablet Se891 + 1006 + 1042 (p. 369) refers to a chariot equipped with ivory *o-mo-pi,* perhaps 'bands'; the reference is quite possibly not to the bridling equipment, of course.

59. See the descriptions in Karageorghis 1982a:131–132; 1973, *Excavations in the Necropolis of Salamis III,* vol. 5, part 1 (Nicosia: Department of Antiquities), pp. 89–94; 1969:92–94, see also p. 82 and plates IV–VI.

60. The translation is that of A. Murray, 1980, *Homer: The Odyssey* (Cambridge: Harvard University Press), p. 233.

61. Karageorghis 1969:94; 1967:168.

62. *Odyssey* translations are those of R. Lattimore, 1965, *The Odyssey of Homer* (New York: Harper Collins).

63. *Docs.*:340.

64. The term used here is not the usual Mycenaean word for silver, *a-ku-ro,* αργυρος ([argüros]), but *pa-ra-ku-we*; see the discussion in *Docs.*:340. In the second edition of *Documents,* Chadwick (p. 496) adduces the thrones from Tomb 79 as support for his interpretation of this form. See also Chadwick's personal communication reported in Karageorghis 1967:168–169, n. 7.

The chair of Ta714 is said to be inlaid with φοινικες ([pʰoinikes]) of gold and of *kuanos.* In the second edition of *Documents,* Chadwick (p. 502), following suggestions of Dessenne and Chantraine, assigns to φοινιξ its meaning 'palm-tree', though in the first edition, the term was translated 'griffin', where it is stated (p. 344), "It has been suggested that the name of the fabulous bird φοῖνιξ (Hesiod, Frg. 171.4) was first applied to the 'griffins' and sphinxes so prominent in Mycenaean art, particularly on the ivories from Mycenae, Delos and Enkomi." Recall that an ivory sphinx cutout occurred on one of the thrones in Tomb 79.

65. Karageorghis 1969:94–95.

66. For D. Rupp, the royal tombs are those "of the first kings of Salamis (and possibly in all of Iron Age Cyprus)" (Rupp, 1988, "The 'Royal Tombs' at Salamis (Cyprus): Ideological Messages of Power and Authority," *Journal of Mediterranean Archeology* 1:124; see also Rupp, 1987a, "*Vive le Roi:* The Emergence of the State in Iron Age Cyprus," in *Western Cyprus: Connections,* ed. D. Rupp (Göteborg: Paul Åströms Förlag), pp. 147–168). Rupp interprets the archaeological record of Cyprus as revealing that "from ca. 1000 until 800 BC there are only limited indications of social differentiation and stratification" (p. 126). The new eighth-century monarchical class sought to legitimate its claim to sovereignty, at least in part, by flaunting its Mycenaean heritage (p. 133; Rupp (1987a:156) even claims, concerning the occupant of Tomb 1, that "the myth that Salamis was founded by the Achaean hero Teukros may have been the invention of this astute political leader"). A continued awareness of a Mycenaean ancestry and conservation of elements of the same clearly underlie Rupp's scenario. Contra Rupp's view of an eighth-century origin of the Cypriot kingdoms, see A. Snodgrass, 1988, *Cyprus and Early Greek History* (Nicosia: Zavalis Press), pp. 7–24.

67. Chantraine 1968:84–85.

68. See Karageorghis 1982b:532; for additional examples of the Cypriot preservation of Mycenaean (and Minoan) cultural features, such as the "horns of consecration," see Karageorghis, 1962, "Notes on Some Mycenaean Survivals in Cyprus during the First Millennium B.C.," *Kadmos* 1:71–77. On Cypriot *wa-na-kse,* see also O. Masson 1983:218. Another Bronze Age Greek relic surviving in Iron Age Cyprus is the use of the chariot in war, a practice which continued into the fifth century B.C.; see Snodgrass 1988:19.

69. Karageorghis 1982b:531.

70. Karageorghis 1962:72.

71. J. Vendryes, 1916, "Les correspondences de la vocabulaire entre l'Indo-Iranian et l'Italo-Celtique," *Memoires de la Société de Linguistique de Paris* 20:265–285.

72. R. Carpenter, 1933, "The Antiquity of the Greek Alphabet," *AJA* 37:8–29.

73. See McCarter's (1975:1–12) valuable survey of nineteenth- and twentieth-century thinking on the dating of the origin of the Greek alphabet. Note also Carpenter's opening remarks (1933:8–9), and see Jeffery 1990:12, n. 4, for a chronologically organized bibliography of works dealing with this topic.

74. Carpenter 1933:10–15.

75. Ibid., p. 27.

76. Jeffery 1990:13–21.

77. Ibid., p. 426.

78. Ibid., p. 12, n. 4; see also McCarter 1975:20, n. 51.

79. Buck 1955:348; it is the case, of course, that the first edition of Buck's work preceded Carpenter's study.

80. Guarducci 1967:70–73; 1964, "Appunti di epigrafia greca arcaica" (review of *The Local Scripts of Archaic Greece,* 1st ed., by L. Jeffery), *Archeologia classica* 16:122–153.

81. W. Albright, 1961, "The Role of the Canaanites in the History of Civilization," in *The Bible and the Ancient Near East,* ed. G. Wright (Garden City, N.Y.: Doubleday), p. 350; G. Driver, 1976, *Semitic Writing,* rev. S. Hopkins (Oxford: Oxford University Press), pp. 171–179; T. Lambdin, 1962, "Alphabet," in *The Interpreter's Dictionary of*

the Bible, vol. 1 (New York: Abingdon), p. 92. See the comments of McCarter 1975:24–27.

82. J. Naveh, 1973, "Some Semitic Epigraphical Considerations on the Antiquity of the Greek Alphabet," *AJA* 77:1–8.

83. That is, 'as the ox turns': going in one direction in one line and in the opposite direction in the next.

84. See, *inter alios,* F. Cross, 1980, "Newly Found Inscriptions in Old Canaanite and Early Phoenician Scripts," *BASOR* 238:1–20; 1979, "Early Alphabetic Scripts," in *Symposia Celebrating the Seventy-Fifth Anniversary of the Founding of the American Schools of Oriental Research I,* ed. F. Cross (Cambridge: American Schools of Oriental Research), pp. 105–111. Among other works by Naveh, see 1991, "Semitic Epigraphy and the Antiquity of the Greek Alphabet," *Kadmos* 30:143–152; 1987, "Proto-Canaanite, Archaic Greek, and the Script of the Aramaic Text on the Tell Fakhariyah Statue," in *Ancient Israelite Religion,* ed. P. Miller et al. (Philadelphia: Fortress Press), pp. 101–113. An even earlier date for the Greek acquisition of the alphabet is proposed in M. Bernal, 1990, *Cadmean Letters: The Transmission of the Alphabet to the Aegean and Further West before 1400 B.C.* (Winona Lake, Ind.: Eisenbrauns). Contrast B. Sass, 1991, *Studia Alphabetica* (Freiburg: Universitätsverlag Freiburg); E. Lipinski, 1988, "Les Phéniciens et l'alphabet," *Oriens Antiquus* 27:231–260; A. Demsky, 1977, "A Proto-Canaanite Abecedary Dating from the Period of the Judges and Its Implications for the History of the Alphabet," *Tel Aviv* 4:22–23.

85. McCarter 1975:17.

86. Ibid., pp. 22–23.

87. Ibid., p. 118.

88. Ibid., pp. 123–124.

89. Ibid., pp. 124–126.

90. For general remarks on the directionality of syllabic Cypriot writing, see O. Masson 1983:78.

91. Mitford and Masson 1982:80.

92. Mitford and Masson 1983:32.

93. O. Masson 1983:65, 78.

94. Mitford and Masson 1983:91–93; Masson and Mitford 1986:109. In Tomb 69 (tenth century) at Palaepaphos-*Skales* was recovered a vase bearing an inscription in an undetermined language, some characters of which appear to be Phoenician; see M. Sznycer, 1983, "Note sur l'inscription gravée sur une cruche de la tombe 69 de Palaepaphos-*Skales*," in Karageorghis, 1983, *Palaepaphos-Skales: An Iron Age Cemetery in Cyprus* (Konstanz: Universitätsverlag Konstanz), pp. 416–417.

95. Mitford and Masson 1982:80.

96. McCarter 1975:120.

97. McCarter (1975:112) states concerning the script of the twelfth and early eleventh centuries (emphasis is mine): "[D]uring the period of transmission from vertical to horizontal writing, an individual sign might occur in its old upright position, or rotated ninety degrees counterclockwise. The inevitable result was much uncertainty and confusion, leading to the *occasional appearance* of a sign in a stance inverted, reversed, or sidelong with respect to the stances of its companion signs in an inscription. This situation was most conspicuous in the twelfth and early eleventh centuries. By the middle of the eleventh it had stabilized, and all the letter-forms had arrived at what would become their traditional stances." With regard to Greek letter orientation, he writes: "The rotation of some of these away from the stances of their Phoenician counterparts was mentioned above. As we have just noted, a similar situation existed in Phoenician itself in the

twelfth and early eleventh centuries, insofar as a particular letter-form might occur in an *incongruous stance* in a given inscription."

98. Naveh also argues that certain early Greek letter-forms suggest an origin of the Greek alphabet ca. 1100. McCarter addresses these and in the end judges most of this evidence to be problematic (pp. 114–118); however, he does find the match between dotted *omicron* of early Greek and the Phoenician dotted *'ayin*, which is attested no later than the early tenth century, to be impressive. Johnston (in Jeffery 1990:426), however, contends that dotted *omicron* does not occur "in the earlier Greek material" and analyzes it as a secondary development within the evolving Greek script. In 1981, a bilingual Assyrian and Aramaic inscription was discovered at Tell Fakhariyah in northern Syria which is dated to the ninth century. The Aramaic inscription is written in a script which is remarkably similar to the eleventh-century Proto-Canaanite script and has been interpreted as evidence of the heterogeneity of West Semitic scripts in the ninth century, contra Naveh (see S. Kaufman, 1982, "Reflections on the Assyrian-Aramaic Bilingual from Tell Fakhariyeh," *Maarav* 3:137–175); Naveh (1987) counters with the claim that this is an intentionally archaizing script. The Tell Fakhariyah inscription preserves a ninth-century dotted *omicron*.

99. Carpenter 1933:27–28.

100. Jeffery 1990:7–8.

101. R. Carpenter, 1938, "The Greek Alphabet Again," *AJA* 42:67. Carpenter cites M. Nilsson, 1918, *Danske Videnskabernes Selskab. Historisk-filologiske Meddelelser* 1:6, and Hammarström, 1920, *Acta Soc. Scient. Fenn.* 49:58.

102. Ibid.

103. J. Justeson, 1976, "Universals of Language and Universals of Writing," in *Linguistic Studies Offered to Joseph Greenberg on the Occasion of his Sixtieth Birthday*, ed. A. Juilland (Saratoga, Calif.: Anma Libri), vol. 1, pp. 61, 65, 71.

104. Sampson 1985:133.

105. Carpenter 1938:67–68.

106. McCarter 1975:78.

107. Carpenter 1938:68.

108. Jeffery 1990:23.

109. Jeffery 1990:10, n. 3.

110. K. Robb, 1994, *Literacy and Paideia in Ancient Greece* (Oxford: Oxford University Press), p. 275; 1978, "Poetic Sources of the Greek Alphabet: Rhythm and Abecedarium from Phoenician to Greek," in *Communication Arts in the Ancient World*, ed. E. Havelock and J. Hershbell (New York: Hastings House), p. 27.

111. Ibid., p. 35. Robb argues that the alphabet was developed in order to record graphically epic poetry and that the presence of vowels in the Greek script, unlike that of Phoenician, was vital since Greek meter is based upon syllable quantity (see pp. 29–32). If it were metrical considerations which dictated the inclusion of vowel characters in the new alphabetic script, it seems probable that some means of orthographically distinguishing long and short vowels would have been incorporated into the script's design, since syllable quantity is a function of the length of the syllable's vowel plus the presence or absence of syllable-final consonants. This point has also been noted by Palaima, to whose comments we will come in chapter 8 (section 8.2.1).

112. A. Heubeck, 1979, *Schrift* (Göttingen: Vandenhoeck und Ruprecht), pp. 85–87. In a footnote (p. 86, n. 514), Heubeck makes mention of Carpenter's thesis that the set of vowel graphemes provided for in the alphabet betrays the influence of the Cypriot Syllabary and indicates that it is "nicht ohne Bedeutung." See our comments above concerning this matter.

113. A. Johnston, 1983, "The Extent and Use of Literacy: The Archaeological Evidence," in *The Greek Renaissance of the Eighth Century B.C.: Tradition and Innovation*, ed. R. Hägg (Stockholm: Svenska Institutet i Athen), p. 66.

114. Ibid.; compare Carpenter's remarks discussed above concerning a Rhodian resident of Cyprus.

115. W. Burkert, 1992, *The Orientalizing Revolution* (Cambridge: Harvard University Press), p. 27.

116. L. Woolley, 1938, "Excavations at Al Mina, Sueidia," *JHS* 58:1–30, 133–170.

117. See the discussion, with bibliography, in J. Boardman, 1980, *The Greeks Overseas* (London: Thames and Hudson), pp. 43–44; on Al Mina generally, see pp. 38–54.

118. Ibid., pp. 426, 476.·

119. Ibid., pp. 40–42.

120. See the discussion in Powell 1991:14–18. Powell (p. 14, n. 32), citing an unpublished lecture by Jeffery, states that these are "the very earliest Greek inscriptions, dated by stratification to as early as *c.* 775–750" (see also p. 15, n. 34). As we have discussed above, the Würzberg alphabet-table is perhaps to be dated to 800 B.C.

121. The inscription of the kotyle dubbed Nestor's Cup is dated to the last quarter of the eighth century; see D. Ridgway, 1992, *The First Western Greeks* (Cambridge: Cambridge University Press), p. 56; Jeffery 1990:235–236, 453–454. On the potential role of the Euboeans in the dissemination of the alphabet, see the summary discussions in J. Coldstream, 1977, *Geometric Greece* (London: Ernest Benn Ltd.), pp. 300–301, and Powell 1991:14–17.

122. Boardman 1980:44.

123. Ibid. Ridgway (1992:22) writes, "That Cyprus emerges at an early stage under the heading 'Euboeans abroad' is no accident. It was indeed far from home, but as a base to explore western Asia Minor it could hardly be bettered."

124. Coldstream 1989:94.

125. See Coldstream's (ibid., pp. 90–96) discussion of Cyprus's intermediary role.

126. A. Reyes, 1994, *Archaic Cyprus* (Oxford: Oxford University Press), p. 139. Reyes adds, "These sites were also ports of call for the Phoenicians, especially those from Tyre, as they travelled from the Levant to the Dodecanese and points further west."

127. Karageorghis 1982a:130.

128. Ibid., pp. 114, 122–123.

129. Ridgway 1992:22. With regard to ninth-century Euboean trade with Cypriot Phoenicians, he notes, "[T]he small-scale and still essentially experimental Euboean overseas operation came into early and mutually satisfactory contact with the much older and much wider Cypro-Levantine network of pan-Mediterranean commerce and communications" (p. 24).

130. See remarks by Coldstream in Johnston 1983:68; see also Johnston's comments on p. 66, n. 17.

131. Boardman 1980:36–37; Karageorghis 1982a:123.

132. Boardman 1980:36–37.

133. A Cretan origin of the Greek alphabet is maintained by Guarducci (1978, "La culla dell'alfabeto greco," *Rendiconti dell'Accademia nazionale dei Lincei* 33:381–388) and Duhoux (1981, "Les Etéocrétois et l'origine de l'alphabet grec," *L'antiquité classique* 50:287–294).

134. See Coldstream 1977:299; Jeffery 1990:9, for example. For supporters of the Rhodian claim other than Carpenter 1933, see Jeffery 1990:10, n. 3.

135. Johnston 1983:66, n. 17.

136. Jeffery 1990:425.

137. Ibid., p. 10.

138. Ian Morris has argued for the continuation of a social and political hierarchy from the Mycenaean demise throughout the Dark Age; see Morris, 1991, "The Early Polis as City and State," in *City and Country in the Ancient World,* ed. J. Rich and A. Wallace-Hadrill (London: Routledge), pp. 25–57. Note his discussion of "rich burials" of Lefkandi commencing ca. 1000–950 (p. 43 with additional references). Changes in the archaeological record ca. 750 B.C., however, suggest "a profound change in social structure in the eighth century" (I. Morris, 1987, *Burial and Ancient Society* (Cambridge: Cambridge University Press), p. 195): "[A] large group of communities in the Aegean . . . were undergoing profound social and economic changes around 750 BC, culminating in the emergence of the polis ideal" (ibid., p. 205; see generally pp. 171–217; I. Morris 1991:49–50). These "profound changes" are occurring at the very time that the Cypriot-born alphabet is able to gain a foothold in the Aegean.

Conclusion

8.0 The Syllabic Predecessors of the Alphabet

8.0.1 An Aegean *Pāṇini*

The so-called syllable-division doctrine espoused by the Greek grammarians and the corresponding word-division practices evidenced by Greek inscriptions had their origins at least a thousand years earlier, in the scribal training centers of Mycenaean Greece or, perhaps, Minoan Crete. It was the Minoans who taught the Greeks how to write (the first time), and quite possibly it was also the Minoans who instructed the Greeks in the notions of sound classes and the relative sonority of sounds. Whether the Linear B (and syllabic Cypriot) practice of utilizing a hierarchy of sonority (i.e., the hierarchy of orthographic strength) for the spelling of consonant clusters was a Minoan or a Mycenaean innovation is undetermined and will remain so until Linear A is deciphered.

If the Greeks acquired a sonority-based strategy for representing sequences of consonants from the Minoans, they probably did not do so in a holistic fashion. The sonority hierarchy of Greek is somewhat unusual, as we saw in chapter 4, to the extent that liquids are more sonorous than glides; crosslinguistically the opposite ranking (one with glides being more sonorous than liquids) is more common. While it is possible that the Minoan language was also characterized by liquid consonants which were of relatively greater sonority than glides, typological considerations would surely lead us to expect otherwise. Thus, if the Greeks acquired from the Minoans the concept of the relative sonority of sound classes (in whatever form this conceptualization took), they, the Greeks, possessed ample linguistic intuition to discover the specific, idiosyncratic sonority hierarchy of their own language.

The idea that some Minoan, or otherwise Mediterranean, scribe of the second millennium B.C. should possess sufficient linguistic sophistication and insight to perceive that language sounds fall into natural classes and that these classes differ in relative sonority may take us by surprise, though it probably ought not. Ancient humanity was no less observant and ingenious than its modern counterpart. It is well known that Pāṇini and other grammarians of ancient India controlled a highly sophisticated knowledge of phonetics and phonology in the middle of the first millennium B.C. and that Pāṇini did not stand at the head of this tradition but was preceded by other grammarians, at least ten of whom Pāṇini mentions by name, but whose works have perished.[1] Beyond this, and of considerable significance for this investigation, J. Watt has recently demonstrated that the characters of the second-millennium B.C. cuneiform consonantal script of Ugarit were assigned an order in the signary on the basis of sound-class membership (the same order which, *mutatis mutandis,* occurs in the subsequently attested Phoenician script—and hence the Greek alphabet—and presumably in its immediate ancestor Proto-Canaanite).[2] The Minoan and Mycenaean scribes were thus not the only scholars in possession of sophisticated phonetic and phonological acumen in the second-millennium B.C. Mediterranean world.[3]

8.0.2 Synopsis

When the scribal component of the community of Mycenaean refugees in Cyprus began to flirt with the Cypro-Minoan scripts which they encountered in their new homeland and, eventually, adapted one of these for spelling their own language, they preserved the highly idiosyncratic practice of deferring to the sonority hierarchy of Greek to determine how consonant clusters should be spelled. The old Linear B deletion strategy was replaced, however, by a regressive spelling strategy, resulting in an orthographically more complete phonetic record of Greek speech (though, as we have seen, the deletion strategy was retained and applied in the spelling of clusters beginning with a nasal consonant). The precise nature of the relationship between Cypro-Minoan and the Cypriot Syllabary is problematic;[4] perhaps, however, the adapted Cypro-Minoan script provided the inspiration for this abandonment of the deletion strategy. That is to say, full consonantal representation may possibly have been a feature of the relevant Cypro-Minoan script. Cypro-Minoan practice might have also supported the decision to represent word-final consonants (to the extent that they are represented) using an empty-vowel strategy. Yet, as we saw in chapter 5, it appears that the germ of word-final empty-vowel spelling and of regressive spelling (which allowed for full consonantal representation) was already a part of Linear B practice.

The Linear B script of the Mycenaean refugees had possessed a set of CV characters representing that consonantal sound which would emerge as the sequence [zd] in the alphabetic period (spelled with *zeta*). At least at the time of the development of the Linear B script the Mycenaean sound was a unitary phoneme, perhaps a palatalized stop. Provision was made by the transplanted Mycenaean scribal community for representing this sound with a distinct set of syllabic symbols in the newly devised Cypriot Syllabary. The early unitary Mycenaean phoneme had probably evolved into a consonant sequence [zd]; in other words, the Mycenaean symbols for the sound had become, as a consequence of phonological change, CCV in value. Thus, the scribes who devised the Cypriot Syllabary were simply preserving their tradition of representing this consonantal sequence with CCV symbols (i.e., <zdV>), rather than innovating by spelling the sequence factorially as CV-CV (i.e., <sV-dV>).

The use of a strategy for spelling consonant clusters which is based upon the sonority hierarchy of Greek coupled with the fuller representation of consonants characteristic of the Cypriot script gave rise to a spelling dilemma with which the practitioners of the more abbreviatory Linear B spelling system had not had to deal. Adherence to the regular Cypriot spelling strategy for representing consonant clusters resulted in a bizarre representation of the sequence *[k] + [s] + stop:* [k] would have to be spelled with a CV symbol whose vocalic component was identical to the vowel which *followed* the entire cluster, while [s] would have to be represented by a CV syllabogram whose vocalic element was identical to that vowel which *preceded* the cluster. A solution to this dilemma presented itself to the adapting scribes; a set of *ksV* symbols was simply introduced into the newly devised writing system (a measure which was possibly suggested by the occurrence of the CCV symbols *zdV*). Perhaps *psV* symbols were also created. At present this remains uncertain, though an alphabetic asymmetry of *ks* and *ps* characters may suggest an absence of *psV* symbols from the Cypriot script; alternatively, the alphabetic asymmetry may simply reflect that *psV* syllabic symbols were less broadly utilized than *ksV* symbols (again as a consequence of phonological change) at the time of the Cypriot adaptation of the Phoenician consonantal script.

At some point in the middle of the ninth century B.C. (or possibly slightly earlier), a significant Phoenician presence began to manifest itself on the island of Cyprus. With the Phoenician settlers came their consonantal script. While the Cypriot Syllabary stands as an advance over the Mycenaean script, at least to the extent that consonantal representation becomes completely overt (with the exception of preconsonantal nasals and certain word-final consonants), it is still far from a tidy system. When the Cypriot Greek scribes encountered the Phoenician writing system, the advantages which it offered must have become readily apparent. To begin with, it operated with fewer symbols than their own script, as each Phoenician symbol represented only an individual consonant sound rather than some specific combination of consonant plus vowel. Moreover, when a Phoenician scribe took writing utensil in hand, each written character that was produced actually represented a speech sound. Because the syllable structure of the Greek language departed significantly from the canonical *consonant + vowel* structure of the units of the Cypriot Syllabary, this syllabic script, though fully functional and adequate for the expression of the Greek language, was less than elegant—spelling required extensive use of vowel elements which had no phonetic reality. Room existed for improvement in the practice of Greek orthography, and the Phoenician system suggested the possibility of improvement.

There are numerous peculiar features of the Greek alphabet which owe their origin to the fact that the people who adapted the Phoenician script for Greek use were individuals already immersed in a literate tradition. That is to say, these seeming alphabetic oddities are simply natural projections of the prior literacy of the designers of the Greek alphabet:

1. The *prima facie* absurd occurrence of an alphabetic character with the biconsonantal value [k] + [s] (in a writing system which has both a symbol for [k] and a symbol for [s]) is accounted for by the presence in the Cypriot Syllabary of syllabic symbols having the biconsonantal value *ksV*—symbols idiosyncratically required by the intersection of Cypriot Greek phonology and the Cypriot orthographic strategy of consonant cluster representation. As noted just above, CCV symbols with the value *psV* (or at least *pse,* for use in word-final position) may have also occurred within the syllabic Cypriot writing system but, if so, would have had a more limited distribution than *ksV* symbols at the time of the origin of the alphabet; this asymmetry is reflected in the early alphabetic traditions.

2. A biconsonantal character with the value [z] + [d] is also redundantly included in the graphemic inventory of the new alphabetic script; such sequences could have simply been spelled $\sigma\delta$, just as [z] + [b] and [z] + [g] are spelled $\sigma\beta$ and $\sigma\gamma$ respectively. The occurrence of the [z] + [d] character *zeta* in the Greek alphabet is again occasioned by the presence of corresponding syllabic symbols in the Cypriot Syllabary as well as in its predecessor Linear B. Though "corresponding," the phonetic value of the consonantal portion of the syllabic symbols was originally something quite different—that of a unitary phoneme and hence, the very reason for the occurrence of characters with the eventual value [z] + [d].

3. The local varieties of the early Greek alphabet preserve, almost in complete complementary distribution, two different symbols with the value [s]: *san* and *sigma.* In origin, however, *san* was the character devised by the Cypriot adapters of the Phoenician script for representing the distinctive Cypriot, as well as Arcadian, sibilant reflex of the Proto-Greek labiovelar *[k^w]. Hence, *san* is preserved in this use in the alphabet which came to Arcadia, the dialect of which place shows evidence of a broader occurrence of sibilant labiovelar reflexes than does its sister dialect of Cypriot.

4. In the earliest stratum (or strata) of the Greek alphabet, there occurred no symbols for the aspirated stops [p^h] and [k^h]. The Cypriot adapters of the Phoenician script were accustomed to operating with a writing system in which no distinct graphemes existed for voiceless aspirated stops, and so this condition was extended to the new alphabetic script, at least in the case of the bilabial and velar articulatory positions. While symbols were devised for distinguishing the voiced stops ([b], [d], [g]) from their voiceless counterparts, the continuation of the tradition of representing the consonantal sequences [k] + [s] and [z] + [d] by a single biconsonantal symbol each (rather than by a sequence of two monoconsonantal symbols each) was prized more highly than utilizing two members of the limited set of Phoenician symbols innovatively to distinguish voiceless aspirated [p^h] and [k^h] from voiceless unaspirated [p] and [k].

5. Early Greek alphabetic writing is variable in direction. This condition contrasts markedly with the thoroughgoing right-to-left direction of ninth-century Phoenician writing. While the practice of the scribes of the syllabic Cypriot tradition was likewise right-to-left across much of the island of Cyprus, the direction of writing at Paphos was, in comparison, mercurial: the predominant direction was left-to-right, but both right-to-left and boustrophedon were also utilized. Perhaps not necessarily those Cypriot scribes responsible for adapting the Phoenician script for Greek use, but at least some early Cypriot users of the new alphabetic script incorporated into this developing tradition the variable direction of writing which characterized their own particular syllabic Cypriot practice. These scribes may have been Paphian or perhaps were from some other region of the island in which such variability in direction of writing was practiced but not as yet attested.[5]

8.1 Concerning Vowels

The creation of the Greek alphabet, a script possessing symbols for representing not only individual consonant sounds but individual vowel sounds as well, was without question a highly significant achievement in the history of writing. Beyond this, the Greek incorporation of vowel symbols into a phonemic script has been hailed as a salient event in the intellectual history of humanity; and this is fitting. Yet even so, the addition of vowel characters to the Phoenician consonantal script was probably not, in the final analysis, crucial.[6] Had the Greeks simply continued the Phoenician tradition of only representing consonants in their writing system, those achievements of the human intellect and spirit realized since antiquity through the alphabetic medium would not, I suspect, have been compromised. The precisely opposite view has been advocated to be sure,[7] but this is to confuse the genius of human thought with the mechanical means of its graphic expression.[8] The literary works produced by Greek and Latin authors which we identify as *classic* would likely still have been produced had a consonantal script been utilized for their recording.

This is neither here nor there, of course. The Greeks did in fact incorporate vowel symbols into the Phoenician consonantal script (and had they not, someone else surely would have done so subsequently). Yet, the fact remains that it is possible to record human speech, human thoughts, human ideas in a sufficiently efficient manner by representing only consonants. While the presence of vowel symbols in a script in which each symbol represents a single sound may indeed be an asset to the reader in the cognitive processing of such writing, the history of Semitic writing (about which I later say more) amply demonstrates that their occurrence is not essential.

Just why *did* the Greeks add vowels to the received Phoenician script? At an earlier period in their history, the Greeks had shown themselves to be quite willing to operate with a writing system which systematically *underrepresented* the sounds of spoken language. As we have seen, the Linear B script of the Mycenaeans omitted consonant characters with abandon—even when such omission could potentially result in significant syntactic ambiguity[9]—and in fact this practice continued at a diminished rate of omission within the syllabic Cypriot system. The answer which would probably most readily be offered to the question which opened this paragraph goes something like this: The Greeks added vowel characters to the Phoenician consonantal script in order to minimize orthographic ambiguity and confusion, to distinguish words which have a homophonous consonant structure. Consider, for example, a Greek consonantal spelling such as $KP\Sigma$; this might represent κηρός ([kɛːrós], 'beeswax'), κέρας (kéras], 'horn'), κόρυς ([kórüs], 'helmet'), or κοῦρος ([kûːros], 'young man').[10] Orthographic imprecision of this sort was indeed avoided by the introduction of vowel characters; that is, such disambiguation was the *result* of adding vowel symbols to the adopted Phoenician script. But was the intent to avoid such fuzzy orthography necessarily the *motivation* for the addition of vowel symbols? Regarding the latter prospect, we need to think further.

Phoenician scribes tolerated a writing system which represented only consonants and so allowed for orthographic ambiguity of the type described above; the same of course holds true for various Semitic scripts related to and derived from the Phoenician system. The claim is often made that the morphology of the Semitic languages naturally suggests that they be written with a consonantal script; that is, (presumably) Semitic morphology is such that the cognitive processing of Semitic writing is unhampered, in some significant way, by the absence of vowel symbols. Canonically, a Semitic root consists of two or three consonants plus accompanying vowels. While the root consonants are rather stable, vowels are quite variable: particular patterns of vowels occur characteristically in various morphological categories, both inflectional and derivational. These vocalic patterns are often accompanied by affixes containing consonants which further mark the morphological category. Between the context in which a given word is found and the consonant-bearing affixes associated with it (when they occur), an ideal reader of a consonantal Semitic text would be able to recognize the morphological category to which the word belongs and, hence, would be able to determine (as a redundant feature) the values of the unwritten vowels of the word.[11]

Vowels do not, however, occur in Phoenician and other Semitic languages only as units in recurring morphological patterns. Precisely as we saw in the previously cited Greek example ($KP\Sigma$), Semitic vowels can also crucially distinguish words which are consonantally identical. For example, the Hebrew consonantal spelling ḥbl might represent ḥĕbĕl ('cord'), ḥēbĕl ('pain'), ḥᵃbōl ('pledge'), ḥōbēl ('sailor'). In other words, in spite of the grammatical predictability of many vowels in Semitic, the problem of lexical ambiguity (as with Greek $KP\Sigma$) still exists. Yet even so, for millennia consonantal scripts have been used and continue to be used with cognitive efficiency[12] by Semitic scribes.

Why is this so? This is so for the same reason that the less than elegant Linear B and syllabic Cypriot scripts could be utilized effectively for writing Greek. Writing systems are "designed" for native speakers of the written language (or at least for readers with something approaching native competence in the language to be read); scripts assume such a knowledge—they are often not user-friendly. Such a reader comes to the written text with an intimate knowledge of the language recorded in the text. The reader's knowledge of the language is primary; the mechanism of giving graphic form to that language is secondary. The reader comes to the text equipped with a knowledge of the possibilities; it is the requirement of the static text only that it provide sufficient graphic clues to direct the language-enriched mind of the reader.

Earlier in this study I mentioned that the Greek acquisition of the Phoenician script must have occurred in a bilingual Greek-Phoenician setting. When Phoenician-speaking Greek scribes learned and began to experiment with the Phoenician script and to reflect upon the possibility of utilizing this system of symbols for writing Greek, was it their conviction that while a consonantal script might be adequate for writing the Semitic language of Phoenician, consonant characters alone would simply not work for spelling their own language? After some deliberation and introspection, did the adapters arrive at the conclusion that the structure of Greek was so different from that of Phoenician that writing Greek with only consonantal characters would yield nebulous spellings and place too great a cognitive burden on the reader? Perhaps they did, but I do not think we can assume so. We should bear in mind that the Greek adapters did in fact introduce ambiguity into the new alphabetic system. As we have seen, in the earliest stratum of the alphabet the voiceless aspirated bilabial stop /p^h/ and velar stop /k^h/ were represented by the characters for /p/ and /k/ respectively. There was also no provision made for graphically distinguishing long vowels from short vowels in spite of the fact that vowel length is phonemic in Greek (though, as I pointed out, this is reported to be a common orthographic phenomenon). Moreover, the Greeks had historically not shied away from orthographies which offered less than orthographic crystal clarity. It is not obvious that *nt^{h}rps,* a consonantal spelling of ἄνθρωπος ([ánthrǫ:pos], 'man') would be more cognitively cumbersome than a syllabic Cypriot *a-to-ro-po-se* (not to mention a yet more abbreviated Linear B spelling *a-to-ro-qo*). Greek words (such as ἄνθρωπος) often consist of a greater number of consonants than is typical of Semitic, frequently occurring in clusters of two or more. This greater consonantal presence would perhaps compensate, with regard to the prospect of consonantal spelling, for vowel occurrence being of a somewhat less predictable nature in Greek than in Semitic.

I suspect that the issue of whether or not the Greek language could be "adequately" spelled with a consonantal script was never broached in any sort of systematic or deliberative way. If we accept the Cypriot scribal origin of the Greek alphabet, the presence of vowel characters in the adapted Phoenician script is practically automatic. For a scribe accustomed to spelling with the syllabic Cypriot script, vowel representation would have been the *sine qua non* of writing. If the Cypriot Syllabary is anything, it is a vocalic script. Every symbol in the system possesses a vowel component. The only symbols in the system which represent only a single sound—in alphabetic fashion—are the V characters, that is, the symbols with the syllabic values *a, e, i, o,* and *u.* Like numerous other orthographic features of the Greek alphabet, vowel characters are remnants of the previous writing tradition of the literate Greek adapters of the Phoenician script.

8.2 Homer and the Alphabet

8.2.1 Powell et al.

On occasion the idea has been advanced that the Greek alphabet was devised for the explicit purpose of graphically recording the Homeric epics. The most recent and expansive expositor of this notion is Powell,[13] prior to whom it was principally associated with Wade-Gery.[14] The idea has not gained widespread acceptance and suffers from some fairly obvious problems which have been pointed out by various reviewers of Powell's book. To begin with, that a writing system would be expressly engineered for such a high-minded and noble purpose as recording poetry and not for some baser, or at least broader, utilitarian end seems not altogether probable.[15] The level of improbability of such a motivation for the Greek alphabet reaches new heights when one considers this prospect in conjunction with the next wrinkle cited by reviewers: there would obviously be no one able to read the epics once they had been penned by Powell's adapter in his novel script.[16] The creator of the alphabet within such a scenario devised a writing system and with it wrote down the *Iliad* and the *Odyssey* for an audience which did not exist.[17]

Another oddity which arises from Powell's scenario has been addressed by Palaima. If the Greek alphabet was devised to record hexameter, then it is curious, notes Palaima, that provision was not made for distinguishing long vowels from short.[18] Vowel length is metrically crucial. I pointed out earlier that writing systems tend not to distinguish phonemically long vowels from their short counterparts. Yet if this writing system, the Greek alphabet, was manufactured for the express purpose of giving written expression to metrical speech, and only that, one might very well indeed expect vowel length to be indicated; this is especially so in the case of the long and short mid front vowels ([e:] and [e]) and the long and short mid back vowels ([o:] and [o]), which differ not only quantitatively but qualitatively as well, and which would eventually be distinguished orthographically (when η began to be used as a vowel character and ω was added to the end of the alphabet).

The origin of the Greek alphabet in the hands of Cypriot Greek scribes steeped in the orthographic tradition of the syllabic Cypriot script does not of necessity exclude the possibility that this new alphabetic system was devised solely for recording epic verse. However, the picture of professional scribes trained and accomplished in one writing tradition seizing feverishly upon the Phoenician script so that they might at long last be able to write down epic poetry is one which oscillates between the comic and the ludicrous. The Cypriot scribes perceived in the Phoenician script the potential for writing their own language with greater simplicity and elegance. This newly devised alphabetic script was no doubt utilized for recording the full range of materials which the adapters had heretofore written with their syllabic script, and it is likely that within this range was found verse.

8.2.2 Hexameter and the Cypriot Script

There is, in fact, one instance of hexameter which is preserved written in the syllabic Cypriot script. The inscription, *ICS* 264, is four lines in length, occurs on a votive relief recovered in 1870 at a temple site in Golgoi, and is dated to the fourth century B.C. Translation of the text presents difficulties.[19] In the course of defending his claim that the Greek alphabet was devised for recording Homer, Powell turns his attention to this document and accurately observes that "many of the difficulties in this text derive from our unfamiliarity with Cypriote dialect and are no different from those we face in reading a dialectal inscription in alphabetic writing."[20] However, he goes on to state:[21]

(1)   Yet while the Cypriote syllabary could in theory have served as a notation for someone familiar with the complexities of the Greek hexameter, and obviously these late hexameters were written down in it, too many uncertainties remain in the phonological information that this script communicates for the script ever to have served as a practical vehicle for recording ambitious poetic compositions. And it never did so serve.

In his provisional study of the uses of the Cypriot Syllabary, Palaima notes:[22]

(2)   A cursory survey of the uses of Cypriote Syllabic script demonstrated that the somewhat greater complexity of a syllabic form of writing did not present an insuperable hindrance in and of itself to broader applications of script or more widespread literacy.

He goes on to state that the Cypriot Syllabary "was a stream-lined (55–56 signs), consistent and efficient tool for writing . . . Greek."[23] The syllabic script of Cyprus was an effective means for recording the Greek language and, as such, could certainly be used for writing verse compositions.

Powell has confused language with script. These are two quite different phenomena, as I have pointed out already, which need to be strictly distinguished.[24] Language is biological; script is mechanical. Language is essential; script is its shadow. Any use of the Cypriot Syllabary as a "practical vehicle" assumes native competence in the Greek dialect of ancient Cyprus—that living linguistic entity in response to which the recording mechanism (i.e., the script) was devised. The script is servant of the language, not vice versa. Undoubtedly the reading of *ICS* 264 would be quite transparent and nonproblematic to a native speaker of the dialect of Greek spoken on Cyprus in the fourth century B.C. About the present spelling system of English, George Bernard Shaw wrote such things as

(3)   The English have no respect for their language. They cannot spell it because they have nothing to spell it with but an old foreign alphabet of which only the consonants—and not all of them—have any agreed speech value.[25]

and

(4)   They spell it so abominably that no man can teach himself what it sounds like. . . . German and Spanish are accessible to foreigners: English is not accessible even to Englishmen.[26]

To claim that the syllabic script of Cyprus was not "practical" for the recording of verse is little different than claiming that the present spelling system of English, phonetically obscure and highly conventionalized, is not a "practical vehicle" for recording rhyming couplets.

Powell's further claim that the syllabic Cypriot script *never* served as a "practical vehicle" for recording verse is unfounded. As he himself explicitly mentions in the context of this claim, the hexametric inscription of *ICS* 264 obviously does exist; the script's use here is in no sense *impractical.* While it is true that this is the only attested metrical inscription, it should be borne in mind that we must possess only a fraction of the total number of syllabic Cypriot inscriptions produced in antiquity,[27] and it is manifestly unlikely that we just happen to have preserved the only verse inscription ever written with this writing system.[28] That the inscription is "late," as Powell notes in his objection cited in (1), has nothing to do with the Cypriot script's practicality for recording verse.

8.2.3   Hexameter and Early Alphabetic Inscriptions

Powell and others have emphasized that hexametric verse is found frequently among the early Greek alphabetic inscriptions.[29] Commenting on this observation, however, Johnston notes:

(5)   Yet a good proportion of this early material is of a different nature; the simple statement of an owner's name is now better attested (a use also common in the near east), and the number of single letters (and non-alphabetic marks) on a good proportion of Pithekoussan amphorae also suggests proprietorial concern.[30]

Marking of ownership was also a principal use made of the syllabic Cypriot script; in fact, in Palaima's tentative statistical survey of trends in the uses of the Cypriot Syllabary (based upon datable texts), marking of ownership on vases is the single most common use of the script between the seventh and fourth centuries inclusively, with the exception of its extensive fourth-century employment for writing wall graffiti.[31] Recall that the earliest known instance of a syllabic Cypriot inscription is one which marks ownership, occurring on an eleventh-century bronze spit. The common proprietorial use of both the syllabic Cypriot script and the early alphabet could be only coincidental; possession is not only nine-tenths of the law but one of the most basic of human instincts. However, Johnston has further remarked that "the personal marking of property [is] frequent in the Phoenician area but not clearly demonstrated for pre-literate Greece."[32] Perhaps we find in the proprietorial use of the syllabic Cypriot script a bridge between Near Eastern and alphabetic Greek practice. One would reasonably expect that when the Cypriot Greek adapters of the Phoenician script began experimenting with their newly created alphabetic writing system, they utilized it for all of the various purposes for which the syllabic script was used, one of which was marking of ownership. When the alphabet went west, it was perhaps accompanied by the idea of using script proprietorially.

The vital connection between Homeric epic and the advent of the alphabet is essentially the opposite of that one promoted by Powell and his predecessors in this effort. The desire to write down Homer did not precipitate the creation of the Greek alphabet. Rather, the creation of the alphabet resulted in a writing down of Homeric verse. This latter statement of a relationship between epic and the alphabet could be assigned its quite trivial interpretation—obviously, neither epic nor anything else could be written down until there existed a system of symbols with which to accomplish such a recording. However, as I have suggested the recording of verse was not in all likelihood *first* achieved utilizing the alphabet.

While a dark age held sway over Greece proper, the Cypriot Greeks were basking in their latter-day Mycenaean or Homeric culture. In the halls of the palaces of the Cypriot kings, we expect that banqueters were entertained by oral poets who composed and recited verses drawn from the old stories about war and adventure, heroes and gods. Some, possibly many, of the verses produced by the Cypriot bards must at various times have been recorded by Cypriot scribes, perhaps by the bards themselves, using the syllabic script; again, much of this recording was likely done on perishable materials. When those scribes involved in the adaptation of the Phoenician script began to experiment with their alphabetic invention, among the old uses to which the new script was put was surely the recording of verse. As a part of the process of the exportation of the Cypriot alphabet westward, a tradition of written verse was likely introduced to the Greeks of the Aegean, a newly literate people who had become literate, however, not for the purpose of reading verse but, no doubt, for much more mundane and practical reasons. Perhaps then the very process of the alphabet's coming to Greece early on established a precedent for the alphabetic inscribing of verse, and for this reason many of our earliest alphabetic Greek inscriptions are hexametric.[33]

8.3 On the Transmission of the Alphabet to the West

In chapter 7, I made passing reference to the possibility that the new alphabetic script was carried out of Cyprus by merchants following the trade routes westward. The notion that traders played an important role in the early spread of the alphabet is not an infrequently encountered one,[34] and perhaps this was indeed one mechanism by which the alphabet was first introduced to points west of Cyprus. However, the establishment of the alphabetic tradition in the Aegean clearly involved more than simply a casual transmission through mercantile use.

8.3.1 Scribal Transmission

We have found that a continuous tradition of literacy links the Cypriot Syllabary with the Greek alphabet. This is a continuity, however, which goes beyond the matter of the presence in the alphabetic script of characters whose value was motivated within the syllabic Cypriot writing system, beyond the earliest alphabet's failure to distinguish graphically the bilabial and velar voiceless aspirated stops from their unaspirated counterparts, beyond the variable direction of writing displayed by early alphabetic inscriptions, and so forth.

In chapter 3 we examined the alphabetic inscriptional practice of word-division at line-end and the teachings of the Greek grammarians concerning so-called syllable-division, which is in fact not based upon syllable structure at all. The grammarians attempt to make sense of their "syllable-division" practices by positing that a syllable-boundary precedes any word-internal consonant cluster which is of a type capable of occurring in word-initial position (phonological and metrical evidence reveals, as we have seen, that in actuality a syllable-boundary generally occurs between the two members of a word-internal biconsonantal cluster, regardless of whether the cluster can occur word-initially or not). For the grammarians, word-internal clusters of the form *[s]* + *stop* prove, however, to be problematic. Though the cluster-type occurs word-initially, the grammarians are divided about whether the word-internal "syllabification" is -*$ [s] stop-*, as per their general rule of "syllable"-boundaries, or -*[s] $ stop-*, as if this cluster were unable to occur at the beginning of a word. A corresponding variation in word-division practice involving *[s]* + *stop* clusters is displayed in inscriptions.

We discovered that the grammatical dogma of syllable-division and the inscriptional word-division practices parallel the spelling of consonant sequences in the syllabic Cypriot script. Those word-internal cluster-types which are treated as tautosyllabic in the alphabetic tradition (but which are actually heterosyllabic) are the same cluster-types which the Cypriot scribes represent using the progressive spelling strategy ($<$-V_i-CV_j-CV_j->). Those types which are treated as heterosyllabic by the grammarians and alphabetic scribes (and which are, in fact, heterosyllabic) are the clusters the Cypriot scribes spell by utilizing the regressive spelling strategy ($<$-V_i-CV_i-CV_j->). In syllabic Cypriot orthography, that word-internal cluster whose division fomented controversy among the grammarians, *[s]* + *stop,* is represented with the regressive spelling technique, and so Cypriot practice agrees with that wing of the alphabetic tradition which advocates division between the [s] and the stop (i.e., -*[s] $ stop-*).

The idiosyncratic doctrine of "syllable-division" which is preached by the grammarians of Greece continues the consonant cluster spelling strategy of Cyprus. With the transition to an alphabetic writing system, what had been a strategy for the spelling of consonant sequences using CV symbols in a syllabic script was ultimately transformed into a strategy of word-division which, sooner or later, was construed as "syllable-division." In other words, what masquerades as a phonological principle of syllable structure in the works of the grammarians has as its historical antecedent a prealphabetic orthographic practice which is itself based upon the phonological phenomenon of relative sonority (a relationship which is formalized in the hierarchy of orthographic strength). As relative sonority intersects with syllable structure, we can see why the grammarians' analysis of Greek syllable structure looks almost right, but not quite.

Thus, not only did the new alphabetic writing system wash up on the shores of the Aegean Greek world, but so did Cypriot scribal strategy. Such a continuity of analytic tradition signals that the passage of the alphabet west from Cyprus was not simply a matter of passive transfer along trade routes at the hands of merchants. It was, at least in part, an active process effected by the movement of scribes out of Cyprus (possibly in response to the alphabet having gained some initial foothold in Greece?). These Cypriot émigrés established there the beginnings of an alphabetic scribal tradition.

8.3.2 Word-Division Further Considered

We also saw in chapter 3 that the Greek grammarians, in discoursing upon "syllable-structure," were able to generalize about *types of consonant clusters* which were capable of occurring at the beginning of a Greek word. Specific clusters which do not occur word-intially ([tʰm], [gd], etc.) but are of a *type* which does occur word-initially (*stop + nasal, stop + stop*, etc.) receive the same word-internal treatment (with regard to division) as clusters of the same type which do in fact occur word-initially ([pn], [kt], etc.). As I pointed out, in making such generalizations the grammarians were wielding the notion of *manner of articulation* (stop, nasal, etc.). The hierarchy of orthographic strength which the Cypriot scribes utilized (in whatever form) in determining how consonant clusters should be spelled is a hierarchy of articulatory manners:

(6)   *stop > fricative > nasal > glide > liquid*

This working knowledge of the concept of manners of articulation displayed by the Greek grammarians must also derive from grammatical knowledge brought by emigrating Cypriot scribes.

Now, the recognition of manners of articulation and their relative sonority is implicit in the word-division (called syllable-division) practice of the grammarians which we discussed immediately above, arising as it does out of a spelling strategy based upon the sonority hierarchy. However, recall that the grammarians' dictum for identifying syllable-boundaries is as follows: a syllable-boundary occurs before a word-internal cluster of a type which is capable of occurring word-initially. At some point, the concept of manners of articulation and their relative sonority (or orthographic strength) ceased to be the operative mechanism in word-division; and the scribes of the alphabetic tradition secondarily acquired the principle of word-division—identified as syllable-division—based upon analogy to word-initial position. It would be easy for such a reinterpretation of strategy to arise.

To see how a shift from a hierarchical strategy of alphabetic word-division to one based upon analogy to word-initial position occurred, let us first look again at the strategy utilized by the Cypriot scribes for spelling consonant clusters:

(7) If the first of two successive consonants occupies a position on the hierarchy [of (6)] which is higher than or equal to that of the second, then it will be written with the CV symbol whose vocalic component is identical to the vowel which follows the cluster; otherwise it will be written with the CV symbol whose vocalic component is identical to the vowel which precedes the cluster.

When (7) was adapted as an alphabetic principle of word-division, the result would have been something like the following:

(8) If the first of two successive consonants occupies a position on the hierarchy [of (6)] which is higher than or equal to that of the second, then word-division will occur before the cluster; otherwise word-division will occur between the two members of the cluster.[35]

For example, ἑπτά ([heptá], 'seven') is divided as ἑ-πτά, but ἔργον ([érgon], 'deed') is divided as ἔρ-γον. Usually sequences of consonants occurring at the beginning of a word are arranged according to progressively increasing, or at least equal, sonority. Hence, when a consonant cluster which is capable of occurring word-initially is found within the word, the word-division practice based on the sonority-dependent hierarchy of (6) and the strategy of (8) will usually divide the word *before* the cluster. Word-division was then eventually reinterpreted as a function of the ability of consonant clusters to occur word-initially.

One consonant cluster is problematic for the reinterpreted doctrine of "syllable-division": namely, the notorious fly-in-the-ointment sequence *[s]* + *stop*. This cluster does occur word-initially but is arranged according to *decreasing* rather than increasing sonority. How is the scribe to divide words with a word-internal *[s]* + *stop* cluster? By the Cypriot imported strategy of (8), word-division would occur between the [s] and the stop, since *fricative* occupies a position lower on the hierarchy of (6) than *stop*. However, once word-division is reinterpreted as based upon analogy to word-initial position, division is made *before* the fricative [s]. Recall that the grammarians are polarized over the proper division of word-internal *[s]* + *stop*—some say division should occur before the [s], some say after—and for this they are mocked by Sextus Empiricus. We can now see quite clearly why the grammarians are so divided: the inherited strategy with its roots firmly set in Cypriot syllabic orthography and the new reinterpreted strategy which is based upon analogy to word-initial position are at odds at this one point. Each strategy produces a different analysis, and this gives rise to the varying traditions concerning the division of word-internal *[s]* + *stop* clusters which are attested among the grammarians, as well as in inscriptions.[36]

Variation is also exhibited in the alphabetic scribal division of word-internal [-sm-] clusters, as we have seen ([-$sm-] versus [-s$m-]). This variation did not arise from a variable treatment in the syllabic Cypriot system, where *fricative* + *nasal* clusters are spelled progressively both word-initially and word-internally. Instead, the deviation found within the alphabetic tradition must be the result of [-sm-] sequences having been drawn into the disagreement over the phonetically quite similar *[s]* + *stop* clusters.

8.4 Parting Words

Having come to a place very near to that one at which I began, my study is concluded. My arguments have demanded the reader's attention; I hope, however, that they have not been found too wearisome. Thank you for your patience. Look to Cyprus.

Notes

1. See S. Katre, 1987, *Aṣṭādhyāyī of Pāṇini* (Austin: University of Texas Press), p. xix.

2. W. Watt, 1989, "The Ras Shamra Matrix," *Semiotica* 74:61–108.

3. Referring to the utilization of the sonority hierarchy in both Mycenaean and Cypriot syllabic spelling, I wrote in Woodard 1994 (p. 330): "[T]he existence of such a tradition would suggest that in the second millennium there lived some scribal figure, or figures, of acute linguistic awareness—a scribal master who, like Pāṇini, . . . was capable of bringing significant analytic abilities to bear on the analysis of language." Commenting on this observation, Watt (1994, "Introduction: Part 2" in *Writing Systems and Cognition,* ed. W. Watt (Dordrecht: Kluwer Academic), p. 109) noted: "Since it is now established that a similar genius organized the Ugaritic or Canaanite alphabet so as to reflect similar insights, at about the same time . . . , it must now be a matter of lively curiosity whether the two ancient linguistic traditions—both preceding Pāṇini and the Sanskrit phonologists by about a millennium—were in any way related."

4. As Thomas Palaima has kindly emphasized to me.

5. Palaima, however, contends that scripts cannot be convincingly linked on the basis of direction of writing (personal communication and Palaima 1988:310–313).

6. Except for historical linguists.

7. See, *inter alios,* E. Havelock, 1986, "Orality, Literacy, and Star Wars," *Written Communication* 3/4:411–420; 1982, *The Literate Revolution in Greece and Its Cultural Consequences* (Princeton: Princeton University Press); M. McLuhan, 1962, *The Gutenberg Galaxy* (Toronto: University of Toronto Press).

8. See the insightful remarks concerning this matter in F. Coulmas, 1989, *The Writing Systems of the World* (Cambridge: Basil Blackwell), pp. 159–162.

9. As in the *a*-stems, in which case only the genitive and dative plural are orthographically distinct from the remaining forms of the paradigm (Palaima, personal communication).

10. The breadth of ambiguity would have been even greater prior to the introduction of distinct symbols for the velar and bilabial stop consonants $[k^h]$ and $[p^h]$.

11. Though perhaps in rapid reading, such determination would not actually be made; see the brief discussion of this matter in Sampson 1985:89–90.

12. This is not to claim that a consonantal script is necessarily *as efficient* for writing Semitic as one which includes vowel characters. On the shortcomings which he perceives to exist in the Hebrew and Arabic scripts (not all of which are the result of

the nonrepresentation of vowels), see ibid., pp. 89–98. In Sampson's opinion (p. 98), "it does seem fair to describe the traditional standard Hebrew script as a relatively cumbersome writing system"!

13. Powell 1991.

14. H. Wade-Gery, 1952, *The Poet of the Iliad* (Cambridge: Cambridge University Press), pp. 11–14. I mentioned in chapter 7 (n. 110) that the idea has also been advocated by Robb; see the discussion at that point. Subsequent to the publication of Powell 1991, however, Robb has sought to distinguish his own position from Powell's (as well as Wade-Gery's): "An important difference between us is that I have defended the inscriptional uses of the alphabet as being primary, whereas Wade-Gery and Powell have not. As a result, I suggested that the first 'texts' ran to a few hexameters at most, not a monumental Homer" (Robb 1994:265). See also A. Snodgrass, 1980, *Archaic Greece: The Age of Experiment* (London: J. M. Dent and Sons), pp. 82–83.

15. On this point, see, for example, the comments of H. Lloyd-Jones, 1992, "Becoming Homer," *The New York Review,* March 5, p. 56. Palaima (1990/91, "Review of Powell," *Minos* 25/26:446–447) writes of "Powell's idiosyncratic explanation" and quotes from the review by J. Hooker (1991, "The Earliest Writers in Europe," *Times Literary Supplement,* June 14, p. 29), who labels Powell's hypothesis as a "scarcely credible theory." The idea is equally dubious if the motivation for recording the poems is claimed to be one of elite class politics; see I. Morris, 1986, "The Use and Abuse of Homer," *Classical Antiquity* 5:122–127.

16. See, for example, Lloyd-Jones 1992:56.

17. Powell makes much of the fact that the Greek adapter of the Phoenician script was, by his reckoning, a single individual: "The Greek alphabet seems to have originated in a single place at a single time, invented by a single man" (1991:66). There must have been some moment in time when the very first spark of the idea of using the Phoenician script for writing Greek entered into the mind of some one person; this is probably the only sense in which we can meaningfully speak of a single individual being responsible for the Greek alphabet. Who made what contributions of experimentation and development beyond this moment is an indeterminable matter. It is possible that a single scribe was responsible for the bulk of the work, but some sort of collaborative scribal effort could certainly not be ruled out; recall that we suggested a scenario by which certain variations in the structure of the Greek alphabet could be reasonably accounted for as early modifications of the new script by various Cypriot scribes or scribal groups.

18. Palaima 1990/91:448.

19. See Masson 1983:284–286; also G. Neumann and K. Stiewe, 1974, "Zu den Hexametern der kyprischen Inschrift ICS 264," *Kadmos* 13:146–155. Making reference to this inscription, Ventris and Chadwick (*Docs.:*27) write: "The inherent difficulty of reading these ancient [Linear B] syllabic texts can be appreciated by comparing the results achieved on the classical Cypriot inscriptions. . . . Though written in a known Greek dialect and in a syllabary whose values have been established since the 1870's, many of them are still as full of uncertainties as, for instance, the notorious Golgoi inscription."

20. Powell 1991:113.

21. Ibid.

22. Palaima 1991:459.

23. Ibid., p. 464.

24. This is obviously not to say that there is no language-script interface. I have argued above that orthography can and does turn to its own use elements of linguistic structure.

25. B. Shaw, 1957, "Preface to Pygmalion," in *Androcles and the Lion, Overruled, Pygmalion,* rev. ed. (London: Constable and Company), p. 195.

26. B. Shaw, 1948, "Preface to Pygmalion," in *Selected Plays of Bernard Shaw,* vol. 1 (New York: Dodd, Mead and Company), p. 191.

27. On the evidence for the use of the Cypriot script with perishable materials, see Palaima 1991:46.

28. We have not even touched on the matter of the "social utility" of a script. Watt (1994:89) writes: "The harder a language's writing-system is to gain control of, the greater is its social utility: Chinese is very high on this dimension; Spanish, whose 'phonemic' spelling borders on one-to-one, is very low. English falls somewhere in between."

29. See especially Powell's summarizing comments on pp. 181–186.

30. Johnston 1983:67. Johnston is responding to claims made by Robb and Heubeck which are similar to Powell's Homeric hypothesis, as noted above.

31. Palaima 1991:470. In the third century the chief use of the syllabary is for inscribing dedications on ceramic vases; these are actually the only third-century occurrences of the script in Palaima's survey, with the exception of Nubian wall graffiti dated fourth/third century.

32. Johnston 1983:67.

33. In his recent article "The Rise of the Greek Epic" (1988, *JHS* 108:173–182), M. West notes that the route by which the Near Eastern elements of Homeric epic were transmitted from southwest Asia to the Aegean (to Euboea for West) must have passed through Cyprus (p. 170). He proposes that these oriental traditions were introduced into Greek epic by "bilingual poets, probably easterners who had settled in Greece and learned to compose epic in the Greek manner" (p. 171). In light of our findings, it is likely that at least some of these easterners were Cypriot Greeks who in Cyprus were already "composing in the epic manner" and who brought their compositions with them to Greece. West further states in regard to these figures that "we need not necessarily set up a separate category of poets. Even a priest or a jeweller might learn how to compose hexameter verse" (p. 172). To this list of potentials I would append "scribe" (on which see further discussion later).

34. See, for example, Jeffery 1990:41: "It is a reasonable assumption that the spread of the local scripts should correspond with what we know of inter-state trade-connexions in the late eighth and early seventh centuries; but in our present state of knowledge it is risky to press conclusions of this kind."

35. We will not at present concern ourselves with clusters of more than two consonants.

36. Note that such variation in the alphabetic division of word-internal *[s] + stop* clusters would not have been precipitated by the Linear B strategy of spelling consonant clusters, as in this system, unlike the Cypriot Syllabary, *[s] + stop* sequences are spelled alike word-initially and word-internally. On the basis of Threatte's study reported in section 3.3.1, it would appear that the "syllable-division" doctrine espoused by the grammarians was not widely incorporated into Athenian inscriptional practice until the third century B.C., and thus that variant scribal traditions of word-division at line-end are suggested.

Phonetic Glossary

Figures G.1 and G.2 follow the terms in the glossary.

aspirated stop   a stop consonant whose articulation is accompanied by a marked rush of air (prolonged voicelessness), as in English *p*ie ([pʰ]) versus English *s*py ([p])

continuant   a sound produced without a complete obstruction of the airflow passing through the vocal tract, that is, sounds other than stops and affricates

emphatic   cover term referring to consonants occurring in various Afro-Asiatic languages; such consonants have been phonetically described as glottalized, velarized or pharyngealized

glottalization   term sometimes used to refer to the articulation of ejective consonants: such sounds are produced by closing the glottis (the opening between the vocal cords in the larynx) and then forcefully ejecting air out of the mouth by raising the larynx

heterosyllabic   occurring within separate syllables

manner of articulation   term referring to the major classes of consonants, as identified, ideally, by the nature of the articulatory movements involved in production of such consonants:

> *stop*—sound produced by completely occluding the airflow passing through the vocal tract: Greek [p], [t], [k] (voiceless); [pʰ], [tʰ], [kʰ] (voiceless aspirated); [b], [d], [g] (voiced)
>
> *fricative*—sound produced by partially occluding the airflow passing through the vocal tract; occlusion is sufficient to create friction: Greek [s], [h]
>
> *affricate*—sound which consists of a stop followed immediately by a homorganic fricative (i.e. a fricative produced at essentially the same posi-

263

tion in the oral tract as the stop which it follows): for example, [tˢ] as in German *Zipfel*, 'tassel'

nasal—sound which is similar to a stop but characterized by a continuous flow of air through the nasal cavity: Greek [m], [n], [ŋ]

liquid—nondescriptive term for consonantal sounds such as Greek [l] and [r]

glide—sound such as Proto-Greek *[y] and Greek [w]; also called *semi-vowel*

obstruents   class of consonants consisting of stops, affricates, and fricatives; as opposed to sonorants

pharyngealized   a secondary articulation effected by constricting the pharynx: essentially involves the articulation of some consonant (the primary articulation) while the tongue and throat are held in the position that they would occupy when producing the vowel [a] (Ladefoged 1993)

place of articulation   term referring to the position within the vocal tract at which articulatory organs are moved in the production of a consonant; the places of articulation of ancient Greek can be broadly identified as follows:

bilabial—[p], [pʰ], [b], [m]

dental—[t], [tʰ], [d], [s]/[z], [n], [l], [r]; some Greek dialects possessed at an early time a fricative [θ] (not to be confused with the Greek alphabetic character *θ*), as in English *teeth*; [θ] is often identified as *interdental* (produced by placing the tongue *between* the upper and lower teeth)

velar—[k], [kʰ], [g], [ŋ]

labiovelar (coarticulation at the bilabial and velar positions)—[w] and early Greek [kʷ], [kʷʰ], [gʷ]

glottal—[h]

sibilant   a fricative which is characterized by high pitch and high acoustic energy (e.g., [s]) or an affricate whose fricative component is of this sort

sonorants   class of consonants consisting of nasals, liquids and glides; as opposed to obstruents

tautosyllabic   occurring within a single syllable

velarization   a secondary articulation effected by raising the back portion of the tongue: essentially involves the articulation of some consonant (the primary articulation) while the tongue is held in the position that it would occupy when producing the vowel [u] (Ladefoged 1993)

voiceless   a sound articulated without accompanying vibration of the vocal cords: for example, [t], [s]

voiced   a sound articulated with accompanying vibration of the vocal cords: for example, [d], [z]

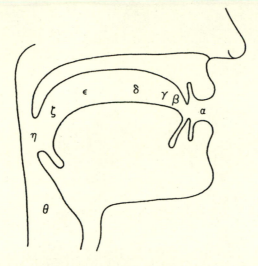

FIGURE G.1 Places of articulation: α bilabial, β dental, γ palato-alveolar, δ palatal, ϵ velar, ζ uvular, η pharyngeal, and θ glottal.

Greek Symbol	Phonetic Transcription	Phonetic Description
α	[a]/[a:]	short and long low central vowels
β	[b]	voiced bilabial stop
γ	[g]	voiced velar stop
δ	[d]	voiced dental stop
ϵ	[e]	short mid front vowel
ζ	[zd]	[z] + [d]
η	[ẹ:]	long lower mid front vowel
θ	[tʰ]	voiceless aspirated dental stop
ι	[i]/[i:]	short and long high front vowels
κ	[k]	voiceless velar stop
λ	[l]	voiced dental lateral liquid
μ	[m]	voiced bilabial nasal
ν	[n]	voiced dental nasal
ξ	[ks]	[k] + [s]
o	[o]	short mid back vowel
π	[p]	voiceless bilabial stop
ρ	[r]	voiced dental liquid
σ	[s]	voiceless dental fricative
τ	[t]	voiceless dental stop
υ	[ü]/[ü:]	short and long high front rounded vowels
ϕ	[pʰ]	voiceless aspirated bilabial stop
χ	[kʰ]	voiceless aspirated velar stop
ψ	[ps]	[p] + [s]
ω	[ǫ:]	long lower mid back vowel

In addition

$\epsilon\iota$	[ẹ:]	long upper mid front vowel
$o\upsilon$	[u:]	long high back vowel
‘	[h]	voiceless glottal fricative

FIGURE G.2 Phonetic exposition of Greek alphabetic characters

Symbols

[ ]	phonetic transcription
/ /	phonemic representation
< >	orthographic representation
#	word boundary
$	syllable boundary
[+]	morpheme boundary
. . .] + [. . .	indicates juxtaposition of two sounds
¢	clitic boundary
[ ]	restoration of inscription
e-ṣọ-lo	inscriptional reading marked by subscript dot is uncertain
[V:]	long vowel (in phonetic transcription)

References

Albright, W. 1961. "The Role of the Canaanites in the History of Civilization." In *The Bible and the Ancient Near East,* edited by G. Wright, pp. 328–362. Garden City, N.Y.: Doubleday.

Allen, W. 1987. "The Development of the Attic Vowel System: Conspiracy or Catastrophe?" *Minos* 20–22:21–32.

———. 1978. *Vox Latina.* 2nd ed. Cambridge: Cambridge University Press.

———. 1974. *Vox Graeca.* 2nd ed. Cambridge: Cambridge University Press.

———. 1973. *Accent and Rhythm.* Cambridge: Cambridge University Press.

———. 1957. "Some Problems of Palatalization in Greek." *Lingua* 7:113–133.

Anderson, J., and C. Jones. 1977. *Phonological Structure and the History of English.* Amsterdam: North-Holland.

———. 1974. "Three Theses Concerning Phonological Representations." *JL* 10:1–26.

Arena, R. 1972. "Greco ὄμβρικος : βάκχος e miceneo *o-mi-ri-jo-i.*" *Minos* 13:182–191.

Aura Jorro, F. 1985–1993. *Diccionario micénico.* 2 vols. Madrid: Instituto de Filología.

Baurain, C. 1984. *Chypre et la Méditerranée orientale au Bronze Récent.* Athens: École Française.

Beekes, R. 1971. "The Writing of Consonant Groups in Mycenaean." *Mnemosyne* 24:337–357.

Bekker, I., ed. 1814–1821. *Anecdota Graeca.* 3 vols. Berlin: Reimer.

Bennett, E., Jr., ed. 1964. *Mycenaean Studies.* Madison: University of Wisconsin Press.

Bernal, M. 1990. *Cadmean Letters: The Transmission of the Alphabet to the Aegean and Further West Before 1400* B.C. Winona Lake, Ind.: Eisenbrauns.

Bhat, D. 1978. "A General Study of Palatalization." In *Universals of Human Language,* edited by J. Greenberg, vol. 2, pp. 47–92. Stanford: Stanford University Press.

Bile, M. 1988. *Le dialecte crétois ancien.* Athens: École Française.

Billigmeier, J.-C. 1978. "The Origin of the Dual Reflex of Initial Consonantal Indo-European *y in Greek." *JIES* 4:221–231.

Boardman, J. 1980. *The Greeks Overseas.* London: Thames and Hudson.

Boardman, J., J. Griffen, and O. Murray. 1986. *The Oxford History of the Classical World.* Oxford: Oxford University Press.

Bonfante, G., and L. Bonfante, 1983. *The Etruscan Language.* New York: New York University Press.

Bonfante, L. 1990. "Etruscan." In *Reading the Past,* pp. 321–378. Introduction by J. Hooker. Berkeley: University of California Press.

Browning, R. 1983. *Medieval and Modern Greek.* 2nd ed. Cambridge: Cambridge University Press.

Brixhe, C. 1982. "Palatalisations en grec et en phrygien." *BSL* 77:209–249.

————. 1976. *Le dialecte grec de Pamphylie.* Paris: A. Maisonneuve.

————. 1975 [1977]. Review of *Note linguistiche a proposito delle tavole di Eraclea,* by Renato Arena. *Kratylos* 20:59–67.

Buck, C. 1955. *The Greek Dialects.* Chicago: University of Chicago Press.

————. 1933. *Comparative Grammar of Greek and Latin.* Chicago: University of Chicago Press.

————. 1904. *A Grammar of Oscan and Umbrian.* Boston: Ginn and Company.

Buck, C., and W. Petersen. 1945. *A Reverse Index of Greek Nouns and Adjectives.* Chicago: University of Chicago Press.

Burkert, W. 1992. *The Orientalizing Revolution.* Cambridge: Harvard University Press.

Carpenter, R. 1938. "The Greek Alphabet Again." *AJA* 42:58–69.

————. 1933. "The Antiquity of the Greek Alphabet." *AJA* 37:8–29.

Catling, H. 1975. "Cyprus in the Late Bronze Age." In *CAH,* 3rd ed., edited by I. Edwards et al., vol. 2, part 2, pp. 188–216, Cambridge: Cambridge University Press.

Chadwick, J. 1990. "Linear B and Related Scripts." In *Reading the Past,* pp. 137–195. Introduction by J. Hooker. Berkeley: University of California Press.

————. 1979. "The Minoan Origin of the Classical Cypriot Script." In *Acts of the International Archaeological Symposium "The Relations Between Cyprus and Crete, ca. 2000–500 B.C.,"* pp. 139–143. Nicosia: Nicolaou and Sons.

————. 1969. "Greek and Pre-Greek." *TPS,* pp. 80–98.

————. 1967. "Mycenaean *pa-wo-ke.*" *Minos* 8:115–117.

————. 1964. Review of *The Interpretation of Mycenaean Greek Texts,* by L. Palmer. *Gnomon* 36:321–327.

————. 1958. *The Decipherment of Linear B.* Cambridge: Cambridge University Press.

Chantraine, P. 1984. *Morphologie historique du grec.* 2nd ed. Paris: Klincksieck.

————. 1968. *Dictionnaire étymologique de la langue grecque: Histoire des mots.* Paris: Klincksieck.

————. 1966. "Finales mycéniennes en *-iko.*" In *Proceedings of the Cambridge Colloquium on Mycenaean Studies,* edited by L. Palmer and J. Chadwick, pp. 161–179. Cambridge: Cambridge University Press.

Clements, G. 1992. "The Sonority Cycle and Syllable Organization." In *Phonologica 1988,* edited by W. Dressler, H. Luschützky, O. Pfeiffer, and J. Rennison, pp. 63–76. Cambridge: Cambridge University Press.

Coldstream, J. 1989. "Early Greek Visitors to Cyprus and the Eastern Mediterranean." In *Cyprus and the East Mediterranean in the Iron Age,* edited by V. Tatton-Brown, pp. 90–96. London: British Museum.

————. 1977. *Geometric Greece.* London: Ernest Benn Ltd.

Collinge, N. 1985. *The Laws of Indo-European.* Philadelphia: John Benjamins.

Comrie, B., ed. 1987. *The World's Major Languages.* New York: Oxford University Press.

Consbruch, M., ed. 1971. *Hephaestionis Enchiridion.* Leipzig: Teubner.

Coulmas, F. 1989. *The Writing Systems of the World.* Cambridge: Basil Blackwell.

Cowgill, W. 1966. "Ancient Greek Dialectology in the Light of Mycenaean." In *Ancient Indo-European Dialects,* edited by H. Birnbaum and J. Puhvel, pp. 77–95. Berkeley: University of California Press.

Cowgill, W., and M. Mayrhofer. 1986. *Indogermanische Grammatik.* Vol. 1. Heidelberg: Carl Winter.

Cross, F. 1980. "Newly Found Inscriptions in Old Canaanite and Early Phoenician Scripts." *BASOR* 238:1–20.

———. 1979. "Early Alphabetic Scripts." In *Symposia Celebrating the Seventy-Fifth Anniversary of the Founding of the American Schools of Oriental Research I,* edited by F. Cross, pp. 105–111. Cambridge: American Schools of Oriental Research.

Crothers, J., J. Lorentz, D. Sherman, and M. Vihman, comps. and eds. 1979. "Handbook of Phonological Data from a Sample of the World's Languages: A Report of the Stanford Phonology Archive." 2 vols. Stanford: Stanford University Department of Linguistics.

Cunliffe, B. 1994. *The Oxford Illustrated Prehistory of Europe.* Oxford: Oxford University Press.

Cunningham, A. 1969. *Coins of Alexander's Successors in the East.* Chicago: Argonaut. Reprint of 1884 edition.

Daniels, P., and W. Bright. 1996. *The World's Writing Systems.* Oxford: Oxford University Press.

Demsky, A. 1977. "A Proto-Canaanite Abecedary Dating from the Period of the Judges and Its Implications for the History of the Alphabet." *Tel Aviv* 4:14–27.

Devine, A., and L. Stephens. 1994. *The Prosody of Greek Speech.* Oxford: Oxford University Press.

Dickenson, O. 1994. *The Aegean Bronze Age.* Cambridge: Cambridge University Press.

Doria, M. 1968. "Strumentali, ablatavi e dativi plurali in miceneo alcune precisazioni." In *Atti e memorie del 1° Congresso Internazionale di Micenologie 2,* pp. 764–780. Rome: Edizioni dell'Ateneo.

———. 1965. *Avviamento allo studio del miceneo.* Rome: Edizioni dell' Ateneo.

Driver, G. 1976. *Semitic Writing.* Revised by S. Hopkins. Oxford: Oxford University Press.

Duhoux, Y. 1989. "Le linéaire A: Problèmes de déchiffrement." In Y Duhoux et al. 1989:59–120.

———. 1985. "Mycénien et écriture grecque." In *Linear B: A 1984 Survey,* edited by A. Morpurgo Davies and Y. Duhoux, pp. 7–74. Louvain-la-Neuve: Cabay.

———. 1982. *L' Etéocrétois.* Amsterdam: J. C. Gieben.

———. 1981. "Les Etéocrétois et l'origine de l'alphabet grec." *L'antiquité classique* 50:287–294.

Duhoux, Y., ed. 1978. *Études minoennes I: Le linéaire A.* Louvain: Éditions Peeters.

Duhoux, Y., T. Palaima, and J. Bennet, eds. 1989. *Problems in Decipherment.* Louvain-La-Neuve: Peeters.

Dunkel, G. 1981. "Mycenaean *KE-KE-ME-NA, KI-TI-ME-NA.*" *Minos* 17:18–29.

Dupont-Sommer, A. 1970. "Une inscription phénicienne archaique récemment trouvé à Kition." *Mémoires de l'Académie des Inscriptions et Belles Lettres* 44:15–28.

Friedrich, J. 1989. *Extinct Languages.* Translated by F. Gaynor. New York: Dorset Press. Reprint of 1957 edition.

———. 1966. *Geschichte der Schrift.* Heidelberg: Carl Winter.

————. 1954. *Entzifferung verschollener Schriften und Sprachen.* Berlin: Springer Verlag.

Fry, D. 1979. *The Physics of Speech.* Cambridge: Cambridge University Press.

Gallavotti, C. 1964. "Le grafie del wau nella scrittura micenea." In Bennett 1964:57–65.

————. 1956. *Documenti e struttura del greco nell'età micenea.* Rome: Edizioni dell' Ateneo.

Gardner, P. 1966. *The Coins of the Greek and Scythian Kings of Bactria and India in the British Museum.* Edited by R. Poole. Chicago: Argonaut.

Gelb, I. 1963. *A Study of Writing.* 2nd ed. Chicago: University of Chicago Press.

Godart, L. 1976. "La scrittura lineare A." *La parola del passato* 31:31–47.

Guarducci, M. 1978. "La culla dell'alfabeto greco." *Rendiconti dell'Accademia nazionale dei Lincei* 33:381–388.

————. 1967. *Epigraphia greca, I.* Rome: Istituto Poligrafico dello Stato.

————. 1964. "Appunti di epigrafia greca arcaica." Review of *The Local Scripts of Archaic Greece,* 1st ed., by L. Jeffery. *Archeologia classica* 16:122–153.

————. 1952–1954. "Iscrizioni vascolari arcaiche da Phaistos." *Annuario Scuola Atene* 30–32:167–173.

Hallager, E., M. Vlasakis, and B. Hallager. 1992. "New Linear B Tablets from Khania." *Kadmos* 31:61–87.

————. 1990. "The First Linear B Tablet(s) from Khania." *Kadmos* 29:24–34.

Halle, M. 1971. "Word Boundaries as Environments in Rules." *LI* 2:540–541.

Hamp, E. 1982. "On Greek ζ : *y-." *JIES* 10:190–191.

Hankamer, J. and J. Aissen. 1974. "The Sonority Hierarchy." In *Papers from the Parasession on Natural Phonology,* pp. 131–145. Chicago: Chicago Linguistic Society.

Harris, Z. 1936. *A Grammar of the Phoenician Language.* New Haven: American Oriental Society.

Havelock, E. 1986. "Orality, Literacy, and Star Wars." *Written Communication* 3/4:411–420.

————. 1982. *The Literate Revolution in Greece and Its Cultural Consequences.* Princeton: Princeton University Press.

Herbert, R., and N. Poppe. 1963. *Kirghiz Manual.* Indiana University Uralic and Altaic Series, no. 33. Bloomington: Indiana University Press.

Hermann, E. 1923. *Silbenbildung im Griechischen.* Göttingen: Vandenhoeck und Ruprecht.

————. 1908. "Zur kyprischen Silbenschrift." *IF* 19:240–249.

Hetzron, R. 1987a. "Afroasiatic Languages." In Comrie 1987:645–653.

————. 1987b. "Hebrew." In Comrie 1987:686–704.

Heubeck, A. 1986. "Die Würzburger Alphabettafel," *Würzburger Jahrbücher für die Altertumswissenschaft Neue Folge* 12:7–20.

————. 1979. *Schrift.* Göttingen: Vandenhoeck und Ruprecht.

————. 1971. "Zur s- und z- Reihe in Linear B." *Kadmos* 10:111–124.

————. 1970. "Nochmal zu griech. –μρ–/–μβρ–." *Glotta* 48:67–71.

————. 1966. *Aus der Welt der frühgriechischen Lineartafeln.* Göttingen: Vandenhoeck und Ruprecht.

Hoffmann, O. 1891. *Die griechischen Dialekte.* Vol. 1. *Der südachäische Dialekt.* Göttingen: Vandenhoeck und Ruprecht.

Hooker, J. 1991. "The Earliest Writers in Europe." *Times Literary Supplement,* June 14, p. 29.

Hooper, J. 1976. *An Introduction to Natural Generative Phonology.* New York: Academic Press.

Householder, F. 1964. "A Morphophonemic Question and a Spelling Rule." In Bennett 1964:71–76.

Hughes, D. 1991. *Human Sacrifice in Ancient Greece.* London: Routledge.

Huld, M. 1980. "The Oldest Greek Sound-Change." *AJP* 101:324–330.

Jeffery, L. 1990. *The Local Scripts of Archaic Greece.* Rev. ed. Supplement by A. Johnston. Oxford: Oxford University Press.

Jeffery, L., and A. Morpurgo Davies. 1970. "*ΠΟΙΝΙΚΑΣΤΑΣ* and *ΠΟΙΝΙΚΑΖΕΝ:* BM 1969. 4—2.1, A New Archaic Inscription from Crete." *Kadmos* 9:118–156.

Johnston, A. 1983. "The Extent and Use of Literacy; the Archaeological Evidence." In *The Greek Renaissance of the Eighth Century* B.C.: Tradition and Innovation, edited by R. Hägg, pp. 63–68. Stockholm: Svenska Institutet i Athen.

Justeson, J. 1988. Review of *Writing Systems,* by G. Sampson. *Language* 64:421–425.

———. 1976. "Universals of Language and Universals of Writing." In *Linguistic Studies Offered to Joseph Greenberg on the Occasion of His Sixtieth Birthday,* edited by A. Juilland, vol. 1, pp. 57–94. Saratoga, Calif.: Anma Libri.

Justeson, J., and L. Stephens. 1981. "Nasal + Obstruent Clusters in Hittite." *JAOS* 101:367–370.

———. "Syllable and Script: A Typological Study." Unpublished monograph.

Karageorghis, V. 1987. "Western Cyprus at the Close of the Late Bronze Age." In Rupp 1987b:115–119.

———. 1984. "New Light on Late Bronze Age Cyprus." In Karageorghis and Muhly 1984:19–22.

———. 1983. *Palaepaphos-Skales: An Iron Age Cemetery in Cyprus.* Konstanz: Universitätsverlag Konstanz.

———. 1982a. *Cyprus: From the Stone Age to the Romans.* London: Thames and Hudson.

———. 1982b. "Cyprus." In *CAH,* 2nd ed., edited by J. Boardman et al., vol. 3, part 1, pp. 511–533. Cambridge: Cambridge University Press.

———. 1976. *Kition: Mycenaean and Phoenician Discoveries in Cyprus.* London: Thames and Hudson.

———. 1973. *Excavations in the Necropolis of Salamis III.* Vol. 5, part 1. Nicosia: Department of Antiquities.

———. 1969. *Salamis in Cyprus: Homeric, Hellenistic and Roman.* London: Thames and Hudson.

———. 1967. "Homerica from Salamis (Cyprus)." In *Europa: Festschrift Ernst Grumach,* edited by W. Brice, pp. 167–171. Berlin: DeGruyter.

———. 1962. "Notes on Some Mycenaean Survivals in Cyprus during the First Millennium B.C." *Kadmos* 1:71–77.

Karageorghis, V., and J. Muhly, eds. 1984. *Cyprus at the Close of the Late Bronze Age.* Nicosia: A. G. Leventis Foundation.

Katre, S. 1987. *Aṣṭādhyāyī of Pāṇini.* Austin: University of Texas Press.

Kaufman, S. 1982. "Reflections on the Assyrian-Aramaic Bilingual from Tell Fakhariyeh." *Maarav* 3:137–175.

Kaye, A. 1987. "Arabic." In Comrie 1987:664–685.

Kent, R. 1953. *Old Persian.* New Haven: American Oriental Society.

Killen, J. 1985. "New Readings in the Linear B Tablets from Knossos." *Kadmos* 24: 26–33.

———. 1979. "The Knossos Ld(1) Tablets." In *Colloquium Mycenaeum: Actes du six-*

ième Colloque International sur les textes mycéniens et égéens, edited by E. Risch and H. Mühlestein, pp. 151–181. Geneva: Université de Neuchâtel.

Kirchhoff, A. 1970. *Studien zur Geschichte des griechischen Alphabets.* 4th ed. Amsterdam: J. C. Gieben.

Krause, W. 1920. "Zum Aussprache des *q* im gortynischen." *KZ* 49:121–126.

Kurylowicz, J. 1968. *Indogermanische Grammatik.* Vol. 2. Heidelberg: Carl Winter.

———. 1958. *L'accentuation des langues indo-européennes.* Kraków: Wroclaw.

———. 1948. "Contribution à la théorie de la syllabe." *Bulletin de la société polonaise de linguistique* 8:80–114.

Labov, W. 1981. "Resolving the Neo-Grammarian Controversy." *Language* 57:267–308.

Ladefoged, P. 1993. *A Course in Phonetics.* 3rd ed. Fort Worth: Harcourt Brace Jovanovich.

———. 1975. *A Course in Phonetics.* New York: Harcourt Brace Jovanovich.

———. 1962. *Elements of Acoustic Phonetics.* Chicago: University of Chicago Press.

Lambdin, T. 1962. "Alphabet." In *The Interpreter's Dictionary of the Bible,* vol. 1, pp. 89–96. New York: Abingdon.

Larfeld, W. 1914. *Griechische Epigraphik.* 3rd ed. Munich: C. H. Beck'sche Verlagsbuchhandlung.

Lass, R. 1971. "Boundaries as Obstruents: Old English Voicing Assimilation and Universal Strength Hierarchies." *JL* 7:15–30.

Lattimore, R., trans. 1965. *The Odyssey of Homer.* New York: Harper Collins.

———, trans. 1951. *The Iliad of Homer.* Chicago: University of Chicago Press.

Laver, J. 1994. *Principles of Phonetics.* Cambridge: Cambridge University Press.

Lehman, W. 1955. *Proto-Indo-European Phonology.* Austin: University of Texas Press.

Lejeune, M. 1982. *Phonétique historique du mycénien et du grec ancien.* Paris: Klincksieck.

———. 1971. *Mémoires de philologie mycénienne.* Vol. 2. Rome: Edizioni dell'Ateneo.

———. 1960. "Essais de philologie mycénienne v 1." *RP* 34:9–30.

———. 1958. *Mémoires de philologie mycénienne.* Vol. 1. Paris: Centre National de la Recherche Scientifique.

———. 1954. "Observations sur le cypriote." *BSL* 50:68–75.

Lejeune, M., ed. 1956. *Études mycéniennes.* Paris: Centre National de la Recherche Scientifique.

Lentz, A., ed. 1867–1868. *Grammatici Graeci.* Part 3, vols. 1–2. Leipzig: Teubner.

Lipinski, E. 1988. "Les Phéniciens et l'alphabet." *Oriens Antiquus* 27:231–260.

Lloyd-Jones, H. 1992. "Becoming Homer." *The New York Review,* March 5, pp. 52–57.

Masson, E. 1977. "Présence éventuelle de la langue hourrite sur les tablettes chyprominoennes d'Enkomi." *Revue roumaine de linguistique* 22:483–488.

———. 1974. *Cyprominoica.* Göteborg: Paul Åströms Forlag.

———. 1973. "La diffusion de l'écriture à la fin de l'âge du Bronze." In *Acts of the International Archaeological Symposium "The Mycenaeans in the Eastern Mediterranean,"* pp. 88–100. Nicosia: Zavallis Press.

Masson, O. 1983. *Les inscriptions chypriotes syllabiques.* Paris: Édition E. de Boccard.

———. 1981. "À propos des inscriptions chypriotes de Kafizin." *BCH* 105:623–649.

———. 1980. "Une nouvelle inscription de Paphos concernant le roi Nikoklès." *Minos* 19:65–80.

———. 1962. "Les noms en 'Εσθλ(ο)—et Εσλ(ο)—dans les dialectes grecs." *Beiträge zur Namenforschung* 13:75–80.

Masson, O., and T. Mitford. 1986. *Les inscriptions syllabiques de Kouklia-Paphos.* Konstanz: Universitätsverlag Konstanz.

McCarter, P. 1975. *The Antiquity of the Greek Alphabet and the Early Phoenician Scripts.* Missoula, Mont.: Scholars Press.

McLuhan, M. 1962. *The Gutenberg Galaxy.* Toronto: University of Toronto Press.

Meillet, A. 1965. *Aperçu d'une histoire de la langue grecque.* 7th ed. Paris: Klincksieck.

————. 1964. *Introduction à l' étude comparative des langues indo-européennes.* University: University of Alabama Press.

————. 1923. *Les origines indo-européennes des mètres grecs.* Paris: Les Presses Universitaires de France.

Meillet, A., and J. Vendryes. 1979. *Traité de grammaire comparée des langues classiques.* 5th ed. Paris: Champion.

Meister, K. 1905–1906. "Arkadische Formen in der Xuthiasinschrift." *IF* 18:77–83.

Meister, R. 1894. "Zu den Regeln der kyprischen Silbenschrift." *IF* 4:175–186.

Melena, J. 1975. *Studies on Some Mycenaean Inscriptions from Knossos Dealing with Textiles.* Supplement to *Minos,* no. 5.

Melena, J., and J.-P. Olivier. 1991. *TITHEMY.* Supplement to *Minos,* Number 12.

Mendel, G. 1900. "Inscriptions de bithynie." *BCH* 24:361–426.

Meshorer, Y. 1967. *Jewish Coins of the Second Temple Period.* Translated by I. Levine. Tel Aviv: Am Hassefer.

Miller, G. 1994. *Ancient Scripts and Phonological Knowledge.* Amsterdam: John Benjamins.

Mitford, T. 1980. *The Nymphaeum of Kafizin.* Berlin: De Gruyter.

————. 1971. *The Inscriptions of Kourion.* Philadelphia: American Philosophical Society.

————. 1950. "Kafizin and the Cypriot Syllabary." *CQ* 44:97–106.

Mitford, T., and O. Masson. 1983. *The Syllabic Inscriptions of Rantidi-Paphos.* Konstanz: Universitätsverlag Konstanz.

————. 1982. "The Cypriot Syllabary." In *CAH,* 2nd ed., edited by J. Boardman and N. Hammond, vol. 3, part 3, pp. 71–82. Cambridge: Cambridge University Press.

Morpurgo Davies, A. 1988. "Problems in Cyprian Phonology and Writing." In *The History of the Greek Language in Cyprus,* edited by J. Karageorghis and O. Masson, pp. 99–130. Nicosia: Zavallis Press.

————. 1987. "Mycenaean and Greek Syllabification." In *Tractata Mycenaea,* edited by P. Ilievski and L. Crepajac, pp. 91–103. Skopje: Macedonian Academy of Sciences and Arts.

————. 1986a. "Folk-Linguistics and the Greek Word." In *Festschrift for Henry Hoenigswald,* edited by G. Cardona and N. Zide, pp. 266–271. Tübingen: Gunter Narr Verlag.

————. 1986b. "Forms of Writing in the Ancient Mediterranean World." In *The Written Word,* edited by G. Baumann, pp. 51–77. Oxford: Oxford University Press.

Morris, I. 1991. "The Early Polis as City and State." In *City and Country in the Ancient World,* edited by J. Rich and A. Wallace-Hadrill, pp. 25–57. London: Routledge.

————. 1987. *Burial and Ancient Society.* Cambridge: Cambridge University Press.

————. 1986. "The Use and Abuse of Homer." *Classical Antiquity* 5:81–138.

Morris, R. 1919. *Runic and Mediterranean Epigraphy.* Gylling: Odense University Press.

Moscati, S. 1980. *An Introduction to the Comparative Grammar of the Semitic Languages.* 2nd ed. Wiesbaden: Harrassowitz.

————. 1964. *An Introduction to the Comparative Grammar of the Semitic Languages.* Wiesbaden: Harrassowitz.

Muhly, J. 1984. "The Role of the Sea Peoples in Cyprus During the LC III Period." In Karageorghis and Muhly 1984:39–55.

Murray, A., trans. 1980. *Homer: The Odyssey.* Cambridge: Harvard University Press.

Mutschmann, H., and J. Mau, eds. 1961. *Sexti Empirici Opera.* Vol. 3. Leipzig: Teubner.

Nagy, G. 1974. *Comparative Studies in Greek and Indic Meter.* Cambridge: Harvard University Press.

———. 1970. *Greek Dialects and the Transformation of an Indo-European Process.* Cambridge: Harvard University Press.

———. 1968. "On Dialectal Anomalies in Pylian Texts." In *Atti e memorie del 1° Congresso Internazionale di Micenologie 2,* pp. 663–679. Rome: Edizioni dell'Ateneo.

Naumann, U., L. Godart, and J.-P. Olivier. 1977. "Un cinquième fragment de tablette en linéaire B de Tirynthe." *BCH* 101:229–234.

Naveh, J. 1991. "Semitic Epigraphy and the Antiquity of the Greek Alphabet." *Kadmos* 30:143–152.

———. 1987. "Proto-Canaanite, Archaic Greek, and the Script of the Aramaic Text on the Tell Fakhariyah Statue." In *Ancient Israelite Religion,* edited by P. Miller et al., pp. 101–113. Philadelphia: Fortress Press.

———. 1973. "Some Semitic Epigraphical Considerations on the Antiquity of the Greek Alphabet." *AJA* 77:1–8.

Neumann, G., and K. Stiewe. 1974. "Zu den Hexametern der kyprischen Inschrift ICS 264." *Kadmos* 13:146–155.

Nöldeke, T. 1904. *Beiträge zur semitischen Sprachwissenschaft.* Strassburg: Karl J. Trübner.

Olivier, J.-P. 1993. "KN 115 = KH 115. Un même scribe à Knossos et à La Canée au MR IIIB: Du soupçon à la certitude." *BCH* 117:19–33.

———. 1989. "The Possible Methods in Deciphering the Pictographic Cretan Script." In Duhoux et al. 1989:39–58.

———. 1976. "La scrittura geroglifica cretese." *La parola del passato* 31:17–23.

Olivier, J.-P., L. Godart, C. Seydal, and C. Sourvinou. 1973. *Index généraux du linéaire B.* Rome: Edizioni dell' Ateneo.

Osborn, H. 1948. "Amahuaca Phonemes." *IJAL* 14:188–190.

Palaima, T. 1991. "The Advent of the Greek Alphabet on Cyprus: A Competition of Scripts" In *Phoinikeia grammata: Lire et écrire en Méditerranée,* edited by C. Baurain, C. Bonnet, and V. Krings, pp. 449–471. Liège: Société des Études Classiques.

———. 1990/91. "Review of Powell." *Minos* 25/26:446–449.

———. 1989a. "Ideograms and Supplementals and Regional Interaction Among Aegean and Cypriote Scripts." *Minos* 24:29–54.

———. 1989b. "Cypro-Minoan Scripts: Problems of Historical Context." In Duhoux et al. 1989:121–187.

———. 1988. "The Development of the Mycenaean Writing System." In *Texts, Tablets and Scribes: Studies in Mycenaean Epigraphy and Economy Offered to Emmett L. Bennett, Jr.,* edited by J.-P. Olivier and T. Palaima, Supplement to *Minos,* no. 10, pp. 269–342.

Palmer, L. 1980. *The Greek Language.* Atlantic Highlands, N.J.: Humanities Press.

———. 1963. *The Interpretation of Mycenaean Greek Texts.* Oxford: Oxford University Press.

Panagl, O. 1971. "Eine 'Interferenz' von nominaler Stammbildung und Linear B-Schrift." *Kadmos* 10:125–134.

Powell, B. 1991. *Homer and the Origin of the Greek Alphabet.* Cambridge: Cambridge University Press.

———. 1988. "The Dipylon Oinochoe and the Spread of Literacy in Eighth-Century Athens." *Kadmos* 27:65–86.

———. 1987. "The Origin of the Puzzling Supplementals Φ Χ Ψ." *TAPA* 117:1–20.

Reyes, A. 1994. *Archaic Cyprus.* Oxford: Oxford University Press.

Ridgway, D. 1992. *The First Western Greeks.* Cambridge: Cambridge University Press.

Riemschneider, K. 1969. *Lehrbuch des Akkadischen.* Leipzig: Verlag Enzyklopädie.

Risch, E. 1966. "Les différences dialectales dans le mycénien." In *Proceedings of the Cambridge Colloquium on Mycenaean Studies,* edited by L. Palmer and J. Chadwick, pp. 150–157. Cambridge: Cambridge University Press.

———. 1956a. "La position du dialecte mycénien." In Lejeune 1956:167–172.

———. 1956b. "Caractères et position du dialecte mycénien." In Lejeune 1956:249–258.

Rix, H. 1976. *Historische Grammatik des Griechischen.* Darmstadt: Wissenschaftliche Buchgesellschaft.

Robb, K. 1994. *Literacy and Paideia in Ancient Greece.* Oxford: Oxford University Press.

———. 1978. "Poetic Sources of the Greek Alphabet: Rhythm and Abecedarium from Phoenician to Greek." In *Communication Arts in the Ancient World,* edited by E. Havelock and J. Hershbell, pp. 23–36. New York: Hastings House.

Ruijgh, C. 1985. "Problèmes de philologie mycénienne." *Minos* 19:105–167.

———. 1967. *Études sur la grammaire et le vocabulaire du grec mycénien.* Amsterdam: Adolf Hakkert.

Rupp, D. 1988. "The 'Royal Tombs' at Salamis (Cyprus): Ideological Messages of Power and Authority." *Journal of Mediterranean Archeology* 1:111–139.

———. 1987a. "*Vive le Roi:* The Emergence of the State in Iron Age Cyprus." In Rupp 1987b:147–168.

Rupp, D., ed. 1987b. *Western Cyprus: Connections.* Göteborg: Paul Åströms Forlag.

Sakellarakis, Y., and E. Sakellaraki. 1979. " 'Ανασκαφὴ 'Αρχανῶν." Πρακτικὰ τῆς ἐν 'Αθήναις 'Αρχαιολογικῆς, pp. 331–392.

Sampson, G. 1985. *Writing Systems.* Stanford: Stanford University Press.

Sass, B. 1991. *Studia Alphabetica.* Freiburg: Universitätsverlag Freiburg.

Saussure, F. de. 1986. *Course in General Linguistics.* Translated by R. Harris. La Salle, Ill.: Open Court.

Schindler, J. 1976. "Notizen zum Sieversschen Gesetz." *Die Sprache* 22:56–65.

Segert, S. 1976. *A Grammar of Phoenician and Punic.* Munich: Verlag C. H. Beck.

Shaw, B. 1957. "Preface to Pygmalion." In *Androcles and the Lion, Overruled, Pygmalion,* rev. ed, pp. 195–199. London: Constable and Company.

———. 1948. "Preface to Pygmalion." In *Selected Plays of Bernard Shaw,* vol. 1, pp. 191–195. New York: Dodd, Mead and Company.

Snodgrass, A. 1988. *Cyprus and Early Greek History.* Nicosia: Zavalis Press.

———. 1980. *Archaic Greece: The Age of Experiment.* London: J. M. Dent and Sons.

Steiner, R. 1982. *Affricated Ṣade in the Semitic Languages.* New York: American Academy for Jewish Research.

Stephens, L., and R. Woodard. 1986. "The Palatalization of the Labiovelars in Greek: A Reassessment in Typological Perspective." *IF* 91:129–154.

Sturtevant, E. 1940. *The Pronunciation of Greek and Latin.* 2nd ed. Baltimore: Linguistic Society of America.

Stuart-Jones, H. 1901. "The Division of Syllables in Greek." *CR* 15:396–401.

Szemerényi, O. 1977. Review of *Dictionnaire étymologique de la langue grecque: Histoire des mots*, vol. 3, by P. Chantraine. *Gnomon* 49:1–10.

———. 1968. "The Attic 'Rückverwandlung' or Atomism and Structuralism in Action." In *Studien zur Sprachwissenschaft und Kulturkunde*, edited by M. Mayrhofer, pp. 139–157. Innsbruck: Leopold-Franzens-Universität.

Sznycer, M.· 1983. "Note sur l'inscription gravée sur une cruche de la tombe 69 de Palaepaphos-*Skales*." In Karageorghis 1983:416–417.

Threatte, L. 1980. *The Grammar of Attic Inscriptions*. Vol. 1. Berlin: De Gruyter.

Thumb, A. 1959. *Handbuch der griechischen Dialekte*. Part 2. 2nd ed. Edited by A. Scherer. Heidelberg: Carl Winter.

———. 1932. *Handbuch der griechischen Dialekte*. Part 1. 2nd ed. Edited by E. Kieckers. Heidelberg: Carl Winter.

Traunecker, C.; F. Le Saout, and O. Masson. 1981. *La chapelle d'Achôris à Karnak II*. Paris: Editions ADPF.

Tronsky, I. 1962. "Slogovaja struktura drevnegrečeskogo jazyka i grečeskoe slogovoe pis'mo." In *Drevnií mir: Sbornik stateí*, pp. 620–626. Moscow: Izdatel'stvo vostočnoí literatury.

Tsountas, C. 1888. " *Ἀνασκαφαὶ τάφων ἐν Μυκήναις*" *Ἀρχαιολογικὴ Ἐφημερίς*, pp. 119–180.

Tsountas, C., and J. Manatt. 1969. *The Mycenaean Age: A Study of the Monuments and Culture of Pre-Homeric Greece*. Chicago: Argonaut. reprint of 1897 edition.

Usener, H., and L. Radermacher. eds. 1985. *Dionysii Halicarnasei Opuscula*. Vol. 2. Leipzig: Teubner

van Windekens, J. 1979. "Once Again on Greek Initial ζ." *JIES* 7:129–132.

Vendryes, J. 1916. "Les correspondences de la vocabulaire entre l'Indo-Iranien et l'Italo-Celtique." *Memoires de la Société de Linguistique de Paris* 20:265–285.

———. 1904. *Traité d'accentuation grecque*. Paris: Klincksieck.

Ventris, M., and J. Chadwick. 1973. *Documents in Mycenaean Greek*. 2nd ed. Cambridge: Cambridge University Press.

———. 1956. *Documents in Mycenaean Greek*. Cambridge: Cambridge University Press.

Vilborg, E. 1960. *A Tentative Grammar of Mycenaean Greek*. Göteborg: Almqvist and Wiksell.

Viredaz, R. 1983. "La graphie des groupes de consonnes en mycénien et cypriote." *Minos* 18:125–207.

———. 1982. "*s entre occlusives en mycénien." *SMEA* 23:301–322.

Wachter, R. 1989. "Zur Vorgeschichte des griechischen Alphabets." *Kadmos* 28:19–78.

Wade-Gery, H. 1952. *The Poet of the Iliad*. Cambridge: Cambridge University Press.

Wall, S., J. Musgrave, and P. Warren. 1986. "Human Bones from a Late Minoan IB House at Knossos." *Annual of the British School at Athens* 81:333–388.

Warmington, E. 1940. *Remains of Old Latin*. Vol. 4. Cambridge: Harvard University Press.

Watkins, C. 1963. "Indo-European Metrics and Archaic Irish Verse." *Celtica* 6:194–249.

Watt, W. 1994. "Introduction: Part 2." In *Writing Systems and Cognition*, edited by W. Watt, pp. 89–114. Dordrecht: Kluwer Academic.

———. 1989. "The Ras Shamra Matrix." *Semiotica* 74:61–108.

West, M. 1988. "The Rise of the Greek Epic." *JHS* 108:173–182.

———. 1973. "Indo-European Meter." *Glotta* 51:161–181.

Wheeler, B. 1885. "Der griechische Nominalakzent." Strassburg: Ph. D. Diss.

Whitney, W. 1960. *Sanskrit Grammar*. 2nd ed. Cambridge: Harvard University Press.

Woodard, R. Forthcoming. "Linguistic Connections Between Greeks and Non-Greeks." In *Greeks and Barbarians,* edited by J. Coleman and C. Walz.

———. 1994. "On the Interaction of Greek Orthography and Phonology: Consonant Clusters in the Syllabic Scripts." In *Writing Systems and Cognition,* edited by W. Watt, pp. 311–334. Dordrecht: Kluwer Academic.

———. 1986. "Dialectal Differences at Knossos." *Kadmos* 25:49–74.

———. 1984. "The Representation of Consonant Clusters in the Writing System of Mycenaean Greek." Paper presented at the Thirtieth Meeting of the Southeastern Conference on Linguistics, Duke University, Durham, N.C.

Woolley, L. 1938. "Excavations at Al Mina, Sueidia." *JHS* 58:1–30, 133–170.

Wyatt, W. 1976. "Early Greek /y/ and Grassmann's Law." *Glotta* 54:1–11.

———. 1968. "Early Greek /y/." *Glotta* 46:229–237.

Index